Sentimental Figures of Empire in Eighteenth-Century Britain and France

Sentimental Figures of Empire in Eighteenth-Century Britain and France

LYNN FESTA

The Johns Hopkins University Press

Baltimore

The Johns Hopkins University Press
2715 North Charles Street
Baltimore, Maryland 21218-4363
www.press.jhu.edu

Library of Congress Cataloging-in-Publication Data
Festa, Lynn M. (Lynn Mary)
Sentimental figures of empire in eighteenth-century Britain and
France / Lynn Festa.
p.   cm.
Includes bibliographical references and index.
ISBN 0-8018-8430-6 (hardcover : acid-free paper)
1. English fiction—18th century—History and criticism.   2. French
fiction—18th century—History and criticism.   3. Sentimentalism in
literature.   4. Imperialism in literature.   5. Colonies in literature.
I. Title.
PR858.S45F47 2006
823'.509358—dc22   2006003549

A catalog record for this book is available from the British Library.

CONTENTS

It is somehow appropriate that a book that describes the shortcomings of benevolence should itself be the product of myriad acts of unstinting generosity.

Many people have contributed to this project. I owe a tremendous debt to Joan DeJean for her unflagging support and inspiration over the years. The critical insight and generosity of John Richetti, Peter Stallybrass, Margreta de Grazia, Lynn Hunt, Liliane Weissberg, and JoAnne Dubil during my years as a graduate student at the University of Pennsylvania created a model of collegiality to which I shall always aspire. Juliette Cherbuliez, Rayna Kalas, Nick Paige, Suzie Verderber, and Amy Wyngaard are and have been for many years the kinds of friends and intellectual community most people only dream of finding.

It would be impossible to list all the people at Harvard who have given me encouragement and support in writing this book (or who have provided welcome respite from it), but particular thanks are due to Larry Buell, Leo Damrosch, Jim Engell, Marge Garber, Stephen Greenblatt, and Barbara Johnson, as well as to Oren Izenberg, Beth Lyman, Luke Menand, John Picker, Leah Price, Ann Rowland, and Sharmila Sen. Many scholars in the field of eighteenth-century studies have helped me over the years, but I would especially like to thank Srinivas Aravamudan, Julia Douthwaite, Beth Kowaleski-Wallace, Sue Lanser, Deidre Lynch, David Marshall, Ruth Perry, Susan Staves, Jim Steintrager, and Cindy Wall, as well as the members of the Eighteenth-Century Seminar at the Humanities Center and the participants in the Bloomington Workshop on the Eighteenth Century. In a book that makes arguments about the ambivalent desire to keep one's self to oneself, it is delightful to find the traces of so many other people.

The writing of this book was made possible by a fellowship at the Radcliffe Institute for Advanced Study. I am grateful to Drew Faust, Judy Vichniac, and the fellows of the 2003 cohort for an extraordinary year. A grant from the W. M. Keck Foundation & Andrew Mellon Foundation enabled me to spend a productive summer at the Huntington Library in 2003. Additional support for this book was provided by the Harvard English Department's Robinson-Rollins Fund.

An earlier version of a portion of Chapter 4 appeared in *Interpreting Colonialism*, a special issue of *Studies on Voltaire in the Eighteenth Century*, edited by Byron Wells and Philip Stewart (Oxford: Voltaire Foundation, 2004). I am grateful to the editors for permission to use this material. I also wish to express my gratitude to Peter Dreyer for his care in copyediting the manuscript. Finally, thanks to my editor, Michael Lonegro, for his support and patience in seeing this project through.

A number of other people have helped me to write this book in ways that may be obscure to them but are perfectly clear to me: Frances Bennett, Dan Carey, Maria Carter, Wendy Chun, Greg Coleman, Tess and Mike Festa, Katy Fogle, Matt Gil, David Harrison, Judy Hershnik, Jill Heydt-Stevenson, Sonia Hofkosh, Jack Killoy, Jacques Lezra, Anna McDonald, Phoebe Minias, Paul Moorcroft, Anita Oliva, Lisa Randall, the Rozetts, John Stevenson, Sally Stiffler, Judith Surkis, Alexis Tadié, Bob and Elizabeth Festa Watson, and Diana Wylie. And I don't know what I would have done without Patty, Kate, Nick, Mark, Sharmila, Elizabeth, and Analia. No one could have been luckier in her family and friends.

This book is for the two people to whom I owe the most: my father, Adam Festa, and my mother, Winnie Festa.

*Sentimental Figures of Empire in
Eighteenth-Century Britain and France*

The Great World Without

> Really, universally, relations stop nowhere, and the exquisite prob-
> lem of the artist is eternally but to draw, by a geometry of his
> own, the circle within which they shall happily *appear* to do so.
> —*Henry James, preface*, Roderick Hudson

A project concerned with the margins of the Enlightenment might as well begin with a footnote. In the first volume of his sentimental novel *The Life and
Opinions of Tristram Shandy* (1759–67), Laurence Sterne describes a village
midwife who, as "she had all along trusted little to her own efforts, and a great
deal to those of dame nature,—had acquired, in her way, no small degree of reputation in the world;—by which word *world*, need I in this place inform your
worship, that I would be understood to mean no more of it, than a small circle
described upon the circle of the great world, of four *English* miles diameter, or
thereabouts, of which the cottage where the good old woman lived, is supposed
to be the centre."[1] Lest readers miss the irony, Sterne's French translator hastened in 1776 to add a footnote: "But do not be fooled: it was not the whole world.
She was not known, for example, among the Hottentot and Dutch women of the
Cape of Good Hope, who are said to give birth like Mother Nature. The world
for her was but a small circle."[2] The relationship between these two worlds—between the "small circle described upon the circle of the great world" and the
great world without—is the subject of this book. The circumscribed area of
"four English miles diameter," the domain of the sentimental novel, jostles uncomfortably against the land of the "Hottentots" and the "Dutch," the domain
of empire. The evident superfluity of the translator's explanation almost raises
the suspicion that it might be yet another layering of irony in the guise of an
earnest interpretive decoding: a sly trick to point out the self-contained nature,
not just of the old woman's world, but of the narrow little world of the sentimental novel.

The sentimental mode held sway over the British and French literary imagination at a time when Europeans were fanning out across the globe in search of commercial and colonial dominion. In the eighteenth century, the great trading companies were consolidated; the sinews of empire were built up in the form of systems of commerce, credit, tax collection, and armed power; the disciplines for the comparative study of man were elaborated, and the slave trade flourished. The British alone transported more than 3.4 million slaves from Africa to the Americas between 1662 and 1807.[3] By 1800, Europeans controlled more than 35 percent of the total land area of the globe; by 1815, the British empire embraced one-fifth of the earth's inhabitants.[4] Why did sentimentality attain such dazzling popularity just when European soldiers, merchants, politicians, and scientists were piecing together colonial empires? Why did a literary form chiefly notable for its preoccupation with the individual self become the mode of choice for writing about colonized populations, about slaves, about the disenfranchised, and the eighteenth-century poor?

This book seeks to connect the turning inward of the sentimental mode and the turning outward of empire in order to offer a history of the eighteenth-century origins of humanitarian sensibility. Focusing primarily on the novel, I argue that sentimental texts helped create the terms for thinking about agency and intent across the geographic expanse of the globe by giving shape and local habitation to the perpetrators, victims, and causal forces of empire. In an era in which imperial reach increasingly outstripped imaginative grasp, sentimental fiction created the tropes that enabled readers to reel the world home in their minds. By designating certain kinds of figures as worthy of emotional expenditure and structuring the circulation of affect between subjects and objects of feeling, the sentimental mode allowed readers to identify with and feel for the plight of other people while upholding distinctive cultural and personal identities; it thus consolidated a sense of metropolitan community grounded in the selective recognition of the humanity of other populations. Sentimental depictions of colonial encounters refashioned conquest into commerce and converted scenes of violence and exploitation into occasions for benevolence and pity. In the process, sentimentality, not epic, became the literary mode of empire in the eighteenth century.

Read in isolation, sentimental writings can be made to tell a tidy story about the emergence of the modern psychological self. Placed in conversation with empire, however, sentimentality invites both psychological and cultural readings of the encounter between self and other. To read the sentimental text alongside the colonial history of the Enlightenment is to recognize the myriad acts of affective piracy that constitute the singularity of the sentimental self. I thus understand the sentimental mode's interest in the interior lives of its characters and readers less as a chapter in the history of the freestanding modern individual than as a response to colonial expansion. Even as global encounters demanded innovative methods of imagining relations to others, the sentimental text sought to anchor and preserve a continuously narrated self in a world whose local attachments were being unmoored by exposure to different cultures and peoples. The protracted attention to the sustained threads of voice and character in sentimental narrative constructed a common language of psychological depth that secured the self in relation to the others it encountered, while the sentimental mode's investment in affective and psychological interiority helped distinguish the particularity of the human from the interchangeability of the commodity, the self-possessed individual from the dispossessed slave.

Sentimentality is defined here as a rhetorical practice that monitors and seeks to master the sympathetic movement of emotion between individuals and groups of people. Whereas sympathy alludes to the mobility of emotion between different individuals, and sensibility describes individuals' susceptibility to particular kinds and degrees of feeling, sentimentality as a crafted literary form moves to locate that emotion, to assign it to particular persons, thereby designating who possesses affect and who elicits it. In distinguishing between subjects and objects of feeling, the sentimental seeks to define what is proper to the self and what can be shared by or exchanged with others: it polices the division of self from world. Sentimentality, in other words, is bound up with the interests of empire, not only because sentimental texts describe and elicit emotion, but also because they *locate* it. By governing the circulation of feeling among subjects and objects, sentimentality helps to define who will be acknowledged as human.

In making sentimental identification the primary means of representing metropolitan relations with colonial populations, eighteenth-century writers give unprecedented centrality to feeling as a form of social and cultural differentiation. The sentimental subject—moved by suffering, sympathetic to others, but alert to the vicissitudes of its own affect—creates a template for the human grounded in the fact that others excite or experience emotion. "Who is it that can read of the poverty and misery of the wretched inhabitants of *Terra del Fuego*," David Henry asks in his 1774 *Historical Account of All the Voyages Round the World*, "who have nothing but the skins of beasts loosely thrown over them, . . . without lamenting the condition of human beings, destitute, as these appear to be, of every comfort and convenience[?] . . . What heart is so callous, as not to sympathize[?]"[5] What heart, indeed? Henry's shivering natives, denuded of all the comforts of civilization and clothing, can only inspire pity in those who have the luxury of sympathy. Although the reader is suffused with emotion, sympathetic identification creates difference rather than similitude; the reader is neither invited to meld ecstatically with these wretched people nor to change places with them. Henry constitutes the natives as human beings and simultaneously sorts them into a separate class: subjects who sympathize and objects who elicit sympathy confront one another across an affective and cultural divide in which one set of people feels *for* another. Colonial expansion means that readers must find ways of recognizing human likeness while maintaining other forms of difference. The sentimental community upholds a common identity, not by forging bonds directly between seemingly like individuals, but by creating a shared relationship to a common but excluded object about which the community has feelings.

In sorting reader from suffering victim, feeling subject from object of feeling, sentimental tropes, I argue, govern the movement of affect not just between different kinds of individuals but between different kinds of individualisms. In eighteenth-century texts, feeling as much as reason designates who has value and who does not. Sentimental writings thus repeatedly confront the gap between what constitutes a "lyric 'person'—emotive, subjective, individual—and a legal 'person'—rational, rights-bearing, institutional."[6] By allowing emotion to be socially distributed, monitored, and culturally validated, the sentimental text both raises and lowers the bar that distinguishes civilized from savage, human from chattel slave, person from thing. The sentimental feeling self is thus the Janus face of the Enlightenment rational subject, the possessive individual, the rights-bearing citizen.

If the ability to inspire feeling demarcates the human community, the reverse is also true. It is difficult to feel for peoples whose customs and manners are alien to our own. Unfamiliarity breeds contempt. "We are," Edmund Burke contends in his 1783 "Speech on Fox's India Bill," "so little acquainted with Indian details; the instruments of oppression under which the people suffer are so hard to be understood; and even the very names of the sufferers are so uncouth and strange to our ears, that it is very difficult for our sympathy to fix upon these objects."[7] Lacking a grasp both of the "Indian details" and of the big picture (the structural "instruments of oppression"), the reader cannot even produce objects with whom to sympathize. Where names are so alien that they will not cleave to the tongue, Burke asks, how is one to find sufficient commonality to create a sense of another's humanity?

Sentimental figures produce the means of drawing the unfamiliar into the listener's ken. Thus it is to the sentimental novel that John Hawkesworth turns in his compilation of South Sea journals. Hawkesworth invents a first-person composite narrator in order to draw "the Adventurer and the Reader nearer together, without the intervention of a stranger." Novelistic technique, Hawkesworth claims, supplements the deficiencies of history. Thus his dilation upon minor details "requires no apology,"

> for it is from little circumstances that the relation of great events derives its power over the mind. An account that ten thousand men perished in a battle, that twice the number were swallowed up by an earthquake, or that a whole nation was swept away by a pestilence, is read in the naked brevity of an index, without the least emotion, by those who feel themselves strongly interested even for Pamela, the imaginary heroine of a novel that is remarkable for the enumeration of particulars in themselves so trifling, that we almost wonder how they could occur to the author's mind.[8]

Spartan descriptions or sweeping statistics make faint impressions; seemingly "trifling" details lend power and verisimilitude to an otherwise affectively unconvincing narrative. The dilation upon "little circumstances" that steeps the reader in another world helps confer imaginary being upon distant peoples; sentimental figures reinvigorate feeling attenuated by distance and make sympathetic identification possible.

Hawkesworth's account describes how sentimental figures wrest readers from indifference, fostering connections between otherwise insular individuals. Recent scholarship on sentimentality has emphasized this capacity to forge social bonds in the face of the self-interested passions of *homo economicus,* providing the training of emotion needed to socialize the uncontrolled passions unleashed by capitalism and simultaneously harnessing individual emotional life to the marketplace.[9] Arguments that emphasize the synthetic capacity of sentimentality to create broader communities of sociability grounded in shared economic, moral, aesthetic, or class-based interests have for the most part shied away from extensive discussions of empire, perhaps because they have difficulty accommodating the antagonisms and contradictions that surface when one enlarges the community too much. My argument departs from this body of scholarship in claiming that sentimental identification operates as a form of differentiation as well as consolidation. Inasmuch as sympathy involves the readers' experience of feelings specifically designated as belonging to another person, it veers towards a perilous absorption in another's affect and interests that may threaten the autonomy of the self. Thus although feelings may serve as social adhesive, the traffic in sympathetic feeling may also spark a struggle to claim feelings for one's own. I endeavor to restore the agonistic element to sympathetic exchanges by acknowledging the tension between the sociable benefits and pleasures of sympathetic affect and the desire to uphold the singularity of the self. Hence, I understand sentimentality not as part of a continuum on which one might also place sensibility and sympathy but as a rhetorical structure that contains the potentially indiscriminate circulation of feeling.

The fact that sympathetic traffic flows beyond the boundaries of individuals challenges the proto-romantic idea that feelings have their origins in unique, interior, personal experience; the emotions sometimes thought to constitute the self may not be one's own. The suggestion that, in Adela Pinch's words, "feelings may be impersonal; that one's feelings may really be someone else's; that feelings may be purely conventional, or have no discernible origins,"[10] calls other contemporary concepts of subjectivity into question. For how can one collate eighteenth-century accounts of the person—the political subject girded round by rights and duties, the self-proprietary individual who enters into market relations with others—with the affective self, whose messy identifications, disruptive passions, inexplicable propensities, and uncertain borders escape precise definition?

Discussions of the management of emotion—the attribution of feeling to specific people or groups of people, the command over one's own emotions, the subjectivity, interiority, and self-propriety that issue from them—have largely centered on gender in recent years.[11] Yet the proclivity of feelings to wander in eighteenth-century texts becomes particularly risky in the context of empire, resulting in a menacing usurpation of the self that threatens to collapse distinctions based on nation, religion, or race. Because sympathy breaks down the borders that support the categories of self and other (a division that sentimentality endeavors to reassert), it interrupts the tidy shot/reverse-shot model of self-other relations that often surfaces in discussions of empire in the eighteenth century. Colonial encounters were messy, ill-assorted things, spawning scenes of mutual unintelligibility marked by confusion, delirium, and violence. As Jonathan Lamb has shown in *Preserving the Self in the South Seas,* the loneliness, wonder, fear, and bafflement experienced by travelers and indigenes could veer towards self-dissolution, imperiling the continuity and unity of the self. By recasting this confusion into scenes of benevolent reciprocity, sentimental depictions of these moments of contact attempt to master a potentially vertiginous relation. The structure sentimental tropes imposed upon vagrant affect enabled Europeans to preserve the identity of the self in encounters that knitted subject and object together in ways that were difficult to disentangle.

This book poses these questions about the continuity of personal identity in the context of recent work on the way eighteenth-century colonial and imperial activity called into being or reoriented categories of nation, gender, family, class, and race.[12] How did these broader concepts of human difference become incorporated into the practices and perceptions of daily life? How did they reshape the identity of the self? There is, as Dror Wahrman has recently observed, "no reason to expect the historical development of understandings of personal identity to mirror that of categories of identity such as gender or race."[13] My argument traces the cultural and literary labor that aligns the felt perception of who is a person with emerging historical categories that delimit the human. The sentimental governance of emotion, I contend, welds the affective response to other people to broader structures of human classification in order both to include *and* to exclude individuals from the class of humanity. The central question I want to pose thus concerns the eighteenth-century concept of the person.

Where critical work on sentimentality has treated empire, it has often focused on the presence of colonial people or objects in sentimental texts, addressing the political labor performed by the sentimental in arousing metropolitan readers' moral and affective responses to the colonies.[14] Where critical work on empire has taken up sentimentality, it has often addressed the ideological sugarcoating that allows, for example, patriarchy to portray itself as paternalism by casting colonial aggression as fatherly protection of helpless, feminized populations at home and abroad. The sentimental heroes of what Mary Louise Pratt calls "anticonquest"[15]—the weak but kindly Hickmans, Détervilles, Saint Preuxs, Harleys, Yoricks, and Primroses of the world—consolidate the role of the compassionate master in order to defend traditional hierarchies against the challenges implicit in the Enlightenment recognition that the freedom, autonomy, and rationality of all are grounds for political and legal equality. Certainly, the dying Indians, grateful slaves, and benevolent savages who populate sentimental texts possess little of the revolutionary agency that Srinivas Aravamudan locates in the figure of the "tropicopolitan" (Aravamudan's name for "the colonized subject who exists both as fictive construct of colonial tropology *and* actual resident of tropical space, object of representation *and* agent of resistance").[16] My argument, however, is not that sentimentality was a blind for pernicious activity going on elsewhere. Rather, I claim that the mode was productively linked to imperial activities, a by-product of the very contradictions it is said to disguise. In exposing the discrepancy between Enlightenment ideals and the realities of human suffering and exploitation, empire begets sentimentality.

This study is thus not primarily concerned with the sentimental mystification of colonial and domestic exploitation. Although the deliberate stimulation of sentimental affect magnifies and mystifies colonial relations, I contend that it does even more than this: sentimentality fashions the tropes that render relations with distant others thinkable. Eighteenth-century readers were obliged to imagine and anticipate the remote consequences of local deeds in the face of global systems—commercial markets, credit, public opinion—that could not be understood through analogies with individual behavior. "[W]hat mighty armies may be put in motion from behind the counter," Adam Ferguson wrote in 1767, "how often human blood is, without any national animosity, bought and sold for bills of exchange."[17] Sentimentality unveils the relationship between anodyne transactions at the corner shop and bloodshed on the other side of the globe by producing some of the terms and techniques by which human agency might be conceived as acting over great distances. In particular, sentimental texts use tropes of personification not only to confer a human face and form upon the victims of empire—the redundant humanizing of the already human—but also to give shape to the abstract forces and collective entities that execute policies and actions in an emerging global system.

Let me say something about what this study does and does not try to do. The colonial and metropolitan worlds described in this book are indisseverable. This is, however, a study centered on European systems of thought and British and French texts. The scope of my argument embraces the triangular Atlantic trade between Britain and France, Africa, and the Caribbean, with a special focus on the use of sentimental tropes in discussions of slavery and the slave trade. Although the figures I analyze surface in discussions of other imperial domains during this period, it would be a mistake to take any one situation to be representative either of other colonial contexts or of a notion of "the" empire as a whole. The French and British colonies in mainland America, the conquests in India, and the voyages of Cook and Bougainville in the South Seas fall beyond my purview here. Nor is sentimentality the key to all imperial mythologies. Although I touch on some of the social and economic anxieties sparked by colonial expansion in Chapter 1, an in-depth discussion of the political and religious arguments that shaped the contesting ideologies of eighteenth-century empire is not possible in a study of this length. By considering the specific nexus of sentimentality and empire in a comparative framework, I have, however, sought to build on recent scholarship in Atlantic studies and on the transnational rise of the novel that dislodges the national and nationalist teleologies that have hitherto structured both imperial and canonical literary histories.

Sentimental tropes, characters, and plots migrate across not only national but also generic borders, surfacing in theatrical and poetic as well as novelistic treatments of empire. Although I primarily focus on the novel, sentimental poetry, much of it by women, dominated the abolitionist press, while Aphra Behn's *Oroonoko*, Richard Steele's version of the tale of Inkle and Yarico, and Bernardin de Saint Pierre's *Paul et Virginie* may have been as well or better known in their popular afterlife on stage than in their original forms. The ballad sung in the street, the play produced in the theater, the poem published in the newspaper or the miscellany, the novel read in the drawing room or the closet, all solicit unique structures of identification and produce different performances of personal or collective affect. Diderot, Rousseau, Edmund Burke, and Adam Smith all raise questions about the origins, authenticity, spontaneity, and depth of the feelings elicited by different generic forms, and it would be a mistake to treat other sentimental forms as if they were simply expressions of a master discourse elaborated in the novel. Nevertheless, the novel was at the vanguard of sentimental fashion. Inasmuch as generic novelty often makes visible objects occluded by more established forms, the novel's lack of rigid conventions made it particularly suited for representations of marginal figures and colonial populations, while its incorporation of minute particulars into narrative helped readers draw the world home in their imaginations. The sustained emphasis on interior affect in the novel—a trait shared with lyric poetry—helps uphold a notion of a continuous self, although, as my discussion of abolitionist writing in Chapter 4 demonstrates, the exemplary suffering figures featured in sentimental verse are often described with a degree of generalization incompatible with dramatic or novelistic plot. Perhaps most important for my purposes, the novel dominated the cross-Channel print market in the eighteenth century.

As the pan-European success of sentimental novels like Richardson's *Pamela* and *Clarissa*, Rousseau's *Julie*, and Goethe's *Werther* suggests, sentimentality forms a kind of affective undertow to the commercial and political currents drawing European nations together during the period. In the eighteenth century, the expanding print trade, the growth of tourism, the decline of religious conflict, the ease of international banking, and close commercial links among merchants of different countries consolidated the cultural and economic bonds among European nations, above all, between Britain and France. "A sort of commerce was established between us [England and France]," the abbé Prévost noted, "through which we exchanged the literary products of our nations—a commerce to be preferred above that which drew the gold of the New World to Europe."[18] French and British reading publics avidly consumed each other's literary fodder, despite the almost incessant wars that raged between the two nations throughout the century (seven declared wars adding up to sixty-two years of the period between 1689 and 1815, plus other minor conflicts).[19]

The degree of exchange between France and Britain is remarkable. Diderot, co-author of the revised third edition of Raynal's *Histoire des deux Indes* (1780) and author of the *Supplément au Voyage de Bougainville* (written 1772; published 1788), translated Shaftesbury's *Essai sur le mérite et la vertu* (1745), wrote an "Eloge de Richardson" (1762), and modeled his own novels *La Religieuse* (written 1760) and *Jacques le fataliste* (written 1771; published 1796) on the writings of Richardson and Sterne; the Swiss Rousseau's *Julie* (1761) was used as a model by the Scottish Henry Mackenzie in his *Julia de Roubigné* (1777), as well as by women novelists including Helen Maria Williams, Elizabeth Inchbald, Mary Hays, Mary Wollstonecraft, and Maria Edgeworth. Sade rewrote Richardson in *Justine* (1791), turning virtue rewarded into virtue punished. The first Canadian novelist, Frances Moore Brooke, translated Marie-Jeanne Riccoboni's *Lettres de Milady Juliette Catesby* (1759; trans. 1760), while Charlotte Lennox translated Madame de Tencin's *Mémoires du Comte de Comminges* (1735; trans. 1756). Sterne's eminently English narrator Yorick triggered an avalanche of sentimental journeys through the Continent and the colonies, and hundreds of *Histoires anglaises* were published in France during the latter half of the century.[20]

Even the term *sentimentality* was tossed back and forth between the two nations like a literary hot potato: Sterne's first French translator said that "the English word *sentimental* could not be rendered into French by any expression which agreed exactly with it, and it has been left to stand as it is," although R. F. Brissenden notes that Sterne thought he "was using the word in a French way."[21] If the French initially perceived sentimentality as distinctively English—a moral mode imported to reform France's corrupt libertine tradition—by the end of the century, the British considered sensibility to be distinctively French. As the Methodist John Wesley wrote with seeming disgust in his *Journal*, "*Sentimental!* what is that? It is not *English;* he might as well say *Continental.*"[22] In James Gillray's famous print "The New Morality" in the *Anti-Jacobin Review and Magazine*, a bedraggled female figure, "Sensibility," sobs over a dead bird, while using the head of Louis XVI as a footrest. The tome of Rousseau clutched in her hand clinches late-century British associations of sensibility with French radicalism.[23] Notwithstanding its claims to a universal humanity, sentimentality was dragged into struggles over national and imperial identities throughout the century.

Anxieties about the mobility of feeling across political borders and personal boundaries surface repeatedly in the mid-century accounts of sympathy surveyed in Chapter 1, where I trace the common threads that unite French and British (mainly Scottish) theories of sympathy and briefly address what distinguishes them, before turning to the problems unfettered sympathy posed for the Enlightenment subject when shifted to the domain of empire. For Hume, Smith, Diderot, and Rousseau, experiencing the feelings of another was disruptive to the "identity" or continuity and unity of the sympathetic subject. These questions of emotional provenance in turn raise questions of propriety: if sympathetic emotion travels, to whom do feelings belong and how do they become my own? What if someone else's feelings overtake me and I cease to be myself? Sentimentality as a rhetorical practice and as a literary form devises strategies to master the seemingly indiscriminate nature of sympathy. It allows the reader to control and assign provenance and proper cause to the ephemeral flow of emotions. The sentimental "location" of emotion, I argue, in turn organizes communal feeling. I examine the tension between the restrictive communities created by the sentimental text's form and its celebration of universal feeling in order to address how sentimental "humanity" simultaneously fosters and supersedes national feeling in an age of empire. Sentimental identification allowed French and British subjects to carve out communal identities based on the distinction between the community of feeling subjects and shared, but excluded, sentimental objects: the poor, the wretched, the old, and the enslaved, who furnished a seemingly infinite supply of emotional fodder for the mode.

Even as the sentimental text seeks to secure the self from dissolution in another's feelings, the particularity of the sentimental self is meant to palliate a market-driven conception of the individual as exchangeable, interchangeable, for sale. Chapter 2, "Sterne's Snuffbox," explores efforts to withdraw persons and things from the fungibility of the marketplace. It focuses on one of the few positive senses of the term *sentimental* still current today: sentimental value, or the attribution of personal significance to an object that transcends its economic price or material worth. By creating a singular and personal relationship to an object, sentimental value creates a sacrosanct domain seemingly exempt from the interchangeability of the market. It binds the world more securely to the subject by appropriating objects (such as the monk's snuffbox in Sterne's *A Sentimental Journey*) in ties that supersede the material or legal connection of property to person. Yet as the eighteenth-century market in "Yorick" snuffboxes attests, sentimental objects and texts were also commodities. Feelings, it seems, can be bought and sold. The fact that sentimental value, far from being inalienable, was up for sale means that Sterne and his imitators were obliged to wrestle with the marketability of human particularity.

Sentimental value enables people to secure the self by personalizing the properties of their things, borrowing personality from their possessions. Chapter 3, "Tales Told by Things," investigates what objects borrow back from subjects, tracing the movement from person to thing to the figure of the person in three clusters of texts: the popular eighteenth-century subgenre of tales narrated by inanimate and nonhuman things, Marx's *Capital*, and the slave autobiography. Not unlike Marx's commodity, the wig, slipper, guinea, and rupee in object narratives traverse the line between person and thing, usurping the attributes and agency of their human owners. The fact that things stir to life and begin to speak in these tales has much to tell us about the uncertain boundaries between subject and object during the eighteenth century, for the period that devoured tales told by things was also the period in which the slave trade was at its height. I reexamine what are perhaps the most famous speaking objects in eighteenth-century literature—the talking books so prominently featured in slave autobiographies like *The Interesting Narrative of the Life of Olaudah Equiano*—in order to address how the trope of personification reanimates another kind of "thing": the *res* the slave legally was. In bestowing the attributes that ostensibly distinguish person from thing upon entities that lack these traits, personifications unveil the properties we associate with the person. At the same time, the uncanny kinship between object narratives and slave autobiographies exposes the way sentimental personification dehumanizes the very figures it animates.

Object narratives and slave autobiographies suggest how easily subject and object, person and thing, can be confused. The abolitionist texts discussed in Chapter 4, "Making Humans Human," endeavor to restore humanity to the slave by emphasizing those aspects of the human that have no equivalents. Abolitionist verse and images like Wedgwood's medallion of a kneeling slave under the inscription "Am I not a man and a brother?" bestow the attributes of the person—a voice, consciousness, a soul—upon the figure of the slave to recreate the humanity of someone who is already human, in what I call a trope of redundant personification. The substitution of self for other meant to restore humanity to the slave through sympathetic identification generates a dizzying double movement of empathy and usurpation in parliamentary debates in the late 1780s and 1790s. The sympathy that authorizes speech on another's behalf can spill over into sentimental ventriloquism, while the feelings aroused by these impassioned parliamentary discourses veer between the sentimental and the sexual.

Abolitionist texts use sentimental figures to enable readers to imagine relations to distant peoples, but they do not yield a sense of the broader structural workings of empire. The final chapter, "Global Commerce in Raynal's *Histoire des deux Indes,*" turns to one of the great Enlightenment attempts to represent eighteenth-century colonial commerce in a systematic fashion. In Raynal's *Histoire,* two contesting views of global relations jostle uncomfortably on the same tabula: a bird's-eye view of commerce as origin and engine of world history, and a sentimental vision of the consequences and human costs of imperial depredations. The absence of a modern vocabulary of systemic causality means that Raynal's depiction of global commerce as a kind of homeostatic body in which the whole exceeds the sum of its parts entails new ways of imagining cause and effect. The *Histoire* personifies abstractions like commerce and collective entities like nations in order to create the means of imagining agency and accountability in a global system that can be understood neither through analogies with individual behavior nor through interlinked causal chains. Raynal alternately addresses and ventriloquizes the victims of colonial conquest, creating a shared tabula on which figures separated by space and time can communicate, as the seemingly spontaneous outpourings of sentimental emotion reaffirm the existence of a common humanity. Raynal's well-intentioned desire to "find" humanity involves arrogation of the title to confer humanity on others—a form of history that is, then as now, sentimental in the best and worst senses of the word.

Eighteenth-century sentimentality was a strategy employed by progressive and reactionary thinkers alike, for ends that were both pernicious and praiseworthy. Although I analyze the sentimental construction of the category of the person, I do not attempt to identify places where the subaltern can speak or has spoken. That sentimental ventriloquism involves usurping others' voices seems pretty much self-evident; what requires greater analysis is the assumption—bequeathed to us, I contend, by eighteenth-century sentimentality—that the attribution of "depth" and "selfhood" is a priori restorative. The projection of subjectivity and personality onto the native may in fact, as Rey Chow has argued, avoid "the genuine problem of the native's status as object by providing *something* that is more manageable and comforting—namely, a phantom history in which natives appear as our equals and our images, in our shapes and in our forms."[24] In questioning what "our" shapes and forms might be, this book seeks to analyze such histories, not to repeat them.

CHAPTER ONE

The Distinction of Sentimental Feeling

Ubiquitous and elusive—the Scarlet Pimpernel of literary history—the term *sentimental* is notoriously difficult to define. Simultaneously a literary style, a mode of self-fashioning, a set of aesthetic parameters, and a model for reader response, sentimentality is almost too volatile to endure the chains of definition. The imprecision of the vocabulary of the sentimental stems from uncertainty about its object: the sentimental is more a way of seeing the world than a cluster of defined symptoms, a structure of reading rather than a set of textual characteristics. Histories of the term tend to focus on its emergence out of the inchoate vocabulary of affect and moral thinking employed by eighteenth-century writers: sense, sensible, sensibility, sentiment. Genealogies identifying seventeenth-century Latitudinarianism, the Cambridge Platonists, Shaftesbury, and the moral sense philosophers as its forebears sometimes look like attempts to acquire respectable ancestral portraits for a slightly vulgar upstart.[1] My interest here is less where sentimentality came from, and whether the sport was good at its making, than the problems its bastard form addressed and solved. What kind of work did the sentimental do in an age of empire?

This chapter traces the common preoccupations of mid-century theories of sympathy—by Hume and Smith, Rousseau and Diderot—in order to address the problems unfettered sympathy poses for the Enlightenment subject when shifted to the domain of empire. I draw on both French and British writers in order to offer a comparative perspective on the concept of humanity fashioned by the sentimental text. The first half of the chapter explores the ways sentimental texts seek to secure the autonomy of the self against the menacing mobility of feeling described in theories of sympathy; the second half addresses the way sentimental identification shapes real and fictive imagined communities. In an era of imperial and commercial expansion, sentimentality invites readers to dabble in the emotional lives of others, while seeking to secure the continuity and unity ("identity" in the eighteenth-century sense of the word) of the metropolitan subject. By monitoring the movement of feeling between bodies, sentimentality—as a formal structure, a set of tropes or figures of reading—produces models or strategies of identification elastic enough to anchor and accommodate both individual and collective identities in the global eighteenth century. It creates a rarefied community of like-feeling souls bonded through their common relationship to a shared but excluded object of feeling. As this chapter explores, it was perversely the aspects of the sentimental that render it so elusive—the malleability of affect, its propensity to travel—that made it an ideal mode for the shifting loyalties and group affiliations of empire.

Sentimental Babel

The meaning eighteenth-century writers assigned to *sentimentality* and *sensibility* can be hard to pin down. It is difficult not to sympathize with the eighteenth-century reviewer who wished novelists "would sometimes inform us what ideas they annex to the word sensibility."[2] The mode is "full of zigzag sentiments and disjointed expressions," the anonymous author of the satirical *Ode to Sensibility* scoffs.[3] "Weak, hybrid and double-hinged," sentimental writing is "a philosophical nightmare of muddled ideas, weak logic and bad writing," Markman Ellis echoes.[4] Not unlike pornography, sentimentality cannot be reduced to ideas that can be paraphrased or summarized; it is appraised, not for its truth value, its logical validity, or its descriptive accuracy, but for its performative efficacy—its ability to affect readers. Since the sentimental is a formal aspect of a text rather than an ideological position, it is promiscuous in its choice of political bedfellows. Janus-faced, the sentimental can be used to argue both sides of a question: thus it is employed as a rhetorical strategy by both proslavery writers and abolitionists, borrowed by supporters and adversaries of colonial trade alike. Sentimentality fosters the sympathy that Lord Kames calls "the great cement of human society" by making "the prosperity and preservation of each individual . . . the care of the whole species."[5] At the same time, it easily devolves into an orgy of narcissism, as in Coleridge's indictment of the tea-drinking "fine lady" who "sips a beverage sweetened with human blood, even while she is weeping over the refined sorrows of Werter [*sic*] or of Clementina."[6]

So supple is the term *sentimental* that it embraces not only the Richardsonian endeavor to train the emotions to moral ends but also the playful effusions of a Sterne, the maudlin excesses of a Baculard d'Arnaud, and the social programs of a Rousseau. Its very imprecision confers a kind of ideological versatility upon the sentimental mode, allowing it to solicit different genders, nations, and classes through the appeal to a common strain shared by all. Feeling is not restricted by social prerequisites: sensibility—"that peculiar structure, or habitude, of mind," as one eighteenth-century magazine writes, "which disposes a man to be easily moved, and powerfully affected, by surrounding objects and passing events"[7]— is accessible even to those lacking a classical education or knowledge of social decorum. Not every one is handsome, clever, rich, and well-born, but every one can feel or, at least, fake it. The sentimental novel prioritizes immediate, individual experience grounded in universal impulses of benevolence or humanity over the derivation of moral sentiments from dispassionate reason or judgment; its emphasis on natural and spontaneous feeling permits the consolidation of a community of readers based on characteristics other than rank, wealth, or birth.[8] This capacity to expand to absorb new populations renders it a propitious genre in the context of empire; with the burgeoning of colonial enterprises, as Peter Hulme writes, "[s]entimental sympathy began to flow out along the arteries of European commerce in search of its victims."[9]

Discussions of the way sentimental texts forge community have largely focused on class. The supple codes of sensibility allow socially aspiring members of the middle ranks to present themselves as genteel, permitting readers to claim authority based on virtue or merit rather than on historically contingent factors like birth, nation, or wealth. Yet arguments that hitch sentimentality too neatly to class interest have trouble accommodating differences among nations. The existence of the middling sort (and their appetite for sentimental literature) has been persuasively documented in Great Britain, but considerable debate persists over the nature and even the existence of a self-conscious middle class in France —a land where sentimental literature also enjoyed tremendous popularity.[10] Seamless parallels between class and sentimental ideology, moreover, oversimplify by homogenizing class (suggesting that it emerges fully formed rather than developing unevenly over a period of time from diverse, even conflicting, interests) and by assuming the existence of an expressive relation between collective economic interests and ideology.[11] Yet, as Stuart Hall neatly puts it, "material interests on their own have no necessary class belongingness."[12] Individuals affiliate with political stances that countermand their own political or financial interests; they identify themselves with subject positions that are not necessarily their own. If one keeps in mind that identifications (who we would like to be) and identities (who we ostensibly are) do not invariably line up, then it is no longer quite as puzzling to contemplate why the working-class English supported abolition rather than putting their own material interests first in the eighteenth century, or why the very poor vote for tax cuts for the very wealthy today. When the "have-nots identify themselves from the position of the haves," Homi Bhabha argues, they remind us that "political positioning is ambivalently grounded in an acting-out of political fantasies that require repeated passages across the differential boundaries between one symbolic bloc *and an other*."[13] By facilitating identification across categories of nation, rank, gender and class, sentimentality exploits this gap between who one "is" and who one desires to be. The sentimental mode thus not only mystifies class interests (a question of content), but also fashions imaginary positions with which individuals might identify even in the face of contradictory interests or rival agendas (a question of structure or form).

Although even eighteenth-century writers depict sentimentality as a wallowing in emotion (as later generations would), contemporaries also perceive its political and moral efficacy. Sentimentality's moral tone helps make the novel a respectable genre, both purveying pleasure in the guise of humanitarianism and smuggling philanthropic arguments into the leisure-time activity of novel reading. Not only are contemporary controversies over slavery or prostitution fodder for novelistic plots, sentimental novels are also seen to possess political agency, inasmuch as they move their readers not only to tears but also to right action. The impressive surge in philanthropic activism in both Britain and France during this period both sustained and was fostered by sentimental writing.[14] The sentimental text's interest in the particular suffering of isolated objects brings the wretchedness of the earth home to the reader in a manner that surpasses appeals to distributive justice and abstract rights. At the same time, the sentimental novel's distinctive images of passive suffering and kindly paternalistic redemption, individual plight rather than mass exploitation, sugarcoat the violence and inequity in emerging commercial systems of appropriation and exchange.

The blurred lines and confused distinctions that characterize the vocabulary of sympathy, sentimentality, and sensibility expose the difficulty of defining what is proper to the self. Simultaneously alluding to emotional affect, intellectual capacity, or sensory receptivity, the vocabulary of sentience (sentiment, sensibility, sense) fluctuates between physical and mental awareness, bounces between mind, body, and soul; it alludes to process (how one senses), power (the capacity or delicacy of the senses), and product (the impressions produced by or the results of thinking and feeling).[15] The proliferation of adjectives in French dictionary entries—"sentiment piquant, aigu, douloureux, agreeable, exquis, délicat," "Sentiment noble, élevé, généreux, bas, lâche," "sentiment d'amour, de tendresse, de haine" (noble, high, generous, low, base sentiment, sentiment of love, of tenderness, of hate)[16]—exposes the need to append a descriptive limiter in order to give a sentiment form: as one moves the vocabulary of affect from exteriorized things to interior sentiments, the referent becomes elusive.[17] Sentimental language must designate the provenance, appurtenance, and quality of a feeling. In the *Dictionnaire de Trévoux,* for example, the adjective is needed to define the sentiment by locating its origin in heart or mind: "it is the adjective, or the matter, that determines whether it goes to the heart or to the mind [*l'esprit*]. An extravagant sentiment, that is, an opinion of the mind. Passionate sentiments, that is, movements of the heart."[18] In distinguishing sentiments from thoughts, John Trusler observes that the former are "guided by the influence of the heart" while the latter "rise greatly, from imagination."[19]

That the nouns that describe sensibility tend to consolidate qualifiers into qualities (i.e., *sentimental* into *sentimentality*) suggests an attempt—only partly successful—to arrest dynamic forces in self-contained terms. The movement between modifier and substantive, between adjective and noun, which characterizes the vocabulary of the sentimental, exposes the problem of ossifying the language of affect around defined objects. Simply propping *the* before the adjective, as in "the sentimental," only provisionally does the trick—although it does mark the emergence of the mode, not as an objective form constituted out of meter, matter, and specific narrative structure, but as a subjective mode, defined by a reader's relation to the text. Sentimental texts are thus crammed with adjectives desperately seeking nouns and nouns clinging to their modifiers, not least in the co-dependent coupling of the word *sentimental* with some—any—noun. As the colonial judge Edward Long puts it in defense of his light-hearted excursion into the genre: "We have Sentimental Comedies, Operas, Sermons, Farces, and Puppet Shows; Sentimental Novels, Histories, Journies, and Voyages; Sentimental Toasts; Sentimental Gingerbread; Sentimental Tobacco-boxes; Sentimental Handkerchiefs; Sentimental Pictures; and why not add to the List, a SENTIMENTAL EXHIBITION?"[20] Long's inclusion of objects from the sublime to the trivial suggests the degree to which the mode had infiltrated cultural consumption at all levels. Notwithstanding its ubiquity, the vocabulary only receives its naturalization paperwork belatedly and piecemeal: in 1787, Féraud's dictionary lists *sentimental* as a "neologism, which still has a bit of precious air"; the word does not reach the *Dictionnaire de l'Académie française* until 1835, and *sentimentalité* never makes it at all. Nor does *sentimentality* merit an entry in Samuel Johnson's dictionary.

As is often observed, the modern usage of *sentiment* has little in common with its eighteenth-century forebears. Feeling and sensibility are notoriously absent from Johnson's 1755 *Dictionary* entry for *sentiment;* both of Johnson's definitions emphasize the moral rather than the affective, the head not the heart. Thus for Johnson, the term *sentiment* refers to the by-products of the mind ("thought, notion, opinion," described without reference to the senses that presented them) or to an idea oddly detachable from words or objects ("the sense considered distinctly from the language or things; a striking sentence in a composition").[21] Johnson does not explain what strikes—carries rhetorical force—in a sentence in which the spirit has been abstracted from the letter; nor does he take up how one sorts out sense from language and things. Whereas the vocabulary of sensibility stresses the interconnectedness of body and soul, Johnson's "sentiment" is a portmanteau for discrete and self-contained notions, aloof from the messiness of the senses and even the looseness of language.

This vocabulary of the sentimental undergoes significant alterations in the course of the century, reflecting the broader currents in the preromantic language of affect traced by Amélie Oksenberg Rorty and Adela Pinch. During the period from Descartes to Rousseau, Rorty argues, emotions change from "reactions to invasions from something external to the self" into "the very activities of the mind, its own motions ... and along with desires, the beginnings of actions."[22] Whereas the term *emotion* at the beginning of the eighteenth century refers to turbulent motions that irrupt into the self from without, by the end of the century, it alludes to specific affect originating from within. *Emotion* in Johnson's *Dictionary* (1755) is a "disturbance of mind; vehemence of passion, or pleasing or painful," referring to intensity and movement rather than to specific affect. In his 1732 *Dictionnaire de la langue françoise*, Pierre Richelet places *émotion* closer to the modern *émeut* (riot) than *ému* (moved), defining it first and foremost as *trouble* or *sédition* and only secondly as *crainte : trouble : éfroi* [sic] : *tremblement* (fear : trouble : terror : trembling), in the sense of "cela me donnait quelque émotion" (it caused me some emotion).[23]

The 1783 revision of Chambers's 1728 *Cyclopaedia* explicitly articulates the difficulty in locating sentiment: "the word *sentiment*, in its true and old English sense signifies, *a formed opinion, notion, or principle;* but of late years, it has been much used by some writers to denote an internal impulse of passion, affection, fancy, or intellect, which is to be considered rather as the cause or occasion of our forming an opinion, than as the real opinion itself."[24] Johnson's neat packet of sentiment as "thought, notion, opinion"—collectively held and easily transferred—here becomes the idiosyncratic internal "impulse of passion, affection, fancy or intellect" behind a particular person's opinion. From an externally held "formed opinion," we move to the shaping forces within, supplanting the communal finished product ("the real opinion itself") with the internal causes that create it. The redefinition of sentiment is correlated with the broader (proto-romantic) transformation of the passions from disruptive impulses to be mastered into motives that issue from within.

The movement from collectively maintained sentiment to internal impulse poses questions about the relation of inner and outer worlds. The sentimental packs affective punch because it lends impetus to reasoned principles by appealing to the volition through the emotions. "Sensibility," the chevalier de Jaucourt tells us in the *Encyclopédie*, "is the mother of humanity, of generosity; it fosters merit, aids the intelligence [*esprit*], and carries persuasion in its wake."[25] As George Campbell writes in his 1776 *Philosophy of Rhetoric:* "what is addressed solely to the moral powers of the mind, is not so properly denominated the pathetic, as the *sentimental.* The term, I own, is rather modern, but is nevertheless convenient, as it fills a vacant room, and doth not, like most of our newfangled words, justle out older and worthier occupants, to the no small detriment of the language. It occupies, so to speak, the middle place between the pathetic and that which is addressed to the imagination, and partakes of both."[26] Lodged between the assertion of a moral principle and the imperative to persuade, the sentimental serves as a kind of *entremetteur* between inner and outer worlds, lending moral interest to pathos and conviction to reason.

Yet even the provisional fusion of inside and outside that Campbell's definition suggests is challenged as the century wears on. The circulation of print commodities allows for a sentiment to be broken off and sold separately. Both the moral and the pathetic moments in sentimental texts could be abstracted from their sources and transported into novel contexts. As early as 1751 with the publication of his *Collection of such of the Moral and Instructive Sentiments, Cautions, Aphorisms, Reflections and Observations contained in the History* [of Clarissa] *as are presumed to be of general Use and Service,* Richardson recognized that bromides might be extracted from their original context for convenient portability and ease of moral digestion. Extracts from Rousseau's *Julie* (1761)—Samuel Formey's *Esprit de Julie* (1763) and the *Pensées de J-J Rousseau* (1763) (the latter pirated by the bookseller Prault in his *Esprit, Maximes et Principes de Monsieur Jean-Jacques Rousseau* [1764])—allow the chaste reader to get the moral minus the naughty bits. Later in the century, readers would snack on sentimental nuggets mined from larger texts (exceptional deeds of charity gleaned from the newspapers, moving scenes like the Le Fever episode from *Tristram Shandy,* and other helpings of chicken soup for the soul) in anthologies like the *Tableau*

de l'humanité (1769), *Les Annales de la bienfaisance* (1772), *Anecdotes de la bienfaisance* (1777), *Les Étrennes de la vertu* (1783), or the stunning popular *Beauties
of Sterne* (which went through seven editions within a year of its initial publication in 1782).[27] As we shall see in Chapter 2, the market in sentiments introduces questions about how much feeling money can buy.

The fact that sentiments might be detached from their original owner, to be
picked up by others and discarded at will, calls into question their authenticity
or sincerity. In the last two decades of the eighteenth century, feeling is increasingly depicted as product not process. Sensibility ceases to be the mark of a
morally acute soul and ossifies into a set of conventional gestures and fashionable expressions. "Efts, toads, bats, every thing that hath life, has a claim to her
tenderest compassion," Vicesimus Knox writes of the lady of sensibility, "but the
excessive sensibility which their slightest sufferings seem to occasion, gives room
to suspect that she is not without affectation. What is so singular and excessive
can scarcely be natural."[28] Sentimental feeling comes to be seen as indiscriminate, self-indulgent, even mechanical. The French coin a new term, *sensiblerie*,
to express the inauthentic affectation of sensibility, leaving the original term intact.[29] By the 1790s, the pathetic passages on Sterne's Maria induced *"genuine
uninstructed Laughter"* even in children, Hester Thrale Piozzi noted, and Lady
Louisa Stuart was famously astonished to discover, during an 1823 group reading
of *The Man of Feeling*, that the stirring passages that had once produced the "secret dread I should not cry enough to gain the credit of proper sensibility" now
elicited uncontrollable mirth.[30]

The stirrings of pleasurable sensibility do not necessarily lead readers to be-
stir themselves on behalf of the unfortunate. Indeed, Coleridge depicts sentimentality as a cultural luxury:

> Sensibility indeed we have to spare—what novel-reading Lady does not over flow
> with it to the great annoyance of her Friends and Family—Her own sorrows like
> the Princes of Hell in Milton's Pandemonium sit enthroned bulky and vast—
> while the miseries of our fellow creatures dwindle into pigmy forms, and are
> crowded, an unnumbered multitude, into some dark corners of the Heart where
> the eye of sensibility gleams faintly on them at long Intervals.[31]

The novel-reading lady, fixed at the gravitational center of the sentimental universe, selectively draws objects into her orbit and casts them away at will in an
arbitrary, self-indulgent game of affective *fort-da*. The solipsistic consumption of
emotion—the contemplation of the sentimental navel—may not carry over into
the social world of ethical enjoinders to end real exploitation; readers may con-

gratulate themselves on their refined sensibility while stepping over a body in the gutter. Worse, sentimental reading may exhaust rather than excite emotion for the suffering of others: "By shedding tears at those representations," Rousseau writes in his *Lettre à d'Alembert*, "we discharge all the duties of humanity, without any other inconveniency: but real miseries require something more; namely, to assist, to console, to ease the unfortunate, which would be making us share in their afflictions."[32] The emotional surfeit wrung out of the sentimental text does not trickle down. Affective wealth does not lead to a redistribution of other kinds of resources.

The charges of self-indulgence and affectation often leveled against sentimental readers should not hide the importance of the underlying question: how can one claim another's feeling as authentically one's own? Even physical sensations can be tough to pin down. The difficulty with assigning emotion to one particular individual stems from the fact that the divisions between subject and object, observer and observed are not always clearly demarcated in the language of the period. Thus, for example, the adjective *sensible* in both French and English marks both the quality of an object and the susceptibility of a subject, both the sensible cold (*froid sensible*) of snow and the sensible hand (*main sensible*) that touches it. We see the same convergence of palpability and delicacy of perception in Johnson's dictionary, where *sensible* is both "having the power of perceiving by the senses" (appertaining to the subject) and "perceptible by the senses" (a quality of the object), both able to perceive and be perceived. (The modern meaning of *sensible* as judicious or reasonable is, Johnson tells us, that used "in low conversation.")[33] What may seem like a lexical quibble in fact defines some of the work performed by the genre. The vocabulary that sorts subjects and objects, inside and outside, helps to police the division of self from world. This triage of inner and outer worlds is one of the central preoccupations of the eighteenth-century theories of sympathy to which we now turn.

Hume, Smith, and the Property of Feeling

One can see the difficulty of locating emotion in David Hume's description of sympathy in his 1739–40 *Treatise of Human Nature*. Sympathy, for Hume, is a spontaneous transfer of emotion whereby the *idea* of another's impressions assumes the force of an impression within the individual: "when we sympathize with the passions and sentiments of others, these movements appear at first in *our* mind as mere ideas, and are conceiv'd to belong to another person, as we conceive any other matter of fact. 'Tis also evident, that the ideas of the affections of others are converted into the very impressions they represent, and that the passions arise in conformity to the images we form of them."[34] The "movements" of another's mind possess the capacity to represent themselves in the commonality of "*our* mind" as "mere ideas" before these ideas are converted into "the very impressions they represent." The person here neither feels for someone else (about them or in their stead) nor deliberately engineers sympathetic feeling, but rather converts the idea of another's feeling into the present and immediate impression of that idea, indistinguishable from the passion itself. It should be remembered that impressions are not, as in Locke, copies received from things in the exterior world, but are themselves sensations, passions, and volitions. Since impressions are distinguished from ideas by their vivacity rather than their provenance, the idea, as an image or reflection of an impression, can be intensified so as to become the impression itself. Reversing the law of affective entropy that dictates "that forceful impressions precede their paler ideas," sympathy, as Adela Pinch points out, "overcome[s] the passivity of mind of the empiricist account as it is usually understood. This mind would not merely suffer the fading of force but could reverse the process."[35] The idea or representation of another's feelings becomes the emotion itself, as the copy is seemingly converted to the original—although not quite, since this original is made after the image of another, "in conformity to the images we form of them."

The fact that emotions possess such agency renders sympathy the very currency of sociability for Hume. The passions are not idiosyncratic but shared, even collectively maintained; they enter from the outside rather than issuing from within. Their spontaneous communication constitutes a common humanity, allowing, as John Mullan puts it, "a sympathetic alignment of feelings" to be projected beyond Shaftesbury's coterie of enlightened gentlemen, for example, and "on to a more inclusive model of society."[36] Sympathy forges connections independent of will. People, it would seem, are possessed of a sheeplike propensity to adopt the sentiments of the herd (or at least those members of it nearby). Rather than treating the passions as Hobbesian appetites or self-interested impulses like Mandeville, Hume sees emotions as constitutively complementary and invariably welcome: we "never remark any passion or principle in others, of which, in some degree or other, we may not find a parallel in ourselves" (318). Feelings, of course, travel with cumbersome socioeconomic baggage: according to Hume, we find it easier to sympathize with the rich than the poor, the near than the far, and property or persons that belong to us are best of all.

But possession by another's passion at times verges on dispossession. For Hume, sympathy is a kind of foreign irruption into the self. "Hatred, resentment, esteem, love, courage, mirth and melancholy," Hume writes, "all these passions I feel more from communication than from my own natural temper and disposition" (317). Such mobile personified emotions suggest, as Pinch has argued, that what modernity defines as most personal to us—our emotions, our thoughts—may not be quite our own. Feelings do not originate from our experience or personal history to authenticate or be authenticated by our individuality. Instead, Pinch notes, emotions assume "autonomous forms, stalking about as personifications, often in vexed and detached relations to the persons presumed to be feeling them."[37] This capacity of emotions to travel makes it possible for others to share feelings, but it presents a logical problem for theories of the self that draw on the rhetoric of possessive individualism to ground their notions of personal autonomy. If emotions can be exchanged, then the affect constitutive of the self from a postromantic perspective is periodically on the verge of dissolving into the elsewhere of another person. How is one to situate emotions in motion: whose are they? Since feelings, once absorbed, cease to be the passion of another and become my own, how am I to know my own feelings from someone else's? How can one grasp another's feelings *and* simultaneously keep one's self to oneself?

Hume's aim in the *Treatise* is to elaborate on the conditions by which we receive the world and the limited nature of our knowledge of it: he tries to explain how we distinguish our perceptions of *other* things from our perceptions of *ourselves*. Feelings are subject to the same epistemological questions Hume poses about the world. How can we come to know which things are self and which are not? Because all impressions, "external and internal, passions, affections, sensations, pains and pleasures, are originally on the same footing" (190), our senses alone cannot distinguish inside from outside objects. For Hume, what identifies an object as external to us is its obdurate consistency in the face of our inner tumult: we "think an object has a sufficient reality, when its Being is uninterrupted, and independent of the incessant revolutions, which we are conscious of in ourselves" (191). External reality does not alter in response to our inner vicissitudes. Passions, being neither stable nor continuous, cannot be subjected to such a test.

Furthermore, what we empirically know of external reality is a set of disjointed snapshots. When we see the world as we truly perceive it (as fragmented impressions), it falls into disconnected parts. The sustained nature of the world within and the world without is thus constantly on the verge of dissolving for Hume. We must quilt together our empirical knowledge of reality and the world as it must be, uniting the discontinuous existence of the object as we encounter it (the coffeemaker in the kitchen) and its presumed external existence (it is still there even when we are at work). The "monstrous" fiction of a "double existence" (215) allows us to suture together inner and outer experiences: it "pleases our reason, in allowing, that our dependent perceptions are interrupted and different; and at the same time is agreeable to the imagination, in attributing a continu'd existence to something else, which we call *objects*" (215). For Hume, then, we project the properties necessary to our own minds onto the world and then behave as if those properties belonged to the objects. To preserve the continuity and unity of things, we rewrite relations into identities, fix processes into products, or transform evolving perceptions into the substance of a self, in an effort to contain a menacing variation.

The fictitious consistency we project onto the world of exterior objects parallels the strategies by which we preserve the self: "what we call a *mind*," Hume announces, "is nothing but a heap or collection of different perceptions, united together by certain relations, and suppos'd, tho' falsely, to be endow'd with a perfect simplicity and identity" (207). If we are a bundle of different perceptions succeeding each other with rapidity, how do we create this false but "perfect simplicity and identity"? How are we to "ascribe an identity to these successive perceptions, and to suppose ourselves possest of an invariable and uninterrupted existence thro' the whole course of our lives?" (253). In a famous passage, Hume argues that we have a "natural propension" to imagine this unity and continuity:

> The mind is a kind of theatre, where several perceptions successively make their appearance; pass, re-pass, glide away, and mingle in an infinite variety of postures and situations. There is properly no *simplicity* in it at one time, nor *identity* in different; whatever natural propension we may have to imagine that simplicity and identity. The comparison of the theatre must not mislead us. They are the successive perceptions only, that constitute the mind; nor have we the most distant notion of the place, where these scenes are represented, or of the materials, of which it is compos'd. (253)

Hume's theater metaphor is, as he acknowledges, flawed, because it implies a location; it presents, however provisionally, a substance or stage upon which these impulses and impressions may strut and fret. The metaphor splits the self into spectator and spectacle, creating an Archimedean observer able to bear witness to the oddly social figures that, as they "pass, re-pass, glide away, and mingle," in fact compose the mind itself. If the act of perceiving constitutes the self, how is one to know the perceiver from the perceived, the dancer from the dance?

Ruthlessly carried to its logical conclusions, Hume's philosophy creates an unlivable world. If we are composed of the fluctuating or fractured impressions we receive, then what sustains our sense of identity, our sameness and continuity over time? "[M]an is altogether insufficient to support himself," Hume tells us; "when you loosen all the holds, which he has of external objects, he immediately drops down into the deepest melancholy and despair" (352). It is precisely this loss of reassuring reference points that precipitates Hume's odd first-person confession of despair at the end of book 1 of the *Treatise*. "Where am I, or what? . . . What beings surround me? and on whom have I any influence, or who have any influence on me?" (269) Lonely, sundered from the sociable world, Hume finds himself a "strange uncouth monster," cast out from human commerce; "unsupported by the approbation of others," he finds that "all [his] opinions loosen and fall of themselves" (264, 264–65, 264). Nothing returns him to himself. Hume is threatened by the loss of "identity"—of continuity of being—in the face of an inconsistent reality. During this anguished interlude, Hume's identity is upheld, not by the objects that surround him, but by the thready continuity of a voice. That is, although the *content* of Hume's apostrophe questions his tenuous ties to the world and his extreme vulnerability within it, the *form* of the address anchors his identity in the repetition of the pronoun *I* that reconstitutes him as the addressee of his own anguished questions. *This* is what creates continuity until he can extricate himself from despair by binding himself to the sociable world by the fire (269).

In the context of eighteenth-century commercial and imperial expansion, Hume's epistemological doubts attest to the powerful moral and psychological disorientation wrought by global transformations. If our ideas of ourselves are anchored by the continuity of the world outside, then how can one secure a sense of self in the face of a world whose boundaries have exploded? When deprived of familiar objects, how do we return the world to its accustomed shape? In eighteenth-century texts, dilation upon an object often reinstates the identity of the bewildered or lost subject. Thus Robinson Crusoe traces the divine hand in the sprouting of barley and Mungo Park discovers Providence in the midst of the Sahara by meditating on the miniature perfection of a moss. Such addresses to objects, as Jonathan Lamb notes, have "little to do with careful observation and discriminate judgment, and much more with an ungovernable yet equivocal emotion, sometimes pathologically intensified, that attaches itself arbitrarily to objects."[38] Instead of describing the causality weaving through the scenes they depict, Crusoe and Park restore order to the world through the attribution of a divine intention behind a minute particular. By addressing themselves to an object, they create the continuity of a voice able to sustain the self. In a range of eighteenth-century texts, above all the sentimental novel, inward-turning characters fasten themselves onto external things in order to create the sustained fiction of the self in the face of a fluctuating reality. Sentimental texts confront the possibility of self-dissolution and create strategies for self-preservation.

Hume's "bundle" theory of the self poses a problem of provenance: where do the impressions that constitute the self come from, and how do they enter into one's world? For Adam Smith, by contrast, the problem is how to get outside the self. If, for Hume, emotions spontaneously travel, for Smith, they are laboriously imparted. "Though our brother is upon the rack," he pleasantly tells us at the beginning of *The Theory of Moral Sentiments*, "as long as we ourselves are at our ease, our senses will never inform us of what he suffers. They never did, and never can, carry us beyond our own person."[39] In Smith's rather unsentimental account, we are all irremediably individual, little islands of insensibility, possessed of feelings all too singular. And yet his text begins with the presumption of an "us" (the awkward plural of "our own person"); we the readers are enjoined to reach beyond our limited faculties to assent to his characterization of "our" insensibility. "By the imagination," Smith continues,

> we place ourselves in his situation, we conceive ourselves enduring all the same torments, we enter as it were into his body, and become in some measure the same person with him, and thence form some idea of his sensations, and even feel something which, though weaker in degree, is not altogether unlike them. His agonies, when they are thus brought home to ourselves, when we have thus adopted and made them our own, begin at last to affect us, and we then tremble and shudder at the thought of what he feels. (9)

Smith's observer attempts to grow the diminished likeness of another's feeling in the petri dish of his isolated being. The intense labor involved in producing and reproducing the feelings of others suggests that empathy is anything but spontaneous and natural, although Smith's assumption that one identifies with the sufferer, not the inflictor of pain, presumes a certain automatic selectiveness on the part of the observer.

Empathy is premised on the capacity to reconstruct another's affect as if it were one's own, but the opacity of others means that the capacity to grasp another's feeling depends on the ability to represent one's projections of another's feelings to oneself. The process of identification Smith describes is a far cry from both the simple swapping of places featured in popular accounts of sympathy and the spontaneous movement of emotion seen in Hume. For Smith, feeling does not travel. Rather like the twentieth-century Pierre Menard rewriting Cervantes, Smith's sympathetic man endeavors to construct a replica of another's feeling from within the citadel of the self. Instead of being impressed by another, the spectator acts upon himself: "we place ourselves in his situation" in order to produce an image within ourselves of his experience. Sympathy does overcome the boundedness of the individual, but it does so less by an extension of the person beyond the confines of the self than through a splintering of the self into multiple personality positions. For the encounter between the spectator and the man on the rack famously turns out to be a kind of ménage à trois: the sufferer on the rack and the witness are joined by a hypothetical "impartial spectator" who calculates the proper measure of affect upon the occasion (that is, the reasonable pitch that may be grasped by the witness). The man on the rack is likewise weighing how much he can rightfully expect the witness to grasp and moderating his cries accordingly; the sympathy in Smith's opening example is thus the labor of both observer and sufferer.

Furthermore, Smith's subjects only know their own feelings by identifying with the perspective of others. Whether victim or witness, "we must look at ourselves," Smith tells us, "with the same eyes with which we look at others: we must imagine ourselves not the actors, but the spectators of our own conduct" (111n). For Smith, as David Marshall puts it, one "becomes a spectator to oneself in order to determine if one can enter into one's own feelings. . . . Smith seems to separate the self from the one self it could reasonably claim to know: itself."[40] His theory of sympathy thus relies "upon an eclipsing of identity, a transfer of persons in which one leaves oneself behind and tries to take someone else's part."[41] In the process, this relation to emotion as one's own becomes more and more distended, but also more social and conventional, as it is calibrated against the ostensible norm of the impartial spectator. By dividing the self into spectator, actor, and third person, Smith forces the self to sympathize (or not) with sentiments of its own making.[42] Yet that sympathy is only possible via a detour through the eyes of another.

Smith acknowledges that sympathy is always mediated in his response to Hume's objections to *The Theory of Moral Sentiments*. If, Hume argues, "the Sympathetic Passion is a reflex Image of the principal, it must partake of its Qualities, and be painful where that is so." What then would impel us to enter into another's unpleasant experience? To claim, as Smith does, that all sympathy is constitutively agreeable, Hume argues, is illogical: were that the case, a "Hospital wou[l]d be a more entertaining Place than a Ball." Sympathy, he concludes, cannot be a matter of duplicating another's feelings; instead, there must be a subtle but necessary difference that shelters the sympathetic spectator from the suffering individual. Smith's rebuttal rests on the delight men take in perceiving imitation. The spectator, Smith argues, derives pleasure from "the emotion which arises from his observing the perfect coincidence between this sympathetic passion in himself and the original passion in the person principally concerned. . . . Two Sounds, I suppose, may, each of them taken singly, be austere, and yet, if they are perfect concords, the perception of this harmony and coincidence may be agreable."[43] We replicate in ourselves the unpleasurable original passion of the sufferer, but in transmuted form, as if it were the same note in a different octave. It is in fact the *difference* rather than the *identity* of these sympathetic feelings that produces delight. The pleasures to be derived from the sentimental stem from mimesis, from the apprehension of the concordance of the passion we have created with the passion of another. It is critical that the two feelings do *not* mingle. Instead, the comparison of original and imitation produces another emotion, a third sound, the harmonious concordance of two feelings. If part of the pleasure of sympathy arises from the synchrony of one's own feelings with those tagged as belonging to another, how is this provenance marked? How does one know these emotions to be another's?

Here we find a signal difference between Hume and Smith. In the *Treatise*, Hume depicts the mind as "a string-instrument, which after each stroke the vibrations still retain some sound, which gradually and insensibly decays" (440–41). Hume's vibrations, however, cannot be rendered as the pure tones of Smith's metaphor. Emotions are confused for Hume; each stroke will not produce a "clear and distinct note of passion, but the one passion will always be mixt and confounded with the other" (441). The passions for Hume are not clearly delimited. They do not inherently possess discrete or self-contained identities as fear or joy; we may not know what we feel. Here is where sentimentality enters the picture. Sentimental language bestows coherent shape upon otherwise inchoate feelings by decanting them into contained linguistic vessels. Only retroactively does affective experience become intelligible.

When another individual is involved, the designation of emotion becomes even more complicated, for others' passions mingle with, reproduce, but also dissipate our own. "[T]he minds of men," Hume announces in the *Treatise*,

> are mirrors to one another, not only because they reflect each other's emotions, but
> also because those rays of passions, sentiments and opinions may be often rever-
> berated, and may decay away by insensible degrees. Thus the pleasure, which a rich
> man receives from his possessions, being thrown upon the beholder, causes a plea-
> sure and esteem; which sentiments again, being perceiv'd and sympathiz'd with,
> encrease the pleasure of the possessor; and being once more reflected, become a
> new foundation for pleasure and esteem in the beholder. (365)

Hume, like Smith, celebrates the pleasure derived from another's sympathy. One consumes one's emotion by witnessing another witnessing it, but the half-life of these emotions—the insensible degrees by which they dissipate—and their immixture as they bound and rebound render origin and image indistinguishable. After multiple refractions, moreover, it is "difficult to distinguish the images and reflexions, by reason of their faintness and confusion" (365). Smith's sympathetic vibrations create a steady harmonious concordance; the refraction of Hume's vibrations or his mirroring minds dissipates rather than augments feeling. Smith's single-tone feeling clearly belongs to a particular individual, while Hume's vibrations confuse emotional belonging. Indeed, as Deidre Lynch notes, sympathy here is "defined in terms that redirect us from the personal to the impersonal. . . . As we proceed through this passage, personal feeling (the pleasure that belongs to somebody in particular) slips away."[44] In Smith, men stand before the mirror as spectators who recognize themselves reflected in others; in Hume, men are themselves mirrors. Both theories, however, emphasize the pleasurable consumption of shared feeling: no hint of envy or competition arises to mar another's tranquil enjoyment of possessions or pleasures.

For Hume, the facility with which we catch the feeling of others obscures the potential rivalry of interests or incompatibility of emotions. Hume's spectator admires an estate by identifying with the proprietor, rather than desiring to usurp his place; he seconds the proprietor's sentiments without anger or rivalry.[45] No covetousness or class-consciousness disrupts our pleasure in another's property and power. Hume blocks out any agonistic dimension to the communication of the passions: even as there is no struggle to appropriate property for oneself, so too is there no desire to claim affect as exclusive. Because there is no scarcity of passions—they fluidly communicate themselves—there can be no competition for their possession. In his fervent natural desire for sociability, Hume's man ostensibly wants to *be* the same or to *feel* the same, not to *have* the same. Sympathetic mimesis is seamless copying, not triangulated rivalry. And yet, as Pierre Saint-Amand points out, although the "mimetic impulse is responsible for initiating social contact through effects of sympathy and pity, and the desire to gather together, . . . imitation as a principle of identity between desires leads people to desire the same objects."[46] Reciprocity, after all, is the principle that underlies both sociable exchange and the lex talionis of vengeance. Notwithstanding Hume's insistence that mutuality of desire leads to balanced exchange, shared passions may spark violent rivalry for the same objects. As Páll Árdal notes, Hume's contagion of passions does not mean that I want you to have a glass of brandy; it means that I want one myself.[47]

Smith's model of sympathy suspends any rivalry to claim emotions as one's own. His man on the rack and his witness are both bent on achieving a normative equilibrium of feeling, allotting affective resources according to the distributive justice of the impartial spectator. Neither Smith nor Hume acknowledges that one might sometimes prefer to keep one's feelings to oneself. Yet Smith also depicts sympathy as a process dogged by potential usurpation. Although his language is saturated with the vocabulary of self-possession, it also describes a process of deliberate dispossession. For Smith, one does not merely endeavor to feel as another would feel, but to become that other person, to personate him or her. As Smith puts it in *The Theory of Moral Sentiments*, "I consider what I should suffer if I was really you, and I not only change circumstances with you, but I change persons and characters" (317). It is not enough to experience the "same" feeling—sadness, joy, fear, or whatever—I must experience that feeling *as if I were you.* The following question surfaces: if I change persons and characters, what sustains the "I"? In what sense are sympathetic feelings one's own? The "I" here has to come out of the margin of inequivalence: the part of the self that does *not* "change persons and characters" but is able both to engineer and to observe the effects of the interchange. In other words, for there to be a self that apprehends empathy, the exchange cannot be perfectly symmetrical; if it were, one would cease to be oneself, becoming utterly immersed in the other.

The descriptions of sympathy offered by Smith and Hume pose a problem of reserve: something must be kept back in order to contain these bodies that keep dissolving (into tears, into sighs) and overflowing (with feeling). What will secure the identity of the sympathetic subject in the face of such absorbing scenes? If sympathy describes the movement of feeling between persons, it also must delineate a kind of leftover, those aspects of the self that are not absorbed by or lost in another. It is here that the literary elements of sentimentality come into play. For literary form designates the relationship that the reader takes to this leftover. In the case of sentimental fiction, the gap between the feeling self (absorbed in another's emotion) and the detached spectator (that part that does not identify) is ostensibly filled in through the self-dissolution of emotion in the form of tears. Alternately, that heightened consciousness of a gap can generate additional displacements of the self and produce irony.

Perhaps nowhere is this oscillation between the sentimental and the ironic more apparent than in Sterne's famous description in *A Sentimental Journey* of a prisoner isolated in a cell. After compiling a battery of touching details—the pile of straw, the rusty nail with which the prisoner etches another day of misery on a calendar of small sticks—Yorick finds the scene *too* touching, and moves to another part of the description. The heightened state of emotion, rather than empathy, becomes Yorick's aim. The prisoner becomes the instrument of augmenting affect. "I darkened the little light he [the prisoner] had," Yorick says self-consciously and vaguely sadistically, debunking his own technique even as he puts it into action.[48] Sterne reconfigures the act of reading by heightening the sense of ironic distance, not from the text, but from the practice of reading (and writing) the reader and Yorick are engaged in.

Sentimentality embroils readers in willful acts of self-manipulation, putting them in emotional leading strings and inviting them to twitch the threads themselves in the puppetlike presence of sentimental figures. The reader, like Yorick, cannot remain absorbed in the moving scene before him or her but must work on his or her own affect in order to maintain or augment the degree of sensation. The risk is that the heightened self-scrutiny solicited by sentimental reading may ultimately precipitate the reader into an ironic posture in relation to both the tearful self and the lachrymose text. Even as Smith's or Yorick's description of sympathy splinters the self, irony, as Paul de Man tells us, "splits the subject into an empirical self that exists in a state of inauthenticity and a self that exists only in the form of a language that asserts the knowledge of this inauthenticity."[49] De Man's ironic subject, repeatedly recognizing the inauthenticity of his position, ceaselessly displaces himself in an endless ironic spiral. The relationship of reader to sentimental object is not the reciprocal, symmetrical substitution of one person for another (a closed figure eight) but a partial identification that splinters and displaces the self (a spiral). The structure of sentimentality closely parallels the structure of irony, but whereas irony produces self-conscious knowledge of its own inauthenticity, sentimentality (which must necessarily not understand its own inauthenticity) produces tears. Both nonironic sentimentality and its parodic hyperbolization produce communities: irony consolidates a community of the archly knowing, while sentimental tears create a community of the tearfully feeling. What I want to underline is that the structural similarity between the sentimental and ironic helps explain the "enlightened false consciousness" that so often characterizes sentimental reader response, in which the reader is aware of the falseness of his or her pleasurable emotion but perseveres without renouncing it. "One would readily create unfortunates in order to taste the sweetness of feeling sorry for them," Mme. de Riccoboni writes to Garrick from Paris in 1769.[50]

The doubleness of the sentimentalist's relation to himself—Yorick's capacity to feel and to manipulate his own affect, Smith's capacity to experience and to applaud his own reaction to the tonal concord—is connected to what the sociologist Colin Campbell has described as an eighteenth-century shift from "traditional" to "modern" hedonism. Whereas the traditional hedonist employs the material aspects of objects to alleviate discomfort, what Campbell calls the modern, autonomous, self-illusory hedonist derives pleasure from the fantasy wrapped around the reality of an object, played out in the hiatus between the encounter with an object and its consumption, between desire and consummation.[51] The modern hedonist consumes experience rather than objects per se— a notion perhaps best exemplified in the ubiquitous enjoinder to modern consumers to "Enjoy" (an injunction to pleasure without a specified object rendered all the more bizarre by its wording as a command). Because the feeling person adjusts his or her relation to the object, concentrating and diluting affect in order to calibrate its intensity and maximize pleasure, she or he is constantly placed in the position of observing or acting upon the self. Like Parson Tickletext, we are "having an emotion" rather than being emotional.

In Campbell's model, the "self" becomes simultaneously subject and object of its own affect, origin and by-product of its own affective experiences. As the proliferation in the eighteenth century of words with the prefix *self-* reminds us, the word (like the French *soi*) is first and foremost a reflexive adjective, closely connected to the term *same* in English and *même* in French. (The word *self* only appears in its modern usage in the seventh entry of Johnson's *Dictionary*, in a citation of Locke: "Since consciousness always accompanies thinking, and it is that that makes every one to be what he calls *self*, and thereby distinguishes himself from all other thinking things; in this alone consists personal identity, i.e., the sameness of a rational being.") This reflexive splitting of the self makes it possible to direct, or at least to monitor, identifications. Not an easy task. As Richardson's efforts to prevent readers from liking Lovelace too much indicate, the unruly reader must be prevented from careening through the text, empathizing with the wrong parties, cheering for the wrong team. The emotions inspired by texts are hard to control. "The tenderness felt there [i.e., in the theater]," Rousseau writes in the *Lettre à d'Alembert*, "has no determinate object of itself, but occasions the want of that object. . . . [I]t does not chuse the person we are to love, but it compels us to make this choice."[52] Although the text may stir up emotions, it cannot designate the object of these emotions; nor can it check the contagion of the wrong kind of feeling. "Who is it," Rousseau asks, "that does not become in some measure guilty of theft, by siding with the thief? For what is siding with a person [*s'intéresser pour quelqu'un*], but putting one's self in his place?"[53] In feeling for another, one may come to feel as another.

Identifications with others tamper with identities. Tales of travelers who "go

native"—from the Gulliver who returns irrevocably transformed from the land
of the Houyhnhnms to the South Seas mariners who refuse to leave paradise—
permit readers to slip out of their skins and traverse the globe in their imaginations. Such stories also ask what happens when a fanciful flirtation turns into a
more permanent relation. Sympathy does not involve the clean-cut substitution
of one person for another (walking a mile in another's well-defined shoes) but
the erosion of borders and the gradual elision of identities as one person embraces aspects of another. Some Britons in Africa, the reformed slave trader John
Newton observes, had "been gradually assimilated to the tempers, customs, and
ceremonies of the natives, so far as to prefer [their new] country to England."[54]
The metropolitan does not necessarily hold sway over the colonial. "By virtue of
living with foreigners," Jean-François Féraud writes, "one unconsciously takes
on their manners, and comes to identify oneself [*s'identifier*] with them."[55]

In its suggestion that emotional lives emanate from interconnectedness, from
the elusive relations *between* rather than the properties *of* particular beings,
sympathetic traffic calls into question the notion of the self as a discrete, self-
contained entity, a cogito, a self-interested island. As Diana Fuss succinctly puts
it, "every identity claim ('I am not another') is based upon an identification ('I
desire to be another')."[56] In sympathy, the lines of demarcation between one person and other people are not always cleanly drawn. The outline of the self is not
made with a cookie cutter. "Rather than thinking of the border as the farther-
most extension of an essential identity spreading out from a core," Michael Taussig suggests, one might consider "the border itself as that core."[57] Sympathy allows readers to catch or replicate others' emotions, suggesting a fluid movement
between subject and object, copy and original, or (in Taussig's terms) mimesis
and alterity. The imperfectly defined borders of empathetic subjects unsettle
easy binaries of self and other, by exposing the messy, shifting identifications and
partial recognitions on all sides of the sympathetic divide.

If sympathy invites readers to become absorbed by and into other people, sentimentality seeks to secure metropolitan readers from a menacing flux. The sentimental text both invites the reader to venture beyond the boundaries of the self
and establishes terms ensuring that there will be a subject position to which one
can return. The users of the sentimental are not lemmings, casting themselves
into an affective abyss, but rather a public engaged in what might be called emotional bungee jumping. And the need to anchor the fall becomes all the more critical when the distance between reader and sentimental object widens, when, as
it were, the other involved becomes even more other. The moment of sentimental identification must therefore contain both an invitation to meld with another

and a check that arrests improper or excessive identifications. Every sentimental union must admit of some impediment.

Rather than being overtaken by emotions that enter from without, the sentimental reader must govern his or her distance from feelings and the objects that incite them. This take-it-or-leave-it relation to feeling means the individual must be able to unhook himself or herself from one object and move onto the next; sentimentality is about both the encounter with the object—the quasi-pornographic usage of sentimental scenes—and the ability to disengage from the scene. It entices one in but also furnishes cues for letting go; pleasure arises from crying *and* from ceasing to cry. The serial structure of sentimental fiction does not invite absorption in the plight of the suffering object (the substitution of self and other) but the substitution of one sentimental encounter for another. We return to the sentimental text not because we are given what we want but because we are left wanting.

The repetitious structure suggests the ways in which the sentimental could turn readers into affect junkies, hardened consumers of deliberately cultivated feeling. And yet the form's quest for new objects, for new scenes of suffering to excite sympathy, is not just the novel moving down the sentimental food chain, as it exhausts one site of affect after another, in search of ever more pitiable scenes for its rapacious maw. Instead, one might understand the sentimental shifting of objects as a function of the political agency the sentimental novel possesses, as Philip Fisher argues. The repetition and rehearsal of emotions in the sentimental novel constitute the genre's contribution to certain kinds of cultural labor: the work involved in engineering a perceptual shift in who is designated as a person, for example. "The redesign of the boundary between the categories of man and thing," Fisher contends, "was an act of cultural work, as well as a legal and military matter, because the moral and perceptual change that alone could make effective a formal change had to be done by means of moral and perceptual practice, which includes repetition and even memorization."[58]

For Fisher, sentimentality does not invent new feelings, but rather applies already experienced feelings to new objects (mad people, women, children, slaves, etc.). Sentimentality uses new objects to trigger old emotional patterns. It "draws on novel *objects* of feeling rather than novel feelings. . . . [It is] a romance of the object rather than a romance of the subject" (98–99). Once absorbed as common sense, Fisher argues, the stock figures or stereotypes of sentimental literature, which are meant to create a change in the larger field of culture, come to seem exaggerated, trite, ossified, and offensive, not (or not only) because they are crudely drawn, overly simplified, but because they betray the effort put into creating the convention. "Where culture installs new habits of moral perception, such as the recognition that a child is a person, a black is a person, it accomplishes, as a last step, the forgetting of its own strenuous work so that what are newly learned habits are only remembered as facts" (4). It is in part because of the overt manner in which sentimentality bludgeons its readers with the essential humanity of its objects that the mode falls out of fashion. (It is also because those sentimental objects increasingly rise up to speak for themselves.)

In its assumption that readers already know who the subjects of feeling are and who the objects are, this model presupposes a clear demarcation between the narrator-spectator and the sentimental object (the slave, the prisoner, the man on the rack). Yet unlike the nineteenth-century American writers in Fisher's analysis, the eighteenth-century theorists of sympathy discussed above do not clearly distinguish between subject and object. Hume and Smith offer us, respectively, a self with improperly policed, porous borders and a subject that keeps splitting into multiple personality positions. The sentimental encounter is not only the mechanical rehearsal of a subject's emotions with an endless sequence of novel objects; nor does it simply absorb these new populations into the broader category of the human. Instead, the distinction of subject from object is part of the work performed by sentimentality. For Jean-Jacques Rousseau, indeed, the idea of the human does not exist before the encounter with another person. As we shall see in the next section, for Rousseau, sympathetic exchanges call into being the class of humanity.

French Sympathy and the Model of the Human

If the utility of the sentimental lies in its capacity to expand and contract the category of the human, the starting point of the French and British models varies: the British begin with the insular individual and seek to coax him or her into relation with the world; the French deploy an exemplary man who condenses universal processes (like the passage out of the state of nature) into a single figure. Whereas Smith and Hume place their individuals in local contexts and linger over the kinds and degrees of relation necessary to facilitate or block sympathy, the French devote greater attention to an abstract concept of the human, to the theoretical elaboration of what the human *de base* might be.[59] The British depict sympathy as fostering connections between discrete individuals. The French seek to unveil the commonality that is already there by deciphering the signs by which men recognize (and misrecognize) each other. Crudely put, for the British thinkers, the individual is more or less already there; sympathy con-

nects him to other men. For the French, the point is to create a thresh[
lows the individual to appear by elaborating a more general templa
sympathy enables the individual to recognize himself by knowing h[
ness in other men.

Several years before his novel *Julie, ou La Nouvelle Héloïse* (1761) enraptured contemporary readers and ignited the sentimental vogue in France, Rousseau elaborated an account of sympathy in his hypothetical history of the emergence of society from the state of nature, the *Discours sur l'inégalité de l'homme* (1755). Before the deforming effects of civilization corrupted him, Rousseau contends, man was naturally sympathetic, susceptible to pity, that "natural repugnance to see any sensitive Being perish or suffer, principally those like ourselves."[60] Anterior to reason and reflection, pity tempers the principle of self-preservation or *amour de soi* in the state of nature. "[A]s long as he does not resist the inner impulse of commiseration," Rousseau tells us, "he will never harm another man or even another sensitive being" (3.126; 3.15). Instinctive pity, as Jonathan Lamb notes, inasmuch "as it cannot be resisted, aspired to, or impersonated, brings everyone to the level of a mechanical impulse of the body, natural to the species under certain circumstances, and operating without any inherent moral value."[61] This spontaneous, even automatic, susceptibility to another's pain is central both to Rousseau's concept of natural man and to the French materialist thinkers; it forms one of the principle differences between the French theorists and the British moral philosophers (who tend to dismiss such mechanistic accounts of human sympathy).

Rousseau's savage does not, however, possess a common template for man, since the concepts necessary to recognize resemblance do not exist in the state of nature. As Rousseau tells us in the *Essai sur l'origine des langues,* natural men "did not know themselves. They had the idea of a Father, of a son, of a brother, and not of a man. Their cabin held all their fellows [*semblables*]; a stranger, a beast, a monster were the same thing for them: outside of themselves and their family, the entire universe was nothing for them."[62] For the primitive, each human exists sui generis, in his relation as father, son, brother. (Women are notably absent here.) In the state of nature, Rousseau contends in the *Discours,* "all individual things appeared to their minds in isolation as they are in the panorama of Nature. If one Oak was called A another was called B" (3.149; 3.32). Since the savage does not understand the properties of and difference between beings, he cannot sort them into classes (3.149; 3.32). It is only when the savage encounters new objects that he feels the urge to generate broader ideas about things through language. As the contiguity of oak trees makes their resemblance apparent, the generic term *tree* supplants "oak A" and "oak B," repressing the myriad differences between them.

And yet when the primitive's circle of humanlike creatures is enlarged, these new beings do not—at least at first—present under the guise of "man." When Rousseau's man of nature first encounters others, he is unable to know them as like and perceives them as threats:

> Upon encountering others, a savage man will at first be afraid. His fright will make him see those men as taller and stronger than himself. He will give them the name *Giants*. After many experiences he will recognize that as these supposed Giants are neither taller nor stronger than himself, their stature does not agree with the idea that he had first attached to the word Giant. He will therefore invent another name common to them and to him, such as the name *man* for example, and will leave that of *Giant* for the false object that had st[r]uck him during his illusion. That is how the figurative word arises before the proper word, when passion fascinates our eyes and the first idea it offers us is not the true one. (*Essai*, 5.381; *Essay*, 7.294–95)

That the other man is seen as a giant arises not from his real properties (he is not larger than the first) but from fear, the "passion" that "fascinates our eyes." The term *giant*, as Paul de Man points out, metaphorically articulates the primitive man's fear by making men seem bigger than they actually are. "The statement may be in error," as de Man puts it, "but it is not a lie. It 'expresses' the inner experience correctly."[63] Language originates in the passions as the individual freezes the inner experience of fear and gives it objective being in a word that crystallizes his apprehension. Crucially, this process of renaming "giants" (beings other than oneself) "men" (beings like oneself) entails a sense of self as the measure of resemblance: the primitive man compares himself to the alleged giants and realizes that they are neither larger nor stronger than himself. The fact that it is so difficult for Rousseau's man of nature to recognize his own likeness in the others he encounters suggests that there is nothing spontaneous or natural about the category of the human or the feelings it evokes.

The moment of comparison that creates the category of "man," moreover, produces two contradictory modes of being. On the one hand, the ability to depart from the self and enter into another's opinions and feelings creates the possibility of sympathy. On the other hand, the capacity to make comparisons produces a fallen self-awareness of the opinion of others, a splitting of the self that Rousseau calls *amour propre* (3.219; 3.91). As David Marshall puts it, "sympathy and *amour propre* both are born in the moment the self compares itself with others. Each is structured by an act of identification through which one transports oneself to someone else's place, a comparison of the self with an other turned *semblable* in which one forgets oneself and imagines the point of view of the other."[64] Whereas for Adam Smith, this splitting of the self produces the very possibility of sympathy, for Rousseau, the comparisons that produce sympathy potentially suspend its operation. Once comparisons between self and other can be made, reflection allows pity to be supplanted by an interested preference for oneself over others. As Rousseau argues in the second dialogue of *Rousseau juge de Jean-Jacques,* people are possessed of a "good" sensibility, affiliated with *amour de soi,* which is "nothing other than the faculty of attaching our affections to beings who are foreign to us."[65] At the same time, social man is plagued with a negative form of sensibility, affiliated with *amour propre,* in which one is only tempted to move "outside oneself in order to assign oneself the first and best place" (1.806; 1.112). The ability to make comparisons may thus create rather than overcome the distance between self and other. The act of sharing another's suffering gives rise to difference and hierarchy rather than similitude and equity.

If pity is the spontaneous instinct of the man of nature, in society it must be laboriously induced. As Rousseau writes in *Émile,* "how should we feel compassion, if not by being transported out of ourselves, and uniting our own persons, in imagination, to that of the suffering animal? by quitting, if I may so say, our own being for his?"[66] The mobility of Rousseau's pronouns—"nous laissons nous émouvoir . . . en nous transportant hors de nous"—indicates that his sympathizing collective "we" must practice upon the self both as subject and as object in "quitting our own being for his." Whereas the Humean conversion of idea into impression collapses another's suffering into oneself, Rousseau, like Smith, does not allow the sympathetic subject to interiorize another's experience as his or her own. Sympathy involves a departure from the self, rather than the irruption of emotions from without: "We suffer only in proportion as we think he suffers; it is not in ourselves, but in him that we suffer" (ce n'est pas dans nous, c'est dans lui que nous souffrons).[67] The fact that "the more you identify with the other, the better you feel his suffering as *his*" paradoxically means that, as Derrida has pointed out, "there is no authentic identification except in a certain nonidentification."[68] To take another's suffering as one's own is to cancel out the other's proper claim to it.

The pity that for Rousseau allows one man to recognize another as human becomes, in eighteenth-century theories of the sentimental, both the sign that one is human and the means of recognizing another as such. It is "sensibility," the sentimental novelist François-Thomas-Marie de Baculard d'Arnaud tells us, "that raises man above other creatures. Reason is not enough to distinguish us from the immense crowd of beings: we must further experience that dear and touching sensation that appropriates for us the misfortunes of our fellows. Pity enlarges our relations; inhumanity isolates us."[69] It is not reason that unites all men; rather, the fact that we feel for others raises us above beasts to the domain of the human. Untempered by compassion, the shared reason of men leads to cruelty and the remorseless exploitation of others. "Remove pity from the heart of man," Arnaud tells us, "and he is first among wild animals! all the more cruel inasmuch as he uses the light of reason to imagine other means to annihilate; should he abandon compassion, this gift he seems to have received from nature, even for a moment, he delivers himself into unheard-of excesses. Open our histories, read, and tremble."[70] Sentimentality's lack of systematic or methodical ordering—its emphasis on spontaneous feeling and action—allow it to mediate between the abstract universal Enlightenment category of "man" *and* the empirical or experiential grounding of a local sense of what a person ought to be like.

Too rigorous or rational a model of the human creates inhumanity. The recognition of "man" is one of the central questions posed in the dialogue between "R" and "N" in the second preface to Rousseau's sentimental novel *Julie, ou La Nouvelle Héloïse*. To the complaint that the characters of the novel are unnatural, impossible, lacking in verisimilitude, Rousseau's *porte-parole* "R" responds: "Do you know how vastly Men differ from each other? How opposite characters can be? To what degree morals, prejudices vary with the times, places, eras? Who is daring enough to assign exact limits to Nature, and assert: Here is as far as Man can go, and no further?"[71] How can one know when anomaly becomes distended to aberration, when hyperbole ceases to be exaggeration and becomes the metaphorical yoking of two different things? "R" protests against the imposition of precise limits on nature, which would place the mark of Cain upon portions of the human race, casting them out of a category that should be capacious, all-embracing. And yet in refusing to impose limits on the category of man, "R" opens the borders to giants and pygmies and untold horrors, chipping away at the common model and posing the crucial question of what ineffable feature will secure human identity. As Rousseau's "N" asks, if we cannot define what man is, how can we know what man is not? How can we know what should be excluded from the class of men? "With such fine reasoning, unheard-of Monsters, Giants, Pygmies, fantasies of all kinds, anything could be specifically included in nature: everything would be disfigured; we would no longer have any common model! I repeat, in Tableaux of humankind, Man must be recognizable to everyone" (2.12; 6.7–8).

It is true, "R" concedes, that novels must present a universally recognizable mock-up of man, "provided one also knows how to distinguish what constitutes variations from what is essential to the species" (2.12; 6.8). Yet how is one to sort out the deviations that produce variety or difference from that which is essential? What is sustained beyond the variations in mores, values, prejudices to confer upon an individual the character of *l'Homme*? In emphasizing the notion that "man must be recognizable to everyone," both "R" and "N" leave us with a perturbingly supple definition of "man," oddly akin to Justice Potter Stewart's definition of pornography. "R" doesn't know what man is, but he knows one when he sees one. That matters of anthropological and political import surface in a discussion of the verisimilitudinous depiction of novelistic character suggests the way literary thresholds shift those in other domains. The task of the novel is not only to paint a "tableau de l'humanité" in which "chacun doit reconnaître l'Homme" but also to establish what the "modèle commun" will be. In questioning how we recognize the humanity of another, Rousseau's preface also asks what the ineffable feature that defines the character of man might be.

Rousseau's discussion of the limits of the human is anticipated by John Locke in his 1690 *Essay Concerning Human Understanding*: *"the boundaries of the Species,"* Locke argues, *"whereby Men sort them, are made by Men."*[72] Locke questions both the arbitrary choice of essential properties and the alignment between real and nominal essences, between, in other words, the real internal constitution of things given by nature (of which we are, says Locke, ignorant) and the names we annex to complex ideas to distinguish species (3.6.13; p. 448). Because we are ignorant of the real essence of a substance, the best we can do is break down the compound into the elements or simple ideas that constitute the specific essence of the name. An enumerative definition of man (i.e., a featherless biped capable of reason) presupposes that we already know what traits—featherlessness, two-leggedness, reason—add up to a man.

But does one know which traits are essential to this equation? The abbot of St. Martin, Locke observes, was as an infant so deformed that he was refused baptism on the grounds of uncertain humanity, and yet he later proved to be a reasonable being. A slightly flatter nose, a wider mouth, and "he had been executed as a thing not to be allowed to pass for a Man" (3.6.26; p. 454). The definition of what essence will constitute the proper qualities of "man" turns into a matter of life or death, demonstrating that Locke's "figure [of man] is not," as Paul de Man writes, "only ornamental and aesthetic but powerfully coercive since it generates, for example, the ethical pressure of such questions as 'to kill or not to kill.'"[73] Minuscule deviation—the shape of a face, the want of a nose or a neck—may be made to morph into monstrosity. Anomaly beyond measured degree casts a being from human creation. "Wherein then," Locke concludes, "would I gladly know, consists the precise and *unmovable Boundaries of* that *Species?* . . . I think, I may say, that the certain Boundaries of that *Species* [of man], are so far from being determined, and the precise number of simple *Ideas,* which make the nominal Essence, so far from being setled [*sic*], and perfectly known, that very material Doubts may still arise about it" (3.6.27; pp. 454–55). Even the most meticulous catalogue of simple ideas making up the nominal essence of man doesn't quite add up. Nature has given us neither category nor epitome; the attempt to circumscribe the "precise and unmovable Boundaries of Species" leads to a circular appraisal using measures that we have ourselves devised. If categories emerge from "complex ideas of our own collecting," then they are constrained by the limits of our own experience. As Locke suggests, operating from generalized particulars can be as perilous as proceeding from absurd universals. The precise lineaments that constitute the just measure of man are uncertain. Even if we define man using an immaterial trait such as reason or spirit, it is unclear where to locate "the utmost Bounds of that Shape, that carries with it a rational Soul. . . . What sort of outside is the certain sign that there is, or is not such an Inhabitant within?" (4.4.16; p. 572).

By studying individuals as the playthings of contingent history and environment, Locke's empiricism fragments the ideal uniformity of human nature. But—as we saw in Rousseau's move from "giants" to "men"—it is language that exposes the pernicious fallibility of inadequate definitions. Words are imperfect vehicles for the ideas in each individual's mind, since the names we bestow upon things "*want Standards* in Nature, whereby Men may rectify and adjust their significations. . . . They are assemblages of *Ideas* put together at the pleasure of the Mind, pursuing its own ends of Discourse" (3.9.7; p. 478). A word takes on a life of its own. Each speaker and hearer thus holds different notions of what a given name signifies, a difference intensified by geographic and historical distance. Locke spells out the consequences of this line of reasoning in a striking example. If we elaborate our ideas of a species by adding up simple elements to form a complex idea that will serve as an umbrella term, the complex interplay between individual example and generalized concept can be exclusionary:

A Child having framed the *Idea* of a *Man* . . . [having] such a Complication of *Ideas* together in his Understanding, makes up the single complex *Idea* which he calls *Man*, whereof White or Flesh-colour in *England* being one, the Child can demonstrate to you, that *a Negro is not a Man*, because White-colour was one of the constant simple *Ideas* of the complex *Idea* he calls *Man:* And therefore he can demonstrate by the Principle, *It is impossible for the same Thing to be, and not to be*, that *a Negro is not a Man.* (4.7.16; pp. 606–7)

Locke intertwines the charged, ostensibly experientially derived concept of man from a child's generalization that all men, whether or not created equal, are created white; he subsequently moves to exclude those possessed of a differing property (here skin color) from the general category of man. The serene march of the child's syllogistic reasoning is Locke's target: specious reasoning dignifies "self-evident" propositions such as "it is impossible for the same Thing to be, and not to be" with the title of a maxim or axiom. However discriminatory Locke's child's remark may seem, the boy is in fact not discriminating enough: by failing to sort essential from inessential traits, he has singled out the wrong descriptive term to govern the category. (Indeed, Locke turns the tables on the boy's logic; his next example shows that children cannot be human if we say that men are defined by their capacity for rational discourse.) Attempts to define a minimal cluster of descriptive features—in Locke as in Rousseau's preface—are doomed to fail.

Sentimental sympathy does not depend upon a preexisting category—instead, it proceeds on a case-by-case basis, finding and affirming humanity based on the ability to excite or experience emotion. In account after account throughout the eighteenth century, fellow feeling is designated as the ineffable, evasive feature that sustains the nature of man in the face of all transformation. "Sympathy with distress," as James Beattie puts it in his *Elements of Moral Science*, "is thought so essential to human nature, that the want of it has been called *inhumanity*."[74] The capacity to experience sympathetic feeling at times defines the very possession of humanity. "[T]hose who feel lively emotions," Mary Wollstonecraft writes in a review of Samuel Stanhope Smith's 1787 *Essay on the Causes of the Variety of Complexion and Figure in the Human Species*, "wish to know if the same string vibrates in another bosom—if they are indeed tied to their species by the strongest of all relations, fellow-feeling—in short, if the world without resembles that within.... The untutored savage and the cultivated sage are [thereby] found to be men of like passions with ourselves."[75] One kind of humanity (the benevolent trait akin to pity) seems to define the other (species membership), as the faltering of fellow feeling marks out the limits of the human.[76] "What," the short-lived journal *Man: A Paper for Ennobling the Species* demanded in 1755, "can be more nobly human than to have a tender sentimental feeling of our own and other's misfortunes?"[77] Sensibility is both the sign by which another's humanity is to be recognized *and* a sign of the humanity of the feeling subject. In controlling the circulation and attribution of emotion, sentimentality helps to demarcate the thresholds of humanity by sorting subjects of feeling from objects. The model of sentimental identification described above is neither ahistorical nor politically innocent. In the context of eighteenth-century empire, the sentimental stakes prove to be high indeed.

The Sentimental Wealth of Nations

The version of "humanity" presented in the sentimental novel claims to embrace all times, all places, all seasons. Benevolence, the *London Magazine* tells us, "is confined by no place, nor connected with any particular number of individuals, but takes in the whole species, and breathes love and social sympathy upon the whole creation."[78] Feeling holds out the promise of universality in an age of global division. The conflicts between individuals and institutions depicted in a sentimental text may arise from a particular confluence of historical circumstances, but the outpouring of feeling is meant to transcend the petty squabbles of nations, the superficial differences of culture and custom. "Sentiment, that universal and invariable language"[79] is a kind of early modern emotional Esperanto, binding the world together. "I suppose," writes one of the Canadians in Frances Moore Brooke's *History of Emily Montague*, "when the heart is really touched, the feelings of all nations have a pretty near resemblance."[80]

The novel does more than depict humanity; it makes the reader a better person, offering exercises to strengthen the organs of sensibility. "The novel," Baculard d'Arnaud tells us, "is the book of humanity. It insinuates into our souls that sensibility, that tenderness, the principle of the true virtues; it tames the ferocity of pride, it inspires compassion, it returns man to nature, and keeps it alive in his heart. The sentiments are like the body; they weaken, become exhausted, and die if one does not give them nourishment. Of all genres of books, the novel is that which gives birth to sentiments, which sustains and strengthens them the most."[81] Sentimental texts nurture the soul to which the sensible body is so tightly conjoined, supplying the recommended daily allowance of humanity that counters the deleterious effects of anti-social appetites. The eternal verities of the human heart enable the sentimental text to soar above cultural distinctions to travel swiftly and fluidly across the globe. As Diderot's "Éloge de Richardson" effuses: "O Richardson! I would dare to say that the truest history is full of lies, and that your novel is full of truths. History paints individuals, you paint humankind.... History embraces but a portion of the duration, but one point on the surface of the globe; you have embraced all places and all times. The human heart, which has been, is and will always be the same, is the model from which you copy."[82] Even as the novel supersedes "fact-based" history, moving beyond narrow local truths to encompass the whole world, the sentimental mode creates a template for the "human heart," unconstrained by the limits of time and geography. The ease with which sentimental humanity absorbs fresh populations seemingly makes it an ideal mode for descriptions of empire.

The sentimental text represents forms of interpersonal communion that transcend national boundaries to embrace all humankind; it produces a community of weeping readers united across cultural and geopolitical barriers by shared tears. As April Alliston has pointed out, the tender ménages that compose and conclude sentimental novels by Sarah Fielding, Sarah Scott, Frances Brooke, Marie-Jeanne de Riccoboni, Françoise de Graffigny, Rousseau, and Bernardin de Saint Pierre only rarely align with social categories or institutions of heterosexual love, family, nation, or rank.[83] It is because it does not remain within these preestablished social forms that sentimentality is such an effective mode in the context of empire. Yet, if such communities mute certain kinds of social difference, they threaten to collapse other kinds: the very traits that render sentimentality so propitious for empire potentially undermine the solidarity of the nation. "The love of our own country," Adam Smith tells us, "seems not to be derived from the love of mankind. The former sentiment is altogether independent of the latter, and seems sometimes even to dispose us to act inconsistently with it."[84] Humanity and the nation are not coextensive. "No nation," Benedict Anderson observes, "imagines itself coterminous with mankind."[85] Although (as I argue below) sentimentality furnishes some of the identificatory tools for imagining the horizontal arrangement of persons associated with the nation, its own premises could not conceive the nation as a limited or bounded entity. If, as Ernest Renan contends, "nationality has a sentimental side,"[86] it is not conversely true that all sentimental feeling has a national side.

At first glance, sentimentality would seem ideally suited to the creation of national feeling. Certainly, it has much to tell us about the way individual affect—often characterized as that which is most personal, most particular to the self—becomes intermingled with communal emotion. Sentimentality, which represents intense shared and reciprocated emotions among novelistic characters in order to incite similar responses in its readers, orchestrates a communion of feeling that conjoins the reader to a larger imagined community, not unlike the "imagined communities" Benedict Anderson has famously described as constitutive of the modern nation. For Anderson, the individual felt experience of sympathy and simultaneity with a largely unseen multitude shapes nationality. This imagined community emerges from like persons engaged in the same actions at the same time—drinking coffee, reading the paper—who come to imagine a connection to others like themselves through the "ghostly intimation of simultaneity across homogeneous, empty time" (145). By inviting the reader to have feelings about or to identify with absent parties, sentimentality gave readers a set of terms and techniques through which to envision these relations to distant others. This argument suggests a structural alignment of national sentiment and the conventions and premises of sentimental reader response. But it produces a disturbingly homogeneous end product: a nation constituted out of the reproduction of sameness.

Nations are rarely uniform in their content, however, and even less so in an age of internal and external colonization. Differences of sex, rank, language, and region create a heterogeneous national body. As Kathleen Wilson notes, "In the early modern period, within the 'nation' mapped out by territorial, linguistic or patrilineal ties, national identities were understood, performed and consumed in a variety of ways by different groups, depending upon the gender, class and ethnicity of their members and hence upon these groups' and individuals' (unequal) access to the resources of the nation-state."[87] Neither the British "island" nor the French "hexagon" (a term that first appears in French geography texts in the 1850s)[88] were uniform, consolidated entities in the eighteenth century. Just as the imperfect union of England with Scotland was violently marked by the Jacobite invasion in 1745, in France, the singularity of *foi, roi,* and *loi* was strained by religious and regional dissension between Huguenots and Catholics, as well as between *franco-français* Franciliens, so to speak, and Alsatians, Occitan-speaking southerners, Bretons, and Basques. The "bardic nationalisms" Katie Trumpener has identified in the Celtic fringe offer a powerful countermodel to a notion of Britishness culled from the English home counties.[89] The Huguenots who settled in England following the Revocation of the Edict of Nantes in 1685, like the Irish and Jacobite refugees in France, are two examples of eighteenth-century diasporic identities that undercut national categories. If the very existence of a nation depends upon the repression of regional difference, local affiliations, individual vagaries, colonial expansion only places additional strain on the body of the nation. From Shaftesbury's perception that a nation grown too large develops factions to Rousseau's ideally sized republic in *Le Contrat social,* eighteenth-century political theorists recognize the deleterious effects of excessive growth upon the solidarity and uniformity of the nation. Like an eighteenth-century Goldilocks, political writers futilely look for a national body that's "just right." The noncontiguous colonies of eighteenth-century empire further undermined efforts to envision a unified nation.

The contesting claims of religion, ethnicity, regionalism, rank, and language suggest that national identity emerges, not from the positive assertion of unified character, but as a reaction to or photographic negative of another: we know who we are by who we are not. It is in distinguishing themselves from others, or in uniting themselves around a shared object, that people come to see themselves as part of the same community. Yet such differential identities are not always easy to define. In the eighteenth century, it was not invariably clear who the so-called other might be. Ongoing political, religious, and economic conflicts between France, Britain, and other European powers, as well as indigenous resistance to metropolitan incursions, meant that colonies frequently changed hands throughout the century. The neat division between Europe and its others subsequently fostered by some nineteenth-century British and French imperial self-definitions did not operate in the absence of a consolidated empire or a consistent "other."

Indeed, throughout the eighteenth century, the French and British principally defined themselves against each other rather than in relation to an extra-European other. Linda Colley has argued that Britons "came to define themselves as a single people not because of any political or cultural consensus at home, but rather in reaction to the Other beyond their shores."[90] And David Bell has identified an equivalent trend on the other side of the Channel: "the essentializing of ethnic and racial differences in fact began at the center as much as it did at the (perceived) periphery. It began as the French struggled to differentiate themselves from the people with whom they often felt the greatest affinity and similarity, yet who had also emerged as the greatest apparent threat to their own honor, prosperity, and understanding of the world: the English."[91] Yet even the opposition between French and British cannot be reduced to a simple binary; contemporaries describe the two nations as torn between longing and loathing for each other. "They fear, and yet despise us," the abbé Le Blanc writes of the English in 1745, "we are the nation they pay the greatest civilities to, and yet love the least: they condemn, and yet imitate us, they adopt our manners by taste, and blame them thro' policy."[92] "Anglomania," the *Observateur françois* remarks in 1770, "has rendered so many Frenchmen singular that if the fear of ridicule does not stifle this rage among us to resemble our neighbors, we will soon be fit to give them lessons in singularity."[93] The mimicry so central to postcolonial theory was played out between Britain and France as each other's internal shadows.

The political stakes of this struggle between Britain and France meant that, until the latter part of the century, the significance of the colonies stemmed largely from their impact on the balance of power—commercial, military, and political—among European states. Colonial possessions were another counter in a system that pitted British naval superiority against French land power, the commercial strength of a trading island against France's greater population and land area. The first three-quarters of the century witnessed a transformation in the economic importance of the colonies both as sources of raw materials (weaning the British in particular from dependence on the Continent) and as markets. Although claims, most notably by Eric Williams, that the profits from the slave trade directly fueled the British industrial revolution have been largely discredited, colonial expansion indirectly wrought massive changes in the British industrial and banking infrastructure.[94] Nor should the impact of global commerce on the French be underestimated. French foreign trade quintupled in the course of the eighteenth century, and France's industrial output increased sevenfold; the Gallic share of European markets grew faster than that of the British (although the British dominated the North American and West Indian markets).[95] Although the archaic plantation economy that produced colonial profits did not transform French industry and banking, as it did in the case of England, the profitability of the French sugar colonies rivaled and even occasionally surpassed that of the British.[96]

Sentimentality came into its own in the 1760s and 1770s, a key transitional moment between what are sometimes called the first European empires (primarily involving the European colonization of America) and the second (involving the European occupation of Asia, Africa, and the Pacific). The Seven Years' War (1756–63), the first protracted European conflict fought primarily overseas, materially altered the geopolitical face of the globe. In the Peace of Paris, the French ceded their possessions in Canada, parts of India, East Florida, Senegal, and the West Indian islands of St. Vincent, Dominica, Grenada, and Tobago to Britain. Although the French retained the three most valuable sugar islands, Guadeloupe, Martinique, and Saint Domingue, Gallic prestige had been dealt a crippling blow. For both nations, the theater upon which states and their citizens acted had gone global.

The Seven Years' War shattered the ideology of the British empire as Protestant, maritime, commercial, and free, necessitating new ways of thinking about

empire. Acquired through conquest rather than established by trade and settlement, the new British empire was territorial, not maritime; it embraced large
populations that were neither white nor Anglo-Saxon nor Protestant. Its administration required the accommodation of different customs, religious beliefs, and
practices. As P. J. Marshall has recently observed, "the alternatives facing British
policy-makers were, put in very crude terms, either to try to assimilate the king's
new subjects to British norms or to accept the existence of a new diversity within
the empire by incorporating into it hitherto alien religions, laws, and modes of
government."[97] The altered nature of imperial possessions required new ways of
thinking about other people that simultaneously acknowledged their common
humanity and upheld hierarchical differences. The qualified recognition of others afforded by sentimentality proved to be an ideal mode for this new form of
empire (a subject to which I shall return below).

Sentimental depictions of the victims of empire fomented doubts about its
morality and legitimacy when colonial insurrections—Tacky's Revolt in Jamaica
in 1760, Pontiac's rising in 1763, and the American Revolution in 1776—threatened to topple the whole edifice. Parliamentary inquiries into the misdealings of
Robert Clive in India and headlines about the savage campaigns to expatriate and
exterminate the Caribs on Saint Vincent in the late 1760s and early 1770s reminded domestic readers of the brutal underpinnings of conquest. The vast extent of British possessions sparked fears of domestic corruption as well. "In the
progress of conquest," Adam Ferguson wrote in 1767, "those who are subdued
are said to have lost their liberties; but from the history of mankind, to conquer,
or to be conquered, has appeared, in effect, the same."[98] An extended empire
might grow beyond the power of citizens to control it; a huge standing army
would compromise the autonomy of the nation, while the influx of luxury goods
would spawn effeminacy, enervation, decadence, and corruption, epitomized in
the reviled figures of the luxurious West Indian Creole and the nabob. The
American Revolution, which seemed to some Britons to be a "massive war effort
aimed at coercing or murdering Protestant English people living in America,"
according to Kathleen Wilson,[99] appeared to be the final sign that the British empire had ceased to be a virtuous one.

In the late 1780s, fear of domestic corruption and disquiet over the moral
governance of empire manifested itself in fevered humanitarian activism both
within Parliament and among the British populace. Edmund Burke's opening
salvo in the seven-year impeachment of Warren Hastings, first governor-general
of British India, in 1787 overlapped with the founding of the Society for the Abolition of the Slave Trade. Drawing heavily on the sentimental rhetoric of sym-

pathy, benevolent governance, and paternalistic protection, Burke, Fox, Pitt, and Wilberforce simultaneously questioned the nature of empire and helped to re-invigorate a sense of imperial legitimacy among Britons. The anti-slavery movement ultimately produced a fresh mandate for British imperial activity through the moral authority to be acquired by abolishing the slave trade. Here we may remark a notable difference between Britain and France: whereas Britons could condemn slavery while supporting other forms of empire, the fact that France's remaining profitable colonial possessions were the sugar islands meant that French opposition to slavery amounted to a wholesale condemnation of the nation's colonial project.

Like the British, the French were uneasy about the deleterious effects of empire (and some gleefully anticipated their rival's decline), but the French crown had not relinquished all imperial aspirations. The losses sustained in the Seven Years' War gave fresh impetus, for example, to speculation about a vast undiscovered landmass in the Southern Hemisphere. Although Louis XV's 1766 orders to the expedition of Louis-Antoine de Bougainville emphasize commerce and exploration, not conquest, it was hoped that markets, restocking ports, and raw materials in the South Seas might redress the balance of power within Europe by supplementing France's sorely diminished empire. Bougainville's circumnavigation of the globe and the Pacific voyages of Captain James Cook were depicted as inaugurating a new era of exploration and gentle civilization, in which commerce would supersede conquest. Nevertheless, eloquent savages like Diderot's Tahitian elder in the *Supplément au voyage de Bougainville* joined the sentimental figures of slaves, Native Americans, and Indians to denounce the destructive incursions of Europeans across the globe.

During this period, the influx of colonial goods and people created tremendous social strains in France and Britain alike. One need only think of Matthew Bramble's cranky tirades against the vile immixture of ranks and bodies in Smollett's 1771 *Expedition of Humphry Clinker* to recognize the anxieties provoked by the foreign infiltration—literal and figural—of the body politic. The proliferation of legislation in the 1770s seeking to regulate the presence of both free and enslaved Africans in metropolitan centers registers heightened anxiety about the impact of empire on the body of the nation. Both France and Britain sought to uphold the maxim that "there are no slaves in England or France," albeit by markedly different strategies. The 1772 Mansfield decision, commonly misunderstood as prohibiting slavery on British soil, prevented owners from kidnapping slaves and returning them to the Indies under habeas corpus, while the French upheld the notion of a free nation by prohibiting the entry of blacks into

France in the 1777 "police des noirs."[100] The intensification of racial discourse during this period was but one response to the question of how one was to absorb these heterogeneous populations into a national community ostensibly rooted in the likeness of all.[101] Sentimentality, I contend, furnished another.

The extension of the imagined community of the nation into the unimagined community of the empire required that citizens find some way of conceiving unity in the face of incontrovertible and intractable difference. Sentimentality attains its greatest popularity at a point when categories of national, ethnic, and cultural difference seem most imperiled, less because it holds out the promise of possible communion with all of humankind, than because of the distinctive structure of readerly identification it puts into place. Sentimental form institutes *restrictive* communities. Sentimental tropes furnish tools for imagining collective relations during this period, because they create the *semblance* of likeness while upholding forms of national, cultural, and economic difference. As Michelle Burnham has argued, imagined communities are grounded not in the real existence of likeness but in its perception. The typical John Bull or Marianne rarely matches the template. It is here that sentimentality is useful to the nation. The sentimental allows us to see things *as if* they were like, *as if* they belonged to the same body. Sentimentality works over its object: it constructs the object with which one identifies and retrospectively names it as coherent (and as like oneself), thereby disguising the labor of making the object in one's own image. The pleasurable similitude one detects and identifies with is itself the product, not the cause, of sentimental identification. As Burnham succinctly puts it, "what is sentimental about the imagined communities that novels create is the obscured fact that they are not based on likeness."[102]

Diderot's 1762 "Éloge de Richardson" describes the process of sentimental identification in terms that make this structure clear. At first glance, the community created by Richardson's novel would seem to issue from the reader's absorption into a world that already resembles him or her. There is, Diderot notes, no exoticism in Richardson:

> he does not transport you to distant countries; he doesn't expose you to being devoured by savages; he does not shut himself up in clandestine sites of debauchery.... The world we live in is the setting of the scene; the heart of his drama is true.... His characters are taken from the milieu of society; his incidents are in the manners of all policed nations [*les moeurs de toutes les nations policées*]; the passions that he paints are just as I feel them in myself; they are moved by the same objects, they have the same energy that I know them to have.[103]

The absence of exotic elements situates the events of the novel in the milieu of a collective "we," to which the reader ("you") is drawn; the novel's claim to truthfulness and reality is derived from the commonality of the reader's experience (the "world *we* live in") and the fact that the events are those of "une nation policée." The rapidity with which Diderot shifts from the reader, to the collective audience, to his own interiority, disguises the way his rhetoric forges a community of readers out of his own sensibility ("telles que je les éprouve en moi"). Diderot's community is not, however, infinitely expandable. To participate in the community of Richardson readers, for Diderot, involves a provisional acceptance of the roles and ideals it celebrates and an implicit refusal of what it excludes or repudiates. Diderot uses Richardson as a "touchstone" to appraise others, banishing those who dissent from his judgment from his community: "those who find [Richardson's novels] displeasing," he announces, "are judged for me" (41). Indeed, when another's position vis-à-vis Richardson cannot be spliced with his own, Diderot is obliged "by an effort of reason" to insulate himself from repudiating the other in a reprehensible "species of intolerance."[104]

In Diderot's description, the sympathetic and involuntary movements of the particular reader conjoin his or her body to the bodies of all readers so moved, creating a homogenized community of crying witnesses: "Men, come, let us weep together over the unfortunate characters in Richardson's fictions, and say: 'If fate overwhelms us, at least honest folk [*les honnêtes gens*] will weep over us too'" (33). The structure of being moved by Richardson involves a shared object ("the unhappy characters") witnessed by a collective readership ("let us weep together"), who simultaneously precipitate themselves into the position of victim ("if fate overwhelms us") being bemoaned by yet another group of weeping "honnêtes gens." The reader does not directly identify with the suffering characters in the text; to become the sentimental object would be to suffer as the victim suffers and hence to lose the pleasure of witnessing it. Instead—and here Diderot echoes Adam Smith—the reader constructs a third position from which to apprehend his or her response to the sentimental text. Simultaneously observer of another and observed by others, the reader is addressed by Diderot ("hommes, venez") not simply to feel and cry, but to model himself, from the position of the sufferer, on an ideal spectator of suffering. The focus on the individual response to the text—on the emotions incited in the reader's own self—trains the many in the "proper" reactions, becoming the means by which to create (and potentially to dominate) the collective. The reader both weeps for another and assumes the position of the suffering object to be apprehended, although his or her projected woes are left to a conditional anticipated state: "*if* fate overwhelms us."

Diderot's model produces a potentially infinite displacement, in which the spectators moved by the characters themselves become the spectacle, recompensed for their sacrificial tears either by the very fact of being moved or by the tears of other witnesses.[105] By creating such recompense, Diderot averts the possibility of agonistic struggle—the potential rivalry implicit in the triangular Girardian structure of these sentimental scenes. Everyone wins, because the moment of sacrifice or lack experienced by each spectator in turn reignites the cycle. The hole that Diderot's self-sacrificing spectator fills is the engine of the sentimental genre, for a hole that never can be filled must be ceaselessly replenished. (In Diderot's *Paradoxe sur le comédien*, we may recall, the ability of the actor to give the same moving performance night after night derives from an emotional vacancy at the heart of his art: it is because he does not feel that he can repeat the performance many times without exhaustion.)

The contagion of tears that transforms each spectator in turn from witness to suffering spectacle is not, however, a pure *mise-en-abîme*. Although Diderot's description of the reading process creates a community of similarly weeping spectators, the precipitation of the self into the role of the other is not a reciprocal and balanced exchange. Some dangling remainder always subsists to unsettle the neatness of the balance sheet. As Burnham puts it, "These tears which are so often a sign of sentimental identification—of the successful establishment of this relation of apparent equivalence—result . . . not from the seamless substitution of self for other but from the necessary margin of inequivalence produced by such an exchange."[106] This inequivalence permits the reader to create a renewable relationship with the sentimental object, because the distance between them has not been dissolved. The seemingly involuted cultivation of sentimental affect can be made sociable because it is *not* about absorption—not about delirious melding with another—but about repetition and preservation.

The plenitude of feeling celebrated in sentimental fiction is created and recreated from this lack. "The heart of the unhappy man," as Prévost's hero Cleveland explains, "is the idolater of its grief as much as a happy, satisfied heart is of its pleasures."[107] In preferring to revel in riotous grief, we seem to love our feelings more than we love the objects that produce them. Thus the "person who grieves," Edmund Burke announces, "suffers his passion to grow upon him. . . . It is the nature of grief to keep its object perpetually in its eye, to present it in its most pleasurable views, to repeat all the circumstances that attend it, even to the last minuteness; to go back to every particular enjoyment, to dwell upon each, and to find a thousand new perfections in all, that were not sufficiently understood before."[108] Like a melancholic, Burke's grief-stricken person lingers over the lost object, preserves it, refusing to relinquish it or to accept substitutions.

Sentimentality draws an object home in order to incite feeling, but it must also keep that object at a proper distance in order to conserve it, allowing that feeling to be revisited and reproduced. In the process, it prevents objects from being absorbed: it keeps things out there, where they can be shared and collectively held. This capacity permits the sentimental to produce sociable (communal, as opposed to personal) feeling. It is the fact that its objects are *not* fully absorbed into the community that makes the sentimental such a useful mode in eighteenth-century discussions of empire. Sentimentality thus creates collective feelings, not through the immediate effusions that ostensibly bond people directly to each other, but by structuring a community's relation to a certain set of objects. We do not feel as though we belong to a nation because we are like the other members, for example, or even because we can put ourselves in their shoes. Instead, we consolidate our affiliation with others who feel the same way about a shared object. The community the sentimental creates is *not* based on the (virtually limitless) objects that produce feeling, but on who is allowed or able to experience certain kinds of feeling about these objects.

In his 1882 essay "What Is a Nation?" Renan famously argues that what binds a nation together is "the possession in common of a rich legacy of memories" and a "present-day consent, the desire to live together, the will to perpetuate the value of the heritage that one has received in an undivided form" (19). But nations share not merely a set of positive values but also collective practices of negation or repression. What constitutes "the essence of a nation," Renan writes, "is that all individuals have many things in common, and also that they have forgotten many things" (11). The labor of bringing subjects together is executed both by what a text overtly represents or performs *and* by what it represses. If part of what creates national unity are collective acts of memory and of amnesia (the repression of multiple origins, the forgetting of the violent acts that created unity, the obliteration of unpleasant historical facts), then nations must preserve not only the past they remember but also the past that they have forgotten. Nations cannot, that is, work through and naturalize loss. They cannot accept substitutions, since it is the monumentalizing of that lost object that fosters national unity. The collective feeling called national mourning by the media is in fact its opposite; it is what Nicholas Abraham and Maria Torok, following Freud, characterize as *melancholia*, the preservation of loss, the refusal to accept substitutions for the lost object. And that melancholic structure of feeling—repetition without absorption—is sentimental. It is this capacity to incorporate without inclusion, to preserve what one has forgotten, that made the sentimental the genre of choice for empire by the end of the eighteenth century.

Romance, Epic, and the Sentimental Rewriting of Eighteenth-Century Empire

The preceding sections examined the way sentimental feeling consolidates individual and collective identities that sympathy threatens to elide. I have argued that the sentimental becomes the privileged mode for discussing colonial activity because it allows for the provisional acknowledgment of the humanity of others while upholding differences between communities. It is not self-evident why the sentimental should have become one of the central discourses of empire during this particular historical period, however, and it is worth examining the generic menu available to eighteenth-century writers on empire to ask whether the two main offerings—romance and epic—might have worked, and to address why they did not. By contrasting the ideological labor executed by epic and romance with that performed by the sentimental novel, I aim to address the specific reasons why sentimental tropes became one of the principal means of representing European relations with other peoples in the late eighteenth century.

It is more customary, certainly, to associate romance and nation or epic and empire. The romance paradigm, as Fredric Jameson argues, is a narrative of social consolidation that emerges in historical periods in which "central authority disappears and marauding bands of robbers and brigands range geographical immensities with impunity."[109] In romance, the defeated knight ceases to be an enemy by revealing his name; the revelation of his identity admits him to the community through a "semic evaporation" that permits him to change from menace to friend. This discovery depends upon a preconstituted world of knights: the unmasking *reveals* an identity that may have been misread in a world of quasi-allegorical signs but that was always already there. Romance *recognizes* characters; sentimentality *creates* recognition between groups that are not always already the same. Thus although the sentimental novel and the romance share a loose, peripatetic structure depicting serial encounters with quasi-allegorical figures, the sentimental community is elastic in a way that romance does not permit: its similitude is not grounded in the preexisting likeness of its members (the community of aristocrats featured in romance), but in their shared relation to a common object (a slave, a prostitute, a child) *unlike* themselves.

This distinction explains why the sentimental mode is particularly useful in the context of eighteenth-century colonialism. Whereas the point of romance, Jameson contends, is the incorporation of the stranger knight into a consolidated community, colonial conquest seeks a *conditional* absorption that preserves differences between parties. The scene of recognition that creates a community in romance does not uphold the hierarchy of power necessary to conduct colonial policy. Because the sentimental distinguishes the subject who feels from the object who produces feeling, it can create the semblance of similitude while maintaining categorical distinctions. In the sentimental text, the moment of recognition is not the pronouncing of another's name—romance's revelation of a shared noble identity—but *tears,* the performed sign of sensibility in response to a shared object of pity.

If romance allows for consolidation of a noble class by unveiling the "other" as the "same," then epic allows the "same" to be construed as "other," turning civil strife outwards towards a common enemy and legitimating a large-scale commitment of resources to war.[110] In epic, conquest furnishes an opportunity for the hero to win honor and prestige through war. Epic celebrates the imperial nation or calls it to arms; as Bakhtin reminds us, it tells the tale of the founding of a nation as inevitable destiny in a closed world. The epic community is already locked into place, the plot already known; detail and person militate towards a predetermined end. While the world of epic is already "completed, conclusive and immutable," however, the world depicted in eighteenth-century accounts of empire is neither closed nor homogeneous.[111] Epic deeds belong to the nation as it is known to be, while the discrete gestures of sympathy and benevolence that make up the sentimental text constitute the community in the performance, turning private acts into public virtues. The knight of romance and the epic hero are always already what they should be: absolutely good, their virtue is neither negotiated out of relations to others, nor contingent upon their deeds. In contrast, the sentimental protagonist struggles to *become* "good" through deeds or signs that manifest pity, charity, and resignation. (Nietzsche has much to say about this in his *Genealogy of Morals.*)

Eighteenth-century accounts of empire sit uneasily with the epic model. In the late seventeenth century, one can still find the kind of moral conviction displayed by François Charpentier in his 1666 *Relation de l'établissement de la Compagnie française pour le commerce des Indes orientales:* "The French nation cannot be contained in the enclosure of Europe; it must expand to the most distant parts of the world; the Barbarians must experience in the future the mildness of her domination [*la douceur de sa domination*] and polish themselves after her example."[112] By the middle of the eighteenth century, however, moral suspicion has crept into every deed. Proleptic tales about the fall of the Roman empire and economists' recognition of the destructive side effects of the influx of Spanish gold into the Old World meant that the colonial enterprise was by no means perceived as an unalloyed good. The horrific depredations in the Americas leave French and English writers scrabbling to differentiate themselves from the Spanish and the Portuguese of the so-called Black Legend. "The older providentialist languages of imperialism," Anthony Pagden writes, had to be "transformed into a pretence to enlightened rationalism."[113] Empire's aims and ends were presented as material goods, not monarchical glory; as commerce, not conquest; as prosperity, not prestige. "Can there be," David Henry asks in his 1774 compilation of English circumnavigations of the globe, "any comparison between the glory of a successful enterprize, founded on the laudable motives of diffusing happiness through regions, whose inhabitants, for ought we know, are yet immersed in savage darkness; and that of engaging in a hazardous war, by which millions of treasure must be expended, and thousands of lives sacrificed?"[114]

Enlightenment writers sing not of epic deeds, of arms and the man, but of colonial misdeeds: the harms done by men. The epic hero is a creature whose time has passed. Thus Adam Ferguson contrasts the ancient hero who, "actuated by a desire of spoil, or by a principle of revenge, is never stayed in his progress by interruptions of remorse or compassion," with his modern counterpart, who "employs his valour to rescue the distressed, and to protect the innocent."[115] Jean Blondel likewise condemns the epic ideal in his 1758 "ouvrage de sentiment" *Des hommes tels qu'ils sont et doivent être:*

> If those illustrious scourges of the earth whom we so fondly call heroes were resurrected, they might perhaps tell us: the frenzy of tormenting humankind went to our heads [*Si ces illustres fléaux de la terre, à qui nous prodiguons si volontiers le nom de Héros, reparoissoient au monde, ils nous diroient peut-être: la fureur de tourmenter le genre humain nous a fait tourner la tête*]. We did not enjoy a single moment of tranquility in our entire lives. We seemed vaguely happy when we had sacked some province that dared to resist us, or when we had cut the throats of several thousand men whom we did not judge worthy of living miserably under our domination. But perpetually renewed desires plunged our souls at every turn into new disquiet.[116]

Seen from the point of view of the victim, epic deeds make the hero into the bane of humankind. Blondel's newly psychologized action figure finds himself burdened with self-consciousness and a conscience to boot: epic valor brings no joy

or respite to the hero or to his nation. Incited by avarice, and fueled by the inca-
pacity to placate these restlessly reignited desires, conquest creates only dissatis-
faction and despair. Virtue belongs not to the victor but to the victim. Whereas
the epic celebration of an enemy's heroically obdurate resistance vindicates the
violence necessary to crush them or to subjugate them as slaves, eighteenth-
century sentimental writers on empire emphasize their status as passive victims
or articles seized on in commercial trade.

Writers in both Britain and France protest against wars waged for the vain-
glory of the monarch. For the better part of the century, empire is represented
as one aspect of broader mercantilist policies bent on bolstering national power
and prestige for the good of the people.[117] The transition from an aristocratic
model of conquest to one grounded in commerce meant that epic was of diminished service to eighteenth-century discussions of colonialism, although the
genre, not unlike history painting, retained its prestige even in the face of the
novel's growing cultural hegemony. As the terms used to justify empire shifted
from the acquisition of specie to commerce, from evangelization to enlightenment, from notions of barbaric others to a shared and potentially civilized humanity, sentimentality comes to the fore. Justifications of empire that rely on
civilization and progress need subjects who *can be* converted and remade in the
conqueror's image. Sentimental claims about common humanity furnished a
necessary underpinning to both the French imperial model, which stressed religious and cultural absorption or assimilation, and the British commercial empire,
with its celebration of reciprocal exchange between similar if not equal peoples.

For British and French theorists alike, commerce not only marks an advanced
state of civilization; it *creates* it by drawing the world together in the reciprocal
exchanges that polish manners. "It is almost a general rule, that where-ever we
find agreeable manners, there commerce flourishes," Montesquieu writes, in *De
l'esprit des lois* (1748), "and that where-ever there is commerce, there we meet
with agreeable manners."[118] Simultaneously symptom and cause of civility,
commerce converts individual passions to collective good, Mandevillean private
vices into public virtues. As Lori Merish has argued, by aligning material and
subjective refinement with the civilizing process, Scottish writers like Smith,
Millar, and Kames "(re)defined capitalism as a system propelled by desire, sympathy, and subjective identification rather than the often-violent expropriations
of labor, land, and resources."[119] The task of the sentimental was to proclaim the
work *already* performed by imperial commerce. Both as a daily practice and as
a rhetorical mode able to articulate economic and sociable relations between individuals and peoples, commerce promised to knit the world together in recipro-

cal, mutually beneficial relations. Commerce established relations between peoples, while upholding the differences between them. It furnished a rhetorical figure through which Britain in particular was able to absorb new possessions in its ever-widening gyre without relinquishing its proper national identity.

In the closing pages of this chapter, I want to sketch some of the differences between the ways French and British writers used sentimental tropes in their vindications and critiques of empire. Notwithstanding the sentimental celebration of universal humanity—its fabrication of a kind of "degree zero" human—categories of human classification developed unevenly in Britain, France, and a range of colonial settings. Comparing French and British models throws into relief the ease with which racial or sexual categories could be elided with national ones, as whiteness, for example, was collapsed into Frenchness or femininity into English domesticity. Recognizing the diversity of colonial practices in the age of Enlightenment may help to dispel the aura of inevitability that sometimes hovers over histories of empire in the nineteenth and twentieth centuries.

French and British colonial policies, institutions, practices, and outcomes differ in important ways. A thorough survey of these divergences falls beyond the scope of this book; indeed, much of this comparative history has yet to be written. The differences sketched out in the next few pages are thus offered as suggestions, in regrettably crude and general terms, of possible avenues for further exploration. The French tended to operate from universalist precepts regarding the common nature of man, while the British were more inclined to conceive of the subject as a rights-bearing or possessive, self-proprietary individual. French colonial policy generally stressed assimilation—the incorporation of others into the great family of humanity and their conversion to the Catholic faith—while the English emphasized trade and reciprocity between individuals in their depiction of imperial endeavors.

French and British colonial practices in the eighteenth century involved varying degrees and kinds of state intervention. French colonies were under the direct political control of the crown, with the mother country's commercial monopoly codified in the *Exclusif*, which prohibited the colonies from trading with any nation other than France. Although British colonies were the king's dominions, their colonial endeavors were frequently undertaken by private initiative (trading companies, charters, religious organizations) and were regulated by parliamentary control of taxation and by the Navigation Acts, which were the backbone of Britannic mercantilism. As a result, the legal regulation of colonial practices had different aims. The common denominator of British policy tended to be the individual as a singular subject girded by rights (or deprived of them), while the French codes sought to define how that individual was integrated into the social fabric through a network of obligations. French policy constituted and regulated subjects in the process of *becoming;* British policy designated the rights of subjects already there. Thus while Anglo-Saxon law emphasized the establishment and protection of rights and property, French law, in keeping with its derivation from the Roman civil code, largely focused on the reciprocal duties of the various orders of society, as well as the regulation of ritual practices, religious and juridical. The British sought to determine whether a right was there or not in order to apply it to a juridically constituted individual, while French law endeavored to regulate the practices, rites, and obligations that confer social being on the subject.[120] Thus the French *Code noir* (1685; revised 1724) that regulated the treatment of slaves in the colonies designated the duties of master and slave towards each other, while English law tended to focus on property rights in slaves and the legal regulation of the trade.[121]

The French emphasis on assimilation, conversion, and cultural absorption means that nothing inherent bars other populations from the doctrine of *une foi, un roi, une loi.* Conducted under the rhetorical auspices of Catholic universalism, French colonial policy dating from Colbert's 1667 directives on Canada sought to assimilate native populations through intermarriage and acculturation: "savages" who were converted were, Colbert instructed, to be "considered and reputed as French," so that "in the course of time, having but one law and one master, they may likewise constitute one people and one blood [*un mesme peuple et un mesme sang*]."[122] Whether Colbert's language borrows from the metropolitan concept of *race* as lineage and noble blood or anticipates the modern formulation of the concept is still disputed by historians; it is notable, as Saliha Belmessous notes, that despite their scant numbers "the French [in Canada] had no fear they could be biologically overwhelmed."[123] Only later in the century did writers recognize the possibility of a reverse influence. "Au-lieu de franciser les sauvages," Mirabeau writes of Canadian intermarriage in 1756, "ceux-ci ont sauvagisé les français" (Instead of Frenchifying the savages, they savagized the French).[124]

Although current eighteenth-century scholarship stresses the role played by the notions of monogenesis (the descent of all from Adam and Eve) and polygenesis (the theory of separate divine origins) in the elaboration of racial categories, the clear demarcation between the elect and the damned drawn by Protestant and especially Calvinist doctrines of predestination created an additional barrier to religious incorporation. Catholic universalist precepts permit, even advocate, the absorption of new souls into the community of saints, while the very name of the Church of England delimits its community. Yet early arguments for colonial ventures contain a strong religious strain. "The historians of the French overseas empire, many of them members of religious orders, assumed that God had approved their venture," Anthony Pagden notes, while "the British, during the period of the Commonwealth, took an astonishingly providentialist view of their exploits in the Americas."[125] The French commitment to evangelization is evident in the religious missions sent by the crown to Canada and the Antilles. Although the English, as Pagden puts it, "made their earliest claim to legitimacy in the name of the seemingly implausible obligation to convert the heathen to the faith," it was only in the 1780s that a broad-based evangelical strain of colonial discourse took hold in Britain, with Charles Grant, a director of the board of the East India Company, advocating the establishment of missions in India and William Wilberforce pleading with Parliament on behalf of Africans.[126]

The French model of cultural assimilation was subtended by a broader acceptance of biological or sexual incorporation among philosophers and natural historians. As Pamela Cheek has shown, French theories of human variety outlined in texts like Maupertuis's 1744 *Vénus physique* or Charles Vandermonde's 1756 *Essai sur la manière de perfectionner l'espèce humaine* stress absorption and the sexual "mixing" of different peoples over the possession of individual descriptive traits: "sex in the British racial model was a descriptive term for identity; it explained what was already there. Sex in the French racial model was generative and degenerative; it created what wasn't there," Cheek asserts.[127] The French generative model anticipated new genetic (and eugenic) groups to be produced, rather than regulating the permissible sexual relations among already-existing individuals. Thus the abbé Raynal advocates intermarriage as a more efficient form of colonialism in his *Histoire des deux Indes*. "Would it not," Raynal suggests, "have been a more humane, more useful, and less expensive plan, to have sent into each of those distant regions some hundreds of young men and women? . . . Consanguinity, the tie that is the most speedily formed, and the strongest, would soon have made one and the same family of the strangers and of the natives."[128] In Raynal's description, sexual union becomes the means of expanding imperial dominion without the need for conquest, assimilating the world into one big happy family.

The British tend to be less receptive towards intermarriage as a form of social and sexual consolidation. Texts ranging from Henry Neville's *Isle of Pines* and Steele's "Inkle and Yarico" depict the ways sexual desires transgress boundaries of culture, rank, nation, religion, and race. Although, as Roxann Wheeler argues, high rank and Christian conversion trump the visible signs of racial difference in mid-century novels about intermarriage, by the end of the century, such unions produce dissension rather than cultural reconciliation.[129] Since sexual attraction and reproductive capacity mark shared species identity, the degree of sexuality admitted into sensibility shapes the breadth of the community and the absorptive capacity of the sentimental courtship plot.

The materialist interests of the French philosophes more readily admit the commingling of bodies as well as souls in sympathy, sanctioning the fleshly component of sensibility that the English would disavow or purge. In Diderot's succinct formulation, "il y a un peu de testicule au fond de nos sentiments les plus sublimes et de notre tendresse la plus épurée" (there's a bit of testicle at the heart of our most sublime sentiments and our most refined tenderness).[130] In contrast, British writers attempt to police the distinction between being "touched" literally and metaphorically, although their efforts to remove the suspicion of prurient interest from sentimental encounters produce passive—even toothless—heroes like Lord Orville in Frances Burney's *Evelina* (1778) or Harley in Henry Mackenzie's *Man of Feeling* (1771). (Infelicitous chapter titles such as "The Man of Feeling in a Brothel" hint at the limits of such delibidinization.) Efforts to disentangle the sexual and the sentimental should be seen in relation to eighteenth-century British models of civic republican autonomy, which, Cheek asserts, sought to represent British public life as "successfully un-sexed, or rid of the troubling intrusions of bodily desire that could compromise rational public discussion and transparent communication."[131] (As we shall see in Chapter 4, the claims of the "man of feeling" to masculine political authority in parliamentary debates on abolition at the end of the century required the strict segregation of sex and sensibility.)

The role assumed by sentimentality in discussions of French and British colonial policy varies. British writers stress reciprocity as the engine and palliative of trade; the French, by contrast, emphasize the universality of humanity, justifying imperial practices by subsuming colonial subjects into a familial, patriarchal model. The starting points of the British and the French models thus differ. Whereas the British model tends to depict the individual as a self-contained vessel who must negotiate social relations and sympathetic feeling from the inside out, the French model situates its subject in a network that constructs and constrains the individual, governing from the outside in. "Nos voisins," as Prévost puts it, "n'ont pas l'esprit de méthode" (our neighbors lack methodical minds).[132]

The sentimental vision of empire propagated in British novels like Mackenzie's *Man of Feeling* gives pride of place to its victims. One of the most popular scenes in Mackenzie's text features the reunion between Harley, the eponymous hero, and his former tenant farmer, Old Edwards, now a beggar. After a rapturous moment of mutual recognition, Old Edwards recounts his fate since they last met. Impressed into the army and sent out to India, Edwards failed to enrich himself, since his "nature was never of that kind, that could think of getting rich at the expence of [his] conscience."[133] Edwards's virtuous restraint is contrasted with the rapacity of his fellow officers, who tortured an "old Indian . . . supposed to have a treasure hidden somewhere" (93). Old Edwards had been so moved by the Indian's "suffering in silence, while the big drops trickled down his shrivelled cheeks, and wet his grey beard, which some of the inhuman soldiers plucked in scorn," that he released the man (93). He was court-martialed for allowing the Indian to escape, given 300 lashes, and turned out of the regiment in the middle of India. The pathetic inverse of the imperial conqueror, Edwards wanders haplessly across India until he (inevitably) meets up with the Indian he has rescued, who "kisse[s] the marks of the lashes on [his] back a thousand times," and confers upon him a purse containing two hundred pieces of gold (94). The treasure that could not be wrested from the tortured Indian becomes the gift bestowed upon the beneficent Edwards as the reward for his pity. "You are an Englishman," the old Indian announces, "but the Great Spirit has given you an Indian heart" (94). Transcending the differences of nation, Harley and the Indian are united by their joint victimization. Mackenzie's text brackets the politics of imperial conquest and state-sanctioned violence, explaining systemic exploitation as the rapacious acts of individual men.

But Mackenzie invites his reader to contemplate the degree of national accountability implied by Old Edwards's anecdote. "Edwards," Harley observes, "I have a proper regard for the prosperity of my country: every native of it appropriates to himself some share of the power, or the fame, which, as a nation, it acquires; but I cannot throw off the man so much, as to rejoice at our conquests in India. You tell me of immense territories subject to the English: I cannot think of their possessions, without being led to enquire, by what right they possess them" (102). Harley's judicious shuffling of pronouns suggests the political implications of the sentimental calibration of distance and engagement. The tension between the English "native" who profits from national policy and the "man" who is moved to repudiate it is never resolved in the passage. The "I" who esteems the prosperity of "my" country shifts to a third-person singular ("himself") in contemplating "our" conquests, which become English ("their") possessions. Here national identity wavers between a claim of collective propriety (everyone appropriates "some share of the power, or the fame which the nation acquires") and personal disavowal ("I cannot throw off the man so much as to rejoice at our conquests in India"). The man of feeling seeks to justify the British presence in India through a defense of commerce over conquest. The English, Harley notes, "came there as traders, bartering the commodities they brought for others which their purchasers could spare; and however great their profits were, they were then equitable. But what title have the subjects of another kingdom to establish an empire in India? to give laws to a country where the inhabitants received them on the terms of friendly commerce?" (102). Exchange here is equitable even if there's an unequal appropriation of surplus value ("however great their profits were"), simply by virtue of the fact that it is exchange. For Harley commerce is acceptable, conquest is not. And yet distinguishing commerce from conquest, as Julie Ellison notes, mystifies their connivance; the passage can only acknowledge "the link between violence and material gain ... through the figure of the victim."[134]

Harley's naïve questions about whether Britons have the right to govern India should be read neither as a straightforward indictment of the English in India nor as an apologetic that justifies conquest by recasting it as commerce. For the fragment that contains these reflections bears a title that undermines their credibility as political commentary: "The Man of Feeling talks of what he does not understand" (102). The impossibility of deciphering whether the heading is descriptive (Harley is explaining those aspects of British foreign policy he does not understand) or satiric (the editor is commenting on Harley's folly in pontificating about matters that he does not understand) places the reader in an interpretive bind: unable to identify with Harley or with the positions advanced in the fragment, the reader is left with a kind of emotional blank check, addressed to an undefined political end for an unnamed sum. Mackenzie fends off the sentimentalist's potential complicity with exploitative economic practices by zeroing in on individual affect, inviting absorption in one's affective responses to other's sufferings rather than an analytic purchase on its material causes and effects. The passage rouses emotions and only ostensibly harnesses them to a political agenda.

Sentimental depictions of empire took off in France in the years following the publication of Bernardin de Saint Pierre's spectacularly popular *Paul et Virginie* (1788). Books like Joseph Lavallée's *Le Nègre comme il y a peu de blancs* (1789) and J.-B. Picquenard's *Adonis, ou le Bon nègre, anecdote coloniale* (1798) and *Zoflora, ou la Bonne négresse* (1800) appeal to shared humanity, singling out exceptional men and women of feeling as the building blocks for a paternalistic society rooted in mutual obligation. Whereas the British sentimental novel emphasizes commerce and social regulation through revised law, the French stress paternalistic reform grounded in a more inclusive template of humanity. Lavallée's hero, Itanoko, is a rare bird indeed: he is a composite of "traits taken from the life of different Negroes" combined in one exemplary model. The text is thus "not exactly a novel; it is the history of a national character offered in the character of a single man."[135] All men, Lavallée proclaims, are the same beneath the skin: "this is the shell: what does it cover? A profound sensibility . . . a pride of soul . . . a goodness of heart" (1.10–11). The task of the sentimental text is to unveil this truth.

Whereas Mackenzie's text extracts the common traits of humanity from shared suffering, Lavallée finds it in the sensibility of heart revealed in moments of transparency. "What has color to do with virtue?" the good son of the slave ship owner demands of his cruel father. "Men are brothers, and . . . they must all love one another" (1.102–3). The sentimental recognition of shared humanity leads, not to liberty or human rights, but to an insistence on the mutual obligations entailed by this recognition. Whites must acknowledge slaves as men— "their form, their services, their courage, does this not tell you that they resemble you?" (3.13)—while the slave must see the man in the master. "We are your brothers," a French abbé instructs the slaves. "Love even the blind hand that strikes you down" (3.14). Lavallée's novel redeems exploitation through paternalism, as the African hero becomes the owner of a sugar plantation and undertakes massive reforms. The whip is replaced by the clock, coercion by Christian conversion. "I rejoiced in my work," Itanoko announces. "I was like a father surrounded by an immense family, who values his hours by the love of his children" (3.47). He eventually retires with his sentimental French friends to Paris, absorbed into their world by virtue of the purity of his soul.

Because sentimentality acknowledges common humanity without requiring spiritual conversion or physical transformation, it allows others to be incorporated into (or expelled from) the sentimental community without formal communion or excommunication. Sensibility allows the happy few to achieve provisional likeness of soul through human feeling. Uniting people without explicit reference to class, ethnicity, region, religion, or race, and reconciling politically contradictory positions in the name of a heightened morality, it allows for the extension of moral or social parity without the risks of political equality.[136] Despite the fact that the sentimental appears to be all-embracing, it proceeds on a case-by-case basis, focusing on extraordinarily moving exemplars. It admits select individuals rather than whole classes of persons into the community of feeling, while withholding the recognition of equal rights. Sentimentality is well suited to a society interested in (the semblance of) a just order, not in equality.

Poised between a restricted cluster of like souls and the seeming universality of all humankind, sentimentality possesses the capacity to seal identificatory bonds within a closed community while ostensibly remaining open to all. The elasticity of sentimental identification, its oscillation between an all-inclusive package and a rarefied emotional elitism, enables it to expand to encompass the broader world of empire and to contract to a relatively constricted circle of right-thinking souls. As Hume puts it in his *Treatise of Human Nature*, "An *Englishman* in *Italy* is a friend: A *European* in *China;* and perhaps a man wou'd be belov'd as such, were we to meet him in the moon."[137] In negotiating between different degrees of separation, the sentimental produces mobile forms of identification that allow the sentimental reader to enlarge the premises of the self to embrace the world, while preserving the ground upon which she or he stands.

CHAPTER TWO

Sterne's Snuffbox

The term *sentimental* has not aged well. It connotes bad novels and greeting card aphorisms, the cheap rush of emotion wrought by commercials for long-distance telephone companies. Modern sentimentality is emotion for emotion's sake—gratuitous, manipulative, solipsistic, mawkish, self-indulgent, insipid, and inauthentic. One of the few positive uses of the word *sentimental* that remains current today is the phrase "sentimental value"—the idiosyncratic assignment of personal meaning to an object that transcends its material or economic worth. Things otherwise worthless (devoid of general use or exchange value) can possess sentimental value: creased photographs, old toys, snuffboxes, and worn-out clothing may all be loved for their own sake. Yet even "sentimental value" is an expression often used in a faintly trivializing and even derogatory sense, as if to condemn the overvaluation of the material, the infusion of inanimate matter with a significance that supersedes the meaning mere things should have.

Sentimental narratives are supposedly forged from purely subjective material—Yorick's sentimental effusions, Julie and Saint Preux's love, Clarissa's suffering. Yet it is material objects that furnish touchstones for these emotions. The monk's snuffbox in *A Sentimental Journey*, Diderot's dressing gown, the miniature of Julie in *La Nouvelle Héloïse*, and Clarissa's coffin are each infused with personal meaning by the hero's or heroine's relation to them. They serve as a means of recalling, calibrating, manipulating the incitement to feeling. Sentimental objects like these are supposedly singular, priceless, incommensurable with other values and other forms of valuation. Unlike the commodity, such objects are not interchangeable; not just any dressing gown will do. They are loved for their own sake and thus transcend their expressive equivalence in other things (their exchange value). This chapter outlines the uses of sentimental value by tracing the peregrinations of what is arguably the most celebrated sentimental object of the eighteenth century: Sterne's (or Yorick's) snuffbox. It argues that

sentimentality—by relegating possession of such objects to a purely private domain—acts as if objects were bound to individuals through exclusively affective
ties. In an era of global commerce, sentimental possession binds the world more
securely to the subject by appropriating objects in ties that supersede the material or legal connection of property to person. Sentimentality palliates appropriation by making property truly personal.

In Chapter 1, I argued that the massive expansion of colonial enterprise fostered a blossoming of sentimentality during the 1760s and 1770s. In the wake of
the Seven Years' War between Britain and France (1756–63), Britons found their
predominantly mercantile Atlantic empire transformed into something dangerously like the sprawling Roman or Spanish model. The acquisition of French possessions in North America, parts of India, and the West Indies meant, as Linda
Colley points out, that Great Britain acquired "too much power too quickly over
too many people."[1] Empire bought power and prestige, but also internecine
strains. Although the war strengthened Britain's maritime infrastructure, ex-
panded its manufacturing, and gained Britain strategically located, expanding
markets and sources for cheaper raw materials, the postwar domestic economy
was in a shambles.[2] The high cost of the war (an estimated £160 million) left the
nation with its powerful sinews overextended. The national debt had nearly dou-
bled, from £74 million in 1756 to £133 million in 1763, at a time when the economy strained to absorb more than 50,000 demobilized men.[3] Britons teetered between global dominion and local impotence.

Sentimentality thus bloomed at a moment when the cherished mainstays of
British national identity—religion, commerce, liberty—had been drawn into
question by the precipitous alteration of Britons' place in the world. "The spoils
of unprecedented victory," Colley asserts, "unsettled . . . longstanding British
mythologies: Britain as a pre-eminently Protestant nation; Britain as a polity
built on commerce; Britain as the land of liberty because founded on Protestantism and commerce."[4] The elaboration of sentimental propriety at this historical juncture reflects the trauma of a nation struggling to absorb too many
worldly goods. The dazzling array of products thrust on the market facilitated social mobility, arousing fears about the malleability of human personality and its
trappings. Sentimentality allowed a society undergoing rapid commoditization
to rope off areas that would not be absolutely fungible, both by stressing the particularity of the feeling self and by withdrawing objects from indiscriminate
circulation. Objects like Yorick's snuffbox, as we shall see, create a sacrosanct domain seemingly exempt from the fungibility or interchangeability of the market. The fact that certain objects cannot be made interchangeable secures per-

sonal and collective identities in the face of commercial and imperial expansion, as the inalienability of sentimental value provides a bulwark both against the incursion of the marketplace into the most intimate spheres of life and against the influx of foreign bodies—goods and persons—into the nation.

To sentimentalize an object is to bestow upon it the kind of singularity that defies the commodity form. And yet the sentimental was forged in the smithy of that great commodity the sentimental text. As the eighteenth-century market in articles like "Yorick" snuffboxes attests, sentimental objects and texts are not simply beloved possessions or gifts; they are *also* commodities, whose strongest selling point is, paradoxically, their sentimental value. The very notion of a sentimental commodity is anomalous, representing the infusion of human particularity into the interchangeability of the commodity as an aspect of its value. The sentimental commodity brings together things that are meant to be kept discrete: the interchangeability of the market and the singularity of a thing that one loves; the authenticity or spontaneity of one's personal ties to the world and the notion that emotional relations (to persons, to things) can be borrowed, rented out, had for money.

By inviting us to have feelings about things—to love them—the sentimental seduces us into taking object for subject; by packaging feelings in a commodity form, the sentimental text replaces subject with object, putting a price on what should not be (cannot be) commoditized. Assigning sentimental value to objects in eighteenth-century narratives poses questions about how we think about the commodity. Commoditizing the sentimental conversely questions the way we can think about the personal nature of feeling. The market in sentiment exposes the potentially impersonal origins of personal feeling: if sentimental consumers in effect purchase feelings, how does one make such feelings one's own? Sterne and his imitators had to wrestle with the fact that sentimental value, far from being inalienable, was up for sale. Simultaneously alienable and inalienable, the sentimental object both expressed and channeled eighteenth-century anxieties about the fungibility of the commodity form and the social relations it produced.

Yorick's Snuffbox and the Paradox of the Sentimental Commodity

Perhaps the most celebrated sentimental object in eighteenth-century literature is the snuffbox Sterne's traveling parson Yorick receives from a begging monk in *A Sentimental Journey*. Upon his arrival in Calais, Yorick famously refuses to give alms to Father Lorenzo and gratuitously adds insult to injury by con-

demning the monk as a parasite. He senses his fault when he later sees the monk
in conversation with an attractive lady, and he accompanies his apology with the
offer of his tortoise-shell snuffbox as the "peace-offering of a man who once used
you unkindly, but not from his heart."[5] Yorick ostensibly seeks to compensate for
his prior rudeness with the gift of an object, but he also wishes to raise himself
in the eyes of the lady, to regulate matters with his own conscience, and to stage
a scene of generosity for his own and the reader's consumption. The compound
motives of Yorick's deed are hinted at but not pinned down. For Sterne to dive
for specificity would be to undo psychological verisimilitude: the *poco più* of too
much clarity—like the *poco meno*—falsifies its object.

In the moment of silence that succeeds Yorick's offer, the monk polishes his
own less valuable horn box and "presented his to me with one hand, as he took
mine from me in the other" (SJ, 101). As the monk giveth, he taketh away: the
exchange balances on the knife blade between affective potlatch, one man out-
doing the other in what the monk calls a "contest" (SJ, 100), and gain—the monk
obtains the difference in value between his box and Yorick's, while Yorick gains
the sentiment. Notwithstanding sentimental claims to reciprocity, there is, it
seems, invariably a profit to be made in such exchanges, either because valuable
objects change hands or because characters siphon off delicious emotion. Indeed,
the fact that Yorick stages the offer cancels out the box's very nature as gift, not
only because recognition creates a symbolic equivalent, but also because, as
Jacques Derrida points out in *Given Time*, the giver's self-awareness means that
he "give[s] back to himself symbolically the value of what he thinks he has given
or what he is preparing to give."[6] The self-consciousness implicit in Yorick's account of the transaction means that the offering of the snuffbox lapses into the
appearance of the gift, because Yorick translates a possible loss into emotional
gain.

Critics who argue that sentimentality disguises unequal commercial transactions as balanced sociable exchanges have tended to focus on this "hidden" surplus, displaying an avid interest in uncovering the profit gleaned from the ostensible good deed. In gleefully stripping off the altruistic veneer to reveal the
self-interest beneath, these analyses of commerce reproduce a set of assumptions
about the origins and aims of exchange that deserve further examination. They
stress what is given and gotten in exchange (the snuffbox, the sentiment), using
equivalence—or inequivalence—to appraise the success of the transaction.[7]
They assume that the pertinent question is what is "really" exchanged, rather
than focusing on the fact that interactions in sentimental texts take the *form* of
exchange.

Although the snuffbox is acquired through exchange, it expresses not a quantitative equivalence between objects but a provisional qualitative relation between persons, a material sign of cross-cultural agreement between English and French, Protestant and Catholic, have and have-not. It is not a swapping of objects that leaves both autonomous parties intact; rather, it is construed by Yorick as a mingling of persons through the transfer of things: a gift. The *manner* in which the object is exchanged is far more important than *what* is exchanged. Sentimental commerce subsists in the transaction itself rather than in its projected outcome: "the ideas of what has happened," Jonathan Lamb writes, "are taking place as what is happening."[8] Simultaneously form and content, deed and description, the exchange of snuffboxes is not supposed to produce signs of sociability; it performs sociability itself.

In Sterne's texts, the way things circulate orders the connection between persons through things. The structure of exchange transforms the individual engaged in it. Thus when Yorick negotiates to purchase a coach, he finds himself becoming sharply appraising, competitive and avaricious. As Yorick bargains with the innkeeper, Monsieur Dessein, he confers upon the latter a pernicious cast of countenance in order to create the enmity necessary to pursue the bargain:

> I looked at Monsieur *Dessein* through and through—ey'd him as he walked along in profile—then, *en face*—thought he look'd like a Jew—then a Turk—disliked his wig—cursed him by my gods—wished him at the devil—
>
> —And is all this to be lighted up in the heart for a beggarly account of three or four louisd'ors, which is the most I can be overreach'd in?—Base passion! said I, turning myself about, as a man naturally does upon a sudden reverse of sentiment—base, ungentle passion! thy hand is against every man, and every man's hand against thee—heaven forbid! said she, raising her hand up to her forehead, for I had turned full in front upon the lady whom I had seen in conference with the monk. (SJ, 89–90)

By looking at Monsieur Dessein from different angles (in profile, en face), Yorick splinters his adversary into multiple demonized types (a Jew, a Turk) before turning his scrutiny back on himself. Yorick's "sudden reverse of sentiment" arises from a *logical* equivalence that first supplements and then supplants the economic one. Weighing the vile passions "lighted up in the heart" against the "beggarly account of three or four louisd'ors," Yorick recognizes the moral price exacted by the transaction.

In Yorick's account, the grasping avarice of the commercial bargain becomes an overreaching for profit that mutates into a hand that would smite another down. The imbricated spirals of the passage—the twist of Yorick's body echoes the "sudden reverse of sentiment" as the hand raised against another becomes the hand of the lady pressed to her forehead—convert anti-social commerce over things into the commerce of the sexes, changing Yorick's solipsistic address to himself ("thy hand is against every man, and every man's hand against thee") into dialogue with another. The adversarial relation between two men bargaining over an object subsides before interpersonal commerce between a man and a woman. Sentimentality reconfigures exchange so that it is not the swapping of discrete objects between atomistic individuals in a market society bent only on gain. It rewrites the scale of exchange (from global to local); the nature of the deed (from economic bargain to interpersonal fusion); its motives (from acquisitiveness to generosity) and its ends (from accumulation to beneficent sharing).

Two different relationships to objects surface in such passages. On the one hand, we have things articulating social relations between persons (a version of what Marx would call commodity fetishism); on the other hand, we have the exchange of objects socializing and consolidating relations (the gift). In anthropological theories, gifts and commodities form a powerful binary that has presided over the division not only between kinds of things but also between kinds of societies—above all, "primitive" and "advanced," "savage" and "capitalist" economies. The way things are exchanged makes visible a social and economic framework that in turn articulates different kinds of personality:

> Gifts, and the spirit of reciprocity, sociability, and spontaneity in which they are typically exchanged, usually are starkly opposed to the profit-oriented, self-centered, and calculated spirit that fires the circulation of commodities. Further, where gifts link things to persons and embed the flow of things in the flow of social relations, commodities are held to represent the drive—largely free of moral or cultural constraints—of goods for one another, a drive mediated by money and not by sociality.[9]

Gifts generate bonds by creating relations of personal indebtedness, whereas commodities cancel out debt through the equivalence of exchange. The gift, John Frow adds, "supposes and enacts a continuity between persons and things and thus the formation of chains of reciprocal obligation by means of the transfer of objects" while the commodity "supposes and enacts a discontinuity between persons and things and thus a reciprocal independence in relatively more abstract processes of transfer."[10] What I want to emphasize here is that the sentimental does not just remove the taint of commercial exchange by depicting the commodity as a gift; it attempts to create an alternate category of objects.

Yorick's snuffbox is neither entirely gift nor commodity; its value inheres in the sentimental uses to which it can be put: "I guard this box," he writes, "as I would the instrumental parts of my religion, to help my mind on to something better: in truth, I seldom go abroad without it; and oft and many a time have I called up by it the courteous spirit of its owner to regulate my own, in the justlings of the world" (SJ, 101). Yorick is careful not to claim property over the monk's box; to do so would be to reinscribe divisions between men. Although it has passed into Yorick's hands, the box has not ceased to belong to Father Lorenzo ("its owner," whose courteous spirit inheres in the object through which it can be called up). Proprietary right subsides before sentimental usufruct. Yorick diverts the proper function of the snuffbox (to carry and serve snuff); instead, he uses the snuffbox to conjure up the absent Father Lorenzo. The material object gives access to the immaterial memory; its permanence preserves the ephemeral experience. What is significant about the object is not just how it is obtained (it is given, not purchased), nor how it is used (as an objective correlative to fleeting emotions) but rather its inalienability (the fact that, irrespective of its ownership, it cannot be detached from Yorick's subjective experience). If the fact of being exchanged as a gift produces the sentimental value of the snuffbox, it also withdraws the box from further exchange, since sentimental associations are meant to be absolutely particular.

Unlike the commodity, the snuffbox is not defined through its relation to other commodities as expressed in the universal language of money and prices. It is not fleetingly "stripped of cultural meaning and social value" at the moment of exchange; instead, it acquires meaning from its exchange.[11] In this sense, the sentimental object is the antithesis of the commodity (at least in theory). Whereas the point of the commodity is its indiscriminate interchangeability, the point of the sentimental object is that it is not interchangeable. Although its initial selection may be contingent or arbitrary—"was I in a desert," Yorick tells us, "I would find out wherewith in it to call forth my affections"—the object itself is not incidental (SJ, 115). Like a child's blanket or teddy bear, only *this* one will do. What is loved *in* the sentimental object is not, however, the object's use value (the child does not love its blanket for its capacity to keep it warm) but something closer to its sensuous capacity to store up the human's living being (thus its softness, its smell, and the fact that it brings warmth have meaning). It is for this reason that we do not usually say a used toothpick has sentimental value.

Whereas the commodity derives its value from its relation to other commodities, the sentimental object gleans meaning from those who possess it. The sentimental object is an extension of the person. "That sort of relation which we own to every object we have long been acquainted with," Henry Mackenzie writes in the Edinburgh periodical *The Mirror*, "is one of those natural propensities the mind will always experience. . . . There is a silent chronicle of past hours in the inanimate things amidst which they have been spent, that gives us back the affections, the regrets, the sentiments, of our former days."[12] "Even for some inanimate things," James Beattie tells us in his *Elements of Moral Science,* "we have a sort of tenderness, which by a licentious figure of speech might be called sympathy. To lose a staff which we have long walked with, or see in ruins a house where we had long lived happily, would give a slight concern, though the loss to us were a trifle, or nothing at all."[13] Indeed, one may come to address one's possessions as companions. "If one has been long accustomed to a certain set of objects," Hugh Blair writes in his 1783 *Lectures on Rhetoric and Belles Lettres,* "when he is obliged to part with them, especially if he has no prospect of ever seeing them again, he can scarce avoid having somewhat of the same feeling as when he is leaving old friends. They seem endowed with life. They become objects of his affection; and, in the moment of his parting, it scarce seems absurd to him, to give vent to his feelings in words, and to take a formal adieu."[14] By establishing a personal communion between subject and object, owner and possession, the sentimental creates a value separate from the economic (the loss is a "trifle"). It renders certain things exempt from exchange, as if they were extensions of a self provisionally free from market relations.

Self and possession bleed together in the sentimental object, breaking down the neat divisions between alienable and inalienable that facilitate commodity exchange. Since sentimental objects cannot be loved by others in the same way, that is, they create a form of *inalienable* value that cannot be replaced by money or goods of like kind. That everything cannot be sold or bought is the repeated enjoinder of the sentimental novel. Thus when Yorick encounters a man grieving for the death of his ass, his servant La Fleur offers him money. "The mourner said, he did not want it—it was not the value of the ass—but the loss of him.— The ass, he said, he was assured loved him" (SJ, 140). Money cannot substitute for what is given, received, and lost in the sentimental object. Thus sentimental characters refuse to part with precious personal objects (or traits like chastity) and disdain recompense for their good deeds. Yorick does not sell the monk's snuffbox; he treasures it. (Of course, sentimental gifts are not necessarily cherished: when Yorick's servant La Fleur presents a young demoiselle with a bouquet, he is appalled to learn that in the two minutes since "the poor fellow had taken his last tender farewel of her—his faithless mistress had given his *gage d'amour* to one of the Count's footmen—the footman to a young sempstress—and the sempstress to a fiddler" [SJ, 256]. As we return to below, objects may be restored to the circuit of exchange from which their sentimental value is meant to withdraw them.)

In reinterpreting the way objects can be valued, sentimental texts devise forms of desire meant to defy avarice and outdo competition. They reinterpret luxury as a form of economic excess back into a kind of religion of sensuous desire, by inviting the consumption of one particular object, which cannot be exchanged against any others because its value lies in its exclusive relation to the individual. Since sentimental objects are ostensibly loved for themselves, one never covets *more* or *better:* they generate a model of desire that is not grounded in accumulation without end but based on the thing as an end in itself. Yorick does not want many snuffboxes; he loves this one. Sentimental possessions like the snuffbox are meant to produce a kind of terminal ownership that arrests further exchange at least temporarily, not only because the creation of sentimental value often also involves the erosion of exchange value (the very qualities that distinguish things as personal possessions of necessity make them secondhand) but also because sentimental value personalizes an object, making it meaningless or worthless to anyone else. (As anyone who has sorted through another person's possessions will know, why people save certain things is elusive, inexplicable, at times obscure even to the person himself or herself.) Sentimental objects thus have no equivalents; when they change hands, their meanings change, because they express a relationship with their owners.

Sentimental objects challenge the assumption—shared by theories of the gift and of the commodity alike—that exchange is driven by a desire to create equivalence through reciprocity. For although sentimental characters try to exchange, they also persistently try to withdraw things from circulation. The emphasis on exchange and commerce in the sentimental novel is in a sense misleading. Things given are not meant to balance out. Indeed, for Sarah Fielding's David Simple, Sarah Scott's Sir George Ellison, or Burney's Cecilia, no return is a good return, since the uncorrected balance sheet of beneficent loss is the mark and medal of charity.[15] Sentimental transactions do not seek to create equivalence, but to create a relation that upholds social and personal difference. They might be better understood in terms of what is kept or withheld, rather than what is given or received. In this sense, objects like the snuffbox should be considered neither as gifts nor as commodities, but as what the anthropologist Annette Weiner has called inalienable possessions.

Weiner argues that the principle of exchange is not reciprocity but withholding: "all exchange," she writes, "is predicated on a universal paradox—how to *keep-while-giving.*" Theories of gift and commodity exchange, Weiner argues, "take for granted, as did [Adam] Smith and others, that there is an innate, mystical, or natural autonomy in the workings of reciprocity. What motivates reciprocity is its reverse—the desire to keep something back from the pressures of give and take. This something is a possession that speaks to and for an individual's or a group's social identity and, in so doing, affirms the difference between one person or group and another."[16] If exchange is analyzed in terms of what is held back, what is *not* given, then it arises, not from a desire to create homogeneity and equality, but from a desire to produce relations while maintaining difference. The agonistic struggle within exchange remains present in Weiner's theory, but it manifests itself as a struggle to *keep*, not to get. In Weiner's terms, sentimental commerce must be seen, not only as mutual giving (whether spontaneous, calculated, or coerced), but also as an exchange of proxy objects motivated by a desire to secure or retain what really matters (one's self, one's singularity, the objects and people one treasures). At stake in giving and getting is personal and social identity. Commerce threatens to dissolve the borders between discrete individuals that sentimental value attempts to uphold. In withdrawing things from the fungibility of the market place, sentimental texts endeavor to uphold the singularity of the self through the particularity of its possessions. We shall return to this in greater detail in the discussion of Sterne's *Journal to Eliza* with which this chapter concludes. For the moment, I want to remark that what makes Weiner's theory particularly useful for sentimental value is that it is premised on objects always already possessed. If, as Derrida succinctly puts it, "*keeping* begins by *taking*," part of the romance of keeping-while-giving involves the repression of this initial arrogation of an object.[17] Sentimental texts repress the origins of the wealth benevolently redistributed by kindly heroes and heroines, disguising the historically specific conditions of the ostensibly universal virtue they claim for their protagonists.[18]

If the account of value that I have just outlined seems suspiciously sentimental, it is because it forms part of the story sentimentality tells about itself. And yet the sentimental value that at first seems pitted against commercial value may become part of the exchange value of the object—indeed, may come to constitute its value.[19] Something like this occurred in the formation of the "cult of

Lorenzo," named for the monk in the snuffbox anecdote. Shortly after the publication of *A Sentimental Journey*, the German lyric poet Johann Georg Jacobi sent fellow poet Johann Gleim a snuffbox inscribed with the words "Pater Lorenzo" in gold letters on the outside of the lid and the word "Yorick" on the inside. An accompanying letter described the purpose of the box. Having read the snuffbox scene to his brother ("who," Jacobi tells us, "feels the same about things as I do") and "to a circle of unfeeling women," Jacobi found himself moved to repeat Yorick's strategy. "How sweet the memory of the sublime monk was to us, and of the one who learned from him so willingly! Much too sweet not to be preserved by something palpable. We all bought a snuffbox of horn, upon which we had printed in golden letters the writing which is on yours." The pleasure derived from reading was to be preserved in "something palpable," so that it could be revisited at will. This public sign of a private sensibility is designed to serve as an outward sign of inward grace. It is a kind of sacrament, a marriage of true hearts in a homosocial ménage from which the "unfeeling" women are banished. Jacobi creates a circle of elite souls marked by an identity of emotion:

> To several we sent the present that you are getting as an insignia of a holy order; this letter is to impart our thoughts to others. Many readers will feel nothing thereby, others will not have the courage to pledge themselves to a struggle with themselves, still others will even be petty enough to appeal to their wealth which a box of horn seems to them to insult. The first we pity, of the second we hope for improvement, and the third do not exist for us. Perhaps in the future I shall have the pleasure of meeting here and there in strange places a stranger who will hand me his box of horn with the golden letters. I shall embrace him as familiarly as a free mason embraces another after receiving the sign. O how I would rejoice if I could introduce such a dear custom among my fellow citizens! Then religion would no longer separate them; they would have a common saint.[20]

The explanatory letter was reprinted in the *Hamburgischer Correspondent* with unexpected results. In his desire to create an insular community that disdained the base values of wealth, Jacobi unwittingly spawned a market in Lorenzo snuffboxes.

Jacobi's letter was published on April 4, 1769; by April 21, a journalist informed Jacobi that at least one hundred snuffboxes had already been manufactured, with the addition of the Latin motto *Animae quales non candidiores terra tulit* ("The world no purer spirits knows," in the poet William Cowper's translation of Horace's fifth *Satire*) in order to provoke "the fair ladies" to ask for an explanation, and exact "kisses for the service." In August, the same journalist sent nine snuffboxes at half a reichsthaler each to Jacobi. In Hamburg, a writer for the *Allgemeine deutsche Bibliothek* sardonically noted, the boxes were sold wrapped in a copy of Jacobi's letter "like Grenough's tooth-tincture in the directions for its use."[21] Merchants sent boxes all over German-speaking Europe. Jacobi was appalled.

Straddling the categories of gift and commodity, the Lorenzo snuffboxes incorporate personal desires and interpersonal bonds (the model of the gift) into the impersonal transactions of the market (the model of the commodity). For Jacobi, the problem is not only that the snuffbox becomes a commodity but also that "personal" value becomes part of the value of the commodity. The market in snuffboxes blurs the distinctions between what is inalienable in humans and what is alienable in things. If the myth of sentimental value is that it cannot be transferred (you can't borrow or piggyback on someone else's sentimental value and retain any claim to authenticity), the fact that sentimental value returns in the form of a commodity (as text, as souvenir, as snuffbox) seems like something of a cheat. "Others," Jacobi writes, "sought to feel emotions through art which they would have liked to have, but which were not theirs, and still others contented themselves with the mere outward appearance of sentimentality" (Howes, 429). The problem for Jacobi is twofold: either the purchasers of snuffboxes are trying to feel emotions "which were not theirs" or they are trying to misrepresent themselves as if they had those feelings by displaying an object.

Jacobi's snuffbox users covet not so much the box itself as the relation to it. What is envied in sentimental value is not possession of the object but the manner in which it is loved: the *how*, not the *what*. The snuffbox buyer aspires to absorb another's capacity to form such intense associations. Sentimental value does not stem from triangulation or the interested gaze of another; indeed, the obtrusive investment of others may undo the object's covert sway over its possessor. The snuffbox loses its value if it is cherished by too many others. The mass circulation of an object meant to be a sign of elite culture turns it into its reverse. As the snuffboxes become common, Jacobi and his friends try to make their particular *mode* of consumption a mark of refined sensibility. Their special grasp of the nuances of Sterne's text is meant, as Deidre Lynch puts it, "to distinguish their own deep-feeling reception of texts from other readers' mindless consumption."[22] Jacobi's disdain for the insufficiently sensitive reader echoes Sterne's own weary contention that "there is so little true feeling in the *herd* of the *world*, that I wish I could have got an act of parliament, when the books first appear'd, 'that none but wise men should look into them.' It is too much to write books and find heads to understand them."[23] Even if the herd of the world can procure the snuffbox or the text, they cannot be counted on to employ them correctly.

It is not that the buyers of the snuffbox or of Sterne's texts have not legitimately obtained them; they have, after all, purchased these items. The problem is that the emotion is still not their own. Mere possession of an object may produce a gush of self-congratulatory feeling, but no object can do the work of feeling for you. Jacobi's accusation is deceptively simple: the owners of the snuffbox "contented themselves with the mere outward appearance of sentimentality." The snuffbox thus may mark a *failed* substitution: it exposes the reader who has *not* identified with the injured monk or the beneficent Yorick, but has bought the snuffbox to stand in its place. Like the Chorus in Greek tragedy or the television laugh track, the snuffbox or the sentimental text performs emotions on behalf of its audience, feeling in our stead.[24] Since the emotions are executed by and in the text, we "have" feelings without feeling, delegating to other persons or even to objects the labor of producing or experiencing our own emotions. The very signs that make communion possible instead become public avowals that such communion has taken place. On these terms, the pleasure of sentimental emotion arises precisely because one is *not* having it: sentimentality involves the procurement of secret enjoyment without anteing up. In a riff on Walter's theory of auxiliary verbs, the sentimentalist, through the object, can enjoy the fact that emotion *is* taking place, *has* taken place, *will* take place, *will have* taken place. The crucial point is that the feeling is taking place elsewhere.

Sterne's vilification of this kind of misuse of objects is reserved for the domain of religion. In the *Sermons*, Sterne condemns the idolatry of the papist, who chooses hollow ceremony over real spiritual labor. It is, Sterne notes,

> easier to put in pretentions to holiness upon such a mechanical system ... than where the character is only to be got and maintained by a painful conflict and perpetual war against the passions. 'Tis easier, for instance, for a zealous papist to cross himself and tell his beads, than for an humble protestant to subdue the lusts of anger, intemperance, cruelty and revenge.... The operation of being sprinkled with holy water, is not so difficult in itself, as that of being chaste and spotless within—conscious of no dirty thought or dishonest action. 'Tis a much shorter way to kneel down at a confessional and receive absolution—than to live so as to deserve it—not at the hands of men—but at the hands of GOD—who sees the heart and cannot be imposed on.[25]

Preferring ritual and empty signs to the true discipline of the heart, the Catholic idolater circumvents spiritual trial; similarly, the facile sentimentalist claims the empty signs of a feeling heart in lieu of real emotion. "They no longer believe," as Slavoj Žižek writes, "*but the things themselves believe for them*" (34). Although

Sterne's sentimental fiction allows the reader to farm out emotion, his sermons do not admit religious labor by proxy. For Sterne, the division of labor that allows the economy to run more efficiently finds its limits in religion. Spiritual work cannot be broken down and hired out.

Popery—what Sterne calls "a pecuniary system, well contrived to operate upon men's passions and weakness, while their pockets are o'picking"[26]—invites its adherent to place his (or her) conscience in the keeping of the priest, "amus[ing] himself with a few instrumental parts of religion"—ritual practices and sacramental objects—in order to "cheat his conscience into a judgment that, for this, he is a religious man, and has discharged truly his duty to God."[27] In his *Sermons*, Sterne ventriloquizes the arguments that would persuade the sinner to commit the task of self-scrutiny and good works to others:

> If your works must be proved, you would be advised by all means to send them to undergo this operation with some one who knows what he is about, either some expert and noted confessor of the church,– – –or to some Convent or religious society, who are in possession of a large stock of good works of all kinds, wrought up by saints and confessors, where you may suit yourself– – –and either get the defects of your own supplied,– – –or be accommodated with new ones ready proved to your hands, sealed, and certified to be so, by the Pope's commissary and the notaries of his ecclesiastic court.[28]

Good works here became commodities available for purchase: new and old, sealed and certified by a papal bureaucracy. The Catholic logic of supererogation allows wealthy sinners to pay cash for the "surplus" meritorious acts of those who have already achieved enough good to get into heaven. The Church becomes a public treasury, its vault the medieval Treasure House of Merits. One cannot however farm out the labor of redemption, Sterne contends: "they who are persuaded to be thus virtuous by proxy, and will prove the goodness of their works only by deputies,– – –will have no reason to complain against God's justice,– – –if he suffers them to go to heaven, only in the same manner,——that is,——by deputies too."[29] Sentimentality is not unlike Catholicism in that it seduces the reader with beguiling promises of moral good at bargain prices, hawking the sentiment that there are some things that money can't buy.

To acquire sentimental feeling in the form of an object like a snuffbox is to shortcut the emotional labor that creates a human relation to the world, which, of course, is part of the reason the sentimental is accused of inauthenticity. Sentimentality becomes disturbing when that which is meant to guarantee the authenticity of the individual—what could be more personal or true than the spontaneous feelings of the true self?—appears to be artificially produced, *made*. That the self should be overtly practiced upon in its most enclosed precincts exposes the hand of man where no hand should be. What is perverse about Jacobi's critique—that others seek to feel emotions through art which "they would have liked to have, but which were not theirs"—is that it describes the very labor of the sentimental mode itself. The whole point of reading sentimental texts is to enjoy the feelings of others. What then differentiates Jacobi's authentic feelings from feelings that readers "would like to have, but which were not theirs"? How can one have feelings that are not "one's own"? What makes sentimental feeling one's own?

Sterne's contemporaries worried about this. Although they eagerly purchased his books, they frequently expressed concern that they might have been duped—that *Tristram Shandy*, for example, might be a textual version of the emperor's new clothes. Thus the French journalist and academician Jean-Baptiste Suard feared that "Mr. S T E R N E had amused himself at their cost, and that his work was a *riddle*, without an *object*."[30] Suard here is precisely the kind of reader Sterne loved to mock: eternally waiting for the punch line, incapable of reveling in the process. By reading as if there were something to be unveiled or an object to be procured, Suard's reader searches for the sentimental kernel hidden within a textual shell. Presumably, this kernel would be fodder for the "invisible cock" that yet another critic finds *Tristram Shandy* to be. This reviewer allegorizes the marketing of *Tristram Shandy* as a tale of Corporal Trim's willingness to pay a showman to see "an invisible cock," but insists, unlike Suard, that the reader has not been cheated even if the book proves empty. The huckster who sells a glimpse of an invisible cock has (Walter observes in the anecdote) kept his word; Trim has not been cheated. So, too, the reviewer contends, the purchasers of Sterne's text have "bought the sight of his invisible cock, without being cheated; for they have been beforehand told he is invisible."[31] The desire for a sign that one has received what one paid for creates a fervent yearning for a material object—for, as it were, a *visible* cock.

But the act of reading does not necessarily produce anything concrete. If the text could be thus ossified, then it would be an artifact (like a starling or a snuffbox) rather than a process. It is tempting to dismiss this longing for an object or souvenir—a readerly proof of purchase—as a trivial impulse or failure to read correctly, but one would be wrong to do so. For the desire to *have* an object marks the difficulty of knowing what one has acquired in or through a text. Although a text inheres in a material form, its physical being may be tenuously connected to its literary value. The physical form of the word—its sound image, its graphic form, the rags or wood pulp of which the book is made—is located midway between the material and the ideational, between interior thought and shared language. In what does a book's value inhere? Where is it located? What does one get out of reading? An object like a snuffbox proves that there was something there to be acquired in the first place. It materializes what has been obtained and proclaims it to be one's own.

In the case of the sentimental text, the question of whether you got what you paid for masks the potentially troubling fact that you paid for it in the first place. For the sentimental novel invites us to purchase in commodity form the sentimental value that can't quite be bought but that can only be paid for in kind. The legitimate acquisition of feeling exacts a particular kind of price. "A sentimentalist," Oscar Wilde wrote to Lord Alfred Douglas,

> is simply one who desires to have the luxury of an emotion without paying for it. ... You think that one can have one's emotions for nothing. One cannot. Even the finest and most self-sacrificing emotions have to be paid for. Strangely enough, that is what makes them fine. The intellectual and emotional life of ordinary people is a very contemptible affair. Just as they borrow their ideas from a sort of circulating library of thought—the *Zeitgeist* of an age that has no soul—and send them back soiled at the end of each week, so they always try to get their emotions on credit, and refuse to pay the bill when it comes in.[32]

For Wilde, to dabble in affect is to live on borrowed feeling; only when one is held accountable for emotional expenditure, when something is given or given up in the exchange, does emotional value issue from the self. That one does not pay in any real sense for sentimental feelings renders them gratuitous. As Wilde puts it, one checks them out as if from a library of commonly held sentiments; they can be borrowed and renewed, used without consequence since they are not permanent possessions but only on temporary loan. If sentiments can be procured without feeling and if emotions can be had without any personal investment, then what guarantees that they belong to the person experiencing them? What price can one pay to know that one's affect is one's own?

Emotions in an Age of Mechanical Reproduction

Laurence Sterne exploits the negotiable boundary between commodities and personal sentiment more than any other eighteenth-century writer, cheerfully flogging feelings in the literary marketplace. "There is a fine print going to be done of me," he writes in a postscript to a letter to Kitty Fourmantel, "so I shall

make the most of myself, & sell both inside & out."[33] Sterne gleefully tabulates
the profit to be gleaned from his books: he decants feeling into marketable vessels for ease of transport and consumption. "I care not a curse for the critics—
I'll load my vehicle with what goods *he* sends me," he writes to his friend John
Hall-Stevenson in 1761, "and they may take 'em off my hands, or let them
alone."[34] *Tristram Shandy*'s dedications are up for auction (TS, 1.9.15); the text
is interlarded with references to the sluggish sales of the volumes and to the
pending publication of Yorick's sermons (TS, 2.17.167). When sales of *Tristram
Shandy* flag, he customizes his texts to cater to the appetite for the pathetic,
evinced in public enthusiasm for the Le Fever episode; he keeps a weather eye on
book reviews to determine how next to proceed.[35]

Sterne, in short, tailors his sentiment to the marketplace. "I have had a lu-
crative winter's campaign here," he wrote to David Garrick from London in
March 1765. "Shandy sells well—I am taxing the publick with two more volumes of sermons, which will more than double the gains of Shandy—It goes
into the world with a prancing list of *de toute la noblesse*—which will bring me
in three hundred pounds, exclusive of the sale of the copy—so that with all the
contempt of money which *ma façon de penser* has ever impress'd on me, I shall
be rich in spite of myself."[36] If the sentimental text, as Sterne acknowledges,
preaches disdain for money, and its form seeks to arrest the fungibility of marketable things, then what is one to make of this deliberate capitalizing on the
sentimental? How does the sentimental grapple with the commodification of its
objects?

Sterne himself recognizes that his texts infuse objects with a value that may
supersede the particularity of the sentimental. The famous anecdote of the starling in *A Sentimental Journey*—an anecdote extensively analyzed by other critics—mockingly anticipates the market in Yorick snuffboxes, as well as the object
narratives to which we shall return in the next chapter.[37] Menaced with impris-
onment for want of a passport, Yorick seeks to master his fear by speculating that
being lodged in the Bastille might after all not be so bad, but his meditations are
interrupted by a repeated cry of "I can't get out," which proves to come from a
caged starling. The bird's cry shatters Yorick's reverie by reminding him, not only
of the very real horrors of bondage, but also of the self-seducing powers of sentimental representation. His consciousness of having been beguiled by art—his
own no less than the bird's—in turn creates a heightened consciousness of himself as both origin and consumer of his own experience.

The fact that Yorick cannot initially identify the source of the cry "I can't get
out" poses questions about the sentimental aesthetic experience. Should the fact

that the voice is that of a bird mitigate the degree or kind of feeling? To what extent does the fact that emotion is artificially procured undermine its authenticity? Yorick's encounter with the starling finds an intriguing parallel in Kant's *Critique of Judgment.* Kant observes that our disinterested delight in "the bewitching and beautiful note of the nightingale" falters before the revelation that the source of the enchanting sound is a boy whistling in the bushes. "As soon as we are aware that it is a cheat," Kant writes, "no one will remain long listening to the sound which before was counted so charming. And it is just the same with the songs of all other birds."[38] By introducing the possibility of a false or feigned note, Kant's mock bird catapults the delighted listener into a disenchanted world in which each object must be measured against its potential imitation. One can never be sure if the represented object is the thing itself. To be moved by a fraudulent tune is to experience the humiliating absurdity of misplaced sentimentality, the peculiar mortification of learning, for example, that a cherished lock of hair was cropped from the wrong head. Yet the unmasking of the artificial source of the sentimental experience may also produce pleasure: our delight in Sterne stems from being simultaneously seduced by and wise to Yorick's sentimental trompe l'oeil. Yorick *is* the boy whistling in the bushes: even as he reminds us that the song of the bird is fabricated, he composes its tune.

The bird, Yorick later informs us, has been taught to repeat the words "I can't get out" by a British groom conveyed into France in the service of his master. Limited to "four simple words—(and no more)" (SJ, 204), the bird has not been taught or at least has not learned to curse. The phrase is descriptive not accusatory; the bird neither protests nor asks to be released. It is, moreover, unclear whether the bird is meant to express the servant's feelings about his lot or to articulate (or mock) the bird's confinement to the cage. Split between the groom and the bird, the utterance does not resolve the question: to whom do the intention and the expression "I" belong? The same problems of portability that surface with Jacobi's improper snuffbox users surface here. To what degree do expressive words culled from another's mouth have meaning for the speaker who borrows them? The joint proprietorship of the phrase is the by-product not of shared feeling but of repetition by rote. Since the bird is not a conscious thinking thing, its utterance cannot be entirely its own; its words are sound rather than expressive language, neither original nor spontaneous. "Mechanical as the notes were," Yorick writes, "yet so true in tune to nature were they chanted, that in one moment they overthrew all my systematic reasonings upon the Bastile" (SJ, 198). It is thus the propitious coincidence of external circumstances and internal state, not sympathy for a like-feeling soul, that stirs Yorick's emotions. The fact that Yorick is moved by accident does not mean that he is not really moved, however: "I vow," Yorick tells us, "I never had my affections more tenderly awakened" (SJ, 198).

Markman Ellis, who sees the starling as an emblem of chattel slavery, notes that the bird unites "the idea of a rational animal (inflected with anthropological discussion of the status of African people) and that of an incarcerated subject (inflected with his surrounding remarks upon chattel slavery)."[39] The notion that parroted words, mimicked without comprehension, are not expressive of subjectivity is fairly unproblematic when the figure in question is a bird; it is quite another story when the speaker is human. The questionable authenticity of sentimental speech ceases to be merely a matter of fashionable affectation (as in Jacobi's improper snuffbox owners) when the person in question is an African, such as the former slave and well-known letter writer Ignatius Sancho.[40] Although Sancho's sentimental effusions are seen as evidence of his humanity—"a specimen of his writings," the children's author Sarah Trimmer notes, "will serve to convince the reader, that the negro race deserve to be ranked among the *human kind*"[41]—what one critic terms "the cant of affected sensibility in Sancho"[42] may also be used to deny the capacities of Africans.

Sterne's interest in slavery is often traced back to his correspondence with Sancho, while Sancho's interest in sentimentality is often traced back to Sterne, whose style Sancho's writings self-consciously imitate. Sancho's July 1766 letter to Sterne on slavery and Sterne's reply were both frequently reprinted in the eighteenth century. Lauding Sterne's call in a passage in his *Sermons* (later recycled in *A Sentimental Journey*): "Consider how great a part of our species in all ages down to this, have been trod under the feet of cruel and capricious tyrants,"[43] Sancho urges in the letter that Sterne "give one half-hour's attention to slavery, as it is at this day practised in our West Indies." Wavering between the implausible suggestion that Sterne's text might alter the material fate of those enslaved in the colonies and the more likely possibility that it might transform metropolitan attitudes, Sancho diagnoses the self-satisfying nature of sentimental discourse: "that subject, handled in your striking manner, would ease the yoke (perhaps) of many—but if only of one—Gracious God!—what a feast to a benevolent heart!—and, sure I am, you are an epicurean in acts of charity." The profits to be gleaned from acts of charity redound upon the benevolent heart; as an "epicurean" possessed of the refined philanthropic palate of a true connoisseur, Sterne will be repaid hundredfold for his sentimental labors. Sancho exhorts Sterne to "figure to yourself their attitudes;—hear their supplicating addresses," rendering the human expressivity of the enslaved multitude both the by-product of Sterne's solipsistic labors and the plaything of the sentimental imagination. Simultaneously example and epitome, the singular figure of Sancho condenses and displaces these suffering throngs, exposing the tension between human particularity and representative interchangeability: "think in me you behold the uplifted hands of thousands of my brother Moors."[44]

Inasmuch as one is ostensibly not meant to love *this* particular individual, but to love all slaves through him, one figure *must* stand in for another, even as the starling alternately represents the groom who has trained him, the chattel slave in the Indies, an anonymous prisoner, and Yorick, as well as Sterne himself. Whereas the particularizing of sentimental value involves the refusal of substitution (only this particular snuffbox is to be cherished), here the interchangeability of the African becomes the precondition for sentimental politics. In a sense, Sancho invites Sterne to produce sentimental value around the figure of the slave by singling out certain exemplary Africans (like himself) to be cherished, not as a source of labor or raw material, but as an emotional indulgence yielding affective gratification. The notion that a person might have sentimental value is unsettling, even repugnant; the value of a human being is always already meant to be sentimental in the sense that people should be inalienable, particular, loved for their own sake. A person should not need the superaddition of sentimental value in order to be kept off the market. More important, a claim to humanity grounded in sentimental value is precarious at best; as Srinivas Aravamudan reminds us in his discussion of Aphra Behn's novel *Oroonoko; or, The Royal Slave* (1688), the "honorary subjectivity" of the sentimentally valued pet is withdrawn the instant the owner decides to return the slave to the marketplace.[45]

This is, of course, the fate of Yorick's starling. Although his servant La Fleur purchases "both him and his cage for me for a bottle of Burgundy," Yorick famously does not set the starling free (204). Instead, he brings it back to England, where the bird becomes a marketable object. After describing the gift of the starling from Lord A to Lord B, Yorick traces the bird's downward mobility from Lord C's gentlemen to Lord D's for a shilling, and thence around the alphabet into the hands of commoners. Constituted as property that shifts from gift to article of sale, the starling remains in bondage *because of* the value given to it by Yorick's encomiums on liberty. Because the bird's plight constitutes its sentimental utility, its suffering must be perpetuated or even replicated in order for it to be of use. The circulation of the bird imitates Sterne's own progress as a celebrity through London and Paris, where he was feted and petted, not unlike the starling, and himself became instrumental in the social mobility of others, just like his books.

Yorick's text renders the bird a mark of status, and hence a desirable, marketable thing. "It is impossible but many of my readers must have heard of him; and if," Yorick adds, "any by mere chance have ever seen him—I beg leave to inform them, that that bird was my bird—or some vile copy set up to represent him" (SJ, 205). Yorick claims the bird, not in order to free it, but in order to make sure he gets credit for it. He is borrowing prestige back from his creation—although his continuing claim to own the bird (*my* bird), even after relinquishing possession of it, must stem either from his emotional labor in feeling for the starling or from the authorial labor of recounting its history. Indeed, this proprietary claim is intensified to the point of subjective solipsism, because the pun on Sterne and starling—grounded in the homophone between the dialectical *starn* (from the Old English *stearn*) for starling[46]—makes the bird a sign of Sterne, not of slavery and certainly not of itself; its placement on Yorick's coat of arms constitutes a kind of aesthetic apotheosis designed to prevent the bird from being appropriated by others. The claim to absolute propriety—sentimental or otherwise—over the bird comes at the price of its life. Although Yorick mocks the circulation of the starling, the text contains no unvarnished indictment of its commoditization. Indeed, since the bird could only possess value *after* Yorick's text is published, the reference *within* the text to its future sale manufactures a future that has not yet been realized (and potentially plants the idea so that it will be fulfilled). The sentimental value attributed to the starling does not withdraw it from circulation but rather creates and augments its market value.

Advertised as the bearer of a ready-made personal significance, the sentimental object (like the souvenir) entices the consumer by promising to confer particularity through exchange. From the love of this stuffed animal, that necklace, we turn outward into the potentially unfillable matrix of the market, moving by imperceptible degrees to matters of personal style, the potentially infinite extension of self into and through things encapsulated in the modern vernacular by the elastic conditional of the expression "the kind of thing s/he would love." To appeal to a connoisseur of affect, objects and texts come presentimentalized. *The Beauties of Sterne*, an anthology of his gems, with the bawdy bits excised, which went through seven editions within a year of its publication in 1782, was marketed for its ability to produce feelings on demand, although its editor confesses that his intention to alphabetize the anecdotes had been abandoned when he realized that "the stories of *Le Fever*, the *Monk*, and *Maria*, would be too closely connected for the *feeling reader*, and would wound the bosom of *sensibility* too deeply."[47]

Yet an object that advertises itself as sentimental, that comes presentimentalized, calls into question the personal nature of the emotion it incites. The mechanical reproduction of the book introduces the troubling prospect of a quasi-mechanical reproduction of readerly experience. Even explanations that derive the value of the sentimental from the consumption of a text, rather than the purchase of an object, encounter this problem of encapsulating value. That our feelings are our own because we feel them (short of demonic possession, to whom else might they belong?) is the kind of pleasant tautology Sterne reveled in. But its circularity begs the question of origins. As we saw in Chapter 1, the fact that emotion irrupts into the self from outside poses troubling questions for eighteenth-century theories of sympathy. How do we assimilate others' feelings or ideas—above all when those feelings and ideas come to us in the form of objects (including texts) that are bought and sold?

Contemporaries who disliked Sterne frequently accuse readers of claiming to have feelings that were not sincerely felt. The proliferation of would-be Yoricks and copycat Shandys who replicated Sterne's style, stole his characters, and impersonated his personae suggests that there was no shortage of readers willing to slip into another's skin.[48] Sterne's language and style are easy to appropriate; his sentiments are too portable. As the *Monthly Review* complained in July 1781: "Every coxcomb who was versed in the *small talk* of love, and who had acquired the knack of writing without thinking, fancied himself to be *another* Y O R I C K ! and as it was exceedingly easy to *assume* the *virtue* of sentiment, and as easy to adopt its *cant*, the E L I Z A s too, were very numerous!" (Howes, 248). The sentimental as a figure of reading lapses into a descriptive term for the affecting postures cast by Hummel figurines, as the experience of authentic emotion becomes a set of hollow gestures to be aped. The proliferation of second-rate copies led the minister and essayist Vicesimus Knox to complain with some asperity that "Mr. Sterne and Mrs. Draper have too many imitators. A goat is a personage of as great sensibility and sentiment as most of them" (Howes, 255). (Given the sentimental nature of Sterne's goats, Knox's comment recoils on its own premises.)

Sterne himself reveled in the capitalization upon his work by others, recognizing it as free advertising—although he took the precaution of autographing the later volumes of *Tristram Shandy* in order to distinguish the originals from pirated editions and knock-offs. Sterne's works bear the ineffable mark of his proper hand, both figuratively in his unique style and literally, in the use of his signature to distinguish one mechanical reproduction from others. "Mr S—," the *Critical Review* observed in 1762, "might have saved himself the trouble of signing his name to each volume of this performance ... as it would be impossible for any reader, even of the least discernment, not to see in the perusal of half a page, that these volumes can be the production of no other than the original author of Tristram Shandy" (Howes, 138–39). The originality of the production creates a desire to discover the precise nature of Sterne's originality, the exact quality that makes Sterne like himself.[49]

It is not an easy question to answer. Sterne's playful appropriation of the figures of Tristram and Yorick both in his letters and in his public life in London and Paris makes him a tough character to pin down. The texts themselves illustrate the fact that personalities casually assumed may come to overtake the person. Not only is Yorick mistaken for the jester in *Hamlet* in *A Sentimental Journey,* he is given legal papers that identify him as such. During his sojourn in Paris, he scrabbles for a place at the table, not unlike Diderot's *Neveu de Rameau,* though Yorick retains his position by falsifying his own sentiments in order to assist in the reproduction of other people's personal lives. "For three weeks together," he notes, "I was of every man's opinion I met" until he sickens of this "most vile prostitution of myself to half a dozen different people" (SJ, 266). If it is vile to live parasitically off of another's feelings and language, it is also degrading to produce the language off of which others live. "It was," he concludes, "the gain of a slave" (SJ, 266). Crucially, it is Yorick's talent as a sentimentalist that qualifies him as a professional sycophant. That Yorick's apostrophe to flattery might easily be mistaken for his praise of sensibility betrays the proximity between the two: "Delicious essence! how refreshing art thou to nature! how strongly are all its powers and all its weaknesses on thy side! how sweetly dost thou mix with the blood, and help it through the most difficult and tortuous passages to the heart!" (SJ, 260). Like flattery, sentimental writing turns out to be a form of "vile prostitution."

Contemporaries, however, sought to protect the sentimental aspects of Sterne's works from accusations of imitation, artificiality, or fraud. Thus, in documenting Sterne's learned allusions or literary larcenies in his 1798 *Illustrations of Sterne,* John Ferriar exempts Sternean affect from allegations of plagiarism. The originality and propriety of Sterne's ideas and language may be open to question, Ferriar acknowledges, but "in the serious parts of his works, he seems to have depended on his own force, and to have found in his own mind whatever he wished to produce."[50] Sterne may well have borrowed opinions and words from Montaigne, Cervantes, Burton, and Shakespeare, but Ferriar insists that Sterne's feelings remain his own. Emotional propriety issues here from a kind of principle of *res nullius* (the right to empty and unoccupied terrain) or perhaps from the right of first or prior possession. This argument solves the problem of Sterne's personal feeling but fails to solve the problem of how the reader can share Sterne's feeling.

Sterne's contemporaries show considerable ingenuity in explaining how "his" affect came to be their own. One reviewer argues that the reader *already* occupies the emotional space sketched out by Sterne's text. He counters accusations of readerly plagiarism with a description of identification so overpowering that it transposes the roles of mimetic text and reader response:

> Sterne, when the reader examines his own heart, has told him nothing new. He recollects, or rather believes that he recollects, having experienced the same sensations on similar occasions, and he cannot conceive how Sterne could have given him so faithful a picture of his own mind. This . . . is the very perfection of writing; namely, to present us with a sentiment or a passion so exactly resembling our own, that we are ourselves deceived so fully, that we believe Sterne has committed plagiarism on us. This we believe to be the only plagiarism of which Sterne has really been guilty.[51]

The reader does not experience Humean sympathy, in which the idea intensifies until it attains the force of an impression; instead, she or he derives the provenance of feeling by comparing (the task of the understanding) the recollection of feelings past with the representation of present emotion. So exact a replication of what one would have felt *had one been there* (not unlike Lady Catherine de Bourgh's boasting of her daughter's skill at the piano "had her health allowed her to learn") allows the reader to reverse the order of imitation. The reader does not imitate Sterne. Sterne, in a curious time warp, proves to have imitated the reader. In reading Sterne, that is, we set ourselves before the text as its object of imitation. As Sterne himself wrote in a letter to Dr. John Eustace, "a true feeler always brings half the entertainment along with him. His own ideas are only call'd forth by what he reads, and the vibrations within, so entirely correspond with those excited, 'tis like reading *himself* and not the *book*."[52] Sentimental identification occurs by repressing the foreign origins of one's sentiments, by forgetting that they are borrowed or bartered from the world outside ourselves.

Yet another explanation of the appropriation of sentimental feeling unto the self may be grounded in what might be called a labor theory of emotional value. Sterne takes up a version of this problem in the form of Walter Shandy's theory of intellectual appropriation. "My father," Tristram tells us, "pick'd up an opinion, Sir, as a man in a state of nature picks up an apple.—It becomes his own,—and if he is a man of spirit, he would lose his life rather than give it up.——" (TS, 3.34.262–63). In constituting ideas as apples, Walter (or Tristram) forces us into a particular logic of appropriation; fluid intellectual exchange becomes staked-out intellectual property, ossifying ideas into opinion in much the same way as Jacobi's snuffbox buyers constitute feelings as goods to be acquired.

Walter's argument for his property over his opinions is itself pillaged from Locke. Like Tristram's plagiarism of Burton's attack on plagiarism and his borrowing from Montaigne on borrowing, this passage reflexively stages the fact that the ideas that we most passionately declare our own are already held by other people. Walter claims Locke's idea for his own by elaborating an argument about intellectual property *using* Locke's idea. The ineffable claim of property assumes (as in Locke) tangible physical form in Walter's account: "the sweat of a man's brows, and the exsudations of a man's brains, are as much a man's own property, as the breeches upon his backside" (TS, 3.34.263). These exsudations "being dropp'd upon the said apple by the labour of finding it, and picking it up" make it his own. The "picker up" owns the "thing pick'd up" through the mixture of "something which was his own" with the "apple which was not his own." Walter owns the apple because he owns himself, although with Shandean circularity, Walter derives his self-propriety from the indubitable ownership of breeches (which are presumably owned because he owns himself).

The very problems that trouble Lockean theories of appropriation also dog Walter's theory of intellectual property. For at what precise moment does the opinion or the apple become his? "[W]as it, when he set his heart upon it? or when he gather'd it? or when he chew'd it? . . . or when he peel'd? or when he brought it home? or when he digested?——or when he———?——" (TS, 3.34.263). Tristram maps out the metaphorical and literal absorption of the apple—its passage through the body—with Shandean relish. For Walter, however, opinions, like apples, are ostensibly made ours through labor not consumption, through what the apple absorbs of the human not what the human absorbs of the apple. Yet, in his example, all that Walter has to do to acquire the apple is to pick it up (which suggests, of course, that his ideas too are *prêt-à-porter*). He does not make the apple, and the example insists that he need not use or eat it. In this sense Walter is exactly like Jacobi's snuffbox buyers. For Jacobi himself, picking up the apple or buying the snuffbox does *not* suffice. If the feeling does not spontaneously arise, it must at least be consumed and digested. (Which, in fine Shandean logic, suggests that the materiality of sentimentality—the snuffbox artifact—is available only in a post-digestive remainder.)

If Walter's labor theory of intellectual property fails to hold water, it is perhaps because there is no state of nature—no *res nullius*—in Sterne's intellectual landscape. The language of feeling, even sentiment itself, is always already preoccupied. Sterne's texts are rife with emotional expressions pillaged from other's mouths and thoughts lifted from other minds. Thus Yorick readdresses a purloined love letter to a different woman in *A Sentimental Journey* (SJ, 153), while Sterne himself recycles a letter he wrote to one "Lady ****" in his correspondence with his "Bramine" Eliza. (In a neat reversal, Sterne's daughter Lydia would later readdress some of the *Journal to Eliza* to her own mother.)[53] In Sterne's texts, words and sentiments melt and resolve into each other; it is difficult, even impossible, to locate them or claim them as uniquely one's own. Even at moments of intense and presumably authentic emotion, Yorick, Tristram, Toby, and Trim have recourse to quotation and imitation of others. Sterne's texts are pieced together from Cervantes, Montaigne, Burton, and Shakespeare; his characters borrow from texts, from each other. Walter's oration upon the death of Tristram's brother Bobby is stitched together from borrowed eloquence. (As Richard Lanham puts it, "The wisdom does not console. The words do.")[54] Just because words have already been used does not make them less sincere. The questions about sentimental propriety with which we began thus extend in Sterne from objects to sentiments and even to words. How can the language of self-expression be properly one's own? If words must be jointly held in order to communicate, what renders them equal to the task of expressing the particularity of the self?

Tristram Shandy and the Befetish'd Word

One can never quite master equivalence in Sterne's world of multifarious definitions and wandering affections, in which a nose may be taken for something more (or less) than a nose. "There is always," as Jonathan Lamb puts it, "some accident in the arrangement or the observation of things to prevent them from being just themselves."[55] Although our sentiments are aroused by and affiliated with exterior, shared things, our impressions and our ideas coalesce only partly, creating an imperfect concordance between inner and outer worlds. Hemmed in by his or her singularities, Sterne's characters carve out a shared language of experience in fractured and imperfect ways, finding commonality by tracing the accidents behind gestures and exclamations: the heat of a chestnut that gives rise to a "Zounds!"; the low-cut pockets in those hard-to-reach-places that produce a face flushed with strain rather than rage; the realization that leads to the gentle withdrawal of pipe from mouth (4.27.377; 3.2.187–88; 9.31.803).

Communication is difficult even under the best of circumstances: a sympathetic listener, a shared set of beliefs, a restricted context. Common points of reference, above all for travelers, are hard to come by. "From the want of languages, connections, and dependencies, and from the difference in education, customs and habits," Yorick announces, "we lie under so many impediments in communicating our sensations out of our own sphere, as often amount to a total impossibility" (SJ, 78). To leave home is to leave behind the familiarity of common references, to abandon the pooled objects that make for ready intelligibility; so little is shared—language, connections, dependencies—that a kind of centripetal force checks "communication out of our own spheres." (Of course, even those who remain at home are subject to miscommunication: *Tristram Shandy* begins with a dispute that arises because *so much* is known. The ill-timed question that opens the novel—"Pray, my dear, have you not forgot to wind up the clock?" (1.1.2)— arises from too much rather than too little being shared.)

What we possess may not be valued in the world beyond our immediate circle; others may or may not have what we need. "[T]he balance of sentimental commerce," Yorick concludes, "is always against the expatriated adventurer: he must buy what he has little occasion for at their own price—his conversation will seldom be taken in exchange for theirs without a large discount" (SJ, 78). More spoken to than speaking, Yorick's traveler uses words as tokens that waver between instruments of exchange and signs of commercial imbalance. In the mercantile economy of sentimental commerce, the home team invariably has the edge. Commerce involves an endless reshuffling of what is to be relinquished and what is to be kept, of *meum* and *tuum;* it constantly renegotiates the inalienable and alienable aspects of the self and its possessions. Sterne's characters are thus careful not to give too much away, in both senses of the expression.

Indeed, for Sterne, absolute transparency is not desirable: enough opacity must subsist to protect the self. Thus Tristram repudiates the notion of fixing "*Momus*'s glass, in the human breast . . . [so that] nothing more would have been wanting, in order to have taken a man's character, but to have taken a chair and gone softly, as you would to a dioptrical bee-hive, and look'd in,—view'd the soul stark naked" (1.23.82). The very notion that one might "have taken a man's character," with its faint whiff of identity theft, suggests that life must not be wholly exposed in the *Life*. Instead of celebrating an intolerable mutual legibility, Sterne offers moments in which the opacity of all humans (to others but also to themselves) gives way to the possibility of momentary translations in a provisionally common tongue.

To speak of anxiety about ownership of one's words, possessions, and personality with reference to Sterne may seem odd in light of the supreme assurance with which Yorick and Toby, Walter and Tristram, divulge and indulge their eccentricities. When astride his hobbyhorse, each seems fearless of others' poaching on his particularities. However sensitive they may be to others' jibes at their foibles, Sterne's characters possess a kind of breezy confidence that no one can take their singularities away. These are coins that will not lose face by rubbing. Notwithstanding the many takes we are given on Walter, Tristram tells us,

> not one, or all of them, can ever help the reader to any kind of preconception of how my father would think, speak, or act, upon any untried occasion or occurrence of life.—There was that infinitude of oddities in him, and of chances along with it, by which handle he would take a thing,—it baffled, Sir, all calculations. . . . [E]very object before him presented a face and section of itself to his eye, altogether different from the plan and elevation of it seen by the rest of mankind.— In other words, 'twas a different object,—and in course was differently considered:
>
> This is the true reason, that my dear *Jenny* and I, as well as all the world besides us, have such eternal squabbles about nothing.—She looks at her outside,— I, at her in—. How is it possible we should agree about her value? (5.24.456–57)

Underlying all Shandean transactions are absolutely particular viewpoints that would seem to annihilate the possibility of shared perspective. The particularity of the Shandean character is such that *any* determination of value verges on impossibility. Sterne's characters don't even recognize the same objects. Walter unpredictably seizes any one of a number of handles by which an object may be grasped; Jenny ostensibly looks to her outside while Tristram claims to peer within; Toby moons over ravelins while Walter rants of names. What is it that hauls the individual out into a shared and conjointly held world? The answer for Sterne is language, but it is an answer proffered with caveats and provisions, which I want to explore in the next few pages.

That "the word in language is half someone else's," as Bakhtin tells us, is a matter of celebration for Sterne. For Bakhtin, the word "becomes 'one's own' only when the speaker populates it with his own intention, his own accent. . . . Prior to this moment of appropriation, the word does not exist in a neutral and impersonal language . . . rather it exists in other people's mouths, in other people's contexts, serving other people's intentions."[56] Words belong to multiple worlds. Individual speakers wrest them away from common keeping, master them by turning them to their proper ends. This "seizure and transformation [of words] into private property" is not a simple process, seamlessly accomplished. Some words remain perpetually alien to their users, "as if they put themselves in quotation marks against the will of the speaker," like Yorick's snuffbox in the hands of one of Jacobi's imperfectly sentimental subjects. "Language," Bakhtin concludes, "is not a neutral medium that passes freely and easily into the private property of the speaker's intentions; it is populated—overpopulated—with the intentions of others."[57] It is, of course, precisely this "overpopulation," this surplus or excess of meaning, that Sterne exploits in his playful movement between the sentimental and the salacious, the pathetic and the bathetic.

Sterne is also, however, interested in the collapse of this free play: what happens when the happy fecundity of Bakhtin's "overpopulation" turns into Malthusian devastation. For a word, as Bakhtin concedes, may also "be perceived purely as an object (something that is, in its essence, a thing). . . . In such a word-object even meaning becomes a thing: there can be no dialogic approach to such a word."[58] For Sterne, the most interesting instances of value ossified into an object occur not in the form of a thing like a snuffbox, but in language. For feelings to become mobile, let alone marketable, on a mass scale in the fashion described above, they must assume a tangible and portable form. They must be given objective form in language. Sentimental commodities, whether snuffboxes or texts, present the feelings the individual would experience as a property of the object tendered. If this assignment of powers to the produced thing rather than to the forms that produce or animate it is one definition of fetishism, then one might say that Sterne delights in exposing the fetishism of words. He is fascinated by what might be called word fetishes: individual and collective investments in shared principles and concepts that hold sway over entire groups by virtue of being ossified into language. "Shall we be destined," Tristram asks, "to the days of eternity, on holy-days, as well as working-days, to be shewing the *relicks of learning,* as monks do the relicks of their saints—without working one—one single miracle with them?" (5.1.408). Like relics whose power lies in their ossified form (or like purchased snuffboxes that stand for feelings never experienced), words may become dead letters that show rather than tell.

Tristram circumvents this problem by embroiling his reader in the production of the text. The draw-your-own-picture of Widow Wadman (6.38.566–67) and the "void space" where the reader may swear "any oath that he is most accustomed to" (7.37.639) acknowledge the human propensity to construct language and objects based on our own willful and errant desires, "our preconceptions having (you know) as great a power over the sound of words as the shapes of things" (8.32.717). Tristram briskly grants us the power of our own inventiveness in the form of a void space, and as quickly withdraws it by reminding us of our own automatism: we seek out our "accustomed" oaths, impose habit upon the space of freedom. If half of the text is the willed discovery of Shandean idiosyncrasy within the self, the fill-in-the-blank model of the accustomed oath (or the more extensive format of Ernulphus's exhaustive curse) reminds us of the mechanical, inelastic, dumb repetition that also governs our choices. Whether all curses are contained in *and* find their origins in Ernulphus (as Tristram insists) or whether Ernulphus is the compiler (as Walter contends) does not affect the fact that *all* words come to us secondhand.[59] They are *used*, in every sense of the term.

Using words does not make them our own; indeed, we often don't know what they mean. The lost liturgical roots of certain curses—*zounds* from "God's wounds," *Gadzooks* from "God's hooks" (the nails of the cross)—efface their origins in bodily injury. Ossified into language, stripped of history, they become fetish words. Bound by their customary use, they reciprocally bind their users— even if only to a twelve-penny fine (following the Profane Oaths Act of 1746, which penalized swearing not by the word uttered but by the rank of the speaker). Thus Tristram warns us not to "give ourselves a parcel of airs, and pretend that the oaths we make free with in this land of liberty of ours are our own; and because we have the spirit to swear them,——imagine that we have had the wit to invent them" (3.12.212). Like words, oaths are not wholly our own. If they were wholly our own, they would be ineffectual, because they would not communicate.

The next line of Tristram's text, of course, demonstrates that Tristram *does* have wit enough to invent words: in criticizing connoisseurs—critics by rote who judge by "rules and compasses" mechanically and indiscriminately applied— Tristram coins the word "befetish'd" to describe the way such critics thrust empty language into the void where thought or belief ought to be. In purveying used words and principles, these connoisseurs are "*befetish'd* with the bobs and trinkets of criticism" (3.12.212). They idolize ornament over substance, using these "bobs and trinkets" to cover a perceptible lack of thought or intelligence. (The notes to the Florida edition observe of the word "befetish'd" that "the OED records this passage as its sole example," suggesting that invented words, however original, do not necessarily communicate.)[60]

Notwithstanding its purported singularity, Tristram offers a genealogy for his metaphor: "I have fetch'd it," he announces, "as far as from the coast of *Guinea*" (3.12.212–13). Constituting the word as an exotic import, Tristram allows it to traverse cultures in a moment of conceptual disembodiment that echoes the passage of the commodity from one country to another. In *Tristram Shandy*, words are described as freight, possessed of their own itineraries, from Walter's Northwest Passage to the intellectual world (5.42.484) to his oration on the death of Bobby, which has been transported from the philosophers of India overland by way of Greece, Rome, France, and England (or by alternate water route via the Ganges, the Indian Ocean, and the Nile [5.3.418–25]). We forget that words acquire meaning by their passage through the mouths of other people when we come to worship language as if its meaning and value inhere in the word itself. The energy of Sterne's text arises from the ability of his idiosyncratic characters to revivify language by wrenching it back into their own particular narratives. Clichés stir back into life under the ministrations of Sterne's characters, as the common stock of the word is replenished by virtue of being literalized or otherwise turned from its worn proper passage.

It is because words potentially ossify that Walter devises his theory of auxiliary verbs: the mind gets hung up. "The highest stretch of improvement a single word is capable of, is a high metaphor," Walter explains. "[W]hen the mind has done with it—there is an end,—the mind and the idea are at rest,—until a second idea enters;——and so on" (5.42.485). Like a character in a Beckett play, Walter's solitary metaphor awaits the entry of a new word to interact with; without stimulus, thoughts idle, "swiming [sic] quietly in the middle of the thin juice of a man's understanding, without being carried backwards or forwards" (3.9.197). In this Newtonian universe, words, like billiard balls, are immobile (at rest) until a second one strikes them. Like the ancillary troops for which Trim takes them, auxiliary verbs—that mobile army of potential conjugations—are implicitly active. They "set the soul a going by herself upon the materials as they are brought her" (5.42.485).

As the engine of the conditional, the auxiliary gives free reign to the imagination, releasing it from the fetters of the strictly referential. It permits one to discourse upon an object sight unseen. "A WHITE BEAR !" Walter exclaims in his example. "Have I ever seen one? Might I ever have seen one? Am I ever to see one? Ought I ever to have seen one?" (5.43.487). Nimbly skipping chronologically and geographically, shifting perspective and cascading from affirmation to negation in a single line, Walter asserts that the mind manipulates an idea rather than being fixed by it. Yet the ebullient stream of questions also suggests that words take on a life of their own: words, as much as ideas and impressions, possess gravity, forces of attraction and association that create patterns only tangentially related to the world. The Shandean linguistic trapeze act does, however, encounter moments of referential touchdown. Thus the concluding question in Walter's discussion of auxiliaries issues from the oppositional association of black and white at the same time as it suggests an electric contact between text and history:

—Is the white bear worth seeing?—

—Is there no sin in it?—

Is it better than a BLACK ONE?   (5.43.487)

Walter's final question deviates from the hypothetical auxiliary. In shifting from possibility ("Might I ever have seen one?") to desire ("Would I had seen a white bear?") to projection ("If I should never see a white bear, what then?") to recollection ("have I ever seen the skin of one?") to an assessment of the white bear's relative properties, Walter invites an appraisal of value that turns his fanciful hypotheses into determinate relations. Only by reverting to the external world can one decide whether a white bear is "better" than a black one. Walter does not state that a white bear is superior to a black one, but his playful comparison of the two finds a real-world echo in Trim's question to Uncle Toby: "Why then . . . is a black wench to be used worse than a white one?" Such questions cannot be answered in the conditional, since they pertain to the world of brute force: "because she has no one to stand up for her" (9.6.748).

The irony of Walter's theory of the auxiliary issues from its source: Walter himself is a living example of how the mind may be fixed by words or by its own ideas. His theory of names, for example, allows a word to dictate the manifest destiny of its bearer in defiance of all the text's lessons about contingency and aleatory play. Sterne joyously mocks those who try to render decisive borders and names better left unfixed, or those who seek to create exhaustive systems that, like Jorge Luis Borges's map, but unlike Walter's bull, will cover all the world. Words like *noses, whiskers, pockets,* and *wax* (Tristram also adds *placket-holes, pump-handles, spigots, night-caps,* and *chamber-pots* [5.1.414]), along with capacious words like *it* and *thing,* are fastened to referents by the reader's caprice. Oddly enough, meanings become fixed through whim or fancy.

Sometimes, however, the word clings so tightly to a particular meaning that the two cannot be prized apart. Thus the word *whisker* circulates through the court of Marguerite de Navarre in a positive miasma of innuendo, oscillating between "gallantry and devotion" (5.1.410) until repetition ossifies its meaning into a single sense—though that sense is *not* necessarily "whisker." When the aptly named La Fosseuse traces "the outline of a small whisker" (5.1.413) upon her lip with a bodkin, the loss of ambiguity inflicts a deathblow. "The word was ruined,"

Tristram announces (TS, 5.1.414). To have mistaken the whisker for the real object—whiskers for noses for the thing itself—is to echo the mistake embodied in the nose in the first place. It is to believe that it is possible to stabilize meaning as if there were a single key code to unlock the world. All whiskers are noses and all noses are phalluses, as "surely as noses are noses, and whiskers are whiskers still," as Tristram puts it (5.1.409). This contraction of the world to a single measure levels its heterogeneity by making everything refer to the uniformity of one thing. In the absence of ambiguity, the opacity of the word—those aspects of it that have no equivalent—disappears.

Yet shared reference to a single object, however arbitrarily selected, permits value to be relayed and measured through a common term. When Tristram argues that "beings inferior . . . syllogize by their noses" (3.40.280), he qualifies his earlier mocking pronouncement of identity—"by the word *Nose* . . . I mean a Nose, and nothing more, or less" (3.31.258). The nose becomes a shared syllogistic principle. "[T]he great and principal act of ratiocination in men," he continues, "is the finding out the agreement or disagreement of two ideas one with another, by the intervention of a third; (called the *medius terminus*)" (3.40.280–81). To syllogize by the nose allows the mind to leap nimbly between heterogeneous things; we move from one thing to another through what is interposed, "just as a man, as *Locke* well observes, by a yard, finds two men[']s nine-pin-alleys to be of the same length, which could not be brought together, to measure their equality, by *juxta-position*" (3.40.281). The third term allows equivalence over distance, admitting comparison without propinquity, but leaves in question the elected measure: the third term upon which the syllogism pivots. Tristram tampers with the terms of Locke's example in a way that subverts the argument. By changing Locke's houses to nine-pin-alleys, albeit both measured by a yard (slang for penis), Tristram slyly invests the syllogism with a bawdy secondary meaning. The reader grasps Tristram's point through a nonlogical substitution rather than the deliberate process of comparison Locke describes. We are drawn into the broader community by our capacity to move between noses and yards—to get the joke—while characters preserve their singularity by refusing to budge from their hobbyhorses.

Each individual at Shandy Hall has his or her preferred *medius terminus*—irremediably private, not interchangeable with others. Thus Walter blithely discourses on noses in the serene assumption that the fingering of Toby's pipe means he "was syllogizing and measuring with it the truth of each hypothesis" (3.40.281). It is only when Walter uses the word *siege* that Toby stirs to attention: "the word *siege*, like a talismanic power, in my father's metaphor, wafting back my Uncle *Toby*'s fancy, quick as a note could follow the touch—he open'd his ears" (3.41.282). The word *siege,* used metaphorically, ignites Toby's interest through its possible military reference; the sound of the word without the meaning possesses the quasi-magical power to attract Toby's notice. Communication and communion here occur without full comprehension (although Walter rapidly veers away from the term *siege* to "keep clear of some dangers . . . apprehended from it" [3.41.282]).

Both knowing and unknowing sympathy bind the characters within the novel. The connections that link individuals are not readily visible to the naked eye, even as, in logic, the *medius terminus* does not appear in the syllogism's conclusion. Sterne's text presents us with words and gestures and then discloses the train of thought that got us there, making this third term visible. It is because Tristram has, so to speak, given us a glimpse of each individual's *medius terminus* that we are able to follow the swivel points that guide Toby's mind from point A to point C. *Nose* and *siege* may seem rather like "befetish'd" words, but they may also function as a kind of transitional object, facilitating movement between inner and outer worlds. (It bears remembering that D. W. Winnicott includes "not only objects but also words, patterns, tunes, and mannerisms in his lists of things that can function as transitional objects.")[61] Shared words, like shared objects, haul us out of the insularity of the self. We grasp Toby's thought processes because we understand his obsession with fortification. Words like *nose* facilitate emotional and intellectual exchange not despite but by virtue of their particularity—what might even be called their sentimental value.

Sterne's mockery of the ossifying of value in language, the conversion of process into product, does not mean, however, that he espouses a world of illimitable flux. His texts acknowledge that there are singularities and beliefs to which people must cling in order to preserve order and intelligibility in an irremediably plural world. It is for this reason that I want to conclude this section with a story—probably apocryphal—about *Tristram Shandy* in the wilderness. The biography of the Victorian writer Samuel Butler contains the story of one Ross, who was

> an engineer making a railway somewhere in Central America in sole command of about 500 black men, only half-civilized. One of the men announced that he was going to marry the cook, who was one of the few women in the camp. Ross thought that it would tend to preserve decency and order if the union were not allowed to take place without a ceremony of some kind; and he, of course, would have to perform it, as there was no parson. He had but one book, which happened to be *Tris-*

tram Shandy. The people, however, only spoke Spanish, so that it did not much matter; at any rate he determined to marry them out of it. A Sunday was fixed for the
wedding, and proclaimed a high holiday. Ross put an old, but clean, night-shirt over
all his clothes, and, looking as solemn as he could, read to the assembled people,
and to the bride and bridegroom in particular, a chapter of *Tristram Shandy;* after
which he declared them, and they were considered to be, duly married.[62]

The prosaic announcement of Ross's situation "making a railway" in the middle
of "central America" masks the potential volatility of its ingredients: "500 black
men, only half-civilized," a handful of women, and a solitary English engineer.
The marriage ceremony mandated by Ross removes one of the few women from
possible circulation; Ross's insistence that a ceremony "of some kind" would
"preserve decency and order" raises the question of who would feel reassured by
it. His pious insistence that the two marry is undermined by the fact that he has
no Bible with him, but what renders the entire anecdote odd and perturbing is
the fact that he usurps and undermines ecclesiastical authority by wrapping himself in a nightgown and employing Sterne as his sacred text. Substituting Sterne's
comic novel for the Bible allows it to serve as an instrument of cultural imposition.

The anecdote may, of course, simply be the conversion of a sacred cow into an
irreverent cock-and-bull story—but the interchangeability of engineer and parson, comic novel for sacred text, calls into question the sacrosanct things that are
meant to anchor the world as we know it. This episode reifies the outer husk of
the ritual, reducing performative language to the fact that some—any—words
were read solemnly from a book. If the words are incomprehensible to the interlocutors, does it matter whether the book is the Bible or *Tristram Shandy?* Neither the words that compose the Bible nor the spirit and belief that infuse it with
meaning, nor even the material object itself, are present in Ross's mockery of a
marriage ceremony. After foisting the ritual upon the couple, he renders it empty.
Yet the passage hints that Ross's intent perhaps renders the object incidental. The
passive voice of the closing lines—"he declared them, and they were considered
to be, duly married"—leaves it unclear who approves the union by considering
the couple to be married.

What the irreverent Sterne, himself a clergyman, would have made of this
story is up for grabs; the sheer impiety of it creates a nervous glee. For *Tristram
Shandy* to substitute for the Bible, like the snuffbox without the sentiment, the
word without the meaning—a symbol where any other object would do—mocks
the limits of liturgical particularity. That the English book (to which I shall re-

turn in the next chapter) becomes interchangeable simultaneously stages and saps its authority. And yet the flip-flopping of texts reminds us that nothing can be fully removed from exchange. I argued at the beginning of this chapter that the sentimental object cannot be traded: only this one will do. Sentimental value arrests fungibility by designating certain objects—and certain aspects of the self—as inalienable; the particularity of sentimental possessions—objects, words, feelings—fends off the menacing mutability of the world. Yet objects are a precarious basket in which to place one's subjective eggs. In a Shandean world of "privation, breach, shortage and emptiness,"[63] things repeatedly disappear and are mislaid, die or are cut off. Sterne's texts are haunted by loss, by the possibility that one may not keep the things one has. Consolation must then be sought in other objects. Yet accepting replacements for such personal possessions potentially undermines the particularity of the self. In Sterne's world, therefore, one must learn both how to accept substitutions and when to refuse them. In the closing section of this chapter, I return to Sterne's snuffbox in order to address how the particularity of a sentimental object provides a bulwark (or a half-moon or a ravelin) against the impending dissolution of its owner.

The Sentimental Deficit and the *Journal to Eliza*

Skin for *Skin* saith *Job nay all that a Man has, will he give* for his
Life.

—*Sterne*, Journal to Eliza

Sterne's own snuffbox had a sentimental value of which his own contemporaries would not have been unaware, for it bore a miniature of Eliza Draper, the young Anglo-Indian wife of an East India Company employee, with whom the 54-year-old Sterne had begun a sentimental correspondence after they met in early 1767.[64] Sterne displayed the box with Eliza's portrait so frequently that it became "something of a joke" amongst his cronies.[65] Traversing the boundary between Sterne's biography and his fictional narratives, both snuffbox and miniature weave in and out of Sterne's novels, private letters, and the *Journal to Eliza*. Sterne introduces her portrait into *A Sentimental Journey* and then comments on it in his *Journal:* "I have brought your name, *Eliza!* and Picture into my work—where they will remain—when You and I are at rest for ever—Some Annotator or explainer of my works in this place will take occasion, to speak of the Friendship which Subsisted so long and faithfully betwixt Yorick and the Lady he speaks of" (166). Aware that the work will outlive both the thing and the person it represents, Sterne envisions posterity's recuperative labor to restore the fullness of reference to the sentiment so fleetingly described. Whereas the monk's snuffbox preserves the ephemeral, sentimental moment, here the text immortalizes the material object. Alternately talisman, memento, admonition to fidelity, apostrophized object, and speaking muse, the miniature assumes different meanings as it is put to different uses. The sentimental value with which we began involves the removal of certain objects from general circulation by conferring personal value upon them; in the closing section of this chapter, I want to turn to the way the individual borrows back from such objects.

Composed after Eliza's return to her husband in Bombay, the *Journal to Eliza*, as Sterne claims in its opening passage, is his translation of a French manuscript of "a Diary of the miserable feelings of a person separated from a Lady for whose Society he languished" written "under the fictitious Names of Yorick and Draper—and sometimes of the Bramin and Bramine" (135). The *Journal* is a kind of anticipatory memento mori, in which Yorick assumes the roles of both sentimental mourner and object mourned. The text oscillates between a direct address and an extended apostrophe to Eliza. Dying "for want of thee" (181), Yorick gazes upon her "passive picture" in order to contemplate a "sweet Shadow! of what is to come! for tis all I can now grasp" (186). The ailing Yorick shadowboxes with his own mortality in the elusive form of his absent beloved, whose portrait anchors his failing reality. He repeatedly tenders sentiments and then anxiously anticipates the return on his emotional investment—one that never comes for us, since Eliza's responses are not included in the *Journal*.

The text's calculus of affect, weaving together the languages of love, debt, and death, anticipates an eternal reckoning. As Jonathan Lamb argues in an electrifying but brief reading of the *Journal:* "It is as if Yorick has planned to antedate his death by dying metaphorically into pure spirit, retaining his consciousness at the expense of everything else and converting all evidence of a real death yet to come into metaphors and tokens of one that has already occurred. . . . With all anchorage in things and bodies deliberately forsaken, the sentiment cannot help but attenuate and get lost in professions that have nothing but scraps of Shakespeare to perform with."[66] For Lamb, the *Journal* is a vaporous text. Only the incursion of the lower body with its Shandean bathos lingers to remind us that "there is still some real life left and also a real death yet to die" (36). But this deliberate sublimation of the spirit—"all anchorage in things and bodies deliberately forsaken," as Lamb puts it—periodically alights on other kinds of objects, like the snuffbox and the portrait. In his effort to retain "his consciousness at the expense of everything else," Yorick fastens himself onto his possessions. These objects in turn become implicated in an elaborate economy of debt and credit. Yorick gives in order to be owed, creating a massive deficit meant to outlast his failing body.

"The human need for continuity," J. Hillis Miller contends of plotlines in *Tristram Shandy*, "is so strong that a man will find some principle of order in any random sequence."[67] In the *Journal*, Yorick asks personal possessions to give continuity to a world otherwise in flux. Things retain their shape despite the inchoate turmoil of Yorick's inner life. He therefore returns to Eliza's portrait throughout the *Journal*. "[I] leand the whole day with my head upon My hand; sitting most dejectedly at the Table with my Eliza's Picture before me—sympathizing & soothing me," he writes on April 16 (136). On June 4, he notes that he has been "employ'd a full hour upon your sweet sentimental Picture—and a couple of hours upon yourself" (158) while on June 12, he effuses: "Every Trincket you gave or exchanged with me, has its force—Your Picture is Yourself—all Sentiment, Softness, and Truth—It speaks—it listens—'tis convinced—it re-signes—Dearest Original! how like unto thee does it seem—and will seem—till thou makest it vanish, by thy presence" (164). On June 22, he travels "with no Soul with me in my Chase, but Your Picture—for it has a *Soul*, I think" (168), while June 27 finds him writing at "Ten in the morning, with my Snuff open at the Top of this sheet,—and your gentle sweet face opposite to mine" (170). He later contemplates moving the portrait from the snuffbox to a locket: "I do not like the place tis in—it shall be nearer my heart—Thou art ever in its centre" (183). So rhapsodic are his effusions that it is vaguely disconcerting to find the following prosaic observation on July 10: "I have just kiss'd your picture . . . I have found out the Body is too little for the head" (180). If objects serve to material-ize the yearned-for beloved, at times their very materiality renders them in-tractable. The more Eliza is present, the less malleable she becomes. As Harriet Guest has argued, Eliza's embodied form and her depicted image possess "per-haps too much expression of individual character, too much of what resists or qualifies Sterne's determination to see in Eliza the sentimental ideal."[68] It is difficult not to suspect that Yorick prefers the portrait because the portrait is more fully his. So arrested is Sterne by the miniature that the woman behind or ante-rior to it becomes incidental.

When his illness becomes too harrowing, Yorick narrows the compass of the world to Eliza's portrait: "in all this Storm of Passions, I have but one small an-chor, Eliza! to keep this weak Vessel of mine from perishing" (159). Eliza be-comes an affective lodestone, sapping all other objects of attraction and weaning

Yorick from the lures of the rest of the world. The literal symptoms of his ill-ness are made into metaphorical tokens of his love: Yorick converts physical loss into figurative offerings, for which he must be repaid. As Lamb observes, "his haemorrhages flow from a lover's bleeding heart and stain handkerchiefs which then become earnests of the absolute fidelity for which, as a ghost and a spectre, he waits to be rewarded."[69] The harrowing suspicion that something is irrep-arably wrong cannot, however, be entirely rewritten into sentimental discourse. "Some thing," he admits, "is wrong, Eliza! in every part of me—I do not gain strength; nor have I the feelings of health returning back to me. . . . The Want of thee is half my distemper—but not the whole of it" (151). When Sterne writes to John Hall-Stevenson at around the same time, he is all body: "I have got con-veyed thus far like a bale of cadaverous goods consigned to Pluto and company."[70] His body wracked, we find Yorick literally and metaphorically beside himself: casting ceaselessly outward in order to be near but not in his pained body, pre-served in objects outside himself that endure beyond feelings that alter and die.

The *Journal* is composed of passages in which Yorick tirelessly empties him-self out and insists that this outpouring must be mirrored and countered by Eliza's affections. Sentiment freely offered as gift starts to resemble sentiment as binding commercial contract. Words of love become counters in a set of partially consummated transactions: "Thou owest me much Eliza!—and I will have pa-tience; for thou wilt pay me all—But the Demand is equal;—much I owe thee, and with much shalt thou be requited.—Sent for a Chart of the Atlantic Ocean, to make conjectures upon what part of it my Treasure was floating" (137–38). Not unlike a merchant tracking the course of his cargo across the sea, Yorick maps Eliza's progress across the globe to India. By doggedly measuring the distance be-tween Eliza and himself, Yorick perversely augments her value. "Objects," Georg Simmel tells us, "are not difficult to acquire because they are valuable, but we call those objects valuable that resist our desire to possess them."[71] Yorick there-fore tries to maintain rather than to collapse distance. He invents barriers (an ocean, a husband, a wife, impotence, illness) in order to be able to consume his feelings about Eliza, rather than attaining the object that would extinguish his desires.

Although Yorick claims that he is striving to balance the emotional budget, he is in fact creating an ever-increasing deficit that Eliza can never possibly re-pay. The perceptible imbalance of trade starts to seem like emotional blackmail; hypothetical moments of reciprocity, meant to cancel each other out, invariably add up to Yorick's proprietary claim to Eliza's being. "[R]emember What I suf-fer.—Thou art mine Eliza by Purchace—had I not earn'd thee with a better price" (155). Sentimental commerce constitutes a form of property that transcends the claims of mere purchase. "Remember You are mine," he admonishes her on July 13, "and stand answerable for all you say and do to me—I govern myself by the same Rule" (182). Yorick's acts of giving are driven not (or not only) by the desire to share but, as Annette Weiner argues, by the desire to acquire and keep. Gifts may be freely given, but their return is a form of obligation. As Sterne writes in his *Sermons,* "we have a right to act according to our own ideas of what will do the party most good in the case where we bestow a favor;—but where we return one, we lose this right, and . . . [must] endeavor to repay in such a manner as we think is most likely to be accepted in discharge of the obligation."[72]

The constant tabulation of his emotional expenses allows Yorick to make a more lasting claim upon the elusiveness of sentimental possession: "tis fit in truth We suffer equally—nor can it be otherwise—when the Causes of Anguish in two hearts are so proportion'd, as in ours.—Surely—Surely—Thou art mine Eliza! for dear have I bought thee!" (145). Sentimental value, I have argued above, rests its claim to absolute possession on the removal of the object from circuits of exchange, and yet Yorick repeatedly reinserts Eliza into transactions that involve giving and taking, owing and repaying. His emotional labors create a massive deficit, which generates an imperative for endless return. Yorick defers payment into the life of the world to come, at the same time disburdening himself of the onerous weight of a tangible object of desire. Borrowing future annuities against present passion, Yorick gambles on the notion that debt will outlast this mortal coil. Here is a gift that yields a perpetual return.

The rhetoric of debt creates a barrier between Yorick and Eliza that oddly enough gives Yorick fuller possession of his beloved. To have her is not to hold her, for once constituted as property, she becomes less fully Yorick's. As Jeff Nunokawa has argued of the Victorian novel, "trouble arises when women are cast as . . . property . . . less because the proprietor's grasp goes too far when it reaches her than because that grasp is always loosened when the shadow of the commodity falls upon the object that it holds."[73] If the dream of absolute sentimental possession is menaced by property's potential return to alienable commodity status, the emotions tendered to Eliza must remain a gift in order to protect Eliza from the shadow of commoditization. Only by *not* possessing can Yorick retain. Immaterial debt is, perversely enough, more permanent than literal possession.

That Sterne himself (as opposed to his alter ego Yorick) was willing to commoditize Eliza (in jest if not in fact) is evident in his rather odd offer to rent Eliza from her husband: "Were your husband in England," he writes in a letter to Eliza prior to her departure for Bombay, "I would freely give him five hundred pounds (if money could purchase the acquisition) to let you only sit by me two hours in a day, while I wrote my Sentimental Journey. I am sure the work would sell so much the better for it, that I should be re-imbursed the sum more than seven times told."[74] Sentimental commerce is infused here with a pecuniary interest that smacks of procurement. Sterne's parenthetical acknowledgment that perhaps there are things money can't buy is superseded by contemplation of the way the surplus emotional value will produce book profits that cancel out the initial seed money. In the exchange between Sterne and Mr. Draper, Eliza becomes a kind of rent-a-muse, with the miniature as her proxy.

Yorick is not the only one to love Eliza; the sentimental value Sterne confers upon her turns out—as in the case of the starling—to be disconcertingly transferable. The abbé Guillaume-Thomas-François Raynal invokes Eliza as a tutelary spirit in his *Histoire philosophique des deux Indes,* a late eighteenth-century encyclopedic compilation of colonial history, to which we shall return in Chapter 5. Even as Sterne wrote with the miniature of Eliza before him, Raynal claims that he "cannot write a line without having before me the monument she has left me"—although the grandiose nature of this claim is somewhat deflated by Anthony Strugnell's identification of the monument as a "Silver ink Standish" given by Eliza to Raynal; Raynal quite literally needed the inkstand to write.[75] Eliza's centrality to the text is suggested by the presence of her name in the frontispiece of the third edition, where the description of Raynal as "Defender of Humanity, of Truth, and of Liberty" is explicitly ascribed to her.[76]

In book 3 of the *Histoire,* Raynal interrupts a discussion of the British colonization of India to trumpet his love of Eliza:

> Territory of Anjengo, thou art nothing; but thou hast given birth to Eliza. A day will come, when these staples of commerce, founded by the Europeans on the coasts of Asia, will exist no more. Before a few centuries are elapsed, the grass will cover them, or the Indians, avenged, will have built upon their ruins. But if my works be destined to have any duration, the name of Anjengo will not be obliterated from the memory of man. Those who shall read my works, or those whom the winds shall drive towards these shores, will say: there it is that Eliza Draper was born; and if there be a Briton among them, he will immediately add, with the spirit of conscious pride, and there it was that she was born of English parents. (3.15.68–69; 3.86)

Even within the motley hodgepodge that is Raynal's text, this digression stands out because of its vertiginous move from colonial context to sentimental object of desire. The sentimental figure overshadows and even occludes the colonial referent. India, Anjengo (the site of the first English East India Company settlement in Kerala, on the southwestern coast of India), and the colonial enterprise disappear: pity for the grosser injustices of the world is here balanced against Raynal's own personal misfortune. Raynal creates a kind of lachrymose round-robin, in which Raynal and Eliza weep for Sterne and the dead Sterne and the living Raynal, in turn, weep for the now-deceased Eliza. "Had it been the will of Heaven," Raynal rhapsodizes, "that you had both survived me, your tears would have fallen together upon my grave" (3.15.69; 3.87). Nor is the reader exempt from this tearful scene. "If I have sometimes moved thee to compassionate the calamities of the human race," Raynal implores the reader, "let me now prevail upon thee to commiserate my own misfortune. I was thy friend without knowing thee; be for a moment mine. Thy gentle pity shall be my reward" (3.15.69; 3.86–87). Inasmuch as Raynal's moving prose has inspired the unknown reader with feelings for the sufferings of distant humanity, the reader owes Raynal recompense in the form of pity for his sufferings. Raynal, not unlike Sterne, converts the gift of sentiment into a form of debt for which he demands the payment of interest.

Raynal's moving elegy was subject to precisely the same kind of critiques as the other forms of sentimental emotion discussed above. If he borrowed Eliza as sentimental talisman from Sterne, the words used to express this attachment appear to have been borrowed from Diderot. Among the many contributors to the *Histoire des deux Indes*, the *Correspondance littéraire* of Friedrich Melchior, baron von Grimm, notes,

> there is one who is impossible to misrecognize, and whose style and ideas are to be found everywhere, even in the outpourings of sensibility in which M. the abbé Raynal wished to appear carried away by a sentiment entirely his own [*avait désiré de paraître emporté par un sentiment tout à fait à lui*]—even so are the regrets on the death of his friend Eliza Draper. . . . [For the] touching epitaph to this Eliza Draper is just a recollection of the one delivered by M. Diderot, several years ago, before twelve or fifteen people, for Mme. Necker. Despite the esteem that one may have for M. the abbé Raynal it is impossible not to find something ridiculous in borrowings of this kind.[77]

Diderot's hand, as inimitable as Sterne's, is immediately apparent in Raynal's epitaph for Eliza, but what draws Grimm's ire is not the plagiarized words but the stolen sentiment, the borrowed feeling—the fact that this purportedly most personal of outpourings in fact flowed from someone else's heart.

These questions about sentimental authenticity have implications for the text's historical project, for Raynal uses Eliza to underwrite his claims to sincerity. "ELIZA, from the highest Heaven, thy first, and last country, receive my oath: I SWEAR NOT TO WRITE ONE LINE IN WHICH THY FRIEND MAY NOT BE RECOGNISED" (3.15.72; 3.90). The truth of Raynal's history is guaranteed, not by its adherence to impersonal facts, but by the authentic sensibility of the historian as affirmed through the gaze of a dead woman. Raynal's fidelity to himself is maintained and guaranteed by Eliza's recognition of his identity. Understood as Diderot's oath, however, the statement "I swear not to write one line in which thy friend may not be recognized" reads as the promissory note of a superior ghostwriter, whose mimicry of Raynal is so exact that Eliza will be fully deceived. We are back in the domain of the imitative starling. The sentimental recognition meant to guarantee authenticity may instead undermine the veracity of the historian, even as Yorick's apostrophe to Eliza—meant to cheat death—only serves to remind the reader of its imminence.

Both Sterne and Raynal lay claim to immortality through Eliza and confer it upon her. Yet the author's purchase on the world proves to be precarious. Objects can be snatched away through death and loss; their transmission can be cut off by the intervening hand of the law. The self cannot be preserved through its possessions. Thus the Sterne of the *Journal* grows nervous at the prospect of his wife and daughter's return from France to Coxwold, their home in North Yorkshire. They would, he notes, take everything: "I shall be pluck'd bare—all but of your Portrait and Snuff Box and your other dear Presents" (157). Likewise, Yorick's passage into France in *A Sentimental Journey* subjects him to the royal *droits d'aubaine* that allow the king to seize the possessions of any foreigner who dies on French soil. Everything, Yorick observes, "must have gone to the King of France—even the little picture which I have so long worn, and so often have told thee, Eliza, I would carry with me into my grave, would have been torn from my neck" (SJ, 66–67). Death does not create a debt everlasting. Instead, it allows beloved things to fall into the hands of strangers.

Sterne's own snuffbox did *not*, however, fall into the hands of people unknown. Although "all Mr Sterne's wearing apparel, & trinkets to the best advantage" were auctioned in order to pay his debts following his death in 1768, Sterne's daughter Lydia instructed the executor to "present Mr. Hall: my Father's Gold snuff-box which he desired to purchase." Even to the end, Sterne's snuffbox waffles between object given and object purchased. It turns out that all of Sterne's possessions fall into the category of the sentimental commodity whose ambivalent half-life this chapter has described. Sterne's things, his daughter Lydia notes, have a value that supersedes their material worth: "many of his friends," she writes, "would have been glad to have purchased his trinkets at even more than their value only because they once belong'd to Mr Sterne."[78] Lingering beyond the limits of self-possession, the sentimental value imparted to Sterne's objects in life is not relinquished in death.

CHAPTER THREE

Tales Told by Things

Things do not usually talk in sentimental novels. In general, narrative is the task of people, not their property; persons not things possess language, consciousness, affect, thought. To invite a thing to speak—to personify it—is thus to transfer the properties of humans to inanimate objects. This chapter addresses the personification of objects in three clusters of texts that may, at first glance, seem to be a counterintuitive, if not grotesque gathering: Marx's writings on the commodity, eighteenth-century tales narrated by objects, and slave autobiographies. It examines the way personifications borrow the attributes that ostensibly distinguish subjects from objects in order to confer agency and intent upon an otherwise taciturn and immobile world. The fact that things stir to life and begin to speak during this period reminds us of the intricate, intimate connections between subjects and objects—of the way the world of persons and the world of things are reciprocally made.

That the line between person and thing was only imperfectly drawn in the eighteenth century is suggested by the proliferation of odd little tales told by inanimate and nonhuman things ranging from English banknote to Indian rupee, tye-wig to lady's slipper, as well as hackney cabs, walking canes, clothing, coins, counterfeit currency, and pincushions. It would seem that the eighteenth century, like a slightly twisted Walt Disney movie, abounded with talking coaches, chatty pens, and long-winded waistcoats. Additional tales were recounted from the point of view of animals: a lapdog, a louse, a cat, or a monkey. These tales were satiric and sentimental journeys, with the role of Sterne's English parson, Yorick, played not by a person, but by a thing. They tender Yorick's encounter with the monk from the snuffbox's point of view.

The previous chapter addressed the way sentimental subjects seek to secure the self by sentimentalizing things and relationships, personalizing the properties of their possessions in order to withdraw them from circuits of exchange. We now turn from what sentimental subjects try to borrow from objects to ask what objects borrow from subjects. The movement from person to thing to the rhetorical figure of the person is the focus of this chapter, which weaves together the theoretical impetus that animates Marx's commodity and the whimsical popular narratives recounted by objects, the talking books prominently featured in slave autobiography and the speaking *res* that is the slave. It is appalling but enlightening to read these sets of texts together, for the period that jubilantly devoured tales narrated by talking objects was also a period in which persons were brutally and persistently seized upon as things in the form of slavery and the slave trade. To contrast personified things with reified persons may seem like a docile replication of the objectifying logic of slavery, but my intention is to retrace this logic in order to ask how (or whether) the tropes of personification may be turned to different ends. What sort of work do we ask "subjectivity" to do when it is bestowed on things, abstractions, or collective bodies? And how do such personifications illuminate the very category of the person?

The People Things Make

The idea of a speaking object would have been familiar to eighteenth-century readers; those with a classical education might have encountered, for example, the *Metamorphoses* (or *Golden Ass*) of Apuleius, while the literate public would have been familiar with the enigmas published in journals and almanacs. These riddles invited the reader to divine what object addressed them—"Ladies if you my parts examine near, / A hero and a goddess will appear: / But tho' true majesty is seen in me, / I'm not esteem'd by men of high degree"[1]—and submit the solution for the following number (in this case, a halfpenny). The success of Francis Coventry's *Adventures of Pompey the Little*, a lapdog, which was reprinted fourteen times between 1751 and 1830, led to a fleeting renaissance of the form. The first two volumes of Charles Johnstone's *Chrysal or the Adventures of a Guinea* met with such an enthusiastic reception in 1760 that two additional volumes followed in 1765. This vogue poses a simple question: what is going on when a society not only publishes but consumes ten editions (twenty by 1800) of a 4-volume, 1,000-page text consecrated to the peregrinations of a gold coin?

The tales are a real generic hodgepodge, combining elements of the picaresque with moral polemic and political satire. The choice of a thing as narrator allows the tale to weave in and out of public and private spaces, as objects gain mute and unobserved access to the secret recesses of human lives, with the added advantage that a thing cannot be prosecuted for libel. Like spies crouched in corners, mute witnesses to human folly, or, worse, like modern paparazzi, the things fetch and carry tales from the boudoir, the council chamber of kings, the back-rooms of thieves and merchants. Like the early eighteenth-century secret memoirs and scandalous histories from which they sprang, these tales cannibalize current events and public figures for their fodder. They require extensive knowledge of eighteenth-century political life even to make sense, so much so that Robert Adams Day's modern annotations of Tobias Smollett's 130-page *History of an Atom* amount to an impressive 1,250 footnotes (130 pages of notes in all). Even in the eighteenth century, keys were needed to unpack the identities of all the persons, places, and things satirized therein.[2]

At times, however, this satiric prose is disconcertingly invaded by sentimental tropes that invite the reader to contemplate the emotional life of property, the affective bond between things and their owners. It is a measure of Sterne's influence and popularity that around 1760, these narratives begin to envision their objects as sentimental travelers, out to accrue affect rather than profit. Many of them begin or end with an invocation of the sentimental reader or writer. "Chance put into my hand an old worn-out pen of Yorick's," the author of the *Adventures of a Hackney Coach* announces, while the rupee begs to be judged by those "whose commerce with mankind has not destroyed every sense of benevolence for your fellow-creatures."[3] Satiric and sentimental allusions to Sterne abound, from references to hobbyhorses and noses to the complaints of an overwound watch on its owner's wedding night.[4] The peripatetic coach and the pedantic black coat never miss an opportunity to "excite virtue, depress vice, and ridicule folly."[5] In the great tradition of Henry Mackenzie's 1771 *The Man of Feeling*, they condemn the evils of corrupt men, recount tales of lost or endangered virtue, and extol the joys of charity bestowed upon worthy objects. Mackenzie's Harley could not feel more than the frame narrator of *The Adventures of a Cork-screw* does upon helping an unfortunate widow and her orphaned children. "I felt a joy superior to what I had ever before experienced," he proclaims. "Say, ye libertines, ye gamblers and others, . . . did you but know the superlative felicity a good action affords, you would quit your favorite sports for proper objects to exercise your benevolence upon."[6] The movement of objects in these tales told by things furnishes occasions for their owners to objectify their virtue, giving it concrete status in the referential world. The coin's passage from the hand of a gentleman to a worthy but poor man is an external manifestation of an interior disposition.

By inviting objects to tell tales about their various owners, these stories told by things bring together the sentimental and the commercial in a quite remarkable way. They contrast the voracious and self-interested pursuit of getting and spending with a kinder, gentler version of the market. If the commodity proclaims the autonomy of things from persons, tales told by things remind us of the intimate connections between the two. Objects create not only a material link between the antipodes and home, but also the capacity to imagine relations to others through the vehicle of such objects. They speak of a world in which the social lives of things are inseparable from the lives and fates of humans. In these tales, the fancy that we in fact inhabit a world in which gregarious objects fall silent upon our entrance is supplanted by the pleasant fiction that one might overhear the inaudible babble coursing beneath the surface of a world only seemingly mute. Provisionally crystallized in these texts is the prose of the world to which we are otherwise deaf. And the prose uttered by that world is at first glance wonderfully reassuring, if not particularly well written: for the things, it turns out, are talking about us. Unlike Marx's commodities (to which we shall return below), the things in these tales are preoccupied with humans: their needs, their desires, their deeds, their power over the thing's material well-being.

These tales told by things communicate, at first glance, the decidedly *un*sentimental message that objects create more of a community than subjects do. The objects create the only relations between otherwise dissociated individuals in a stratified society. "Without me," the Birmingham counterfeit announces, "trade and commerce would dwindle to a shadow, and the retail trader be totally ruined."[7] In the gold cane, or the coin, or the waistcoat that travels from master to servant, from thief to lord, we find the unacknowledged bonds that link a society together. What unites people are things and, as Aileen Douglas puts it, the "impersonal" ways they circulate.[8] Because they are narrated by things rather than people, the narratives implicitly draw attention to the absence of any community other than that produced by money and commodities. Thus the hackney coach carries Samuel Johnson and Oliver Goldsmith before picking up, as it were, a prostitute, but there is no other relationship between these characters. In these narratives, the human at times seems to drop out of the loop altogether: the goose quill writes, not to a body of human readers, but to his friend, Mrs. Midnight's tye-wig; the lady's slipper speaks to the lady's shoe, and the waistcoat addresses a petticoat.

On these terms, it would be easy to say that these stories are just taking a consumer society's misplaced idolatry of objects to a new extreme, to the point where they rise up against their owners and unmask them. Like Marx's table, which frisks and capers on its four legs, the object narratives feature things that have realized their autonomy to such a degree that they can now proffer their own histories. Relations between persons would seem to have been supplanted by relations between things in a disturbingly exact exemplification of Marx's commodity fetishism, in which "the social character of men's labour appears to them as an objective character stamped upon the product of that labour," and social relations among humans assume the "fantastic form of a relation between things." And yet the tales told by things are not harbingers of the commodity fetishism fully realized in Marx, since the things are not preoccupied with each other, but with the people who own them. "But I must recollect I am writing my own history, not theirs," the pin exclaims after a long excursus into the lives of its owners.[9]

In the context of these eighteenth-century tales, the interest of Marx lies, not in his description of the reification of people, but in his description of the animation of things. For what Marx's account shares with the tales is a heavy reliance on the trope of personification. It seems that even an explanation of the way objects overtake subjects and usurp their agency (i.e., commodity fetishism) cannot quite do without the figure of the person. Where people are absent, personifications abound. The question this chapter poses is not why commodities are said to propel capitalism along, why "the relations connecting the labour of one individual with that of the rest appear, not as direct social relations between individuals at work, but as what they really are, material relations between persons and social relations between things."[10] The question is why this process is represented in the form of personifications.

The Commodity's Soliloquy

Marx invites objects to speak, of course, in volume 1 of *Capital:* "Could commodities themselves speak," he tells us, "they would say: Our use-value may be a thing that interests men. It is no part of us as objects. What, however, does belong to us as objects, is our value. Our natural intercourse as commodities proves it. In the eyes of each other we are nothing but exchange values."[11] The use-values of objects that interest humans—the properties of the coat that keep us warm, the capacity of food to nourish us—do not matter to the commodity. Once it mysteriously absorbs the labor of the subject, the commodity finds the subject—its labor, its needs—to be oddly superfluous. When endowed with a voice of its own, Marx's commodity uses it to snub us.

It is not only the person that disappears in the commodity form but also the thing. For commodities "in the eyes of each other" are not things, but exchange values, and as exchange values, they are oddly immaterial. In a world of economic equivalence (in which one coat equals twenty yards of linen equals three clocks equals twelve CDs), the specific properties of a thing evaporate. "Commodification," as Margreta de Grazia, Maureen Quilligan, and Peter Stallybrass have argued, "is thus not only the vanishing point of the subject into the commodified object but also of the object into pure exchangeability."[12] Value does not inhere in the object proper, but outside of it, in its differential relation to other commodities. As Marx wryly puts it, "The reality of the value of commodities differs in this respect from [Shakespeare's] Dame Quickly, that we don't know 'where to have it'" (15). Marx's talking commodity, this object that claims to possess value as well as a voice, would seem to be oddly dispossessed. Indeed, its very immateriality is what necessitates its voice. "In order to inform us that its sublime reality as value is not the same as its buckram body, it [the commodity] says that value has the appearance of a coat, and consequently that so far as the linen is value, it and the coat are as like as two peas" (20).

That things look different when seen through each other's eyes is perhaps less surprising than the notion that they might have eyes to begin with; that things scorn men when endowed with voices of their own is less surprising than the fact that they should have voices at all. Why does Marx bestow a voice upon his commodity? Given Marx's insistence on the elusive immateriality of the value form of the commodity, what exactly is being personified? Marx, it seems, personifies the commodity in order to have it proclaim the disappearance of person and thing alike. By bestowing upon the commodity desires, forcefulness, and agency, Marx gives shape and local habitation to the ineffable abstraction and mysterious activity of the fetishized commodity.

Even a perfunctory reading of Marx reveals that one of the dominant rhetorical modes of *Capital* is personification. Marx's commodities have voices, eyes, faces, even "natural intercourse" and active social lives (although perhaps not as active as that of Dame Quickly). In the absence of a personal agent, commodities perform exchanges, confer and appraise value; they see and are seen, strutting and fretting their hour upon the stage in a decisively animated manner. In the opening chapter of *Capital*, persons are replaced by things as commodities, which are in turn replaced by personifications.

At first glance, personification looks like the ideal trope for *Capital*.[13] To personify things is to follow, quite docilely, the logic of *Capital*'s opening chapters: if the person (or his or her labor) is objectified in commodities, then the neat reciprocity of balanced exchange would dictate that things become personified. The mistaking of subject for object that occurs in the fetishism of the commodity is neatly turned on its head in the mistaking of object for subject that is personification. The fetishistic inversion is revealed (and reversed) by a trope that confers agency upon a thing under the pallid mask of a personified object, the commodity that addresses us.

To make a thing speak—to personify it—is to enact a qualified form of fetishism: it is to make an object provisionally into a subject. Even the most anodyne of personifications borrows qualities from the human in order to animate the material and immaterial world. Personification thus implicitly confers capacities upon a being that does not possess those capacities. In this, personification might be seen to bear an uncanny kinship to the religious fetishist's worship of inanimate and nonhuman things—the wooden stumps, snakes, statues, and masks so derided in Enlightenment texts. But the fetishism of commodities Marx describes in the opening chapter of *Capital* is not the overvaluation of the material of which religious fetishists stand accused: it is instead the worship of intangible value refracted into objects. Commodity fetishism is, as Peter Stallybrass has argued, "one of Marx's least-understood jokes." To fetishize commodities is "to reverse the whole history of fetishism. For it is to fetishize the invisible, the immaterial, the supra-sensible. The fetishism of the commodity inscribes *immateriality* as the defining feature of capitalism. Thus, for Marx, *fetishism* is not the problem; the problem is the fetishism of *commodities*."[14]

What makes Marx's personification of the commodity so bizarre is that Marx bestows voice, eyes, faces, upon commodities—garbs them in the habit of the human—in order to have them proclaim this immateriality. "What belongs to us as objects," his commodities declare, "is our value." Marx uses personifications where people are wanting, where things have moved beyond the grasp of the human; he borrows the properties of subjects to explain the abstract agency of the economy. The theoretical impetus that spurs Marx's commodity into speech thus has much to tell us about the way personifications give shape to the operation of the overarching economic system. In these terms, the personified things in the eighteenth-century tales, like Marx's commodity, articulate not only the sinews that bind otherwise dissociated persons and things together, but also the systemic workings of markets at a point when the vocabulary of economic abstraction has not yet fully emerged.

Yet the story told about the circulation of objects in the tales told by things does not match up with Marx's account in many respects, and this is in part because of the role played by the sentimental in the eighteenth-century narratives. The objects exist not to express the value of other objects (although they occasionally do so), but to express their feelings about their owners. In these narratives, people do *not* exist in self-evident autonomy, aloof from objects, detached from and prior to the things that make and unmake their world. Moreover, the object itself does not exist in self-evident autonomy, establishing value in that "language," as Marx puts it, "with which alone it [the commodity] is familiar" (20). Things still need people in these narratives.[15] The waistcoat may exist without a wearer or tailor, the stagecoach without a driver, the wig without a head, but without people, there is no narrative, which is part of the reassurance of the tale. Objects may have histories but without people, there is no story to tell. Whereas Marx animates his commodity to have it proclaim its relation to other commodities (and its indifference to humans), the object narratives animate their objects in order to have them describe their relations to people. The world that Marx's commodity inhabits is not yet fully realized in these books. Indeed, the purpose of these narratives is to fend off that day.

The tales cannot be read as neat allegories of commodity fetishism for the simple reason that these things are *not* just commodities. The objects in the tales possess the kind of cultural biography that the anthropologist Igor Kopytoff suggests all commodities possess.[16] Thus we are given the birth, stormy adolescence, banal career, midlife crisis, and old age of the watch, the petticoat, the coin and its counterfeit. Things, as Kopytoff tells us, move in and out of their status as commodities: the watch is a commodity on a jeweler's shelf, an heirloom within a family, a sentimental trinket, a repository of value to be pawned or sold. Addison's coin is raw material, miserly treasure, currency, gift, and medal, before being clipped and defaced to the point where it is unrecognizable.[17] Things are no more fixed in their meaning than persons; they too have stories, and those stories are inseparably bound up with the stories of people.

The tales told by things transform commodities from repositories of economic value to objective correlatives of interior emotions and personal experiences. Thus the cast-off objects up for sale in a pawnshop produce the histories of their former owners (but not of their makers): "That ring," the rupee tells us, "was perhaps in remembrance of the purest flame that love can excite, and may have been worn by some gentle maid.—This one is a wedding ring; it has been a witness of the fairest pleasures that heaven bestows on mortals.—Sad misfortunes alone could force its mistress to expose it to sale; perhaps this step was the only to [*sic*] one by which she could support the helpless offspring of that union it was made to celebrate."[18] The sentimental becomes the means of revaluing commercial objects: things are coveted *not* because of their economic value but because of the personal bond felt between owner and object. The reader who is moved by the misfortunes of the mother who pawns her wedding ring to feed her children finds in the ring a connection to her suffering. In these narratives, the rapacity of a market that tempts the individual to hoard is supplanted by an invitation to share, whether through consumption of the object or through consumption of the tale. Sentimental commerce thus establishes bonds between human beings by establishing a shared relation not *between* objects (as in commodity fetishism) but *through* objects.

These are not stories about commodities among themselves, but about things' relations to people. Indeed, the narrative is driven by the fact that people and things can't quite stay together. The fact that loss is necessary to propel the narrative forward even dictates the choice of narrating object: because the separation of things from their owners is the engine of the plot, the object narratives must focus on superfluous things (feathers, watches, canes) or objects that inherently circulate (coins, banknotes). Necessities like food are not appropriate for these narratives because they *cannot* be parted with—we need them to live—and because they get used up. Even clothing in these texts is valued for its sartorial properties rather than its ability to shelter a body from the elements. (It is a mark of desperation, the rupee points out, that pawnshops contain "the very necessaries of life, which hunger has torn from their masters. Good heavens! what has become of those wretches which these rags used to defend from the inclemency of the weather. This is not a temple where wealth has deposited its superfluities; it is a cell loaded with the spoils of the afflicted, and the very necessaries of necessity.")[19] The things featured in object narratives are usually the kinds of things one parts with in order to acquire the *absolutely* necessary. And it is this fact that makes their loss such a blow to human particularity, for the things that transcend the urgent imperatives of base necessity are also, perversely enough, the things that are most particular and personal to us.[20] Superfluities are chosen, the objects of election, the bearers of the sentimental value discussed in Chapter 2.

The fact that these objects, however loved, however needed, must be parted with for there to be a narrative betrays the possibility that the right things will not fall into the right hands. If things can go astray, then the bond between person and thing is made, not natural. Perhaps things *should* recirculate and be redistributed in a more equitable manner? The tales told by things rarely veer towards such a revolutionary premise, however. And here we come to the ideological labor being performed by these texts: the law of diminishing resources and increasing scarcity is applied in these tales not to things, but to people. The tales depict a pathetic game of musical chairs, in which there is one place fewer to sit at each round. But the tales perversely reverse the game: the problem is not that there are not enough good *things* to go around, but that there are not enough good *people*. It is the objects that are looking for a place to reside, not people who are desperately looking for things to possess. The worst fear of a thing is to be ownerless. As the watch writes,

> For about a week I remained in a dull kind of uncertainty of my next servitude. This is the state which, of all others, is the most perplexing; and is strikingly depicted by the first of poets as a damned state. A watch of quality may surely be allowed to feel as well as a dog of quality; humanity is the darling characteristic of a free and enlightened people, and should extend to every quarter of the globe— The poor African[']s servitude would then be light as the machine that points the hours.[21]

To be unowned is to be in a state of perplexity, even damnation. The proclamation "I will not serve" of Milton's Satan becomes the watch's "I serve, therefore I am." Identity is gleaned from one's position of subordination within a system of orders. Thus the watch uses the third person to describe itself as a member of a class, as "a watch of quality" comparable to "a dog of quality" like the narrator of Coventry's 1751 *Pompey the Little*.

Although the logic of the passage is obscure, the humanity of "a free and enlightened people" ostensibly confers the right to feel upon dog and watch alike. Extended to "every quarter of the globe," such humanity eventually moves from dogs to things to people: "the poor African[']s servitude," the watch concludes, "would then be light as the machine that points the hours." The ambiguous wording might mean that the African would suffer as little as the narrating watch, a machine that records the hours of toil, or it might mean that the metaphorical weight of African suffering would become as light as the literal weight of a watch. No matter: for the watch soon forgets the suffering Africans in an apostrophe to those noble souls sensitive enough to feel for another's suffering:

> Colour ought to furnish no colour for barbarity—Sordid interest may in the end prove of a darker hue than the negro's face! But enough of this; darkness, ignorance, nay sordid interest, will, I trust, be dispersed by the refulgent lustre of heaven-born humanity. Ye noble partizans of Universal Freedom, hail! Distant shores, with rapture, shall repeat your names! Myriads yet unborn shall hereafter chaunt your praise![22]

"Colour" is rhetorically reworked from epidermal layer into a mask that disguises or "colors" over exploitation, as self-interest proves to be "darker" than "the negro's face." Placed in the mouth of a provisionally masterless object, the watch's rhapsodic meditations on the compassionate "partizans of Universal

Freedom" suggest that the problem is not with the fact of ownership but with the moral character of particular owners. By implying that the problem lies not in institutions but in the character of those who use them, the watch personalizes systemic exploitation. Good owners redeem unjust property claims.

Sentimentality, as we saw in the previous chapter, surfaces in these tales in order to bind the world more securely to the subject by appropriating objects in bonds that supersede the material or legal connection of property to person. From the one-night stand of commodity exchange, we move to the protracted engagement of true love. The reason certain things belong to particular people is not class or economic privilege, nor even commonplace rapacity or greed. Instead, you own objects because objects want to be owned by you. Indeed, in these texts, the intimacy that exists between things and their owners is eerily reciprocal: the young gentleman may shrug into the black coat, but the black coat "contract[s] every thread to clasp him."[23] Property, it turns out, is not personal, but interpersonal: that the coat shrinks to fit the man, that the watch clutches at chains to stay attached to a desirable owner, legitimates the ownership of the many by the few. If the ostrich feather of quality is devastated to fall into the hands of a prostitute, the watch is elated to wind up in the hands of William Trueman.[24] When restored to its virtuous first owners, the pin claims to have "gained my P O I N T of brightest glory."[25] Objects objectively confirm the earthly rewards of virtue by desiring to belong to the good.

When these texts shift to the domain of empire, they use the sentimental to reinforce the prerogative of appropriation: the most absolute form of propriety is sentimental possession. Thus Helenus Scott's *Adventures of a Rupee* depicts colonial commerce as a mutually beneficial set of exchanges with distant lands, but it takes this vision a step further by having the thing itself proclaim the superiority of the English nation. The Scottish hero and heroine who transport the rupee to England are both virtuous exemplars of nonviolent conquest. They are present in India, the rupee proclaims, to "protect the trade of [their] country, against the insults of European powers, or of the Indian nations, who ignorant of the blessings that commerce diffuses, even to themselves, are often disposed to interrupt its equitable course."[26] Indeed, the sole ambition of the Indian rupee is to emigrate to England: "I wish, said I, that fortune may some time or other carry me to England; for without doubt, that great East India Company, which can keep black men in such good order at so great a distance," will be even better at home. That all spoils should go to the British is not the malevolent desire of a rapacious colonizing nation, but a neutral desire voiced by the thing itself. Condemning the avarice of the Indian priests, the rupee declares that "it is surely not so in England, where men, I have been told, are acquainted with the true religion" and even goes on to celebrate the "Happy women of England, whom custom and religion have made the equals of men! . . . You are not placed under the dominion of tyrants, who possess nothing in common with men but the figure."[27] The teleology that directs all commodities into the hands of the virtuous (or at least the British) is proclaimed by the most objective of sources: the object itself. If all things wind up in the hands of the British, it is because all things in their hearts yearn to belong to the British.

I have been arguing that sentimentality infuses objects with personal meaning in order to incorporate them into the body of the nation. And yet the provenance of these objects is cause for alarm. The consumption of foreign goods carries the threat that one will turn into the thing one consumes; you do eventually become what you eat. Foreign products may leech away national identity. In the tales told by things, the objects themselves are able to disavow this malevolent intent: they exist to absorb Englishness, not to purvey foreignness. Thus the rupee approvingly quotes an immigrant's avowal that his "greatest boast shall ever be, that as a Briton, I can feel my heart beat at the very name of liberty."[28] The gold-headed cane notes that he was "by the hands of savages, pagans, Mahometans, and unbelievers, all cut down in a few hours," but reassures us that he is "now entered Christianity and civilization, and furnished with an elegant and accomplished European dress."[29] The coin bears the violent imprint of its English nationalization on its body: "after I had gone through a deal of torture," the shilling announces, "I discovered, by the letters imprinted on me, that I belonged to *George the Third, King of Great Britain, France, and Ireland, Defender of the Faith.*"[30]

If the objects model themselves on their masters, they also, however, hope to mold them. In object narratives, human personality proceeds from personal property (which was also, in the eighteenth century, called personalty), not vice versa. Rather than one's things bearing the stamp of the personality one already possesses, one gets personality in and through one's property. In the 1791 "Adventures of a Mirror," the mirror prides itself on its capacity to fashion its owners in its own image: "[I]t was I only that could sanction the work when finished . . . from me there was no appeal," it boasts. "I was always consulted for the finishing and completing of their persons."[31] Whereas for Marx the object incorporates the subject's labor into itself, so that the subject's labor appears to be a property of the object itself, here the object makes the subject. The object narratives derive their human characters' lives and selfhood from the things they own. For part of the reason objects come to possess personality is that they bestow it. In a world in which money talks (metaphorically speaking), why shouldn't money talk (literally)? If things confer social character and personality upon people, why should they not possess character and personality themselves? And if they do possess character and personality, how is one to prevent them from overtaking persons? At times they do. As Chrysal the guinea puts it, "when the mighty spirit of a large mass of gold takes possession of the human heart, it influences all its actions, and overpowers, or banishes, the weaker impulse of those immaterial, unessential notions called *virtues*."[32] People are possessed, or rather dispossessed by what they own. They are ventriloquized, as Aureas the sovereign contends, by their property and their wealth: "money has the power to move the tongue . . . and thus, by proxy, it often speaks unutterable things."[33]

These narratives recognize (and fear) the transformative power of things themselves: you are or you may become what you own. The gold cane, the guinea, the shilling, and the rupee explain their alchemical powers to convert people from idiots to geniuses, from paupers to princes. In transforming the surface appearance of their owners, these objects misrepresent the "real" social status of the human: by making their owners appear more prosperous than in fact they are, the embroidered waistcoat and the petticoat facilitate all sorts of deception. The black coat is so agitated by the frauds it helps perpetrate that it disavows accountability for its owners' actions: "When I . . . meditate on the vile schemes I have been obliged to countenance in those whose sole merit and reputation arose from my close attachment to them," it announces, "my very threads blush at the indignity" (3–4). The boundaries between persons and things become increasingly precarious in these tales; people come to seem curiously thinglike. Humans take on the attributes of objects both as the means of representing themselves *and* as they come to circulate as commodities themselves, not only as prostitutes or pawns in family marriages, but even to the child who sells its front teeth to an "old lady of quality."[34]

All things are not your friend, however. Underlying these tales is a kind of hostility or antagonism between the world of things and the world of people: the things *despise* many of their masters; they wage a secret war on their owners. People are in the clutches of these objects—not only at the mercy of the wealth they signify but also bound by the privileged knowledge of their personal life that the objects have obtained. The coach meant to proclaim one's hard-won rank might instead snitch about one's true origins, and the confidences of a nightgown or a sofa might be even more revealing. "By Means of my Intimacy with my Lady," the petticoat proclaims, "which was greater than any other of her Servants, save her Smock, I may make bold to affirm that I know more of her secret

Story than any Body else."[35] The French instances of the object narrative exploit this pornographic potential; Crébillon fils's *Le sopha* (1742) and the speaking female genitals in Diderot's *Les bijoux indiscrets* (1748) expose the deeds and proclivities of their possessors, while suggesting unsavory parallels between the ways objects and women's bodies circulated in the eighteenth century.[36] The notion that no place is private or sacrosanct is made even more explicit in Victorian examples of the genre: "Never, gentle reader," the feather tells us in a paranoia-inducing lecture on the panoptic powers of our possessions, never "so long as you have a stitch about your anatomy, believe yourself alone. . . . Ignorance of man! to believe that what is borne upon the body has no intelligence with the moral good or evil dwelling in the soul."[37] The mastery or would-be mastery of people holding sway over a world of things is challenged by the image of a society enslaved to wealth, to accumulation, commerce, and consumption without end. If, at times, persons and things snuggle up together in sentimental reciprocity, at others they are locked together in a kind of eighteenth-century version of Sartre's *No Exit.*

But the object that makes feigned or assumed identities possible is ultimately called to the bar to testify against its own transformative capacities. The objects *see through* the duplicitous surfaces of the humans they encounter, purveying a reassuring message about their fundamental humanity. The perversity of these texts should be apparent: they animate things and allow them to speak in order to proclaim their impotence. In story after story, the rupee, the guinea, the watch, and the wig tell of the *failure* of the thing to reconstruct the person within. A whore may buy a fancy gown and pass for a lady, but she is still in essence a whore (usually marked as such by a name like Mistress Bourdel or Bet Careless). What lies below the surface is the truth of a character that resists commercial transformation, that is not fungible. Once deciphered, the deceptive exterior reveals a fixed interior truth: "you will find the sanctify'd clergyman, an arch Hypocrite; the bluff Captain, a kick'd Coward; the noble Count, a *Swiss* Peasant."[38] Chiron the looking glass promises to teach the reader to see through men "as well as a painter knows an original from a copy, or a woollen-draper a good, from a bad commodity."[39]

The stripping away of misleading surfaces does not lead to infinitely plural selves but to an essential and unproblematic core. As Deidre Lynch points out, these narratives depict characters, not "deep" personalities in the modern sense of the term.[40] The fact that goods do not alter the essential identity of the person who acquires them conveys the reassuring message that you do not become what you consume. Object narratives elect to reassert the primacy and particularity of the human at the point where they begin to blur the distinctions between what is inalienable in humans and what is alienable in things. The language of interiority and sentimental feeling furnishes a vocabulary by which identity, be it personal or national, can be located or anchored, aloof from objects. It allows a nation of shopkeepers to participate in bustling traffic with foreign bodies and to remain English to the bone.

Thinking Through Things

The eighteenth-century sentimental novel typically restricts itself to specific, usually domestic, locations. By contrast, the household goods that supported the life of the self in the metropole were often the product of colonial materials and labor. Things and persons moved from the farthest reaches of the British empire to the home, creating tangible but unacknowledged bonds between bodies and contexts otherwise unconnected to each other. The mere presence of a foreign thing thus warps sentimental texts, creating a kind of Narnian wardrobe into a world extending far beyond the particular and local sphere of the novel. Although its domestic setting may seem to construct a precinct from which the violence of colonial life has been expelled, the sentimental novel also uses material objects to enable the reader to imagine broader communities of nation, of empire, of humanity. By restoring the history of an object's relations to people, the sentimental intimates that there is a double "truth" to be told about things— both an economic and a novelistic account of their origins, meanings, and ends. Read sentimentally, imported objects constitute not only a material link between home and the far side of the world but also a means of imagining relations with the distant others who inhabit it. Material things provide the necessary underpinning for the imagination.

In the sentimental text, humanitarian feeling about distant others is only infrequently generated through the presence of the suffering individuals themselves. Rather, anti-colonial and anti-slavery writings retrace the histories of commodities to give affective import to actions and persons so remote as to defy imagination. Even where objects are not literally given a narrative voice, as in the tales told by things, their materiality can be used to retrace the history silenced by their commodity form. Thus anti-slavery writing tries to bring home the fact that domestic pleasures are purchased through labor and exploitation elsewhere by inviting the reader to recognize the suffering of the slave in its objectified form in the commodity. The strategy persists over several decades. Andrew Burn's invitation to readers in 1792 to recognize "that every Hogshead of

Sugar . . . is more or less impregnated with . . . liquid from the human body" is succeeded in 1824 by the declamation of "Anthropos":

> May every man, who casts his eye over this page, who bears that name, before he
> again indulge his appetite with the blood-bought luxury, *reflect upon the price it*
> *cost*. . . . As he sweetens his tea, let him reflect on the bitterness at the bottom of
> the cup. Let him bring the subject home to his heart, and say, as he truly may, this
> lump cost the poor Slave a groan, and this, a bloody stroke with the cart-whip; and
> for this, perhaps, worn down by fatigue, and wretchedness, and despair, he sunk
> under his misery, and died! And then, let him swallow his beverage with what ap-
> petite he may.[41]

Even as the tales told by things recount the stories of persons through their passage from one hand to another, here we find the slave literally transmuted into
thing. The term "cost" moves from the price paid for the sugar to the sum of human suffering ("this lump cost the poor Slave"); sugar, the Englishman's "blood-
bought luxury," is paid for in the suffering of the West Indian slave, parsed out
in sighs, groans, and whip strokes. The reader is invited to "bring the subject
home to his heart," telescoping time and distance by identifying *not* directly
with the slave (who sinks under misery and dies before the passage's close), but
with the position of a sentimental observer who feels pity by using the sugar
as a mediating object. Each lump implicates the tea drinker in compound horrors, adding another stroke of the whip, another groan. (In a widely circulated
1791 pamphlet, William Fox even went so far as to specify that for "every pound
of sugar used . . . we may be considered as consuming two ounces of human
flesh.")[42] The commodities that motivated colonial expansion became a means
of inciting feelings of revulsion against exploitation.

As Deirdre Coleman and Charlotte Sussman have noted, the association of
sugar with the slave's body in anti-slavery polemics makes a cannibalistic other
of the English sugar eater, who ingests the slave's body and blood both metaphorically (the slave's labor and tragic fate) and literally (actual sweat and blood transferred to the sugar during its production).[43] These passages incite disgust both at
the blood-soaked sugar ingested and at what one becomes by virtue of having
eaten it (a cannibal). The sugar moves between laboring body and consuming
body, eclipsing the distinction between metropolitan self and colonial other by
creating a physical hybrid of African and European flesh. Anti-slavery discourse
wavers on a knife-edge between sympathy and revulsion, between the fusion of
bodies and the desire for differentiation.

Object narratives also invite readers to recognize that their daily lives are sustained by goods drawn from the farthest reaches of empire. Thus Smollett's atom conjoins the antipodes to the metropole in a scatological satire that fuses high and low. Originating in Japan, the atom

> was enclosed in a grain of rice, eaten by a Dutch mariner at Firando, and, becoming a particle of his body, brought to the Cape of Good Hope. There I was discharged in a scorbutic dysentery, taken up in a heap of soil to manure a garden, raised to vegetation in a sallad, devoured by an English supercargo, assimilated to a certain organ of his body, which, at his return to London, being diseased in consequence of impure contact, I was again separated, with a considerable portion of putrefied flesh, thrown upon a dunghill, gobbled up, and digested by a duck, of which duck your father, Ephraim Peacock, having eaten plentifully at a feast of the cordwainers, I was mixed with his circulating juices, and finally fixed in the principal part of that animalcule, which, in process of time, expanded itself into thee, Nathaniel Peacock. (*Atom*, 7)

Not unlike Matthew Bramble, Smollett's benevolent crank in *Humphry Clinker*, the atom depicts a world of overwhelming immixture. If a king may go a progress through the guts of a beggar, an atom is able to traverse ranks, bodies, nations, and even species, allowing foreign and domestic, food and waste, animal, vegetable, and mineral, to commingle. The atom infiltrates bodies literally and figuratively, binding them together in a world in which nothing can be held apart. Indeed, the atom excreted from one body becomes the origin of another in the form of an "animalcule."

That we are framed of common materials does not mean that we are all equal or alike. As the atom observes: "Of the same shape, substance, and quality, are the component particles, that harden in rock, and flow in water; that blacken in the negro, and brighten in the diamond; that exhale from a rose, and steam from a dunghill" (*Atom*, 6). Broken down into elements, all things are leveled into likeness, yet the atom's proclamation that we are all composed of "the same shape, substance, and quality" opens up on a vista of social and objective differentiation. The passage is constructed around a set of implied contrasts: the solidity of rock versus the fluidity of water; the sweet aroma of the rose against the stench of dung, and, rather oddly, the "blackness" of the Negro and the brightness of the diamond. The opposition of earth and water, rose and dung, does not quite lock the unconventional pairing of Negro and diamond in place. That blackness in a "negro" should be contrasted with brightness in a diamond—rather than, say, whiteness in a "Circassian" or dullness in a coal—leaves us with the puzzling question of what valence to assign to the two implied extremes: the relative value of the Negro or the diamond? their contrastive complexions? The atom's foot-loose movement through person and thing places them on a continuum, although the indeterminacy of satire leaves it unclear whether the passage incorporates the Negro into the circle of life or mocks efforts to banish the African from the great chain of being.

These fused material qualities are invisible on the level of the body. Unto themselves, the bodies the atom composes—like sugar, like rum, and even, as we shall see, like the slave—remain obdurately uncommunicative. As Elaine Scarry puts it, "the notion that everyone is alike by having a body and that what differentiates one person from another is the soul or intellect or personality can mislead one into thinking that the body is 'shared' and the other part is 'private' when exactly the opposite is the case. The mute facts of sentience (deprived of cultural externalization) are wholly self-isolating."[44] However porous the body may be—and sugar and atoms attest to its permeability—it is also guarded and secret, from the mouth that opens onto the darkness of the esophagus to the contracting intestines so central to Smollett's scatological imagination. Without the atom's explanation, the cultural externalization of language, we would be unable to recognize the way bodies are conjoined to each other. By having otherwise mute things speak, object narratives unravel the stories behind Scarry's "self-isolating facts." They bestow characteristics like language, thought, life history, and personality upon things, producing the *effect* of subjectivity in a thing that does not "really" possess personality, selfhood, a Christian soul. In part because the traits associated with subjectivity are seemingly immaterial, it is easy to forget that the narrator is a thing. The things disappear—or at least our consciousness of them does: if you don't know the title of the book, it can be hard to tell whether you're reading the adventures of a pincushion or a peg-top, a clock, or a coach.

Things, as Bill Brown has argued, become most present to us when they balk or stall out regular processes, deviating from their "natural" allotted function. (Part of the reason objects are able to eavesdrop so easily on their possessors in the object narratives is that the latter don't even notice they are there.) What Brown calls "misuse value" frees objects from "the systems to which they've been beholden,"[45] allowing them to be recognized as "things." It is only when the goose quill notes that the hack writer uses "one End of me to get him a *Dinner,* and the other to cleanse the corrupted Filth from his rotten Teeth"[46] that we remember a quill is composed of a feather. Objects remember their materiality when reminded of their mortality. Thus we become aware of the banknote's fragility when it is most imperiled; the bill lives in terror of being ripped, burned, buried alive (in a miser's hoard), used as toilet paper, even, at one point, eaten by

the irate mistress of a nobleman. Above all, the banknote fears being brought
back to the bank, where "a fellow with a hangman-looking face, takes us by the
nape of the neck, and in a moment twitches some talismanic letters (which to us
are the spinal marrow) from the north-east corner of our skirts" (*Bank-note*,
1.167). But the greatest "misuse" of these objects is the fact that they tell their
own tales. It is in the production of speech and text that we become most aware
of their material being.

The need to account for the material production of the object narratives means
that these texts focus on the manual labor of the author—the flexing of the writing hand, the transcription of a voice—rather than the ideational aspects of literary production and consumption.[47] The goose quill pen overcomes the author,
turning the labors of the writer into the mechanical activity of a lowly transcriber.
The banknote converts the author into a kind of dictaphone—"a secretary," as he
puts it, "or more properly speaking . . . a machine" (*Bank-note*, 1.3). Object narratives repeatedly return to the gap between text and material book. The talking
Bible refers to the library as a "Jail for books" and complains about the fact that
nobody reads anymore: its owners admire the Bible's external appearance but
never crack its spine.[48] The quire of paper, after describing its transition from
plant to cloth to rag to paper, dissevers literary content from material form. As a
"fast-day prayer," the quire indignantly announces, it was used "at the bottom of
some mince pies. . . . In the form of a pastoral I was rubbing the grease off a grid-
iron in an eating house; and as A Kind Warning to Christians, clapped under a pot
of porter just taken from the fire, over which a chairman and a drayman were
quarrelling, and damning each other with all their might."[49] From the quire's
standpoint, only rarely is literature worth the paper it's printed on.

That objects can speak without (not in) tongues and write without hands be-
speaks the ways we cancel out the material and social aspects of literary production. The personification of things renders subjectivity effects immaterial traits
that can be infused into any kind of entity, inhering in language, intent, memory, and ideology. It is only when the texts attempt to account for the physical capacity of the thing to speak that language ceases to be the immaterial expression
of interior spirit. The mystery by which a fan acquires a voice reminds us of the
flexing of the tongue by which *all* humans attain speech, as the words we use to
describe speech—gravity, weightiness—become literal as well as metaphorical.
Lewis Carroll's Cheshire Cat, one may recall, only speaks "as soon as there was
mouth enough for it to speak with," and Alice waits for the Cheshire Cat's ears
to materialize before answering.[50] For a thing to have a voice, it must have face,
form, mouth, tongue.

This material dimension of personification is produced through the trope of prosopopoeia, which Paul de Man defines as "the fiction of an apostrophe to an absent, deceased, or voiceless entity, which posits the possibility of the latter's reply and confers upon it the power of speech."[51] Because voice requires the giving of bodily form, de Man contends, the trope must call into being the shape of the person: "Voice assumes mouth, eye, and finally face, a chain that is evident in the etymology of the trope's name, *prosopon poien*, to confer a mask or a face (*prosopon*)."[52] Thus Addison's shilling "that lay upon the Table reared it self upon its Edge, and turning the Face toward me, opened its Mouth, and in a soft Silver Sound gave . . . [its] Account."[53] The needle only sees once it has acquired an eye; the clock when it gains a face; the pin is "sharp" because it has "a good head."[54]

The tales told by objects add an additional twist to the trope of prosopopoeia, for coins and watches do not literally have faces, any more than needles have eyes, canes and pins have heads, or banknotes backs. Properly speaking, faces and eyes pertain to bodies (human or animal). The face of a coin is a substitute figure borrowed from human anatomy; it is a figurative expression for which there is no literal term, a catachresis. Catachresis is a distinctive figure. Whereas other tropes involve the substitution of figural for literal meaning, the exchange of one word for another (part for whole, like for like), in catachresis, the substitution of figural for literal meaning—exchange itself—breaks down.[55] Instead of creating relations that allow one word to be substituted for another, catachresis marks the place-holding function of language: its ability to stand for a thing lacking a name. Catachresis thus exposes "the positional power inherent in language"—its capacity both to create and to "dismember the texture of reality and reassemble it in the most capricious of ways."[56] Tables do not strictly speaking have legs; the borrowed word *leg* is the only term we have for it. One need only literalize the image of a table leg and see a table capering on goat's legs to understand why catachresis is called an abuse of language, the trope of monstrosity. The personification of things in the object narratives is a form of monstrous catachresis: the things borrow, wholesale, terms proper to persons.

Inasmuch as personifications borrow the property of a person to lend shape, purpose, or agency to something lacking definable form, personification invariably involves some form of catachresis. Personification, that is, gives form to what would otherwise be a there that's not quite there. "It is as though," as Barbara Johnson has argued in a different context, "the operations of personhood could not be eliminated but only transferred—which does not necessarily imply that their rightful place is within the self."[57] That the "operations of personhood" may be transferred beyond the borders of the subject poses complicated questions about agency and accountability both historically and theoretically. I shall return to this later in this chapter and in Chapter 5; it suffices here to note that personifications are figural proxies that arise in the *absence* of subjectivity. They mark the *non*appearance of a person. The problem is knowing when one is dealing with personifications and when one is dealing with people.

Personifications are the unobtrusive but ubiquitous power brokers of the trope world, silently allocating agency, intent, and form to things otherwise immobile and ineffable. They borrow aspects of the human to animate both abstractions—systems or collectives (capitalism, the commodity, nations)—and inanimate particulars. The world is peopled in this way by entities that are not people. Through personification, as Ephraim Chambers puts it in his 1728 *Cyclopaedia,*

> not only different Objects, but different Systems and Worlds, are combined and blended together; and what belongs to one Kind of Beings, Man, is attributed to every other: each Object, either of Sense or Imagination, being occasionally invested with all the Characters and Properties belonging to the human Kind. Thus, an Arrow grows *impatient,* and *thirsts* to *drink* the Blood of a Foe; or *loiters* and stops half way, *loth* to *carry* Death. *Etc.* So an Action of the Body, *Laughter,* is above represented as it self laughing, ready to burst its Sides. And in the same Piece we have one of the Planets, the Moon, represented as *trick'd up,* and *frounced;* and again, as *kerchief'd,* and in a decent Undress, and thus going a *Hunting.*[58]

Chambers gives personification positional power to immix dissimilar things. The trope not only creates relations between "different objects" but also parlays among epistemologies ("different systems and worlds") in order to recast the world in the image of man. When we borrow human traits to animate a nonhuman being, we appropriate qualities that that being lacks as the only language available to describe it. By transferring human characteristics or properties to things, personifications delegate intention or will to a surrogate object (the arrow that thirsts for blood); they give form to what otherwise lacks shape, intent, and agency (laughter as an act is morphed into a graspable, describable entity; a celestial body like the moon is given motive for its movements). But personifications don't just help us imagine or animate objects; they are ways of imagining what a person is as well. To treat personification as a figure of substitution like any other—in other words, to insist that personification is not a kind of catachresis—is to take for granted that we know what a person is. But persons (as the things suggest in their tales) are not always what you think they are, and there is a sense in which "person" is a term for which we have, properly speaking, no referent. If personifications, as Chambers puts it, borrow "what belongs to one Kind of Beings, Man," then they may tell us something about "the Characters and Properties belonging to the human Kind." It is to these properties that we now turn.

Subject and Object in Olaudah Equiano's *Life*

The worth of a soul cannot be told.
—The Interesting Narrative of the Life of Olaudah Equiano, or
Gustavus Vassa, the African, Written by Himself

The intimacy and enmity of thing and owner that we have seen in the object narratives is also to be found in late eighteenth-century slave autobiographies. Tales told by things exist in harrowing proximity to tales told by slaves (or rather vice versa). Both sets of texts display and enact a disturbing confusion of subject and object, person and thing. The title pages of object narratives, as Jonathan Lamb has pointed out, bear a disturbing resemblance to the title pages of slave autobiographies (recounted by himself, written by itself).[59] There is even a perverse sense in which slave autobiographies are themselves tales told by (former) things, given the legal status of slave as chattel or *res*. The talking object in the slave autobiography is not only the speaking book, the animated clock, the watchful portrait; it is also the slave himself or herself. The very existence of a slave autobiography such as Olaudah Equiano's 1789 *Interesting Narrative* counters the characterization of slave as chattel or *res* by asking what happens when the object protests. The slave narrative brings out a question the object narrative never poses: if such "things" possess subjectivity, do humans have a right to subjugate them?

The simple bestowal of voice upon a coin and the waving of an authorial wand that stirs a watch to life are thrown into grotesque relief by the slave's laborious attainment of literacy. If the object narratives are monstrous or catachrestic because they give heads to coins, backs to banknotes, eyes to needles, and so on, slave autobiographies are grotesque because they labor to lay claim to human traits that the slave already possesses. Unlike the thing in the object narrative, the slave possesses all the physical accoutrements necessary to speak: face, mouth, tongue. And yet the slave, like the things in the object narratives, must acquire the means to recount his or her tale. The trope that confers human traits and voice upon a narrator is prosopopoeia—which is also, for Paul de Man, the trope of autobiography. Prosopopoeia, de Man argues, is a form of apostrophe to a "dead, silent, or absent other" that invites the addressed other to respond. It is the appropriate trope for autobiography, because the person writing at the present time is not the same as the past person who is written about: the "I" in the text and the "I" of the text are aligned but separate, mirrors of each other. Thus a present, writing subject calls up past selves through an apostrophe in order that they may recount his or her tale. Perhaps more than any other form of autobiography, slave autobiographies stage a raising of the dead through apostrophe: they describe the author's reanimation from the social death of slavery and the moral death of sin.

The fact that the present, writing self addresses a "dead, silent, or absent other" suggests that the subject in de Man's theory is split, and indeed, the unity of Equiano's "I" is called into question even before we arrive at the text of the autobiography itself. The title page indicates that this is the apostrophe of a double or split subject: Gustavus Vassa and Olaudah Equiano. The autobiography is composed partly under a name other than the one by which the author is nominally called; indeed, in the text, Equiano is variously called Jacob, Michael, Olaudah, and Gustavus.[60] The apostrophe that calls the shape of the self back into being cannot even assign it a proper name, a singular form. Recent speculation about the authenticity of Equiano's autobiography complicates the nature of this apostrophe even more. If, as Vincent Carretta has speculated, Equiano was actually a native of South Carolina, not Africa, then the "I" of the narrative does not call into being a prior self in an act of textual mirroring.[61] If Carretta's hypothesis is correct, the "I" called into being in the autobiography is a fiction—an apostrophe to a dead or absent other that is not himself. Equiano's first-person account of the Middle Passage might then be read as a kind of collective biography (or collective personification)—the experience of many condensed into a single narrative strain.

The unity of the autobiographical "I"—like the subject of Lacan's mirror stage—depends upon the capacity of language to impose wholeness upon the fragmentary self; the coherence of the subject is wrought out of the substitution of what de Man calls the privative word for the life. De Man fears that the trope may turn; the word may replace the person, as the living subject that conjures a past self is supplanted by the mask of the other. Riveted by his reflection, Narcissus may fall through the looking glass and drown. It is for this reason that Equiano must both revive a past self and maintain a certain distance from the being thus apostrophized. He must try to siphon off the animating force of prosopopoeia without getting caught by the turning of the trope; he must seize the face without being arrested by the mask. What de Man describes as the peril of prosopopoeia finds an uncanny counterpart in eighteenth-century writers' disquiet about personification's power to "transform abstract concepts into animated beings." Eighteenth-century writers, Steven Knapp contends, found personification troubling not because of "its inherent primitiveness and irrationality," but rather because of "its *reversibility*. Once the boundaries between literal and figurative agency were erased, it seemed that nothing would prevent the imagination from metaphorizing literal agents as easily as it literalized metaphors."[62] It is this tension between the giving and taking of voice, of face, of life, that gives autobiography its peculiar energy and distinctive form.

The trope of personification in the slave autobiography demonstrates the need to *make* the slave into a person. Indeed, the genre endeavors to literalize personification: to make a man through a literary form that is written by a person legally constituted as a thing. In this sense, what Homi Bhabha remarks of mimicry and national identity—"to be Anglicized is *emphatically* not to be English"[63]—might be extended to personification: to be personified is *emphatically* not to be a person. At the same time, the labor of making a personification—of finding in an object a similitude with one's human self—is itself a uniquely human act. In personifying himself (in showing the negation and reaffirmation of his human being), the slave demonstrates that he needed to be made into a person, and he makes himself into a person. Slave autobiographies are thus personifications in both a transitive and an intransitive sense: they depict the making of a person into a thing (enslavement) and then back into a person (manumission); the making of a man through God's calling (conversion) and the making of a self through an act of writing (autobiography). (Personification, it should be remembered, also meant the conferring of human being upon God in the form of Christ. I shall return to this below.)

To tailor an argument about an autobiography is to select those things that seem more or less essential to a particular model of the human: the proprietary possessive individual, the representative African, the mimic Englishman, the convertible religious self, the juridical subject, the reflexive narrator. The episodes included or omitted by abridgers, the annotations of editors, and the examples excised by critics expose assumptions about the very nature of the human subject. Thus readings of Equiano that stress the religious tacitly insist upon a model of the individual grounded in the distillation of body into spirit, while materialist readings often emphasize the notion of a self-proprietary individual. Still others pit one form of personality against another, as if individuals could only possess one identity at a time: "Equiano's successes, spiritual and commercial, seem to come at the cost of his identity as an African," one writer observes.[64]

Yet the commercial and the theological blend together in Equiano's autobiography, suggesting the permeability of the boundaries between the material and the spiritual that nevertheless create a palpable schism in scholarship on the *Narrative* even today.[65]

The very plot of Equiano's *Narrative* offers different itineraries, depending on how the reader wishes to balance economic or spiritual accounts. Thus Equiano's description of his childhood in Nigeria from his birth in 1745 to his kidnapping into slavery at the age of eleven has been read alternately as a precapitalist idyll, meant to recuperate accounts of Africa as retrograde, and as a typological precursor that allows Equiano to understand his life "as mirroring the movement of Biblical history from the Old Testament to the New."[66] After surviving the crucible of the Middle Passage, Equiano was purchased by a British naval officer, who renamed him Gustavus Vassa after the sixteenth-century hero of Swedish independence featured in a popular eighteenth-century play on the London stage. Equiano worked as a sailor in the British navy during the Seven Years' War—including stints under General Wolfe and Admiral Boscawen—where he learned to read, before being resold to a Philadelphia Quaker merchant, Thomas King. While laboring on King's trading vessels between the American colonies and the West Indies, Equiano earned enough money by selling goods to buy his freedom, but he continued to work as a freeman on King's ships. During the 1770s, he traveled to England, throughout the Mediterranean world and even to the Arctic, as well as engaging in a British enterprise among the Moskito Indians of Central America with a former employer.

Converted to Anglicanism (though he also inclined to Methodism), Equiano construes the events of his life as a series of providential deliverances. On October 6, 1774, he experienced a spiritual rebirth that forms the religious center of the text read as a spiritual autobiography. By the 1780s, he was in the thick of the anti-slavery movement. It was Equiano who, in 1783, informed the abolitionist Granville Sharp of the 1781 *Zong* atrocity, in which 133 slaves were thrown alive into the sea in the course of the Middle Passage in the hope of recuperating insurance costs. As a member of the "Sons of Africa," he wrote letters to the newspaper in 1788 excoriating James Tobin's 1785 attack on the abolitionist James Ramsay's 1784 *Essay on the Treatment and Conversion of African Slaves*. His appointment in 1786 as commissary for the ill-fated Sierra Leone settlement by the Committee for the Relief of the Black Poor was terminated due to his whistle-blowing about administrative corruption. The failure of the expedition did not prevent him from concluding his autobiography by trumpeting the market possibilities presented by a continent of African consumers. Published in 1789 at a point when the first great parliamentary debates on abolition had not yet been overshadowed by the French and Haitian revolutions, his *Narrative* is explicitly directed to the "Lords Spiritual and Temporal, and the Commons of the Parliament of Great Britain" and is both the account of a conversion and an attempt to convert the British public to an anti-slavery stance. The book met with tremendous success, with nine English editions before Equiano's death in 1797; it was also translated into Dutch, German, and Russian.

The lucidity of Equiano's retrospective account does not prevent him from recounting his youthful experience as if through the eyes of a child. The young Equiano encounters a world filled with unknown people—red-faced sailors who may, for all he knows, be cannibals—and objects—ships and snow—apparently possessed of mysterious qualities and magical powers of animation. The world in which the object narratives fancifully dabble is that encountered by a youthful Equiano when the eleven-year-old is summoned into the house to fan his sleeping master:

> The first object that engaged my attention was a watch which hung on the chimney, and was going. I was quite surprised at the noise it made, and was afraid it would tell the gentleman any thing I might do amiss: and when I immediately after observed a picture hanging in the room, which appeared constantly to look at me, I was still more affrighted, having never seen such things as these before. At one time I thought it was something relative to magic; and not seeing it move I thought it might be some way the whites had to keep their great men when they died, and offer them libations as we used to do our friendly spirits. In this state of anxiety I remained till my master awoke, when I was dismissed out of the room, to my no small satisfaction and relief; for I thought that these people were all made up of wonders.[67]

The clock and the picture take on the kind of animistic abilities we saw in the object narratives, but not just any subject animates these things; they are surrogates for a particular kind of person. The master's dominion extends to objects that answer his will, even when he is asleep. Equiano's "improper" understanding of these objects, as Henry Louis Gates notes, estranges them from the ready intelligibility of customary use, giving the reader correct insight into their real usage. Equiano's talking clock and watchful portrait expose European misrecognition of their own proper fetishism. Portraits *are* a means of venerating the dead; clocks *do* hold sway over master and man alike.[68] In seeing the clock and the portraits in his master's bedroom as sinister animated proxies of his master's will, the young Equiano gives shape to the fleetingly visible forces that hold him in terrified subjugation.

And yet the master is mastered by the object both he and Equiano see as his servant. Like the object narratives, the scene depicts humans overtaken by their possessions. Anodyne objects seem omnipotent, while the master who ostensibly holds a monopoly on force is prone, vulnerable, speechless, asleep. Although Equiano fans "with great fear," he does so not from any apparent agency within the master; indeed, the sleeping form of the master is the closest the scene comes to an inanimate thing. The master—like the stoic surrounded by a bustling household of slaves—remains aloof, oblivious, so pure of consciousness that he is unconscious. The master exists as if prior to and separable from things, although Equiano's parting shot—that "these people were all made up of wonders"—suggests that the master is made or made up by what he owns.

Before Equiano is "surprised" by the clock, and "affrighted" by the hanging picture, he is however "astonished" by something else. In their haste to reach the portrait and the clock, readings of this passage forget the cook Equiano encounters en route to the master's bedchamber, a "poor creature . . . cruelly loaded with various kinds of iron machines." Above all, Equiano notes "one particularly on her head, which locked her mouth so fast that she could scarcely speak; and could not eat nor drink. I was much astonished and shocked at this contrivance, which I afterwards learned was called the iron muzzle" (44). All objects take on the sinister cast of the iron muzzle: "I was very much affrighted at some things I saw, and the more so as I had seen [this] black woman slave," Equiano tells us (44). The device blocking the cook's mouth is implicated in the animation of the portrait and the clock, as if there were only so much speech to go around. Equiano's "misunderstanding" of the nature of the object is thus grounded in the master's misunderstanding of the nature of the subject. Whereas object narratives demonstrate how objects make or remake the people who own them—the black coat does make the man, money does speak for the wealthy—slave autobiographies illustrate how objects *unmake* subjects, are refused to them, and are used violently to deprive people of their humanity. The muzzled cook is only one of many descriptions in Equiano's text of things turned against people to harm or even to kill them.

Equiano's improper animation of the clock and the picture (mistaking objects for subjects) masks the improper reification performed by the Europeans who mistake subjects for objects in the form of slaves. One need only think of the pejorative terms we use to describe the taking of subject for object and vice versa to recognize that their confusion is almost invariably accompanied by violence. As de Grazia, Quilligan, and Stallybrass have observed, "to treat a subject like an object is to *reify, objectify*. To treat an object like a subject is to *idolize, to fetishize*. In the modern idiom, the substitution of one term for the other is a theoretical and political problem—a category mistake of the highest order."[69] If Enlightenment discussions of fetishism demonize those who worship or are "enslaved" to objects, what should we make of humans who do not confuse objects for subjects, but subjects for objects? The woman who makes food that she cannot eat, the boy transformed into an extension of the "fan put in my hand" become pure instruments, rather than ends in themselves. In Equiano's account, it is Europeans who are improperly arrested on the material, unable to see through surface complexion to the human spirit within, "limiting the goodness of God," as Equiano puts it, by "supposing he forbore to stamp understanding on certainly his own image, because 'carved in ebony'" (31).[70] Although, as Gates argues, Equiano is fixed in "a status identical to that of the watch, the portrait, and the book" as the master's object, Equiano does not observe as a surrogate for the master (unlike watch and picture). His shock at the sight of the cook is not the reaction of the owner's proxy.

The scene forcibly reminds us that *all* subjects are themselves also objects. "[M]ateriality," Peter Pels observes, "is not some quality distinguishing an object from a subject."[71] It is not that people are subjects in relation to which things are objects; if things are objects, so too are persons. But the recognition provided by objects also *constitutes* subjects. Where some object narratives invite texts and writing materials—Bibles, quires of paper, pens and quills—to speak, slave autobiographies draw attention to the fact that these objects do not speak impartially to everyone. Nowhere is this more evident than in what is perhaps the most famous speaking object of the eighteenth century: the talking book that Gates has traced through the hands of the black British and American authors John Albert Ukawsaw Gronniosaw (1770), John Marrant (1785), Quobna Ottobah Cugoano (1787), Equiano (1789), and John Jea (1815). The talking book is a book that perversely refuses to talk. It speaks to the literate white master who reads from it, but presents an obdurately silent face to the slave who addresses it. That the book is also the Bible gives a theological dimension to this failed call and response, because the Christian book that speaks apostrophizes the faceless sinner into spiritual being, wrenching him or her from the grip of sinful death.[72]

The trope of the talking book first appears in Gronniosaw's 1770 *Narrative*. His master, Gronniosaw tells us,

used to read prayers in public to the ship's crew every Sabbath day; and when first
I saw him read, I was never so surprised in my whole life as when I saw the book
talk to my master; for I thought it did, as I observed him to look upon it, and move
his lips.—I wished it would do so to me.—As soon as my master had done reading I followed him to the place where he put the book, being mightily delighted
with it, and when nobody saw me, I opened it and put my ear down close upon it,
in great hope that it would say something to me; but [I] was very sorry and greatly
disappointed when I found it would not speak; this thought immediately presented
itself to me, that everybody and everything despised me because I was black.[73]

Gronniosaw *sees* speech and speaks unobserved ("when nobody saw me"); he
wishes to be all ears, but he is instead a black face. The explanation that the book
will not speak because it sees that he is black comes from the outside (the thought
"presented itself to me"), as Gronniosaw interprets silence as intentional; he hy-
pothesizes a cause (his black skin) to explain the absence of an effect (the book's
failure to speak). "The text's voice," Gates writes of this passage, "presupposed
a face; and a black face, in turn, presupposed the text's silence since blackness was
a sign of absence, the remarkably ultimate absence of face *and* voice."[74] Gronniosaw's prosopopoeia bestows a face and eyes upon the book, and as a result, it
looks upon him and refuses to speak.

Gronniosaw's incomprehension of oral prayer as well as written text suggests
that the problem arises not so much from literacy per se as from the structure of
address that constitutes persons as subjects or objects. The minister, Mr. Free-
landhouse (who bequeaths to Gronniosaw his freedom), "took me home with
him, and made me kneel down, and put my two hands together, and prayed for
me. . . . I could not," Gronniosaw observes, "make out what it was for, nor the
meaning of it, nor what they spoke to when they talked—I thought it comical,
but I liked it very well" (42). It is necessary to have the means to speak or read
or write, but one also needs an addressee. Without a divine interlocutor to anchor
its meaning, prayer is nothing but empty sounds and gestures to the unconverted
mind—at best, a pleasant amusement. For one to pray, there must be someone
to pray *to*. As Gronniosaw's confusion of the father "who lived in heaven" and
"*my* father [who] lived at Bournou" (42) suggests, it is both the *fact* of an addressee and his or her precise nature that is important. Prayer, like any kind of
performative language, has meaning, not simply because of its content (the expression "I do" of itself tells us nothing about the deed it performs), but also because of the social field in and through which it operates. The speech acts of the
master ostensibly elicit the desired effect, but Gronniosaw's speech is impotent,

because performative language is only effective when a social field "captures those words and enables them to register as actions."[75]

Equiano's encounter with the talking book famously works off of Gronniosaw's version:

> I had often seen my master and Dick employed in reading; and I had a great curiosity to talk to the books, as I thought they did; and so to learn how all things had a beginning: for that purpose I have often taken up a book, and have talked to it, and then put my ears to it, when alone, in hopes it would answer me; and I have been very much concerned when I found it remained silent. (48)

Neither Gronniosaw nor Equiano apostrophize the book in the present tense (O Book! Why would you not speak to me?); each writer tells the reader of his prior failed addresses from a retrospective position. Equiano's spoken apostrophe is not meant to be overheard (he speaks to the book "when alone") *until* it is converted into the retrospective written form of the autobiography. Gates argues that the shift in verb tense from the past to the present marks "the difference between the narrator and this character of his (past) self," permitting the older Equiano to take on the younger Equiano as an object of his discourse.[76] Thus we encounter the Equiano who desires to read the book and the Equiano who reads himself reading the book. If Equiano fails to animate the book in the scene described, he succeeds in animating the child he once was.

Equiano speaks to the book in order to wheedle it into responding: *you* talk. In addressing an object, the speaker wills it to function as a subject, enjoins it to respond, so that in responding, the object may constitute the addressee as a subject. Reading here is construed, not as a doubling of the written text into verbal speech, but as an answer to the book (which places the master in the position of responding to another's address.) Reading thus becomes an effect, the master's speech, arising from a personified cause, the book's address to the master. The book does not speak to Equiano, because he cannot read and because he is not a Christian, but also, Gates claims, because he is a slave, and hence an object.

> Of course the book does not speak to him. Only subjects can endow an object with subjectivity; objects, such as a slave, possess no inherent subjectivity of their own. Objects can only reflect the subjectivity of the subject, like a mirror does. When Equiano, the object, attempts to speak to the book, there follows only the deafening silence that obtains between two lifeless objects. Only a subject can speak. Two mirrors can only reflect each other, in an endless pattern of voided repetition. But they cannot speak to each other, at least not in the language of the master. When the

master's book looks to see whose face is behind the voice that Equiano speaks, it can only see an absence, the invisibility that dwells in an unattended looking-glass.[77]

Gates's argument presumes that the subject exists anterior to objects, that objects do not make subjects; they only reflect. But objects, as the tales show, both mirror *and* make the subject. The two are interdependent. Instead of reflection, one might speak of specular construction and mutual animation. It is true that "only subjects can endow an object with subjectivity" (and strictly speaking, that is precisely what Equiano does in personifying the book); it is also conversely the case that only objects can endow a subject with subjectivity.

For Gates, the trope of the talking book is an allegory of the slave's entry into a literary tradition that confers authority and legitimacy upon the writer: "black people could become speaking subjects only by inscribing their voices in the written word."[78] The portability or transferability of literacy—the fact that it is a capacity that some people possess and others do not—should, however, warn us that it is not a defining trait of humanity. To name literacy as the threshold marker by which the black man or woman becomes a speaking subject is, as Srinivas Aravamudan has contended, to collapse "the category of subjecthood with the agency that comes from the complex technology of literacy."[79] The ability to enter into language, Aravamudan notes, is not governed by the acquisition of technologies of literacy or literateness. People who cannot read and write are still subjects who use language. Although literacy crystallizes the ephemeral manifestations of a particular life in a written and readable text, signs of agency can assume myriad forms.

Literacy constitutes and excludes specific constituencies. Writing thus puts in place a structure of address that is as significant as the technology of language at work. Indeed, one of the moments in which Equiano is most empowered by the book does not involve literacy or reading at all, but the simple presence of the book as an object. For Equiano addresses the book not as text but as material object when—in imitation of Columbus—he uses it to terrorize a group of Moskito Indians into compliance. "I would take the book (pointing to the Bible), read, and *tell* God to make them dead. This," Equiano informs us, "was something like magic" (158). Here Equiano speaks to and through the previously taciturn book in order to claim power over an illiterate populace. If the book works "like magic," it is because Equiano uses it as if it were magical. The passage corrals the reader into complicity; those who see through Equiano's ruse are empowered by the same rules of recognition that structure his address to an otherwise mute object.

Texts—words, words, words—assume only provisional shape in a book made of rags bound in the skins of animals. Although books are tangible material objects—the thirty or so copies of the Gutenberg Bible printed on vellum used the hides of some five thousand calves[80]—their value and their powers are understood to inhere in their immaterial contents. Yet Equiano's use of the Bible in the episode involving the Moskito Indians is oddly arrested on its existence as an object. Here, as on the ship, the book does not answer. The incident allows the "exterior signs of religion" to usurp the place of spiritual worship, in a troubling incursion of idolatry into Protestantism.[81] Equiano's emphasis on the material form of the Bible rather than its spiritual content suggests the fetishism of the Europeans' relation to the book as much as that of the Indians.

A passage from John Gabriel Stedman's *Narrative of a Five Years Expedition Against the Revolted Negroes of Surinam* tenders a critical perspective on the book as an object of European worship. Noting that the Negroes "bring their offerings to the wild cotton tree which they adore with high reverence," Stedman asks "an old black man" for an explanation.

> Having no churches on the coast of Guinea, and this tree being the largest and most beautiful growing there, our people assemble often under its branches to keep free from the heavy showers of rain and scorching sunshine, when they are going to be instructed. Do not you Christians pay the same homage to your Bibles &c.? We well know that our tree is but a wooden log covered with leaves of green, nor is your book assuredly any more than a piece of lumber composed of leaves of paper.[82]

What the English deride as an incorrect or fetishistic relation to objects—a means of affirming their own superiority—turns out to be the Christian relation to the book as well. Refusing to allow Africans to be characterized as fetishists, the "old black man" instead unveils the fetish character of the Christian Bible. Claiming a position of superior epistemological insight—"we well know that our tree is but a wooden log"—the old man implies that *Christians* fail to recognize the proper nature of their own worship. The catachresis of leaves of paper for tree leaves reminds us that the borrowing of one kind of language from another form of object stems from the absence of a proper term: the faltering of language belongs here to the Bible, not to the tree. Spirit and letter lie in the lumber and paper of book and of tree alike.[83]

For Stedman's old man, it is the Europeans who are guilty of fetishizing the book. Yet what exactly is fetishized in the form of the book? The trope of the talking book, like the narratives of speaking objects, confuses subjective *effects* (language, memory, thought) and objective being. It confers on the book as object the power of text as language. A talking book, that is, attributes to things the power of agency we associate with persons. At the same time, it reminds us of the materiality of language, the tactility of memory, the objective forms assumed by thought. For memory, language, and thought can act in the world because they have material form (words are not immaterial; they are sound and ink.) Subjectivity must have some kind of material being in order to act upon the world. Subjects, that is, must also be objects.

On these terms, the problem is not that the slave is an object. Quite the reverse. To be human is to be an object; the problem is that the slave is *nothing but* an object. (Here it is significant to remember that the commodity is the vanishing point of *both* the subject and the object.) As a slave, Equiano cannot assume the relation of subject to himself as object. It is for this reason that writing becomes so central to the slave's claim to be a person. By allowing the subject's voice to attain objective status as written text, autobiography describes and enacts the slave's move from the status of chattel to that of person through his written mastery over the self. (Here again, however, literacy's "transitive role—agency rendered self-reflexive"—should not, as Aravamudan argues, be mistaken for proof of "subjecthood or its lack.")[84]

If Equiano's autobiographical writing makes him a self-making man, Equiano is also a self-made man in the more colloquial sense of the expression: in his business transactions. The kind of reversal permitted by the acquisition of literacy—the reflexive construction of self as subject and object—reappears in Equiano's doubling of self as slave and trader. Equiano as a slave is a form of merchandise, but he incorporates himself into the system as an agent, trading goods on voyages that included transporting slaves. "The pure product of trade," Houston Baker writes, "becomes a trader, turning from spiritual meditations to canny speculations on the increase of a well acquired and husbanded store."[85] The profits earned on these voyages enable Equiano to buy himself back, precipitating him into the familiar torturous circular logic of slavery: to buy himself back, Equiano must be a subject already, but only manumission can make him into the subject able to execute the contract he has already performed in order to become that subject. The paradox of the manumission certificate—that one must be a man or woman to become one—is also the paradox of the autobiographical text, which calls into being the writing subject who must exist for there to be a text.

The manumission certificate, Baker argues, marks the "West Indian slaveholder's willingness to substitute one form of capital for another," although Mr. King's expressed reluctance to part with Equiano acknowledges the surplus value he has reaped from Equiano's labors.[86] Equiano is worth far more than the price paid for him. The buy-back exposes the want of equivalence between these two versions of the same transaction: the making of man into thing (as we shall see in the next chapter) is not a reversible mathematical function from the standpoint of the human commodity so transformed. The fluid equation of one commodity with another described by Marx breaks down in the equation of human and money. Slaves as commodities proffer a different tale of expressive equivalence from that tendered by Marx's personified commodity. When the freed Equiano speaks, he does not articulate his exchange value. Instead, Equiano's rhapsody upon receiving the certificate of manumission reclaims his particularity through a series of cancelled comparisons:

> Heavens! who could do justice to my feelings at this moment! Not conquering heroes themselves, in the midst of a triumph—Not the tender mother who has just regained her long-lost infant, and presses it to her heart—Not the weary hungry mariner, at the sight of the desired friendly port—Not the lover, when he once more embraces his beloved mistress, after she has been ravished from his arms!— All within my breast was tumult, wildness and delirium! (105)

The passage moves beyond the spartan communication of an idea to almost excessive rhetorical ornamentation, an arena beyond the mere necessities afforded to the slave. In piling one comparison upon another, Equiano compels the reader to trace the roles—hero, parent, free worker, lover—denied him by his status as chattel. Each of these roles, as Baker notes, figures either in fact or in fantasy at different points in the narrative. In sketching out an alternate, negated biography, Equiano prevents us from limiting the meaning of humanization to a single aspect of freedom.

What I want to underline is that Equiano tries to "do justice to [his] feelings" not by describing them directly, but through a sequence of failed parallels (mother, hero, sailor, lover). None of them fills the linguistic void he wishes to mark. The repetition of the litotes in this passage underlines the incommensurable and immeasurable losses suffered by the slave. Litotes, the trope of understatement and double negation, expresses an affirmative by the negative of the contrary ("no small feat"; "I do not hate you"). It refines meaning through indirection, through a series of negations that invoke an absent meaning to be inferred by the reader who fills in the blank. Equiano's repetition of the litotes works towards rendering unambiguous a meaning that is never explicitly stated; the passage implies the possibility of linguistic equivalence through a sequence of comparisons before refusing to allow these equivalences to stand: nothing can live up to his elation upon manumission. His feelings defy language both then (at the moment of freedom) and now (at the moment of writing). The litotes thus functions as a metacritical or metalinguistic trope that invites *repeated* appraisal of the failure of its own language: the experience is not like this, nor like that, nor like that. No literal equivalent exists for Equiano's movement from loss to restoration; even figurative substitutions prove unequal to the occasion. The impossibility of "doing justice" to his feelings—the refusal to allow any comparison to stand in the place of his experience, the negation of substitution—both shows the problem of taking feelings to be one's own *and* stakes a proprietary claim over the particularity of Equiano's feelings and experience. These emotions are his own, and the reader can have no claim over them. The essential truth to be expressed is confusion: "tumult, wildness and delirium."

Equiano's inability to express what he has regained through manumission indicates the difficulty of naming what makes a person human. For the buying back of Equiano's body that makes him a legal "person" does not make him a spiritual one: manumission gives Equiano the habit of the free man, but without the inward form. The conversion manuals Equiano reads by Richard Baxter, Joseph Alleine, Thomas Wilson, and Lawrence Harlow all confirm that external transformation will not suffice. As the Puritan nonconformist Alleine writes in *The Solemn Warnings of the Dead:* "You may cast the lead out of the rude mass into the more comely proportion of a plant, and then into the shape of a beast, and thence into the form and features of a man, yet all the while it is but lead still: so a man may pass through diverse transmutations, from ignorance to knowledge, from profaneness to civility, thence to a form of religion; and all this while he is but carnal and unregenerate, whilst his nature remains unchanged."[87] The individual may refashion his mind, his manners, even his mode of worship, but without divine grace, he cannot remake his own nature. One can work to be free, but faith cannot be made, nor belief coerced. It is for this reason that Equiano's moments of greatest abjection are experienced *after* he is freed. In terror of being damned, uncertain that he will be saved, he blasphemously wishes "to be any thing but a human being" (137). "I would then," he adds, "if it had been possible, have changed my nature with the meanest worm on the earth" (137). The buying back of his body must be followed by the redemption of his soul through Christ's suffering.

If the first half of the text describes Equiano's struggles to acquire a self and to avoid being made an object by other men, the second half describes his struggles *against* self to become an object of God. What for de Man is the privative projection of a face—the turning of the symmetrical trope of prosopopoeia that supplants the speaking subject with the mask of the addressed other—is in Equiano's theology the moment of calling. Conversion tracts ask the reader to make himself into a blank so that God can write him or her. The self-reliant individual must learn to rely exclusively on Christ. "Now," Equiano tells us, "the Ethiopian was willing to be saved by Jesus Christ, the sinner's only surety, and also to rely on none other person or thing for salvation. Self was obnoxious, and good works he had none, for it is God that worketh in us both to will and to do" (144). From speaking matter (the animated *res* that is the slave), Equiano turns to someone addressed in, through, and by spirit:

> in this deep consternation the Lord was pleased to break in upon my soul with his bright beams of heavenly light; and in an instant as it were, removing the veil, and letting light into a dark place, I saw clearly with the eye of faith the crucified Saviour bleeding on the cross on mount Calvary: the scriptures became an unsealed book, I saw myself a condemned criminal under the law, which came with its full force to my conscience, and when "the commandment came sin revived, and I died." I saw the Lord Jesus Christ in his humiliation, loaded and bearing my reproach, sin, and shame. I then clearly perceived that by the deeds of the law no flesh living could be justified. (143–44)

Equiano doesn't achieve his humanity from manumission or literacy, but from becoming a being who can be addressed by a book, by other men, by himself, and ultimately, by God.

The rhetoric of exchange that pervades discussions of Christian conversion suggests that readings of Equiano that emphasize spiritual autobiography and those that focus on the economic and the material may be closer than they at first glance appear. Yet important differences between economic and spiritual conversion persist. Whereas the redemption of manumission involves the exchange of money for man, Christian redemption involves Christ's sacrifice: he accepts Equiano's sin and in exchange gives the gift of grace. Although the chain of substitutions that allows men to be made commodities is always potentially reversible (as Equiano's persistent fear of being reenslaved shows), spiritual conversion, this divine gift, cannot be taken back. It is irrevocable.

The passage from Acts 4:12 that is singled out in the frontispiece to Equiano's text reaffirms that Equiano finds in Christ a proper name that fixes identity: "Neither is there salvation in any other, for there is none other name under heaven given among men whereby we must be saved, but only Christ Jesus" (145). Successively called Olaudah, Jacob, and Michael, and then finally renamed Gustavus Vassa against his will, Equiano ultimately rests his value on a proper name beneath other names: that of Christ. As Adam Potkay notes, "that Jesus Christ's is the only *name* that can save neatly caps Equiano's earlier concern with the weight of nomenclature, signifying that the chain of nominal substitutions that constitutes his earlier career might now come to a close."[88] The (potentially reversible) personification performed by his manumission must be made permanent through a kind of anthropomorphism that fixes his being in its transmuted form. Anthropomorphism, as de Man reminds us, "is not just a trope but an identification on the level of substance. It takes one entity for another and thus implies the constitution of specific entities prior to their confusion, the *taking* of something for something else that can be assumed to be *given*. Anthropomorphism freezes the infinite chain of tropological transformations and propositions into one single assertion or essence which, as such, excludes all others."[89] It is a moment of referential touchdown in a sequence of figurative transformations that makes the individual definitively human. Anthropomorphism is a kind of personification that has gotten stuck. (Equiano's conversion also alludes to anthropomorphism in the eighteenth-century sense of the term: Christ made man. For anthropomorphism is not merely the symbolic assumption of the shape of a man, but the real conversion of divine into human so that God may experience human suffering, not by proxy, but in the flesh.)

The conversion manuals cited by Equiano—Baxter's 1658 *Call to the Unconverted*, Alleine's 1673 *The Solemn Warnings of the Dead, or, an Admonition to Unconverted Sinners*, Wilson's 1740 *The Knowledge and Practice of Christianity Made Easy for the Meanest Capacities, or, An Essay Towards an Instruction for the Indians*, and Harlow's 1774 *Conversion of an Indian* (Equiano, 88, 143, 57, 140)—are riddled with images of animism and prosopopoeia that animate both human and divine. Wilson's dialogue and Harlow's narrative are recounted in the voices of Native Americans; Baxter's call is an address to a silent or absent other. Alleine, whose very title claims to ventriloquize the dead, oscillates between an address to the converted and the unconverted, the animate and the inanimate, the living and the dead. "Do I speak to the trees and rocks, or to men? To the tombs and monuments of the dead, or to a living auditory?" Alleine asks. Conversion manuals address humans in the same way that Equiano and Gronniosaw address the book: as an object to be reanimated or brought to life by an address. Whereas Gronniosaw lays himself upon the ground and Equiano presses his ear to the book, Alleine prostrates himself upon the grave:

> Alas, wherewith shall I pierce the scales of Leviathan, or make the heart to feel that's hard as stone, hard as a piece of nether millstone! Shall I go and lay my

mouth to the grave, and look when the dead will obey me and come forth? Shall I make an oration to the rocks, or declaim to the mountains, and think to move them with arguments? . . . thou, O Lord, canst pierce the scales and prick the heart of the sinner: I can but shoot at rovers, and draw the bow at a venture, but do thou direct the arrow between the joints of the harness, kill the sin, and save the soul of a sinner that casts his eyes on these labours.[90]

Those who have not been called to God are depicted as inanimate objects—millstones, the dead, the mountains—to be reanimated by the Word. Alleine apostrophizes the divine to address the sinner, treating God as a marksman capable of guiding and animating the arrow loosed by his minister. His text can animate the recalcitrant souls who refuse to open their ears to the Word only by conferring a shape, a voice, a will upon God.

It is perhaps useful in this context to recall the double meaning of *anthropology* in the eighteenth century. The first definition offered by Chambers's *Cyclopedia* is "a Discourse or Treatise upon Man, or Human Nature . . . [including] the Consideration both of the Human Body and Soul, with the Laws of their Union, and the Effects thereof, as Sensation, Motion." But anthropology as the study of man is also the making of God, as Chambers's second definition suggests: "in theology, for a way of speaking of God, after the manner of Men; by attributing Human Parts to him; as Eyes, Hands, Ears, Anger, Joy, &c. We have frequent Instances of *Anthropology* in Holy Scripture; by which we are only to understand the Effect, or the Thing which God does, as if he had Hands, &c."[91] Even as prosopopoeia confers a voice and mouth to make speech, here anthropology creates a cause capable of producing the effect to be explained. Not only must the world be peopled with intentional entities, but these entities must possess the means to execute these intents. For God to make, he must have hands.

If God needs hands to make, then Equiano and others must make a God with hands. Equiano's conversion involves this kind of anthropology of the divine. At his moments of greatest despair Equiano gropes for and finds the hand of God: "the kind and unknown hand of the Creator (who in very deed leads the blind in a way they know not) now began to appear, to my comfort" (45), he announces early on. No event is contingent in Equiano's world: "In these, and in many more instances," he tells us, "I thought I could plainly trace the hand of God, without whose permission a sparrow cannot fall" (64). Because God's "invisible but powerful hand" is everywhere, Equiano comes to look "for the hand of God in the minutest occurrence" (71, 178). Every incident is part of God's design; no detail is superfluous. This principle of economy and thrift offers us a hermeneutics for reading his *Life* that echoes that for reading his life: "there is scarcely any book or incident so trifling that does not afford some profit" (178). If Equiano seeks a God able to form his life into a providential pattern, a secondary task of the autobiography is to fashion a self able to make a God that can make that self.

When Equiano gives God hands that they may shape his life, he engages in the act of prosopopoeia that, David Hume argues, constitutes natural religion. Equiano models his maker after a human image to give intelligible shape to the inchoate forces that preside over his fate. This chapter has explored the way personification confers intent and purposiveness upon the increasingly abstract systems that govern the movement of persons and things across the globe. In its final pages, I want to turn to "the mist-enveloped regions of the religious world" to which Hume, like Marx, has recourse in explaining how the "productions of the human brain appear as independent beings endowed with life, and entering into relation both with one another and the human race" (*Capital*, 43). For the animation of things is connected not just to the fetishism of the commodity but to the fetishism of the divine.

The propensity for anthropology—the molding of the world in our own likeness—is identified by Hume in the *Natural History of Religion* as a "universal tendency amongst mankind."[92] For Hume, primitive man is no Adam, in full possession of his faculties, but "a barbarous, necessitous animal"[93] who inhabits a world of violent contingency. Polytheism, idolatry or fetishism are, for Hume, the logical outcome of a universe experienced in fragmentary form. Religion— the hands Equiano bestows upon the divine—emerges from the desire to make an intentionless world purposive. Hume's primitive man scares up a vision of gods in human forms in order to explain the arbitrary events that tear apart his world. The inconsistency of nature, which creates a field of crops and then blights it, which makes a human body sound and whole and then cripples it, does not intuitively lead back to a single cause. Lacking leisure to contemplate, beset by a world of contrary impulses and subject to the ravages of nature, prescientific peoples lack an abstract notion of the system of nature. It is for this reason, Hume argues, that "primitive" peoples "unite the invisible power with some visible object," seizing on objects before them as the cause behind the effect.[94] They seek a one-to-one correspondence between invisible or divine causes and arbitrary inconsistent effects: hence the proliferation of imaginary personifications—warring gods, discrete, arbitrary deities, or fetishes like idols, animals, snakes, stones, and trees.

For Hume, only progress and contemplation allow humans to move from sensed objects to an abstract idea of a single divine cause. And that one anterior cause is modeled on an image of the human. (The old joke: God made man in his own image, and man, being a gentleman, returned the compliment.) People, Hume says, have a universal tendency

> to conceive all beings like themselves, and to transfer to every object, those quali-
> ties, with which they are familiarly acquainted, and of which they are intimately
> conscious. We find human faces in the moon, armies in the clouds; and by a nat-
> ural propensity, if not corrected by experience and reflection, ascribe malice and
> good-will to every thing, that hurts or pleases us. . . . No wonder, then, that man-
> kind, being placed in such an absolute ignorance of causes, and being at the same
> time so anxious concerning their future fortunes, should immediately acknowl-
> edge a dependence on invisible powers, possessed of sentiment and intelligence. . . .
> Nor is it long before we ascribe to them thought, and reason, and passion, and some-
> times even the limbs and figures of men, in order to bring them nearer to a re-
> semblance with ourselves.[95]

In projecting a face upon causes of which they are ignorant, people personify "invisible powers" (prosopopoeia); they bestow a human form upon a causality lacking a proper referent (catachresis). Projecting our own traits onto the external world is a natural propensity of human beings, Hume asserts in his *Treatise of Human Nature:*

> There is a very remarkable inclination in human nature, to bestow on external ob-
> jects the same emotions, which it observes in itself; and to find every where those
> ideas, which are most present to it. This inclination, 'tis true, is suppress'd by a lit-
> tle reflection, and only takes place in children, poets, and the antient philosophers.
> It appears in children, by their desire of beating the stones, which hurt them: In
> poets, by their readiness to personify every thing: And in the antient philosophers,
> by these fictions of sympathy and antipathy. We must pardon children, because of
> their age; poets, because they profess to follow implicitly the suggestions of their
> fancy: But what excuse shall we find to justify our philosophers in so signal a weak-
> ness?[96]

The imaginative extension of powers to objects—of rocks to wound, for exam-
ple—is a controlled act of personification that infiltrates our every moment: we project the capacity to render or to rend our world onto inanimate things, at-
tributing cause and intention to the effects they produce. The child who goes Johnson's refutation of Berkeley one better by beating the stone that hurt him is simply acting out mental processes of accountability that we all imaginatively sketch. Hume cannot entirely dismiss this process of animating the world, since

it is not all that different from the kind of imagining that gets us, for example, from flame as cause to burning as effect. In other words, the kinds of relations—resemblance, contiguity, and cause and effect—that permit the mind to make connections between discrete objects and persons in his *Treatise* govern Hume's theory of religion. Each relation possesses its proper trope: if metaphor is the trope of resemblance, and metonymy and parataxis are the tropes of contiguity, then personification is, for Hume, the trope of causality; by attributing the capacity to act to inert objects, personifications create causal links between discrete entities. Personification is the very engine of thought.

The religious problem Hume describes here—how to make a cause that can produce an effect; how to make an entity that does what seems to have been done—is a version of an economic problem: how to confer form upon the forces governing a global marketplace, whether in the object narratives, the slave autobiography, or the theoretical writings of Marx. In all these cases, the desire to project a human countenance upon a cause anterior to or beyond the boundaries of the self reminds us that all agency is not personal. In lending the attributes of a subject to an object (or an abstraction), personification postulates agents capable of acting as causes for the effects to be explained. Things thus wind up in certain hands because they wish to be there; the horrors to which Equiano is subjected can thus alternately be made intelligible as the deeds of malevolent men or the presiding intentions of divine will. But personification also embodies the agency of collective entities like nations, abstract entities like the economy or capitalism, or obscure first causes: the just-so stories that explain how things came to be.

The things that speak in tales foreshadow the entities that routinely solicit us today and it is for this reason that I conclude this chapter with a relic of American advertising. During the 1980s, the now defunct investment banking firm E. F. Hutton broadcast commercials that featured well-dressed people chatting over lunch in a busy restaurant (the kind with tablecloths) or perhaps sipping drinks at a posh cocktail party. From the hum of conversation, one would pick out the phrase "My broker is E. F. Hutton, and E. F. Hutton says . . ." Instantly the room would fall silent, as everyone sought to overhear the wisdom culled from the lips of E. F. Hutton, while a voice-over announced the point we were meant to absorb: "When E. F. Hutton talks, people listen." In an era of Wall Street scandal, the slogan may simply look like a reminder of the perils of eavesdropping, but I want to linger over how truly odd this advertisement is: "E. F. Hutton"—a person constituted as a corporate entity reconstituted as a person—ostensibly addresses people, who listen because they are being spoken to. The advertisement is rendered all the more bizarre by the fact that E. F. Hutton does not speak or even show up in the commercial: we are never party to the initial utterance that interests so many. We are hooked by the promise of words that we never in fact hear, attributed to a being who never appears. The question here is less why we allow ourselves to be hailed or interpellated by such personified entities than why we personify such entities in the first place.

The personification of E. F. Hutton lends the attributes of a subject to a collective entity (a corporation). Indeed, under American law, a corporation may be a person.[97] If E. F. Hutton "himself" is absent, so too are the people who make up the company, as well as those who labor to produce the wealth that such firms manage. My point is not just that we lose track of the real people and real things behind the abstraction of the economy. (Although we may need to be reminded to imagine the worker who made the shirt we wear or the paper we read, we can imagine him or her without tremendous difficulty.) What defies imagination is the nature of an economic system that seems to obliterate such particularity. The capering commodities of Marx's *Capital* pale before the grotesque incarnation of capitalism in the modern multinational corporation.

In an era in which global reach increasingly outstrips intellectual and imaginative grasp, personifications give shape and local habitation to abstract and immaterial forces. Without them, we may wind up with what Foucault calls—alluding to the toothy smile of the Cheshire Cat in *Alice in Wonderland*—a series of "grins . . . without the cat," manifestations emanating from god-knows-what, lacking proper or tangible cause.[98] Hume's prosopopoeia personifies causes, making an entity able to do what seems to have been done; figures like E. F. Hutton give shape to the agencies that supersede our ideas of immediate or contiguous causality. Personifications carry out deeds performed by abstractions, collectivities, or inanimate things, stealing from the riches of subjectivity to give to a relatively impoverished understanding of who is doing what and why. In endeavoring to "think globally"—either about the eighteenth century or today—it is good to ask what we think with.

CHAPTER FOUR

Making Humans Human

Eighteenth-century discussions of the slave trade create a kind of readerly vertigo. They shift precipitously from descriptions of slave families torn asunder to the banal catalogues of objects exchanged in the trade, from testimony about the incalculable suffering of the Middle Passage to the capacious abstractions that describe the global balance of trade, the gleanings of the customs house, the gains and losses of a voyage. These various orders of representation—eyewitness depositions, account ledgers, mercantile dictionaries, moral jeremiads—jostle uncomfortably on the same tabula. Inviting different logical and affective responses, they share a common grammar, the conjugation of things and people, people and things. Both proslavery accounts of the trade and abolitionist texts endeavor to traverse the porous boundaries between human and commodity, albeit in opposite directions. Accounts of the sale of slaves describe the process by which an individual was seized upon as a commodity and stripped of his or her rights to self-propriety and self-determination. Abolitionist texts, by contrast, try to restore the humanity of the slave by emphasizing those aspects of the human that are inalienable, that have no equivalents. Whereas the slave trader's ledger describes the process by which the slave was made (the conversion of a person into chattel), abolitionist texts try to reverse this process by capitalizing on what escapes the equation of price and person.

This chapter traces the way sentimental figures alter the threshold of the human in a range of literary and rhetorical forms: autobiographical memoir, abolitionist verse, parliamentary polemic, and pro- and anti-slavery propaganda. As sentimental tropes migrate across generic boundaries, they change the structure of sympathetic identification, altering the ways in which the humanity of others can be recognized. Poems like Thomas Day's "The Dying Negro" or William Cowper's "The Negro's Complaint" and images like Josiah Wedgwood's medallion of a kneeling slave (fig. 4.1) bestow the attributes of a person (a voice, a soul, a consciousness) upon the figure of the slave in order to supplant the economic substitution of persons and things with the sympathetic substitution of self for other. These texts invite the reader to humanize slaves by attributing feeling to them, by finding his or her own likeness in their form, or by feeling *for* them (having feelings about them or in their stead). Yet the carefully structured invitations to feel for others issued by sentimental texts only selectively recognize the humanity of certain categories of people. Sentimental writers do not issue a carte blanche on feeling; not all suffering individuals are qualified candidates for sympathy. Thus although Janet Schaw's *Journal of a Voyage to the West Indies* (1774–76) celebrates the transformative power of the sentimental gaze to excite feelings about lower-class Britons, it also betrays the way sentimental tropes may curtail the ostensibly spontaneous movement of sympathetic affect. Not only does Schaw refuse to acknowledge the suffering of the slaves she encounters, she also argues that they are not possessed of human feelings. Sentimental tropes, when not used as directed, block emotion as well as channel it.

In the late 1780s and early 1790s, when popular agitation for abolition was at its height, awareness of the volatile and vagrant nature of sympathy produced verse—for example, Hannah More's "Slavery," William Cowper's "Sweet Meat has Sour Sauce, or, the Slave Trader in the Dumps," and Anna Letitia Barbauld's "Epistle to William Wilberforce"—that sought less to excite the reader's feelings for others than to draw attention to the limits of a politics based on sympathy. Influential images like the plan of the slave ship *Brookes* (fig. 4.2) notably make no direct appeal to emotions; instead, they compel the reader to enter into the very logic of the trade in order to inspire revulsion against it. By creating a reflexive consciousness within the reader of the very structure of identification at work in sentimental texts, these abolitionist works foster a heightened awareness of the ways sympathy may go astray.

The stakes involved in policing sentimental identification are raised to new levels in the British parliamentary debates on the abolition, where the manipulation of emotion is meant to shift the status of different kinds of persons, facilitating the movement of feeling not just between kinds of individuals (lyric personality) but between kinds of individualisms (legal or political personality). The parliamentarians must monitor the circulation of sympathetic feelings, both because the attribution of lyric personality paves the way for legal personality and because sympathy at times menaces the autonomy of the feeling subject. The parliamentary speakers are preoccupied with feeling gone haywire. Impassioned oratory may transport the speaker or listener beyond himself or may fail to move him at all; the enjoinder to imagine the suffering of others may produce not just sentimental but also sexual pleasure. Given the deleterious "hardening" effects

of witnessing scenes of torture in the West Indies, how could one ensure that the
Britannic audience did not become either inured to or turned on by the testimony? If the privileged relation to another's feeling furnishes a claim to feminine poetic authority within these public and political debates on slavery, it
threatens to undermine individual masculine self-possession. The excitation of
abolitionist sentiment becomes a testing ground for a contest between masculine
and feminine versions of the sentimental, as the act of extending imaginative
being to distant others comes to menace the continuity and unity—the identity—of the metropolitan self.

Of Price and Men

Eighteenth-century accounts of the transactions that made people into merchandise are disconcertingly prosaic: "Mr Cumberhatch came on board," the
trader John Newton writes in his *Journal,* "paid me a woman and a boy (4 foot 1
inch) for his debt, and sold me 2 boys (of 3 ft 10 inches each). He had an old man
but I would not buy him. Mem: he owes me still 26 bars."[1] Seemingly unruffled
by the grotesque use of humans for currency, Newton moves from the deracinated particulars (woman, boy), their quantities and qualities (4 foot 1 inch), site
and date of acquisition, and thence to the remainder in the form of "26 bars"
and an old man left unbought. The ledgers from slave ships, like that of the *Judith* (see table 4.1), likewise record the methodical conjoining of human and
thing. The *Judith* began purchasing slaves at Junk on the Grain Coast (modern-
day Liberia) and subsequently traveled east to the Gold Coast (today's Ghana)
before departing for the West Indies in late February; 214 slaves survived the voyage to be sold in Barbados and Jamaica. The ledger records the order of their acquisition, deriving the equivalence of person and thing from their proximity on
a page. The promise of interchangeability is held out by the contiguity of two
dissimilar objects that disguises the strangeness of their juxtaposition.[2] The
bookkeeper's monotonous tabulation reduces the individual to a number and a
gender (No. 1, a boy; No. 2, a boy; No. 3, a man) in order to facilitate the conversion of human beings into units of labor, values in the balance of trade. Unlike
the autonomous monad postulated by theories of possessive individualism, the
isolated slave's individuality is confined to his or her status as a numbered singular entity. The assigned number marks the order of acquisition and registers
the quantities exchanged for the slave; it creates a continuity of identity as the
slave is moved from one set of books to another, sold from dealer to captain to
plantation owner. The serene march of numbers and balances that characterizes

TABLE 4.1
Accounts from the Slave Ship Judith

JUNKE the 3rd	To twoo Bucenear gunns Each Seaven Aceyes		14	
of Sep'br	To four Brass panns at One Aceye Each		4	
1728		1	2	
A boye				
No. 1				
	One Bucenear gunn at Eight Acceyes		8	
Ditto the 3d	To One Treaden gunn at four Acceyes		4	
A boye	To twoo twoo pound Beassens		1	6
No. 2			13	6
	To twoo Bucenear gunns at Eight Acceys Each	1		
Ditto	To One quarter Barrell of powder at Eight Acceyes		8	
the 3d	To twoo treaden gunns at four Acceyes Each		8	
A man	To Twoo twoo pound Beassens		1	6
No. 3		2	1	6

the slave traders' ledgers seems to be a noninterpretive representation of particulars: what distortion could possibly be implied by the dispassionate register of impersonal transactions? Such ciphers set forth what should be counted under the laws of bookkeeping.

The ledger of the *Judith* describes the objects bartered for slaves, measuring the value of the European goods exchanged in ackies. The ackie equaled one-sixteenth of the trade ounce, the unit of currency that prevailed on the Gold Coast throughout the eighteenth century. On the north Windward Coast, the unit was called the bar; on the southern Windward coast, it was the "piece" (of cloth). Usually worth about half an ounce of gold, the "trade ounce" and the "bar" permitted the reckoning of value for the vast range of goods and persons embroiled in the trade.[3] Such units were necessary, since traders gave many kinds of equivalents—gunpowder and pottery, calico and rum—for African slaves in the eighteenth century. When the Bristol slave ship *Pilgrim* sailed for the coast of Africa in 1790, it carried, among other things, "1858 bars English iron, 40 casks corn spirits, 65 chests muskets, 2 casks felt hats, 11 casks gun flints, 1 cask wrought iron knives, 5 butts cotton."[4] These commodities had no fixed rate in relation to each other, since prices within the triangular trade were based on the available assortment of goods, the values for which they could be exchanged, and their first or prime cost in Europe. Thus while the purchasing power of the "trade ounce" might remain the same (a male slave might consistently cost ten trade ounces), the cost of the goods that constituted the ounce might fluctuate dramatically for the European trader. "A slave in cowries costs us above four pounds in *England*," one English trader explains, "whereas a slave in coral, rangoes, or iron, does not cost fifty shillings."[5] The price might remain constant while its cost fluctuated.

The protracted explanations of exchange rates in eighteenth-century texts on Africa betray the difficulty of finding something common across cultures and value systems that will permit persons and things to be interchanged. Marx famously solves the problem with the category of human labor, and there is a sense in which the journal of the slave trader describes the labor expended to make a human into a commodity. Even as a tree must grow, be cut down, and the lumber planed and joined together to make a table, so too a slave had to be seized and shackled, transported and stored, turned out for market, weighed and scrutinized as goods. On these terms, what confers value upon the slave is both the labor that goes into the making of the slave and the labor power that *is* the slave. Because of the moral culpability associated with the trade, however, the work of the trader in converting man into merchandise must be disguised, because the slave must be represented as an article *found*, not produced. Thus Francis Moore's elaborate explanation of the relative value of bars and ounces, goods and slaves, treats the slave as a commodity always already there:

> A Barr is a denomination given to a certain Quantity of Goods of any Kind, which Quantity was of equal Value among the Natives to a Barr of Iron, when this River was first traded to. Thus, a Pound of Fringe is a Barr, two Pounds of Gunpowder is a Barr, an Ounce of Silver is but a Barr, and 100 Gun-Flints is a Barr, and each Species of trading Goods, has a Quantity in it called a Barr; therefore their Way of reckoning is by Barrs, or Crowns, one of which does not sometimes amount to above one Shilling Sterling; but that happens according to the Goods which they are in Want of, sometimes cheap, sometimes dear. These five Articles, *viz.* Spread-Eagle Dollars, Crystal Beads, Iron Barrs, Brass Pans, and Arrangoes, are called the Heads of the Goods, because they are dearest. When you agree with the Merchants for Slaves, you always agree how many of the Heads of the Goods you shall give him upon each Slave, which is three or four, if Slaves are worth forty or fifty; but when Slaves are dearer, as they oftentimes are, at eighty Barrs per Head, then you must give five, and sometimes six of the Heads upon every Slave; and there is an Assortment made of the Goods, by Barrs of different Species, which come out to the Price of the Slaves.[6]

Like the trade ounce, the bar is a convention, a historical invention (created "when this river was first traded to") that fluctuates in value based on the going rate of exchange. The bar contains no intrinsic properties; it is an abstract unit contained "in" objects as diverse as fringes and gunpowder, silver and slaves. The democratic interchangeability of objects undermines the bar's role as the measure of value; the bar as governing metaphor disintegrates into chains of metonymic detail: "Spread-Eagle Dollars, Crystal Beads, Iron Bars, Brass Pans."

As an abstraction, the bar denotes something that has no independent material existence, and its lack of a defined referent creates a kind of vacuity within the passage that discloses the instability at the heart of these exchanges: the bar can be supplanted by "crowns" or "shillings" or "heads of the goods," which are in turn given value based on their capacity to purchase slaves at a price agreed upon with the "merchants for slaves." That goods are also "heads" is that abuse of language literary critics call catachresis, the use of a borrowed word (eye of a needle; arm of a chair) for which there is no proper term discussed in the previous chapter. "Something monstrous," Paul de Man reminds us, "lurks in the most innocent of catachreses: when one speaks of the legs of the table or the face of the mountain, catachresis is already turning into prosopopeia [the projection of a human face onto an absent or inanimate other], and one begins to perceive a world of potential ghosts and monsters."[7] Haunting Moore's description is the monstrosity of his referent. The "heads of the goods" becomes a macabre literalization of the exchange enacted, capping the acephalous objects given for the slave with a human head. The figural language that describes the trade cannot fully cover its literal barbarism.

Indeed, a "pièce d'Inde" (a prime African male slave in his early twenties) becomes the base currency to which other slaves are compared: three children from ten to fifteen might equal two pièces d'Inde; two children from five to ten might count as one.[8] The value of the individual is derived from a set of arithmetical relays, dividing and adding children and bodies to achieve a balance of trade. As Lieutenant John Matthews notes, "Slaves are the medium, instead of coin, for the purchase of every necessary, and the supplying of every want; and every article is estimated, by its proportion, to the value of a slave."[9] Slaves wobble between medium and object of exchange; they are both measure of value and repository of wealth. As a universal equivalent, the slave loses all particularity: indeed, Matthews tells us, it is not "very material whether a guinea, a sheep, cow, or a slave, are the denominations of value" (176).

As the existence of the trade ounce and the bar both reveal, the exchange of bodies and things in global commerce perforce involves an abstraction of value. By definition, commodities experience a moment of conceptual disembodiment at the moment of exchange: a commodity is defined through its relation to other commodities as expressed in the universal language of money and prices. However fleetingly, in the moment of exchange, the object belongs in "a world-picture of functional objects stripped of cultural meaning and social value."[10] For objects and persons to be exchanged as commodities across cultural boundaries, in other words, they must be wrenched from the social context that confers value and meaning upon them and precipitated into a world in which their value is defined by the commodity form in which their value is expressed. Commerce in slaves suggests that it is possible to find an expressive equivalent for a person, that the particularity of a purportedly inalienable subject can be objectified as a cluster of things apart from the self. By contrast, the abolitionists repeatedly assert the absolute incommensurability of price and person. "Money," the earl of Mornington declared in the parliamentary debates of 1792, "ought not be considered as of equal value with blood."[11]

Yet the growing importance of wage labor to the metropolitan economy places this incommensurability on shaky ground. For what exactly does one buy in buying a person? When Granville Sharp calls the slaveholder an "imaginary proprietor" and asserts that the property held in the slave is "imaginary Property,"[12] he is drawing attention to the phantasmal nature of the slave owner's claims: what is it that one can own in another human being? This "imaginary Property" is seemingly materialized in the things given in exchange (the expressive equivalent of the commodity), but there can be no equivalent for the immaterial rights an individual holds over the self. As William Blackstone asserts, "Every sale implies a price, a *quid pro quo*, an equivalent given to the seller in lieu of what he transfers to the buyer: but what equivalent can be given for life, and liberty, both of which (in absolute slavery) are held to be in the master's disposal?"[13] The person is not reducible to the things for which he or she is exchanged—something human persists, a kind of leftover that escapes from the equation. "There is no proportion between Twenty Pieces of Silver and LIBERTY," the New England Puritan Samuel Sewell affirms. "The Commodity it self is the Claimer."[14] Lurking behind the ostensible exchange of money for liberty is something that cannot be alienated.

Sewell's language presents us with a familiar paradox: the prior claim upon liberty belongs to "the commodity itself," the human who has been turned into the thing exchanged. How is one to reverse the equation? If the ledgers that describe the transformation of man into slave make the catalogue of commodities into the expressive equivalent form of the person sold, is it possible to make the person sold into the expressive form of these commodities? Something of the sort ostensibly occurs when a slave buys back his freedom, but—as we saw with Equiano in the previous chapter—the irrecuperable losses experienced by an enslaved person can neither be compensated for in economic terms nor expressed in literary ones. The equivalence promised by the economic substitution goes only one way. Although the substitution of self for another is meant to restore humanity through sympathetic identification, the disturbing reversal in the slave trade of subject and object, agent and commodity, cannot be corrected by a simple transposition of terms. Indeed, the representations meant to humanize the slave may perversely erode the absolute claim to possess humanity by lending to the slave the human traits he or she ostensibly already possesses.

Day, Cowper, Wedgwood, and the Tropes of Redundant Personification

Abolitionist texts typically make a plea for the humanity of the slave by conferring a voice upon the slave. They capitalize on the figure of prosopopoeia examined in the previous chapter, creating an apostrophe to a dead, silent, or absent other that confers voice, life, and consciousness upon the slave, enabling him or her in turn to address the reader. The animating effect of the apostrophe becomes both the form and the theme of abolitionist verses like Thomas Day's 1773 "The Dying Negro" and William Cowper's 1788 "The Negro's Complaint," which articulate the sufferings of the slave in the first person in order to stir the reader-interlocutor into action. In both poems, the metropolitan reader veers between a first-person identification with the slave speaker (the "I" of the poem) and his or her "real world" identification with the British audience (the "you" or "thee" addressed in the poem). This oscillation between the position of speaker and interlocutor executes the political agenda of the poem; it enables the reader to sympathize with the suffering slave and asks him or her to recognize, if not to alter, the oppressive structures in which the slave is enmeshed.

"The Dying Negro" was composed by the Oxford-educated social reformer Thomas Day and his friend the barrister John Bicknell after they read a newspaper account of an African who, upon being returned to the ship anchored in the Thames from which he had fled to marry a white fellow servant, killed himself rather than return to slavery in the Indies. The poem reconstructs the sentiments of its unnamed hero in a series of addresses to a variety of individuals and groups in turn: Fortune, his beloved, his fellow slaves ("dear, lost companions in despair"); the sailors who trapped him into slavery, the cruel West Indian masters, and even the Christian God.[15] The address takes the form of the complaint—an expressive plea that is also, as Lauren Berlant has argued, a form of "self-circumscription[,] in that the complaint implicitly marks the conditions and the probability of its failure to persuade the addressed subject."[16] The fact that the Negro of the title is dying suggests the futility of his complaint—its belatedness with regard to the plight of *this* particular slave—and defers the immediacy of any call to action on the part of the reader. Indeed, the continuous present of the "*dying* negro" only provisionally suspends recognition that the poem's speaker is already dead.

The power of Day's poem to humanize its speaker rests in part upon a sentimentalized vision of the encounter between innocent African victims and rapacious British traders. Day's Africa is a land of wild beasts and guileless primitive warriors, who "melt with pity" (10) for the English sailors cast helpless upon their shores. The scene of benevolent reciprocity quickly turns to treachery, as the British merchants trap the Africans. "From Lord to Lord my wretched carcase sold, / In Christian traffic, for their sordid gold" (14). The heroic Oroonoko-like African of epic deeds is degraded to merchandise and only restored through the Desdemona-like pity of his fellow-servant and bride, who listens to "the story of my woes, / With heaving sighs" and "trick'ling drops of liquid crystal" that "mark'd thy pitying soul" (15). Pity rehumanizes the slave both from his interlocutor's perspective, and, significantly, from his own vantage point; it is because his beloved sees him as human that he regains his will to become so. "For thee I bade my drooping soul revive," he proclaims, "For thee alone I could have borne to live; / And love, I said, shall make me large amends, / For persecuting foes, and faithless friends" (2). The white servant's feeling response to the speaker's suffering models the correct posture of sympathy for the reader. If the reanimation of the speaker from the social death of slavery comes from the compassion of his beloved, his afterlife will issue from the reader's reception of his dying words. Pity and love become recompense for the injustice done to the slave.

Melding the discourses of romantic loss with anti-slavery polemic, the poem shifts from one register to the other whenever the poem veers towards too overtly political a claim. The dying Negro attributes his suicide less to his unwillingness to return to slavery than to his refusal to lose his beloved bride: "This hour I triumph over fate and love" (17). To understand the speaker's kidnapping as the romantic sundering of lovers is, however, to mute the significance of the poem's date of publication in the year following the 1772 Mansfield decision, which ruled that the forcible removal of slaves from British soil constituted a violation of habeas corpus. Notwithstanding Day's remarks in the second edition's dedication that "it is in England alone, that laws are equally favourable to liberty and humanity," the poem's story exposes the fragility of Britons' idealizations of their nation's liberty and the inadequacy of the law to uphold such ideals.[17] Yet the closing lines of the poem do not call Britons to account; instead, Day's speaker displaces the culpability onto the crew immediately responsible for his plight, begging God to destroy their ship: "while they spread their sinking arms to thee [God], / Then let their fainting souls remember me" (19). Stripping away the sentimental buffer that allows the reader to extract pleasure from shared feeling, the Negro wishes his persecutors to experience his sensations, not his sentiments: "may these fiends, who now exulting view / The horrors of my fortune, feel them too" (19).

Like "The Dying Negro," William Cowper's ballad "The Negro's Complaint" humanizes an individual slave by having him describe his plight in the first person. Set to the tune of "Admiral Hosier's Ghost," a well-known political ballad of 1739–40 attacking Walpole's administration, "The Negro's Complaint" was the most popular of the four anti-slavery verses Cowper composed at the behest of the Committee for the Abolition of the Slave Trade.[18] In March 1788, Cowper's friend John Newton, a reformed slave trader and evangelical minister, had conveyed to him the committee's request that he compose "some good Ballads to be sung about the street" in order to facilitate the dissemination of abolitionist sentiment among the lower orders.[19] Because it is cast in the first person, the poem requires the singer to take the role of the slave. "To speak this poem," as Suvir Kaul argues, "or to sing it as a ballad, is to assume the position of the slave, a rhetorical identity that puts into play precisely the circuit of sympathy and identification that the antislavery movement sought to inculcate in the British public."[20] In taking the slave's part, the British singer levels accusations against himself or herself. The political efficacy of the poem depends upon both identification with and differentiation from the slave.

The very title of Cowper's poem indicates that it is an address that articulates the woes suffered by a particular individual. If the definite article in the poem's title allows the unnamed first-person speaker to stand for *all* Negroes, the possessive apostrophe suggests the Negro's title to his complaint. The poem's speaker, however, avoids the self-defeating logic at work in Day's "Dying Negro." He ruptures the circularity of the complaint by moving from the description of his plight to a catalog of injuries inflicted upon him, in what Anne Anlin Cheng evocatively describes as "the conversion of the disenfranchised person from being subjected to grief to being a subject speaking grievance."[21] The speaker addresses a series of questions to British traders, Parliament, consumers, and Christians, interrogating the rights of Britons to enslave and exploit him. As he shifts from victimized object to subject and agent in the course of the poem's seven stanzas, Cowper's speaker questions the humanity of Europeans rather than Africans.

The first stanza of the poem describes the speaker's departure from Africa and his—or possibly her, since the gender of the speaker is never identified— sale into slavery. The opening lines grammatically and semantically locate the speaker as an object: "Forced from Home and all its pleasures / Afric's coast I left forlorn, / To encrease a stranger's treasures / O'er the raging billows borne" (1– 4). Pushed to the second line, the speaker's "I" is the object of an agentless force that sunders him from his home, leaving either Africa or the speaker "forlorn." The first stanza nevertheless confers a vestigial agency upon the speaker that challenges his status as merchandise. Although he is rendered a commodity, inasmuch as the English have "Pay'd my price in paltry gold," the speaker claims an autonomous subjectivity: "minds are never to be sold" (6, 8). It is only if the speaker's interiority remains unshackled that he can logically pose the questions articulated in the second stanza: "Still in thought as free as ever / What are England's rights, I ask, / Me from my delights to sever, / Me to torture, me to task?" (9–12).

The following stanzas turn from complaint to inquisition, shifting from a description of the slave's own sufferings to an interrogation of the rights of his victimizers. "Fleecy locks and black complexion," the speaker argues, are the only recognizable explanation for the barbaric treatment of Africans, and yet they constitute an irrational justification for slavery: "Skins may differ, but Affection / Dwells in White and Black the same" (13, 15–16). The poem neither lingers over the suffering of the slave in order to inspire a benevolent tear nor simply affirms that the slave possesses human qualities (the "affections" that dwell in white and black alike). Instead, the feeling and reason that the (hypothetical) Negro possesses are enacted in the very logic and structure of the poem. Because the poem invites the reader to speak or sing as the slave, it *performs* its argument regarding the essential humanity and rationality of its speaker.

The invitation to identify with another—to "be" the slave for the space of a song—asserts a possible equity or exchange between the intradiegetic and extradiegetic speakers of the poem. And yet the British speaker must confront the knowledge that his or her place is more properly with the accused "you" rather than with the accusing "I." Part of what complicates the conversion from subject of grief to subject of grievance in abolitionist poetry is that this transformation is often enacted in and through the imagination of another. That is, it is not the Negro himself who speaks, but Cowper who speaks through and for him.

To complain on someone else's behalf (as opposed to for oneself) is to pose questions about whose grief it is anyway. If the movement from the recognition of injury to the recovery of damages implies a "logic of comparability and compensation,"[22] allowing loss and restitution to be weighed together, what happens when the speaker who voices the grievance in the first person is not the one injured (and may even be the one inflicting damage)? Grief cannot be seamlessly exchanged for grievance.

The oscillation between identification with the speaking "I" of the slave and identification with the addressed white Briton opens up a gap between the context from which the poem is ostensibly spoken (the world of the slave) and the real place of the speaker (as part of an oppressive system.) This gap is *necessary*, since only insofar as the reader is *not* in the position of the Negro does she or he possess the agency within the political system to change it. In this sense, the poem exposes and exploits the gap between sympathy and identification, between the capacity to share another's feelings and structural alignment with his or her plight. By the final stanza, the speaker has reversed the position of African and Briton:

> Slaves of Gold! Whose sordid dealings
> Tarnish all your boasted pow'rs
> Prove that *You* have Human Feelings
> 'Ere ye proudly question *Ours.*   (53–56)

The chiastic structure of the closing lines reverses the position of slaves and masters: not only are the latter enslaved to gold, but their "boast'd pow'rs," like precious metals, also become "tarnished" by their "sordid dealings." The final lines send us into a familiar logical tailspin: the very fact that Britons enslave Africans proves that they are devoid of the human feeling that they deny the slave. If the poem begins with the speaker creating the grounds for his own speech acts ("Still in thought as free as ever" [9]), here he undermines the speaking position of the Briton and the moral claims that vindicate British imperial endeavors.

"The Negro's Complaint" eventually became, after *John Gilpin*, the most frequently reprinted of Cowper's poems; "many thousand copies" of the poem, Thomas Clarkson tells us, were printed "on the finest hot-pressed paper" under the title "A Subject for Conversation at the Tea-table," making it one of the two most effective arms of the abolitionist movement.[23]

The other was Josiah Wedgwood's small black and white medallion featuring a kneeling slave beneath the question "Am I not a man and a brother?" (fig. 4.1).[24] Designed as the official seal of the London Committee of the Society for the

Figure 4.1. Josiah Wedgwood, slave medallion. 1787. Black on yellow jasper. By courtesy of the Wedgwood Museum Trust, Staffordshire, England.

Abolition of the Slave Trade in 1787, Wedgwood's medallion appeared on brooches, hairclips, stationary, tea sets, bell pulls, cushion covers, and fire screens. The conflation of sentimental and economic value discussed in Chapter 2 resurfaces here once again in the form of a snuffbox: Clarkson notes that "some had them [the medallions] inlaid in gold on the lid of their snuff-boxes."[25] The medallion was even printed on trade tokens (ersatz coins that circulated as money because of a shortage of specie), placing its circulation as coin in harrowing proximity to that of the slave as commodity.[26] It was in order to avoid infelicitous parallels between the sale of the image of the slave and the sale of the slave that the committee distributed the medallions as gifts rather than selling them. "I understand they are not purchaseable," Cowper notes in a 1788 letter, "which makes it all the more valuable. Wedgwood refused to sell them, affirming that it should never be said of him that he had sold a Negro."[27] The medallion's itinerary demonstrates the critical difference between the mobility of representations and the mobility of what they represent: the *Tale of Wedgwood's Medallion* would be nothing like the *Tale of the Slave* who is depicted on it.

There are many things to say about this medallion, and many of them have already been said by others. The single figure, black on yellow jasper, is evidently meant to stand in for the suffering millions in a mute tableau. The medallion takes the individual slave and raises him to the status of miniaturized exemplar, transforming the slave's fetters into the human bonds of transcultural fraternity. This slave is a synecdochal substitution for—or perhaps a condensation of—countless others: for the purposes of the medallion, one male slave is as good as another (Anyslave, if not Everyman). Depicted in a pose of supplication, the slave begs rather than demands, kneels rather than revolts. Isolated and abject, he is in no position to unite in revolution and therefore poses no threat to the reader's contemplation of his suffering. Relegation to the category of sentimental object would seem to consign the slave to the class of things devoid of agency, and part of the pleasure to be derived from the medallion stems from this very asymmetry, as the consumption of images of a victimized other affirms the wholeness of the observing self. Yet militating against a reading that emphasizes the total passivity of the slave is the flex of his right foot, which may either stabilize his kneeling posture, holding him in place, or may suggest muscles tensed as if he is poised to rise.

It might seem as if a single slave is necessary to particularize suffering, since contemplation of the anguish of millions catapults the reader into the boundlessness of a sublime incoherence. "[T]he miseries of five hundred thousand wretches, noticed in general terms," as Thomas Cooper notes in his 1787 *Letters on the Slave Trade,* "seldom produces a permanent effect among persons, who would shudder at the detail of the complicated misery, which any individual of the ill-fated group has been doomed to undergo."[28] And yet the medallion is curiously devoid of pointers that might allow us to particularize or to reconstruct the slave's story. Wedgwood does not contextualize the "African-looking" figure in a "colonial-looking landscape." There is no agent inflicting suffering on the slave; we are given an atemporal decontextualized effect without a cause. The things the wearer is meant to change—the abusive hands that torture the slave, even the injury inflicted upon him—are conspicuously absent from the image. Indeed, Wedgwood's slave might be better seen as the allegorical personification of an abstraction (Africanness, slavery), characterized by "the virtually total saturation of its 'personality' by the thematic idea it represents."[29]

The fact that the medallion lends a voice to an otherwise mute slave returns us to the object narratives and slave autobiographies discussed in the previous chapter. One might say that the medallion engages in the personification of that which (she or he who) is already a person, the redundant animation of someone who is already a living human being. Personifying a tree does not make a tree human, and neither does personifying a slave; extending the *representation* of humanity is evidently not the same as treating others as human beings. Indeed, it may make the absence of humanity more apparent. As Lord Kames observes in his *Elements of Criticism*, "a thing inanimate acquires a certain elevation by being compared to a sensible being. And this very comparison is itself a demonstration, that there is no personification in such expressions. For, by the very nature of a comparison, the things compared are kept distinct, and the native appearance of each is preserved."[30] The provisional lending of human traits and voice to the slave creates the *effect* of humanization without any necessary real transformation. If anthropomorphism (as we saw in the previous chapter) is a trope that alters the essence of its object, then it might be said that Wedgwood's medallion is a personification that is trying to pass itself off as an anthropomorphism.

The text—"Am I not a man and a brother?"—placed over the head of the figure apparently makes these words his utterance. The question makes the motto into an address—one that does not elicit a response, since the question is left suspended, unanswered. (In this, the medallion returns us to the mute Bible in the previous chapter.) The relationship between consumer and slave remains purely hypothetical: the reversibility of grammar allows the slave to be (or not to be) a man and a brother.[31] The question invites the reader of the medallion to *find* likeness in the slave—to attribute the similitude to the figure that will render him human—but it also implicitly negates the slave's humanity by inviting the reader to *restore* that humanity. The question thus presupposes the difference it claims to cancel out: the slave is made unlike in order to invite the reader to make him like. In other words, Wedgwood's slave is made less than human so that we can make him human again. "[I]t is," as Laura Wexler reminds us, "the sentimental reader who is dangerous for his or her 'novel' object, precisely *because* he or she newly discovers in that object the possibility of a primary relation to itself that has been there all along, but must then be denied its history so that the discovery can be made."[32]

It is not, of course, self-evident to whom the slave's question is addressed. It may be directed at those who enslave him as a plea for freedom; it may be an appeal to a third party for sympathy and assistance; it may be addressed to God either in prayer or in reclamation of the humanity of which he has been unjustly deprived. By addressing God, the slave claims a singular and potentially revolutionary relation to the divine—a relation that takes the form of an implicit accusation. Although in Christian theology, the chains of sin that bind humans in their mortal coil weigh upon all alike, here those chains are borne by those sinned against rather than those sinning. Slavery has perverted the relation not only between human and human but also between divine creator and creature.

Finally, shadowed in the question "Am I not a man and a brother?" is an intimation of self-consciousness that renders the slave himself the reflexive addressee of his own query.

The question posed by the slave on Wedgwood's medallion suggests that humanity is not an attribute possessed by particular individuals, but a relation that can only be known and expressed in relation to others. This argument finds a homology in Marx's description of the way commodities acquire value. For Marx, value and identity emerge out of expressive relations with others. A thing by itself has no value; it is only when it is placed in relation to other commodities that it acquires value: "In a sort of way, it is with man as with commodities. Since he comes into the world neither with a looking glass in his hand, nor as a Fichtian philosopher, to whom 'I am I' is sufficient, man first sees and recognizes himself in other men. Peter only establishes his own identity as a man by first comparing himself with Paul as being of like kind. And thereby Paul, just as he stands in his Pauline personality, becomes to Peter the type of the genus homo."[33] In slavery, it is literally "with man as with commodities." The relation then is not just a matter of *analogy*—that human relations mirror relations among things—but of the literal treatment of persons as things described in the first section of this chapter. The possibility of an identity that goes beyond the uninformative tautology of "I am I" depends upon comparisons among men as if they were "of like kind." Identity rests on the recognition of oneself through a likeness to another: Peter knows his humanity through Paul as the type of genus homo. It is to that resemblance— one denied in slavery—that Wedgwood's slave appeals.

The analogy here opens up a set of questions that the medallion cannot resolve. If Peter knows himself through Paul as the type of "genus homo," then does Paul reciprocally know himself through Peter? In the case of the medallion, who is Peter and who is Paul? If the slave is meant to know himself through the medallion owner as the type of "genus homo," then does the medallion owner reciprocally know himself through the slave? Is the ventriloquized slave who asks if he is a man and a brother comparing himself to the European addressee? Or is it the user of the medallion, who reads and interprets the question, who seeks his humanity in his response to the question? (When one considers that the female counterpart to Wedgwood's male slave didn't materialize until 1826, the question that irresistibly surfaces is: "Is the female human?"[34] What role does gender play in the creation of the general category of humanity?)

If man only recognizes himself *in other men*, then in the case of the medallion, the template of the human seems to be curiously lacking. Whereas Peter and Paul can only know themselves through each other, the owner of the medallion is solicited to recognize another as human from his position as the type of genus homo. And yet, the type of genus homo can only emerge from relations to another—what Marx (following Hegel) calls a reflex-category. Reflex-categories like king and subject, master and slave, Marx tells us, "form a very curious class. For instance, one man is king only because other men stand in the relation of subjects to him. They, on the contrary, imagine that they are subjects because he is king."[35] Even as the king knows himself as such through his subjects, so too the slave knows himself in relation to the master (and vice versa). Through a fetishistic inversion, these relative identities come to appear to be a property inherent in the object itself. The king, that is, acts as if his kingship is not a function of his relation to his subjects but a property of himself (and, most of the time, his subjects concur in this). Instead of thinking about how that value is produced, how it's made, we are meant to think of it as always already within the object, as if it *were* how it is (the tautology here is deliberate).[36] Wedgwood's medallion tries to capitalize on the logic of the fetishistic inversion. The owner of the medallion acts as if humanity is an absolute property of the self, even as its relative nature is dramatized through the slave's postulated question. Only by forgetting that humanity is a reflex category, defined relationally, can the medallion's addressee assume his or her role as gatekeeper over admission to the enchanted kingdom of the human. Perversely, that is, Wedgwood's medallion uses the logic of commodity fetishism to humanize the slave, robbing Peter to pay Paul, as if there were only so much humanity to go around.

The medallion's question binds the humanity of the slave to the humanity of the master by drawing on the reciprocity of brotherhood (if you are my brother, I must be yours). But the term *brother*, as David Hume points out, in fact implies a kind of deceptive equivalence, a false reciprocity. The question "Are you my brother?" is not the same as the question "Am I your brother?" As Hume puts it in the *Treatise of Human Nature:*

> If a person be my brother I am his likewise: But tho' the relations be reciprocal, they have very different effects on the imagination. The passage is smooth and open from the consideration of any person related to us to that of ourself, of whom we are every moment conscious. But when the affections are once directed to ourself, the fancy passes not with the same facility from that object to any other person, how closely so ever connected with us.[37]

The relation of brotherly mirroring that is supposed to produce a reciprocal identity produces a nonreciprocal hierarchy. The flow of emotion is not equal and balanced: it is more difficult to pry interest away from the self and direct it towards another than to nudge it back into the natural slipstream of self-absorption. Self is our default mode. Categories that appear to be symmetrical thus prove to be differential.

The commonality of brotherhood would seem to derive less from the reciprocal ties of sympathy than from the bonds that lock both parties together in an unequal but indisseverable relationship. The comparisons that create the likeness of men also produce the desire for distinction. As Hume points out, in our relations with others, we derive our sense of self *not* from mirroring or equivalence but from superiority and inequality:

> the vanity of power, or shame of slavery, are much augmented by the consideration of the persons, over whom we exercise our authority, or who exercise it over us. For supposing it possible to frame statues of such an admirable mechanism, that they cou'd move and act in obedience to the will; 'tis evident the possession of them wou'd give pleasure and pride, but not to such a degree, as the same authority, when exerted over sensible and rational creatures, whose condition, being compar'd to our own, makes it seem more agreeable and honourable. (315)

The enslavement of others is not a matter of services rendered; robots give less validation than the delicious knowledge of lordship over our fellow rational creatures. On Hume's terms, we *prefer* to subjugate our own kind because the human qualities of the slave exalt the pride of the master. The greater the degradation of the owned, the more rarefied the pleasure of the owner. For Hume, the reciprocal relations between men and brothers implied by the medallion's question produce hierarchy rather than equivalence or similitude. One compares in order to distinguish.

Although the reciprocal logic of the question "Am I not a man and a brother?" would *seem* to invite the reader to exchange places (or to recognize the mutual constitution of master and slave, brother and brother), the medallion never actually invites the reader to identify with the position of the slave. For what makes the use of Wedgwood's medallion sentimental (and not just sympathetic) is the fact that the reader does not put himself or herself into the position of the suffering slave. She or he *answers* the question the slave asks. The consumer of the medallion identifies not with the slave but with the community of moved souls, and that identification with other like-feeling souls is connected to the repudiation of being another, of being a slave. Sentimental readers do not melt in ecstatic identification with the sentimental object; they bond with each other through the medium of the sentimental object. The precipitation of the self into the role of the other is thus not a reciprocal and balanced exchange that produces a community of like equals, of men and brothers together. Instead, Wedgwood's medallion creates likeness among the community of its consumers by creating a shared relation to an object that is seen as different.

For what the medallion *did* help do, as Sarah Parsons has argued, was to gloss over factional differences of religion and class in the eighteenth-century abolitionist community by soldering them together around a binary of black and white.[38] The medallion did not bind slave to British subject, but fostered greater unity within the abolitionist movement by creating oppositions that allowed other types of difference sundering the sentimental community (religion, class) to seem less significant. At a time when large segments of the British public were agitating for Catholic emancipation, electoral reform, poor relief, unionization, and industrial legislation, slavery formed a moral cause around which almost all political and religious persuasions could rally.[39] "The country," as Samuel Whitbread, MP for Bedford, put it, "never has, and I fear, never will, express a feeling so general as they have done about the slave trade."[40]

Figures like Wedgwood's slave consolidate metropolitan identities over and against the objects of pity and compassion, inviting sentimental identification not with the suffering other, but with the compassionate observer. Indeed, as Elizabeth Kowaleski-Wallace has pointed out, the medallion may draw attention to the wearer's "deeper, more 'humanitarian' female subjectivity," rather than to the suffering of the slave.[41] It is as much the humanity of the Briton as the humanity of the slave that is staged and interrogated in the medallion. The popular success of the medallion, like that of Day's and Cowper's verse, attests that acts of provisional identification stir political sentiment. And yet the question posed by sentimental form—"How does one come to feel for another human?"—proves to be contingent upon another question: "How does one know what the class of the human *is*?" Not every candidate who applies for pity possesses the right qualifications. As Janet Schaw's *Journal* of her voyage to the West Indies in 1774–76 demonstrates, sentimental tropes block as well as facilitate the recognition of likeness in other people.

Discriminating Figures in Janet Schaw's *Journal*

It is not the softness but the restrictive element in pity which makes it questionable; for compassion is always inadequate.

—*Max Horkheimer and Theodor Adorno,*
Dialectic of Enlightenment

In October 1774, Janet Schaw, a thirty-something Scotswoman, embarked for the West Indies with her brother Alexander, two young nephews, a female cousin, and two servants. Schaw was to accompany her brother to St. Kitt's, where he was to assume his post as customs officer, before continuing on to visit another brother in North Carolina. Circulated in manuscript form during her lifetime, Schaw's *Journal* of the voyage out and of her sojourn in the colonies furnishes a valuable account of social relations in the Indies and the southern colonies on the eve of the American Revolution. Analyses of Schaw have focused on the complex strategies of sociable and rhetorical self-fashioning of a woman writing from a politically turbulent context to a coterie of friends in the metropole.[42] Although much has been said about her representation of Africans and Europeans, little attention has been paid to Schaw's use of sentimental tropes to qualify the people she encounters as human.

Upon departing from Scotland, Schaw stumbles upon a cluster of emigrants smuggled on board by the captain. "Never did my eyes behold so wretched, so disgusting a sight," she remarks. "They looked like a Cargo of Dean Swift's Yahoos newly caught."[43] Undifferentiated in their bestial aspect, these huddled masses are classed as merchandise ("cargo") and stripped of humanity as "Swift's Yahoos newly caught," animals not yet domesticated. Unlike Swift, Schaw excises the abject and the excremental elements that fuel Gulliver's ambivalent identification with the Yahoos. What binds us together, for Swift, is the fact that we are all mired in our own moral and literal dirt: we repudiate in the Yahoos what we know ourselves to be. By contrast, Schaw's Swift reference maximizes the distance between Schaw and the Yahoos, drawing attention to her literary cleverness rather than the plight of the steerage passengers. Her disgust is not the negation of a recognized or recognizable kinship, but the revulsion of an observer confronted with "so wretched, so disgusting a sight." The jarring intrusion of sordid circumstance undermines the pleasure of witnessing suffering.

For Schaw, the Yahoos must be remade in a sentimental image in order to become suitable objects of feeling. Thus it is only when she witnesses the emigrants' last glimpse of their former home that she is moved by their plight:

> [they] stood in silent sorrow, gazing fondly on the dear spot they were never more
> to behold. How differently did the same sight affect them and me? What chilled
> my blood and disgusted my eye, filled their bosoms and warmed their hearts with
> the fondest, the most tender sensations, while sweet remembrance rushed on their
> minds and melted the roughest into tears of tenderness. The rude scene before us,

with its wild rocks and snow-cover'd mountains, was dear to them, far more dear than the most fertile plains will ever appear. (33–34)

Schaw describes a process of humanization through feeling, both the feeling attributed to the "Yahoos" and that experienced by Schaw in watching them. Yet sentimental feeling arises here not from resemblance or imitation (the Yahoos are *not* like Schaw) and not from spontaneous sympathy (she does not feel the same thing they feel). In fact, Schaw feels the opposite of what the Yahoos feel. Where their bosoms are filled with tender sensations, her blood is chilled; she witnesses with disgusted eye what the emigrants regard with yearning. By having feelings about the Yahoos' feelings, Schaw cranks the steerage passengers into the category of the human. Her feelings arise not from the recognition of similitude but from the production of likeness in the emigrants.

Schaw herself marvels at the transformative power of feeling to alter its objects in an apostrophe to pity:

Pity, thou darling daughter of the skies, what a change do you produce in the hearts where you vouchsafe to enter; from thee the fairest social virtues derive their being; it is you who melt, soften and humanize the soul, raising the man into a God. Before the brightness of thy heavenly countenance every dirty passion disappears—pride, avarice, self-love, caution, doubt, disdain, with all which claim Dame Prudence for their mother; and how different a set appears in thy train, those gently-smiling Goddess[es]—charity, meekness, gentle tenderness with unaffected kindness. What a change has she wrought on me since my last visit to the deck. Where are now the Cargo of Yahoos? they are transformed into a Company of most respectable sufferers, whom it is both my duty and inclination to comfort. (36)

No closeted interiorized emotions these; here we are in a world of allegorical passions, in which feelings easily supersede the bounds of the particular person. Personified pity stalks into the soul like a power-sharing superhero, "raising the man into a God" by humanizing the soul, and vaporizing "dirty passions" with her "heavenly countenance." Pity performs a kind of emotional triage, dispensing with "pride, avarice, self-love, caution, doubt and disdain," while admitting "charity, meekness, gentle tenderness." What shifts the status of the Yahoos is not the perception of a hitherto overlooked attribute, but an alteration in Schaw. Indeed, Schaw's lofty flight, with its apostrophe to pity and its self-dramatizing rhetorical question ("Where are now the cargo of Yahoos?"), places her own transformation at central stage, with herself as chief spectator. The emigrants themselves are unchanged; only her relation to them has altered. The similitude

Schaw detects and identifies with in the Yahoos is thus the product rather than the cause of the act of identification.

This passage from Schaw performs what Philip Fisher has described as the sentimental work of humanization, enlarging the sphere of feeling creatures to embrace previously excluded groups (women, children, slaves) within the reader's purview. Sentimental stereotypes, Fisher argues, perform the heavy lifting in elevating debased populations; they repeat the moral lessons that need to be absorbed. Once the renegotiated status of these groups has been accepted, the ostentatious labor performed by these stereotypes must be forgotten or repressed in order for this newly acquired status to seem natural. It is for this reason, Fisher argues, that sentimental descriptions come to appear as maudlin, offensive, trite, and contrived: "we are left looking at the sinking, overdone, too-insistent images that now offend us precisely because they have done their work and we no longer even remember the images that they were designed to correct."[44] The passage from Schaw describes the changes in the sentimental object—the "Yahoos" become worthy, suffering people—but it is also strikingly self-conscious about the labor involved in producing this change. Schaw seems acutely aware both of the gaze she trains upon these objects, and of the way her perspective will make her look to other people.

In a discussion of the structure of psychoanalytic identification, Slavoj Žižek reminds us that we must consider not only with what position the reader is invited to identify, but also from what point of view that position is attractive. We must ask, that is, not only with whom an individual identifies, but also "*for whom* is the subject enacting this role? Which *gaze* is considered when the subject identifies himself with a certain image?"[45] Thus when a sentimental text depicts "good poor people" as charming and virtuous or farm laborers as happy rustics, it is offering us the gaze of the affluent upon the poor, not necessarily the gaze of the poor upon their own lives. That perspective might be attractive to a bourgeois audience and repellent to the good poor people themselves (or vice versa). Similarly, the vision Schaw offers of the emigrants is not necessarily the gaze that they would turn upon themselves, but the sentimentalized vision of a privileged observer. Schaw even wishes for the presence of a "Miss Forbes, with her pencil of Sensibility, to have done justice to this group of heart-affecting figures" (35). Such sentimental tableaux suspend the narrative, permitting the leisurely contemplation both of the moving object and of the fact that we are moved. What is important for my purposes is that the pleasure derived from this sentimental image issues from the identification with a moved, emotionally correct spectator, rather than with the suffering individuals themselves.

The sentimental mode cajoles readers into aligning themselves with a particular perspective by creating a position from which to enjoy the image of the suffering object in comfort. But the text must also elaborate a second position, which allows this sentimental posture to be seen as likeable. That is, it must also create a position from which to enjoy the image of oneself enjoying the image of the suffering object. We must identify both with the feeling subject within the text (Schaw as a sympathetic observer) *and* with the point of view from which Schaw's description of her self is appealing. (Seen from another angle, the sentimental gaze Schaw trains on the Yahoos might seem self-indulgent, patronizing, repellent.) The sentimental lapses into inauthenticity when the artificiality of the gaze for which one performs becomes apparent—or when it becomes clear that the artificial gaze for which one performs is oneself. It is for this reason that the sentimental masters never depict the torturer's horse scratching its rump: such details interrupt the seamless identification with this gaze. "Poverty," as Anna Letitia Barbauld notes in her *Inquiry into those Kinds of Distress which Excite Agreeable Sensations,* "if truly represented, shocks our nicer feelings; therefore, whenever it is made use of to awaken our compassion, the rags and dirt, the squalid appearance and mean employments incident to that state, must be kept out of sight."[46]

Although the objects available for sentimental feeling are virtually limitless, not every object elicits a sentimental response. Schaw's inability to be moved by the suffering of the Yahoos *until* they are converted into sentimental figures shows that suffering by itself is inadequate to arouse emotion. We do not feel for all who suffer; we are, as Adam Smith points out, unmoved by injuries done to our enemies in war. How is one to explain this selectivity? Smith argues that our indifference, even delight, in the damage done to the other side stems from the fact that we attend to the nationality of the victims rather than the nature of the deed or its violation of an abstract principle.[47] Sympathy, that is, discriminates by objects rather than by acts.

That the principles of selection for these objects are culturally bound is apparent in what is perhaps the most famous passage from Schaw's *Journal:* her misrecognition, upon her arrival in Antigua, of a group of "negro children." "Just as we got into the lane," Schaw writes, "a number of pigs run out at a door, and after them a parcel of monkeys. This not a little surprized me, but I found what I took for monkeys were negro children, naked as they were born" (78). The passage is interested in *how* Schaw sees rather than *what* she sees; otherwise, Schaw would have simply noted that she saw a group of "negro children, naked as they were born." Even as the initial misrecognition of the emigrants as Yahoos is amended, so that we understand them to be people, here Schaw narrates the error and its correction. But this time Schaw omits the process that precipitates this perceptual revolution.

Whereas the initial confusion of emigrants for Yahoos is cleared up by an injection of corrective sentiment, here nothing engineers the shift that allows Schaw to differentiate the children from the scurrying animals with whom they are metonymically affiliated. Indeed, their metonymic proximity produces a metaphorical substitution in which one thing is "taken" for another: the children are both mistaken for and supplanted by monkeys. In Warren Montag's analysis of this passage, skin color initially leads to a mistake that is rectified by recognizing that whiteness is not an essential or universal property of humanity. "The apparently different," he writes, "is restored to its place in the identical."[48] In forcing us to oscillate between the determination human/not-human, Schaw's initial error and immediate correction of it remind us that categories are known through the uncanny threshold of the "not-quite." But Schaw's confusion seems neither to be intended as a reflection on Enlightenment philosophical categories nor to issue from a lapse in sentiment. Instead, it seems intended for a joke. Not logic, not feeling, but a grotesquely playful racism polices borders in Schaw's text.

Although Schaw differentiates primate and person in this example, she elsewhere collapses human into brute. Whereas the inclusion of the Yahoos in the order of the human involved the labor of feeling, the banishment of Africans from this sphere involves what might be called the labor of unfeeling: the work necessary to justify the failure of sympathy. Thus Schaw's description renders slaves visible objects before the reader's observing eye before trying to curb his or her feeling response:

> Every ten Negroes have a driver, who walks behind them, holding in his hand a short whip and a long one. You will too easily guess the use of these weapons; a circumstance of all others the most horrid. They are naked, male and female, down to the girdle, and you constantly observe where the application has been made. But however dreadful this must appear to a humane European, I will do the creoles the justice to say, they would be as averse to it as we are, could it be avoided, which has often been tried to no purpose. When one comes to be better acquainted with the nature of the Negroes, the horrour of it must wear off. (127)

The neutral tone that opens the passage—the ratio of slaves to driver, the length of the whips the latter holds—rapidly cedes to an address to the metropolitan reader, soliciting him or her to fill in the blank ("You will too easily guess the use of these weapons"). The lashed naked back, the whip, and the wound-inflicting hand disappear, sandwiched between present observation and past-tense injury ("you constantly observe where the application has been made"). We are given the site of the scars, which are then immediately erased, as "the application" of what and by whom is left unstated. Indeed, the entire passage is littered with obscured agents and unclear pronouns (the antecedents of "they," "this," and "it" being—one presumes—slaves, whipping, and whipping). The pronouns by which the reader is solicited also shift: "you" becomes the abstract position of "a humane European" before the collective "we" shifts to an impersonal "one." The European exists in the present and imperative tense ("this [whipping] must appear" dreadful; "we are" averse to it) whereas the Creole exists in the conditional ("they would be"). Emotions hang in the balance in a set of projected equivalents between the revolted feelings of the European and the potential but contained revulsion of the Creole.

If Schaw were endeavoring to bring home the slaves' sufferings, she might go on to concretize the means of inflicting injury, giving the insular experience of torture objective being in a shared language. All the ingredients are here for pain to be rendered visible, and this is certainly a scene with great potential if suffering is the cue for a riotous bout of sentimental feeling. What checks Schaw—her political convictions, her underexamined cultural assumptions, her own subjectively dicey position in the Indies—is less important for my argument than *how* she cuts off our contemplation of their suffering. For Schaw excuses her lapse of feeling by depicting the Negroes as constitutively devoid of feeling. "It is the suffering of the human mind," she announces, "that constitutes the greatest misery of punishment, but with them it is merely corporeal. As to the brutes it inflicts no wound on their mind, whose Natures seem made to bear it, and whose sufferings are not attended with shame or pain beyond the present moment" (127). Her failure to feel or incite sympathy for the slaves' physical suffering is accompanied by a meditation on why we fail to feel sympathy. It is not a question of putting oneself in the position of another to ask what *we* would suffer if we were in a similar plight. Instead, we must consider what *they* suffer in a categorical projection of their sensibility and their mental capacities. The ethical enjoinder to respect the individual sanctity of another's experience becomes an excuse for quiescence. The witness's want of emotion is perversely depicted as a closer approximation of the slaves' experience than revulsion, anger, or sorrow. Thus "the horrour," Schaw tells us, "must wear off" upon further acquaintance with the "nature of the Negroes." The absence of sympathy comes to be the object's failure of affect; our failure to feel stems from their absence of feeling.

If the metropolitan subject here becomes a kind of moral Etch A Sketch®, whose ethical obligations can be erased at will, it is because the scars indelibly graven into the flesh leave no trace upon a mind "whose sufferings are not attended with shame or pain beyond the present moment." Whereas sentimentality, as we saw in relation to the snuffbox in Chapter 2, at times involves the experience of emotion by proxy—through the medium of the text—here the *failure* of feeling is farmed out, attributed to the object itself. One need not feel for others if they do not feel for themselves. When Schaw cuts off sympathy by discounting the slave's capacity for human feeling, she uses the attribution of affect to restrict the universality of the categorical imperative. Her refusal to admit that slaves suffer in effect banishes them from the class of the human. Schaw's circular logic (one cannot feel for those who have no feeling; because one does not feel for others, they have no feelings) is in fact the flip side of sentimental reasoning (sympathetic feeling expands the class of the human, but the class of the human is defined by the ability to inspire or to experience feeling). It is for this reason that sentimentality is ultimately inadequate to overturn the political impasse wrought by Schaw's claims.

Schaw's text reminds us that acute sensibility and proslavery sentiments may go hand in hand; abolitionists did not possess a monopoly on sentimental feeling. The political volatility of the mode is apparent in—to single out one example— Thomas Bellamy's 1789 dramatic afterpiece *The Benevolent Planters.* Although the play begins with an abolitionist prologue spoken by an actor in the character of an African sailor, it ends with the slaves literally singing the praises of their British masters, Goodwin, Steady, and Heartfree, to the tune of "Rule Britannia." "[U]nder subjection like yours," the play concludes, "SLAVERY IS BUT A NAME."[49] The appropriation of sentimental figures by proslavery writers like Bellamy or Schaw drives abolitionist writers to experiment with the form, replacing the straightforward attempt to humanize the slave through ventriloquism with an interrogation of the proper limits of sympathy. Although the plan of the *Brookes* and William Cowper's "Sweet Meat has Sour Sauce" directly and indirectly appeal to the same models of identification discussed above, they simultaneously recognize the fallibility of a politics based on sympathetic feeling.

Political Sympathies and the Sympathetic Misfire

It is notable that one of the most powerful tools of the abolitionist movement makes no direct appeal to the emotions of its reader. I refer of course to the famous image of bodies crammed into the *Brookes,* a Liverpool slave ship (fig. 4.2). Based on a design created by the Plymouth branch of the Society for Effecting the Abolition of the Slave Trade, the plan was intended to stimulate support for the passage of a bill proposed by the MP for Oxford University, William Dolben, to limit the number of slaves to be packed in each individual slave ship. It was part of a massive public relations campaign launched by the Society's London committee, which embraced the composition of verses by Cowper and More, the publication of John Newton's *Thoughts upon the African Slave Trade,* and the staging of Thomas Southerne's dramatization of Aphra Behn's *Oroonoko* at Covent Garden (a proposal made by Hannah More "on condition that they will leave out the comic part, which is indecent and disgusting" and add "an affecting prologue, descriptive of the miseries of these wretched negroes").[50]

The depiction of the bodies in the *Brookes* sought to give the reader an idea of the suffering of the Middle Passage. Using measurements provided by a captain in the Royal Navy, the committee calculated the maximum carrying capacity of the vessel by dividing an allotted portion of space for each body into the dimensions of the ship. The committee's recommendations to Parliament for restrictions on the numbers to be transported on each slave ship were based on these calculations. Circulated as a pamphlet, posted on the street, framed and hung on the walls of homes, the plan of the *Brookes* was published as a broadside in a print run of more than 8,000 copies in 1789 and became, Marcus Wood notes, "the most famous, widely reproduced and widely adapted image representing slave conditions on the middle passage."[51] Hannah More herself carried a copy of the plan of the *Brookes* to dinner parties, at times creating awkward social situations: "I was," she reports to her sister, "in a large party one evening, showing a section of the African ship in which the transportation of the negroes is so well represented, to Mr. Walpole, &c., when, who should be announced but Mr. Tarleton, the Liverpool delegate, who is come up to defend slavery against humanity. I popped the book out of sight, snapped the string of my eloquence, and was mute at once."[52]

The *Brookes* plan is not grounded in verisimilitude, but in something that feels like it. Seven cross-sections (both top-down and side views) are offered. The multiplication of images suggests exhaustively presented empirical truth, incontrovertible fact, clinically documented. As Clarkson describes it:

> The committee ... thought that they should now allow certain dimensions for every man, woman, and child; and then see, how many persons, upon such dimensions and upon the admeasurements just given [for a slave ship], could be stowed in this vessel. They allowed, accordingly, to every man slave six feet by one foot four inches for room, to every woman five feet by one foot four, to every boy five feet by one foot two, and to every girl four feet six by one foot. They then stowed

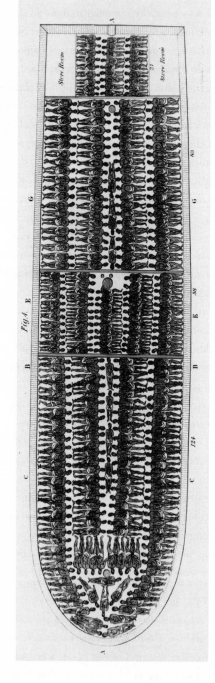

Figure 4.2. "Plan of the Slave Ship, the *Brookes*." From Thomas Clarkson, *History of the Rise, Progress and Accomplishment of the Abolition of the African Slave Trade by the British Parliament* (London: John W. Parker, 1839). By courtesy of the Andover-Harvard Theological Library, Harvard Divinity School, Harvard University.

them, and found them as in the annexed plate, that is, they found . . . that only four hundred and fifty could be stowed in her, and the reader will find, if he should think it worth while to count the figures in the plate, that . . . they will amount to this number.[53]

The plan graphically depicts the distribution of bodies on the slave ship, in which the slave is reduced to the quantity of space required for shipping the body as cargo. The small coffinlike black marks recreate the claustrophobic conditions between the decks. The invitation to count the number of bodies in the various portions of the plan interpellates the reader into the text: by minimizing the little labor involved in counting the figures, Clarkson augments the magnitude of the object contemplated.

The image both visualizes the plight of the slaves and, as Marcus Wood notes, underlines "their total passivity . . . their status as helpless victims." Seen from an Archimedean purchase point, the isolated prone figures become the objects of a surveying gaze that prevents them from uniting in revolt. The image thus replicates the logic it ostensibly repudiates. Reduced to an opaque figure, the slave is stripped of gender, nation, all particularizing features; she or he becomes an abstracted quantity in goods, in space, in money.[54] Only by squinting closely at the image can one discern the minute variations in posture: heads turned or cocked, arms folded or crossed or akimbo, legs straight, twisted, or splayed.

The bird's-eye perspective, aloof from the messiness of the trade, allows the reader to see the entire ship in one comprehensive glance. The diagram reduces whole bodies to details in a neat composition that follows the curves of the ship's hull in perfectly distributed symmetry. As Wood points out, "in terms of compositional balance the white spaces where the slaves are not are as important as the black spaces of ink which represent their bodies." It is in these white spaces, I would add, that one can glimpse what the plan of the *Brookes* seems to represent but in fact effaces. Notwithstanding Charles James Fox's claim to Parliament that the image allows the "the eye [to] see what the tongue must fall short in describing," the plan is in no way mimetic.[55] There were no neatly demarcated spaces between the bodies of the people immured in the hold of the slave ship. Thomas Clarkson's transcription, in a letter to Mirabeau, of the testimony of an African survivor of the Middle Passage hints at the inaccuracy and inadequacy of the plan of the *Brookes:* "Heat—Stench—Suffocation— . . . Yelling the whole night—Screaming for Air and Water—the Tongue parched—Wallowing in Excrements and Gore—amidst the dying and the dead."[56] Disintegrating into sentence fragments, the description omits reference to an observing or acting subject, steeping the reader in the present continuous of verbs lacking agents. One cannot tell whether the narrator hears others' screams or is himself screaming. Mired in excrement and gore—again, his own or another's?—the speaker is reduced to the partiality of a parched tongue that is not even described as his own (*my* tongue).

The abolitionists hastened to fill in these spaces verbally in the testimony offered to the select committee of the House. Thus the *Brookes*'s surgeon, Dr. Trotter, attested that he had seen slaves "drawing their breath with all those laborious and anxious efforts for life, which is observed in expiring animals, subjected by experiment to foul air, or in the exhausted receiver of an air pump; has also seen them, when the tarpalwings have inadvertently been thrown over the gratings, attempting to heave them up, crying out, 'Kickeraboo, kickeraboo', i.e., 'We are dying.'"[57] Dr. Trotter's comparison draws the traffic in human beings into the affective and scientific purview of the metropolitan reader by creating a sinister kinship between scientific scrutiny and sadistic experimentation, depicted in images like Joseph Wright of Derby's 1768 painting *Experiment on a Bird in the Air Pump.* The array of spectatorial responses depicted in paintings like Wright's—horror, sympathy, distress, sorrow, indifference—are likewise available to the witness of Trotter's testimony. At the same time, the grotesque conjunction of the death of a single bird and dying masses of people sends the reader into an affective tailspin. The reduction of enslaved Africans to expiring animals makes the traffic in humans into a cruel and profitless experiment, and places the reader or the parliamentarian in the position of the godlike natural philosopher who wavers between killing the bird and giving it air. Surely, Charles James Fox assured Parliament, "mankind, who certainly were not naturally cruel, would not be cruel where there could be no end."[58]

Trotter's comparison exposes the lack of any adequate metropolitan analogy capable of describing the horrors of the Middle Passage. It is a theme to which writers on abolition repeatedly return. As James Stanfield puts it in his 1788 *Observations on a Guinea Voyage,* "no pen, no abilities, can give more than a very faint resemblance of the horrid situation. One *real* view—one MINUTE, absolutely spent in the slave rooms on the middle passage, would do more for the cause of humanity, than the pen of a *Robertson,* or the whole collective eloquence of the British senate."[59] In the face of such inexpressibility, writers have recourse to metaphors whose flagrant inadequacy opens up an imaginative abyss, creating a kind of inverted sublime. Thus John Newton describes slaves lying "in two rows, one above the other, on each side of the ship, close to each other, like books upon a shelf. I have known them so close, that the shelf would not, easily, contain one more."[60] Comparing human bodies forcibly stowed on a slave ship to an overcrowded bookshelf sets the luxury of Enlightenment intellectual labor in disconcerting proximity to the material practices that support it. By the end of the passage, the metaphor overtakes the object represented, as the planks on the ship become shelves on which bodies are crammed. In making the comparison, Newton simultaneously obscures the colonial referent and incorporates it into the familiar world of the home.

The plan of the *Brookes* does not attribute feeling or thought to the figure of the slave; it unveils the brutal treatment of persons as chattel by obliging the reader to enter fully into the barbaric logic of the trade. William Cowper's "Sweet Meat has Sour Sauce or, The Slave Trader in the Dumps" likewise pitches its reader into the mentality of the slave captain, dwelling not on the agony of the slave, but on the financial woes of the trader upon abolition. To embrace the perspective of the captain is to create a travesty of correct feeling; the plea for inappropriate pity is meant to trigger a critique of sympathy—one that exposes the very mechanisms at work in abolitionist texts. As Robert Mitchell puts it, "[r]ather than assuming that the function of sympathy in a poem was to enable readers to *feel* the sufferings of others, Cowper's poem is effective to the extent that it encourages readers to *reflect* on the limits and proper objects of sympathy."[61] Mistaken identification with the slave trader spurs the reader into negative action by forcing him or her to repudiate the repugnant plea for sympathy he has just voiced in the guise of Cowper's slave trader. Either because of its oddly jaunty tone or perhaps because of fear that singers might not recognize the irony, the poem was not disseminated by the Society for Effecting the Abolition of the Slave Trade like "The Negro's Complaint," and it was only published in Southey's edition of Cowper's poems in 1835–37.

The slave trader overtly demands both the pity and the financial assistance of his interlocutor: the ending of the trade has obliged him to sell his stock, "a curious assortment of dainty regales, / To tickle the Negroes with when the ship sails, / Fine chains for the neck, and a cat with nine tails."[62] The stanzas of the poem hawk the trader's wares, converting the sympathizing reader into a potential buyer ("Come, buy off my stock," he implores [42]). The fact that the poem would have been sung in the street, blending in with the other street-sellers' tunes, shows how the slave trade is imbricated in the broader economic prosperity of the kingdom. The trader advertises his goods by showing how handily they fulfill the tasks for which they are intended (torturing and confining slaves); the uselessness of these objects for any other than barbaric purposes is apparent in the grotesque metaphors employed in the stanzas. "Here's padlocks and bolts, and screws for the thumbs, / That squeeze them so lovingly till the blood comes, / They sweeten the temper like comfits or plums" (17–19). The agency of the trader drops out, as the thumbscrews "lovingly" puncture the flesh until blood, like the juice of a fruit, spurts out. The fullness of the pad of the thumb is echoed in the rotundity of the plum, as the torture that enforces compliance is said to "sweeten the temper" in much the same way as sweetmeats are used to bribe schoolchildren. The poem's depiction of bodily injury subsequently moves to an *improper* demand for pity; the anticipation of his losses threatens to "break my compassionate heart," the trader says (35).

Marcus Wood has argued that the poem gives us "the way the abolitionist liked to see the slave trader seeing his slaves. In its extremity, vulgarity, cruelty, and stupidity, this version of the slave trader's views represents an abolition ideal, or anti-ideal." Wood contends that the poem is unable to "see the slave as anything but the site for a white moral contest,"[63] and this is true, inasmuch as the repellent nature of the trader carves out a complacent position for the reader ("Whatever my faults, at least I am not that!"). Yet in its form and in the structure of readerly identification it incites, the poem has a disturbing effect that carries it beyond Wood's thematic analysis of its content. Its efficacy lies in the fact that the reader or singer *only retroactively* recognizes his or her own complicity in the way the poem animalizes the slave, who under torture "clenches his teeth and thrusts out his paws" (22). The rhyme scheme initially glosses over the words, as the cadences of the poem carry the singer from withdraws to paws to jaws; only belatedly, after one has been caught singing along, is it possible to recognize one's error. In this, as Jennifer Keith points out, "Cowper exposes the dangers of highly regularized forms—of poetry, of thought, of commerce in humans—that too readily make cruelty familiar."[64] The familiarity of the tune thus moves us unwittingly past the point of what is pleasing until it is too late: the unpalatable truth that would ordinarily be disavowed has already issued from our lips. What "nobody can deny, deny," as the refrain puts it, is the complicity that always already exists in the reader. The seemingly ironic structure of the poem allows the real complicity of all to surface in the contained guise of the trader, because the identity of the speaker serves as a kind of negation that enables the idea to enter into the reader's consciousness. Nobody can deny these unspoken truths, yet everybody does; these truths cannot be misrecognized and yet they are only allowed to surface in the disavowed language of the trader.

Identification with the trader is meant to produce a corrective revulsion in the reader. Only by entering fully into his repulsive logic, humming along with the torturer, as it were, will one be impelled actively to differentiate oneself from his corrupt position. Yet the seamlessness of the poem's logic is such that no prob-lem is visible if one reads at face value. The slave trader's blithe enumeration of the qualities and uses of his wares is not accompanied by the standard-issue pieties of regrettable necessity; he seems jubilantly unaware of the moral flaws in his stance, and—for as long as one remains absorbed in the song, or in the slave trader's vantage point—no error of perspective is evident. The recognition of the ethical issues at stake depends upon the *nonidentity* of the reader with the posi-tion of the speaker, upon the ability of the reader or singer of the poem (as op-posed to the speaker within the poem) to create a dialectically mediated distance from the persona assumed in singing it. In other words, the reader must assume an ironic distance from the words she or he has just uttered. This distance makes emotions the objects of election, introducing an ethical element to sentimental feeling: if feelings are chosen, then the decision to have them or to resist them can be judged.

What if the trader's failings *feed* the reader's identification with him, inciting joint commiseration over the financial losses incurred by abolition, rather than leading the reader to disavow his stance? One does not only identify with others because they represent ideals; identification may also stem from the possession of shared but unattractive traits. Cowper's poem revels in its perversity; it seems, as Kaul notes, "to enjoy its own proslavery soliloquy too much."[65] In order to dis-rupt this pleasure, to kick-start change, the poem has to tamper with the relation between what psychoanalysis calls imaginary and symbolic identification, by minding the "gap between the way I see myself and the point from which I am being observed to appear likeable to myself."[66] We enjoy the slave trader's *blind-ness* to the gap between how he sees himself and how the right-thinking person sees him. Yet the pleasure of seeing through the trader also potentially obscures the reader's own lack of self-awareness, fostering complacency rather than self-critique. The reader may be caught in precisely the same trap as the trader, obliv-ious to the moral repugnance of his or her own position.

In his description of pity as self-pity, Cowper suggests sympathy is blind to anything but itself: "For oh! how it enters my soul like an awl! / This pity, which some people self-pity call, / Is sure the most heart-piercing pity of all" (37–39). Juxtaposed with the images of chains, whips, and padlocks, the trader's depiction of pity as a weapon that pierces the heart hints at the literal underpinnings of real suffering and embroils the reader in the calculus of relative pain. The com-peting claims to sympathy—the torture of the slave versus the fiscal losses of the trader—force the reader to enlarge or contract his or her perspective in order to appraise the degree to which the needs of the self should outweigh the competing claims of the rest of the world. If the most powerful form of pity is that which takes self for its object, the reader need not, as Robert Mitchell observes, "feel for anyone but him or herself."[67] This essentially narcissistic vision of pity suggests that sentimental politics can at best piggyback on self-interested emotions. If it is only by provisionally considering another's plight as one's own that one can be moved, then there is no such thing as disinterested pity (pity felt for the other *as* other, rather than as a disguised version of the self.) Although the poem does not (ideally) incite pity for the trader, nor does it redirect sympathy towards the slave as its "proper" object. Instead it leaves the reader with the recognition both of the inadequacy of sympathy as an impetus to right action and of its propensity to misfire.

"[S]ympathy," Edmund Burke states, "must be considered as a sort of substitution, by which we are put into the place of another man, and affected in many respects as he is affected."[68] As we saw in Chapter 1, the imaginative placement of oneself in the position of another allows one provisionally to grasp his or her experience. And yet these sympathetic exchanges cannot be perfectly symmetrical; if they were, one would cease to be oneself, becoming utterly absorbed in the other. Absolute equivalence does not secure identity; it menaces it with total substitution. Governing the spontaneous movement of feeling is thus crucial both to upholding the autonomy of specific individuals and to creating distinctions between kinds of men. We must be affected in "many" ways, Burke reminds us, but not all. Sentimental writers on slavery rely on the symmetry of sympathetic substitution to create empathy; at the same time, they capitalize on the asymmetry of these exchanges, preserving the self through the failure to identify absolutely with the suffering other.

The parliamentary debates on the abolition of the slave trade from 1788 to 1792 to which we now turn were likewise marked by tremendous anxiety about the vagrancy and volatility of affect.[69] In part this anxiety stemmed from the ways the abolitionist movement enlarged the political nation, giving a voice to those without property, connections, or influence. The petition drives in 1788 (and again in 1792) as well as the large-scale campaign to abstain from the consumption of West Indian sugar forced Parliament to bow to public pressure; select committees of the Privy Council, the House of Commons, and the House of Lords began gathering evidence on the trade in 1789.[70] The central role assumed by women in the movement placed the abolitionist man of feeling in close proximity to the lady of sensibility, while the extraordinary groundswell of popular agitation posed questions about the independence of the MPs. Thus at the same time as the parliamentarians derive moral authority from the claim to feel and

speak for the slave, they must define themselves against potentially perilous models of excessive, mobile, or inadequate feeling. The dispassionate torturer, the
sexualized slave master, and the whipping white Creole woman are used in the
parliamentary debates as models of the kind of feeling *not* to have. The debates
struggle to reconcile the tempered imperatives of reason with the humane claims
of right feeling by elaborating a model of compassionately conservative masculine sentimentality designed to enter provisionally into the feelings of others
while upholding the prior claims of the metropolitan self.

Usurpation and Empathy in Parliamentary Debates

Reason is, and ought only to be the slave of the passions.
—*David Hume*, A Treatise of Human Nature *(1739–40)*

Perhaps the most astonishing facet of the parliamentary debates on the abolition of the slave trade is the spectacular display of emotional plumage by these
political men of feeling. Each group of parliamentarians exhibits the best, the
right, kind of affect, turning themselves inside out, hearts on sleeves, in an initial public offering of emotion. Claims to possess the proper sentiments anchor
masculine political and moral authority through what might be called affective
distinction, because the kind and degree of emotion one experiences define one
as a particular type of political subject. The emotions of the parliamentary man
of feeling produce a homosocial sympathy that creates what Julie Ellison calls a
kind of "nervous equality among elite men and a few good women."[71] Affective
affinities create nonfamilial bonds among men, reinforcing the social ligature
that binds civil society together. Sentimentality does not authorize feeling for all,
but rather claims it for the happy few.

The parliamentary debates on abolition waver between the celebration of
sympathy as the bonds of humanity and the disquieting recognition that sympathy excites roving passions that may abrogate the claims of self-possession so
critical to eighteenth-century theories of masculine political autonomy. The fact
that sympathetic feeling courts a kind of affective dissolution threatens the self-
contained political personae of these Englishmen; the extravagant passions
elicited by the lurid testimony leave these ostensibly autonomous and self-
possessed men beside themselves. If, as Claudia Johnson has argued, sentimentality in the 1790s entailed "the 'masculinization' of formerly feminine gender
traits,"[72] the masculine appropriation of sentimentality causes gender trouble

not only because the appropriation by men of female feeling unsettles conventional gender positions, but also because the feelings the sympathizing reader experiences may not be entirely his or her own. That feelings course through subjects from without, that they stir into life in ways that exceed the will to master them, mocks assertions of masculine autonomy and civic republican self-sufficiency. The form of the debate must therefore master the incendiary content of the testimony.

Wilberforce opens the debate on abolition in 1789 by proclaiming that he wishes "to guard both myself and the House from entering into the subject with any sort of passion." Although he tells the members that he will ask "only for their cool and impartial reason,"[73] he rapidly slips into an inflammatory rhetoric meant to kindle other men's moral feelings. One must stir up the passions of otherwise unmoved men in order to excite their humanity. It is, Wilberforce claims, "sympathy, and nothing else than sympathy, which, according to the best writers and judges of the subject, is the true spring of humanity" (28.49). His endeavors to move men to right action leave him, as Burke puts it, "knocking at every door, and appealing to every passion; well knowing . . . that mankind were governed by their sympathies" (28.70). Yet even Burke invites his listeners to "surrender . . . up their hearts and judgments to the cause" (29.358).

In the previous chapters, we saw how augmented commercial systems allow individuals to influence events, acts, and systems beyond their immediate purview. The parliamentarians use this understanding of the enlarged scope of individual agency to show how the metropolitan subject is implicated in deeds and crimes committed on the far side of the globe. Even those not directly embroiled in the trade are held accountable for its perpetuation. Irrevocably bound up in a system of global markets, the individual cannot help but profit from the exploitation of others. "We are all guilty," Wilberforce proclaims, "we ought all to plead guilty, and not to exculpate ourselves by throwing the blame on others" (28.42). If Wilberforce's self-flagellating perorations seem like a riotous bout of liberal guilt, it is because this sense of complicity is the Janus face of the powers of individual agency and choice to which abolition appeals. The high premium placed on personal feeling means, however, that the pleas for abolition rest less on the obligation to alleviate others' misery than on the imperative that the members of the House "extricate themselves from that guilt and that remorse which every man ought to feel for having so long permitted such cruelties to have been suffered by human beings" (27.598).

The task of the abolitionist is to translate the suffering of the Africans into incontrovertible terms so that natural humanity can reassert itself. One must focus on particulars in order to bring home the suffering of the slave: "if the wretchedness of any one of the many hundred negroes stowed in each ship could be brought before their view, and remain within the sight of the African merchant," Wilberforce suggests, "there is no one among them whose heart would bear it" (28.45). Such speaking scenes will inevitably move the interlocutor to right action. "[T]he natural and unerring feelings of every man upon this subject," the abolitionists insist, can lead to only one outcome (29.335). Those who do not feel as Pitt, Fox, and Wilberforce are monstrous by default, marked as unfit for civil society. "He would not believe," Fox declares, "that there could be found in the House of Commons, men of *hard hearts* enough, and of such *inaccessible understandings*, as to vote an assent to the continuance of the Trade; and then go home to their houses, their friends, and their families, satisfied with their vote, after being made fully aware of what they were doing, by having opened their ears to the discussion."[74] Those who vote against abolition are accountable before the tribunal of the human heart. Inasmuch as the descriptions of suffering "would excite pity in the most callous heart, that still had one human sensation left in it" (Cobbett, 29.291), the anti-abolitionist does not *disagree* with a political position—he displays his want of humanity.

The abolitionists depict the perfectly rational individual as one who fails to grasp the *real* situation because he does not possess the mediated capacity to move between remote or abstract objects and immediate particulars. Those who perpetuate "this cool, reflecting, deliberate, remorseless commerce" (29.1240) can only do so because they deal in abstraction, banishing from their sight and consciousness the consequences of their trade. The very scale of suffering produced by the Liverpool merchants, Wilberforce claims, blinds them: "if it were not for the multitude of these wretched objects, if it were not for the enormous magnitude and extent of the evil which distracts their attention from individual cases, and makes them think generally, and therefore less feelingly on the subject, they never would have persisted in the trade" (28.45). The greater the suffering one causes, the less evident one's accountability for its effects.

Reason without sentiment could not lead to abolition, since slavery's violation of the Kantian categorical imperative found its vindication in the pitiless calculus of maximal utility. From the perspective of national interest, the proslavery faction contended, abolition was a bad idea. However unsavory, the trade sustained British prosperity. "Gentlemen had displayed a great deal of eloquence in exhibiting, in horrid colours, the traffic in slaves," one opponent to abolition declared. "He acknowledged it was not an amiable trade, but neither was the trade of a butcher an amiable trade, and yet a mutton chop was, nevertheless, a very good thing" (29.281). Abolition of the trade, the proslavery contingent argued, would cast the British manufacturing economy into disarray, creating suffering among British laborers. The loss of the African trade as the "nursery of seamen" would devastate the British navy and leave the sector open to the French and to other competitors. The impoverishment of the planter would worsen rather than improve the condition of the slaves, and the appropriation of West Indian property would violate the cherished rights of all Britons. The debates thus expose the tension between reason as a tool of Enlightenment, "aimed at liberating men from fear and establishing their sovereignty,"[75] and reason as a means of dominating disenchanted nature and exploiting other human beings. Only sentimental discourse can dislodge the implacable dictates of economic rationalization, and yet the volatility of affect introduces an unpredictable element into the debates. Because emotion cannot be rationalized in either sense of the term (subjugated by reason or subordinated to the ruthless logic of economic maximization), it was a volatile weapon in the hands of pro- and anti-slavery speakers alike.

Whereas the abolitionists accused their opponents of embracing reason without sentiment, the proslavery forces argued that the abolitionists embraced sentiment without reason. If slavery were an abomination to all reasonable men, the Lord Chancellor declared, then "he could not imagine why those crimes had not been discovered by our ancestors, and were now to be so conspicuous in the year 1792" (29.1354). The abolitionists were said to be possessed—or rather dispossessed—by heightened emotion, "carried away by the meteors they had been dazzled with" (29.358). Opponents of abolition railed against the "infatuation almost bordering on frenzy, which had taken possession of the public mind without" (28.713). "[T]he unwary and uninformed," as one member put it, "were tricked out of their humanity, by inflammatory extracts" based on "flimsy hearsay evidence" (29.1093). Not only the public but also the MPs had purportedly been seduced out of their self-command. Lord Sheffield could "trace nothing like reason, but, on the contrary, downright phrenzy, raised, perhaps, by the most extraordinary eloquence" in Parliament (29.358).

At times, however, the graphic accounts seem to become ends in themselves rather than the means of moving the reader to right action. One of the most frequently reproduced anecdotes from the testimony heard before the select committee involved Hercules Ross, a resident of Jamaica from 1761 to 1782, who reported having "heard the shrieks of a female, issuing from a barn or outhouse; and as they were much too violent to be excited by any ordinary punishment, he was prompted to go near, and see what could be the matter."[76] Peering through a gap in the wall, Ross saw a young female suspended by the wrists to a tree, swinging to and fro; her toes could barely touch the ground, and her body exceedingly agitated. The sight rather confounded him, as there was no whipping, and the master just by, seemingly motionless; but on looking more attentively, [Ross] saw in his hand a stick of fire, which he held so as occasionally to touch her about her private parts as she swung. He continued this torture with unmoved countenance, until the witness calling on him to desist, throwing stones at him over the fence, stopped it.[77]

The reader is initially aligned with the peeping Ross; we, like him, do not grasp the relation between the seemingly motionless master and the thrashing body of a female. The seeming absence of a physical cause of the body's writhing at the beginning of the passage renders its revelation all the more ghastly. The immobility of the torturer augments the horror of the event, as does the absence of a narrative to frame or justify it. Nothing in the passage, however, constrains the interlocutor to identify with a particular position in this triangulated scene of torture. He or she may be alternately victim, torturer, or witness. The possibility that one may identify with any of these positions allows such scenes to skid easily towards the pornographic, a point to which I shall return below.

The anecdote is never fully explained in the testimony; indeed, no moral cause is conceivable for such an effect. "What crime this miserable wretch had perpetrated [*sic*]," Fox proclaims, "he knew not; but that was of little consequence, as the human mind could not conceive a crime, in any degree, warranting such a punishment."[78] No crime can justify the criminality of the system, as the disproportion between unnamed transgression and represented punishment opens up the possibility that the torture is an end in itself. The contrast between the screaming woman and the stolid master suggests that the problem is not that an impassioned individual might go savage, but that a fully rational man might deliberately devolve into a monster.

If the mere representation of this torture is so troubling, the referent behind it must harrow the very soul: "the tale was so horrid," Fox observes, that the House "could not listen to it without shrinking. Will the House then (said he) sanction enormities, the bare recital of which is sufficient to make them shudder?" (ibid.). Fox questions the moral status of witnessing and the obligations imposed by such knowledge: "Let them remember that Humanity consists not in a squeamish ear. It consists not in starting or shrinking at such tales as these, but in a disposition of heart to relieve misery, and to prevent the repetition of cruelty. Humanity, he observed, appertained rather to the mind, than to the nerves; and it would prompt men to use real and disinterested endeavours, to give happiness to their fellow creatures."[79] Drawing on Adam Smith's contention that "humanity is the virtue of a woman, generosity that of a man,"[80] Fox distinguishes between the mere aversion to another's suffering and the reflection and judgment involved in its alleviation. Like Smith's generous man, the parliamentarian must suspend his immediate self-interest (which might simply involve the removal of the unappealing object from his sight), command his passions, and subordinate them to a greater need. Manly deeds, not effeminate feeling, must issue from the testimony. Circumventing the nerves, sensibility must be converted to useful benevolence. One can only justify the reproduction of such a scene if one moves beyond squeamish sensibility to end it. Likewise, the potentially pornographic circuit of the scene Ross witnesses is only broken when he moves beyond passive witnessing to terminate it.

In order to protect sensitive readers—and in an effort to avoid accusations of pandering to their reader's taste for sensational tidbits—abolitionist writers employ a version of the inexpressibility topos. Texts were often bowdlerized (a practice called "castrating" or "gelding," until those terms themselves were politely excised from common parlance.)[81] Yet such self-censorship at times smacks of literary striptease. "One instance more of brutality I would, however, willingly relate," James Stanfield writes,

> as practised by the captain on an unfortunate female slave, of the age of eight or nine, but that I am *obliged* to withhold it; for though my heart bleeds at the recollection, though the act is too atrocious and bloody to be passed over in silence, yet as I cannot express it in any words, that would not severely wound the feelings of the *delicate* reader, I must be content with suffering it to escape among those numerous hidden and unrevealed enormities, the offspring of barbarity and despotism, that are committed daily in the prosecution of this execrable trade.[82]

The delicate mind of proper sensibility would be overwhelmed by the horrors Stanfield is tempted to describe, as the wounded bloody body of the slave produces the bleeding heart and wounded feelings of the reader. Stanfield's willingness to bear witness is superseded by the obligation to shelter the "delicate" reader. He thus must "suffer" the scene to escape unseen. Such gaps invite the reader to fill in the blank—interpolating his or her own ideas into the gap—while sketching out the boundlessness of the horrors that might be found within an unexpurgated text.

The owners' brutal reduction of the slave to the mere matter of the tortured body leaves the domain of the soul open to the dominion of the abolitionist. "[I]t

was not in his power to impress the House with what he felt," Wilberforce announces: "the description of their conveyance was impossible, *so much misery
condensed in so little room,* so much affliction added to misery, that it appeared
to be an attempt by boldly suffering to deprive them of the feelings of their
minds."[83] So overwhelming is the suffering inflicted upon the enslaved that they
may not even apprehend it, and their lack of consciousness becomes the engine
of humanitarian intervention; the more disempowered the slave, the broader the
scope of the abolitionists' intervention on his or her behalf. Sentimental representation potentially usurps the place of the enslaved person, or, worse, compels
the slave, as Laura Wexler puts it, to play "the human scenery before which the
melodrama of middle-class redemption could be enacted, for the enlightenment
of an audience that was not even themselves."[84] Feeling for others (having empathetic emotions) can easily become feeling in their stead.

Writers like Benjamin Rush in his well-known *Address to the Inhabitants of
the British Settlements in America, upon Slavekeeping* (1773) tender exhaustive
menus of possible scenes for their readers to envision before faltering into theatrical silence:

> Think of the many thousands who perish by sickness, melancholy and suicide, in
> their voyages to America. Pursue the poor devoted individuals to one of the West
> India islands, and see them exposed there to public sale. Hear their cries, and see
> their looks of tenderness at each other upon being separated.—Mothers are torn
> from their daughters, and brothers from brothers, without the liberty of a parting
> embrace. . . . But let us pursue them into a sugar field, and behold a scene still more
> affecting than this—See! the poor wretches with what reluctance they take their
> instruments of labor into their hands. . . . But, let us return from this Scene, and
> see the various modes of arbitrary punishments inflicted upon them by their mas-
> ters. Behold one covered with stripes, into which melted wax is poured—another
> tied down to a block or a stake—a third suspended in the air by his thumbs—a
> fourth obliged to set or stand upon red hot iron——a fifth,——I cannot relate
> it.——[85]

Rush's interlocutors are invited to represent to themselves lurid tableaux in
which they alternately witness the suffering of the victim and the deeds of the
perpetrator. They frame and reframe the scenes of suffering, preserving maximal mobility in selecting a point of entry into the scene. A disturbing plasticity
emerges out of such a fantasy sequence, as the reader "pursues" the slaves from
one scene to the next in pursuit of ever greater stimulus. Each scene is "still more

affecting" than the last, until we achieve the apotheosis of suffering sensibility (our own, not the slaves) in the wracked body whose disfigurement is described in an abruptly truncated catalog of tortures.

The abolitionists acknowledge that the moral obligation to bear witness is a kind of torture. They (less frequently) acknowledge the rhetorical turns necessary to prevent the evil they describe from becoming banal. "Were I to transcribe a regular journal of the usage of the slaves on the middle passage," Stanfield acknowledges, "it would be but a repetition of acts similar to the above, and varied perhaps only by the circumstances that attended it."[86] One is reminded of Sade's explanation, in the midst of the orgies in *La Philosophie dans le boudoir,* that "fear of becoming monotonous prevents us from rendering those expressions that in such moments are all alike" (la crainte d'être monotone nous empêche de rendre des expressions qui dans de telles instants se ressemblent toutes).[87] Indeed, the rhythmic cadences and repetitious content of Wilberforce's discourse at times collapse the distinction between the representation of torture and torture itself. "[W]hat right [had] any one . . . to do so inhumane a thing," Lord Carhampton demanded, "as to inflict a speech of four hours long on a set of innocent, worthy, and respectable men[?]" (Cobbett 29.1281). The testimony, drummed into its captive audience day in and day out, becomes as repetitious and relentless as a beating. It bores into the listeners and it comes, even, to bore them. The notion that horror may turn to banality suggests that the parliamentarians, as interlocutors of these secondhand accounts, may become as inured to the testimony as the pitiless West Indians.

It is a commonplace that those regularly exposed to the horrors of the trade become oblivious; they are, the former slave trader John Newton writes, "liable to imbibe a spirit of ferociousness, and savage insensibility, of which human nature, depraved as it is, is not, ordinarily, capable."[88] Excessive contact with representations of such horrific scenes might callous the heart. The parliamentarians' awareness of the deleterious effects of both first- and secondhand witnessing creates fears that the listeners may themselves become hardened—either inured to or aroused by the testimony. Is the sympathetic willingness to listen a sign of willful self-punishment, or conversely, does it yield a sadistic enjoyment? The possibility that such testimony might elicit sentimental or sexual pleasure undermines the dignified claim to disinterested beneficence that ostensibly justifies the presentation of such explicit scenes.

Sentimental tropes provide the means of bringing home the suffering of others, but in reconstructing such suffering in one's own imagination, such figures potentially become the marionettes of self-pleasuring fantasies. The well-known use of Harriet Beecher Stowe's *Uncle Tom's Cabin* as a source of masturbatory fantasies, described in both Richard von Krafft-Ebbing's *Psychopathia Sexualis* and Freud's essay "A Child Is Being Beaten," suggests the erotic satisfaction to be obtained from sentimental reading.[89] To consume parliamentary testimony for a personal payoff, the extraction of sexual or sentimental gratification, is to treat the suffering of others as if it were fictional—an explanation that blocks the more troubling possibility that one may be turned on all the more by the fact that the suffering *is* real.

The intense passions incited by the testimony thrust the listener into close proximity with the impassioned men of the colonies. "The abolitionists' rhetoric," Mary Favret argues, "delivers their listeners into the practice of slavery itself, imagined as a realm where bodies are subjected to vicious men whose own self-possession has been sacrificed to sexualized excitement."[90] Once severed from the tempering effects of sympathy, the passions become terrific forces that drive all will, all compassion, before them. As the abolitionist parliamentarian Philip Francis put it, "It is a horrible truth, that when once the lash is lifted by an angry man, with despotic power over the object, his rage is inflamed by every stroke he gives. The cries and writhings of the creature are called resistance; even his patience is called sulkiness: even his sufferings are an offence. The decrees of passion are executed by passion. Admitting the power to be necessary, is there any protection against the abuse of it?" (29.289). The whipping man who finds himself delivered over to uncontrollable urges is converted into the implement of a barbaric system that overtakes his will. Even as men who enslave others are overtaken by passions, so too MPs may find themselves swept away. The mobility of feeling does not threaten to dissolve the distance between the man of feeling and the slave, but between the parliamentarian and the master. The fear expressed by the speakers is not that they will become like the slaves but that they *already are* like the masters.

It is perhaps in order to distance the man of feeling from the impassioned master that so many of the popular accounts single out the stunning acts of violence committed by white Creole *women* (or it may be that such lurid scenes were even more of a turn-on). The male witnesses who parade before the subcommittees repeatedly testify to the barbaric Creole lady who superintends the punishment of male and female slaves alike and even wields the whip herself, "ordering the number of lashes, and with her own hands flogging the Negro driver, if he did not punish the Slaves properly."[91] Lieutenant Baker Davison, surgeon in Jamaica from 1771 to 1783, reported that a clergyman's wife at Port-Royal was accustomed to "drop scalding hot sealing wax on her Negroes, after having punished them by flogging" and testified to having seen "a woman order a Slave's nose to be slit in both nostrils out of jealousy."[92] A Captain Cook described a mistress who "beat [a female slave] about the head with the heel of her shoe, till it was almost all of a jelly; she then threw her down with great force on a child's seat of a necessary, and there attempted to stamp her head through the hole; she would have murdered her had she not been prevented by the interposition of two officers."[93] Cook added that the "girl's crime was, not bringing money enough from aboard ship, where she was sent by her mistress for the purpose of prostitution."[94]

So twisted are social relations in the West Indies that even that icon of civilization, the beneficent domestic white woman, has been denatured into a sadistic harridan who slakes her unconstrained appetites by beating her slaves without mercy or utility.[95] Creole white women, William Alexander notes in his 1779 *History of Women*, "have been often hardly less distinguished for debauchery and cruelty than the men. A virago of this sort in the East or West-Indies, seldom meeting with any opposition to her whim and caprice, assumes at last a spirit of presumption and tyranny; and lost to feeling and humanity, wields the whip with such dexterity, as to fetch at every stroke blood from the back of the naked and unresisting slave; whose only fault was, that he did not anticipate the wishes of his mistress, or because he let fall some hints, that he was a creature of the same genus as herself."[96] Once taken out of her proper domestic sphere, the white Creole woman's sensibilities know no proper restraint. Caprice unchecked turns to presumption and tyranny. The beating of men by women exposes the tangled hierarchies operating in the colonies. Race trumps gender when a white woman lords it over a black man. The whipping lady violates gender norms that both pro- and anti-slavery forces uphold: she is one of the few points of agreement between the two factions.

Worse, in the Indies such behavior was consonant with feminine domesticity: "it was indeed," a Jamaican physician notes, "thought necessary for an industrious wife to be rigid in the punishment of her slaves."[97] Flogging did not conflict with domestic duties: it fulfilled them. The whipping woman thus illustrated the degree to which Creole society had fallen away from worthy Britannic norms. Female savagery exposed the decadent turn of an empire in decline. One visitor to England towards the end of the century compared the West Indian women to "the Roman ladies . . . [who] had their slaves sometimes fixed on the cross without their having committed any thing; they had them frequently and most severely whipped in their presence, for the sake of amusement, or being capricious, and in an ill-humour."[98] Torture alternately purges the lady's ill humor on the body of another or furnishes distraction in an idle hour. What at first sight appears to be a sign of excess—of sensibility gone too far—proves to be a matter of essence—of sensibility betraying its true nature.

In her 1790 *Vindication of the Rights of Man*, Mary Wollstonecraft describes a scene of reading set in the Caribbean where a fair lady of sensibility composes her spirits through recourse to a novel. "Where," Wollstonecraft asks, "is the dignity, the infallibility of sensibility, in the fair ladies, whom, if the voice of rumor is to be credited, the captive negroes curse in all the agony of bodily pain, for the unheard of tortures they invent? It is probable that some of them, after the sight of a flagellation, compose their ruffled spirits and exercise their tender feelings by the perusal of the last imported novel.—How true these tears are to nature, I leave you to determine."[99] The passage insists that we recognize that sensibility can be suspended in order to inflict torture and obliges us to acknowledge that the fair lady's exercise of feeling does not provide solace to the victimized slave. Indeed, one almost wants to read the expression "exercise her feelings" as "exorcise," in order to make the passage mean that the sentimental novel expunges the horror of a whipping. But when Wollstonecraft says that the sentimental novel allows the lady to "exercise her feelings," as if a sentimental workout were necessary in order to be ready for another hard day at the rack, she reminds us that a taste for the sentimental may veer dangerously close to a taste for another's pain.

Or perhaps vice versa. For the lady is not just an inadvertent witness to the slave's whipping or even simply the pleased consumer of his suffering; she is complicit in the production of his suffering. The proximity of the two acts of whipping and reading (as readers of Sade already know) suggests that the sentimental may not ensure a humane reception of descriptions of torture, but may instead feed an appetite for such scenes. This is not just a failure of sympathy; it is sympathy gone utterly awry. The avid inventive torturer is not at odds with the lady of sensibility: one makes the other, as if the intimate knowledge of the subtle workings of the body's nerves gleaned from sentimental reading helps the lady to refine the "unheard-of tortures" she devises. The passage is further complicated, of course, by the way Wollstonecraft solicits her reader's presumed sensibility: we are supposedly right-feeling enough to recognize the suffering slave and to indict the misplaced tenderness of the lady of so-called sensibility.

For Wollstonecraft, the problem issues *not* from the faltering of sensibility but from its correct implementation. It is not that the Creole woman falls out of her proper gender category by taking the whip hand; rather Wollstonecraft's women whip *because* they have learned the lessons of sentimental femininity all too well. These whipping ladies have, she claims, "read your [Burke's] Enquiry concern-

ing the origin of our ideas of the Sublime and the Beautiful, and, convinced by
your arguments, may have laboured to be pretty, by counterfeiting weakness . . .
[and choosing] not to cultivate the moral virtues that might chance to excite respect, and interfere with the pleasing sensations they were created to inspire."[100]
Wollstonecraft's morally infirm women have no strength of will or mind, no reason, no tempered and measured command of their passions. Rendered "slaves to
their persons," they concentrate on making themselves desirable so that "man
may lend them his reason to guide their tottering steps aright."[101]

   Unlike many abolitionist women writers, Wollstonecraft refuses to exploit the
moral power of feminine sensibility—a sensibility "unmixed," according to the
1789 *Monthly Review,* "with those political, commercial, and selfish considerations which operated in steeling the hearts of some men against the pleadings of
humanity"[102]—as a means of claiming political authority.[103] Instead, in much
of her writing, she depicts sensibility as a vitiating force that undermines the
powers of male and female alike, rendering them simpering sycophants or weak
and luxurious sentimentalists. The masculine takeover of these formerly feminine attributes leaves Wollstonecraft and other women with "only two choices:
either the equivocal or the hyper-feminine," Claudia Johnson argues.[104] The
whipping woman whose excessive sensibilities have led her to such savagery *col-
lapses* the two categories. The hyper-feminine produces the equivocal, as the ric-
tus of sentimental femininity comes full circle to produce the woman who takes
the whip hand. The whipping lady is the Janus face of sentimental masculinity:
she is what happens when men leave their proper cultural position empty. For the
parliamentarians, the lady who whips both shows how sensibility may go awry
when decanted into the weaker, feminine vessel and creates a vessel for sentiment
gone wrong that *cannot,* by virtue of their gender, be occupied by masculine MPs.
Notwithstanding the prominent role played by the barbarically whipping white
West Indian lady in the sensational testimony before the select committee, she
all but vanishes in the parliamentary debates. And, of course, like the enslaved
human beings said to excite these feelings, she never appeared in person before
the British Parliament.

   Notwithstanding Wollstonecraft's attacks on sentimentality in the *Vindications,* in later works such as her novel *Maria, or the Wrongs of Woman* (published
in 1798), she employs sentimental figures to exhibit "the misery and oppression,
peculiar to women, that arise out of the partial laws and customs of society" and
to move her readers to right action.[105] It was, oddly enough, Wollstonecraft's rival Anna Letitia Barbauld who ultimately declared sentimental politics dead.[106]
Barbauld's "Epistle to William Wilberforce, Esq. On the Rejection of the Bill for

abolishing the Slave Trade" serves as a kind of obituary for the abolition movement. Notably, Barbauld does not claim that sentimental tropes have failed; the horrors of African suffering have indeed been drawn home to the reader:

> The Preacher, Poet, Senator in vain
>
> Has rattled in her [Britain's] sight the Negro's chain;
>
> With his deep groans assail'd her startled ear,
>
> And rent the veil that hid his constant tear;
>
> Forc'd her averted eyes his stripes to scan,
>
> Beneath the bloody scourge laid bare the man,
>
> Claim'd Pity's tear, urg'd Conscience' [*sic*] strong controul,
>
> And flash'd conviction on her shrinking soul.[107]

The religious, literary, and political enjoinders of Preacher, Poet, and Senator have "assail'd" the public with images of the suffering slave, rending the "veil that hid his constant tear" and compelling the reader to look upon the suffering she or he would prefer to ignore. The passage depicts the task of the abolitionist as itself a scourge: even as the whip tears away the clothing, so too has the abolitionist's rhetoric "laid bare the man." The "constant tear" of the slave has "Claim'd Pity's tear," and yet even the labors of the "soon awak'd" Muse have not sparked political action (11). The British public understands exactly what is happening and remains tenaciously quiescent: "She [Britain] knows and she persists—Still Afric bleeds, / Uncheck'd, the human traffic still proceeds" (15–16). What might be called Barbauld's critique of cynical reason offers us a nation of individuals who "know very well what they are doing, but still, they are doing it."[108] Inasmuch as the sentimental text enables the reader to pay the tribute of a tear and thus to dismiss his culpable participation in the broader system, sentimentality becomes part of the reproduction of the very ideology it ostensibly attacks.

Julie Ellison argues that "Barbauld replaces the conventions of sensibility, which rely on vicarious emotion to induce pity, with the threat of contagious corruption."[109] And yet the rhetoric of contagion does not supplant but rather exploits the sentimental model of mobile feeling. If sensibility enables the passage of sentiment from one bosom to another, in Barbauld's poem, infectious feeling turns to the debased and sexualized contagion of minds and bodies:

> Each vice, to minds deprav'd by bondage known,
>
> With sure contagion fastens on his own;
>
> In sickly languor melts his nerveless frame,

And blows to rage impetuous Passion's flame:

Fermenting swift, the fiery venom gains

The milky innocence of infant veins. (47–52)

The symptoms of decadence bear all the markings of sensibility gone bad. Bondage leaves slave and master alike depraved, as the passage waffles between sexual excess and effeminate impotence, the "rage" of "impetuous Passion" and the "sickly languor" of the exhausted, "nerveless frame." Corruption travels across generations, converting "milky innocence" into venomous blood.

The imagery of the degeneration and contagion pervades Barbauld's description of the languishing "pale Beauty," who has been alternately identified as a decadent Briton or a corrupt Creole:[110]

Lo! where reclin'd, pale Beauty courts the breeze,

Diffus'd on sofas of voluptuous ease;

With anxious awe, her menial train around,

Catch her faint whispers of half-utter'd sound;

See her, in monstrous fellowship, unite

At once the Scythian, and the Sybarite;

Blending repugnant vices, misally'd,

Which *frugal* nature purpos'd to divide;

See her, with indolence to fierceness join'd,

Of body delicate, infirm of mind,

With languid tones imperious mandates urge;

With arm recumbent wield the household scourge;

And with unruffled mien, and placid sounds,

Contriving torture, and inflicting wounds. (57–70)

The echoes of Pope's *Rape of the Lock* render the "pale Beauty" a debased version of Belinda, the very figure of feminine sensibility gone wrong; her "faint whispers of half-utter'd sound," her "body delicate, infirm of mind," turn the (overly) refined body and comportment of the lady of feeling into an unnatural and wasted shell. The reader is enjoined to "see" the vices of a decadent civilization made visible in the lady's degenerate form; in her body, the luxurious Sybarite and the Scythian whose martial virility has degenerated into effeminacy unite. As the embodiment of *masculinity* (Sybarites and Scythians) gone wrong, the white mistress scrambles conventional gender categories. Like the whipping Creole woman in the parliamentary testimony and in Wollstonecraft's polemic, Barbauld's Beauty exists on a continuum with the domestic lady. If she urges "imperious mandates," it is with languid tones; if she "wield[s] the household scourge," it is "with arm recumbent."

For Barbauld, these degenerate men and women betray the price of empire. Colonial practices lead to metropolitan decadence and moral degeneracy, so that "injur'd Afric, by herself redrest, / Darts her own serpents at her Tyrant's breast" (45–46). Not even self-interest can check Britons' self-destructive seeking, as the "seasoned tools of Avarice prevail" (25). "By foreign wealth are British morals chang'd, / And Afric's sons, and India's, smile aveng'd" (104–5). If, as Kaul has noted, the colonial subject here "emerges as the shadowy, triumphant, agent of British degeneration" (Kaul, 263), he or she, in the guise of the slave, also becomes the occasion for the individual abolitionist to redeem himself (if not the nation). Barbauld's praise for Wilberforce and other members of the "generous band! / Whose efforts yet arrest Heav'n's lifted hand" (110–11) falters into a defeatist stance: "seek no more to break a Nation's fall / For ye have saved yourselves—and that is all" (116–17). While failing to save the slave, the abolitionist succeeds in saving himself.

The test of the African's humanity invariably boomerangs back upon the speakers: "it is we," Wilberforce declaimed in a speech of 1792 before the House of Commons, "that must confess ourselves deficient in tenderness. From these despised beings, whom we would degrade to the level of the brute creation, let us discover what it is to have human feelings; let us learn from them the mystery of compassion, and borrow the sympathies of a nature superior in sensibility to our own."[111] In exalting the victimized slave to the position of sentimental template, Wilberforce shoves the burden of self-correction onto the shoulders of the disenfranchised ("Teach me how not to be racist"). Britons must "borrow" back from the slave the very humanity that the slave trade has sought to stamp out. What makes the identification between Wilberforce and the slave sentimental in this case is that it substitutes the recognition of human kinship for acknowledgment of structural complicity. For the MP is not like the slave; he seeks his likeness in the slave to avoid recognizing his likeness to the master.

Reversible Figures

> We have seen that the native never ceases to dream of putting
> himself in the place of the settler—not of becoming the settler
> but of substituting himself for the settler.
>   —*Frantz Fanon*, The Wretched of the Earth

This chapter has addressed the ways in which different types of representation facilitated the conversion of humans into chattel slaves and the abolitionists' efforts to reverse them. In closing, it seems appropriate to turn to the points where the invitation to MPs to see themselves in the mirroring visage of the slave threatened to become reciprocal. The African slave who sought out his image in the form of the British master could raise a fearsome specter, Whitbread warned in a speech before the Commons in 1792. Whitbread used Shylock's speech from Shakespeare's *Merchant of Venice* to give a voice to the silent figure of the slave:

> The cruelties practised by the blacks in St. Domingo they have learned from their oppressive masters:—"Hath not an African eyes? Hath not an African hands, organs, dimensions, senses, passions? Is he not fed with the same food, hurt with the same weapons, subject to the same diseases, healed by the same means, warmed and cooled by the same summer and winter as we are? If you prick him, does he not bleed? If you tickle him, does he not laugh? If you poison him, does he not die? And if you wrong him, shall he not revenge? If he is like you in the rest, he will resemble you in that. If an African wrong a white man, what is his humility?—Revenge. If a white man wrong an African, what should his sufferance be by our example? Why, revenge. The cruelty you teach him, he will execute.—But I fear it is not possible to better the instruction."[112]

An absolute symmetry between master and slave would lead to carnage, not communion. For at the heart of the debates was the possibility of a revolt by these objects of feeling, their claim to become subjects in the political rather than the sentimental sense of the word. What if the slaves put a radical construction on the self-dramatizing proclamations of the parliamentarians? "The negroes," the duke of Chandos remarked, "read the English newspapers as constantly as the ships from England came in; and from what was then doing [in Parliament], they would conclude their final emancipation was at hand" (27.647). Sir James Johnstone noted that in Grenada "the common exclamations among them [the slaves] were, 'Mr. Wilberforce for negro! Mr. Fox for negro! The Parliament for negro! God Almighty for negro!'" (27.505), but he did not question whether the slaves might circumvent such indirect representation and seize these rights for themselves. In seeking to tether the slave's humanity to Britons' acknowledgment thereof, the parliamentarians block out the possibility that the slave might claim humanity without reference to their beneficent gaze.

The clamor for abolition subsided before the specter of revolution in the early 1790s. Its association with radical ideas of equality alarmed those eyeing the rising tide of violence in revolutionary France and the emergence of popular radicalism (English Jacobinism) in Britain. (One writer alluded to "the J A C O B I N S of E N G L A N D, the *Wilberforces*, the *Coopers*, the *Paines*, the *Clarksons.*")[113] The St. Domingue (Haitian) Revolution in 1791 nourished fears that abolition might lead to slave insurrections in the British sugar islands as well. Although a vote in the House of Commons in 1792 resolved on a gradual abolition of the trade, the Lords rejected the resolution. The abolitionist campaign dwindled in the face of the war with France declared in 1793, the difficulty of collating the interests of the Commons and the Lords, and a generalized fear that public expression would overturn the social order altogether.

In confining their deliberations to the abolition of the slave trade, parliamentary anti-slavery advocates sheered away from questions of emancipation. By defining humanity in sentimental terms, the speakers avoided constituting the (potentially) emancipated slave as a rights-bearing individual with a claim to liberty, autonomy, self-ownership. Sentimental feeling allowed the parliamentarians to ratchet the enslaved Africans into the category of the human without admitting them to the rights of juridical or civil subjects. "No man," Wilberforce proclaimed, "could in reality be their friend, who proposed any thing that could lead them to hope for their emancipation. The way to alleviate their misery was, to render them attached to their masters, governors, and leaders" (29.1061). The slave of feeling was not a citizen: "they had the same feelings, and even stronger affections than our own," Wilberforce insisted, "but their minds were uninformed, and their moral characters were altogether debased. Men, in this state, were almost incapacitated for the reception of civil rights."[114] The protracted degradation of the slaves barred them from political equality. Indeed, it reduced them to unconscious bodies. Thus Wilberforce describes the restoration of the slave to civil status as the resuscitation of a fainting body: "The first return of life after a swoon, was commonly a convulsion, dangerous, at once, to the party himself, and to all around him. Such, in the case of the Slaves, Mr. Wilberforce feared might be the consequence of a sudden communication of the consciousness of civil rights. This was a feeling it would be dangerous to impart, till you should release them from such humiliating and ignominious distinctions, as, with that consciousness, they would never endure."[115] The slave about whom one has feelings does not possess feelings or consciousness of his own; he must wait until these feelings are "imparted" to him. The attribution of lyric subjectivity does not translate into the attainment of political subjectivity.

Acts of sympathetic substitution may imperil the sympathetic object by usurping or ventriloquizing the position of the suffering other. Such sympathetic interchanges may, however, also end by inviting yet another form of exchange:

between the place of the master and that of the slave, the supplanting of sympathetic reciprocity with the quid pro quo of the slave's vengeance. The next chapter turns to these revolutionary possibilities in the abbé Raynal's widely read history of European colonial contact, the *Histoire des deux Indes*. Whether in the form of spiritual accountability in the hereafter or the immediate and violent reprisals of a slave revolt, the transactions that made the slave into chattel were eventually translated into the moral price to be paid for the violation of the slave's rights to self and liberty. For pro- and anti-slavery writers alike, the anxieties about the injustice of the trade, or the incommensurability of price and person, were ultimately superseded by terror in the face of another kind of reckoning.

CHAPTER FIVE

Global Commerce in Raynal's
Histoire des deux Indes

In the opening paragraphs of his *Histoire philosophique et politique des éta-blissements et du commerce des Européens dans les deux Indes,* the abbé Raynal stakes out an Archimedean point from which he claims to compose his text: "Raised above all human considerations," he writes, "it is there we soar above the atmosphere, and behold the globe beneath us."[1] With the planet at his feet, aloof from its petty prejudices and self-interested pursuits, Raynal can deliver the world to the reader in one comprehensive glance, diminished in scale but unified in form. Raynal's imaginary purchase point above the globe allows him to weigh impartially the value of kings and slaves, executioners and victims; he is able to depict the currents governing global history, creating a rapprochement between causes and consequences across space and time. "Divested from passions and prejudice" and stripped of the historical fingerprints of nation, religion, and occupation, Raynal's first-person narrator is a kind of degree-zero human being, a citizen of the world, above the partiality of passions, the sway of profit, the prejudice of personal interest (1.intro.3; 1.3). Yet Raynal's philosophe is no nail-paring deity, indifferent to the petty squabbles of mice and men. One climbs aloft the better to weep:

> From thence it is that we let fall our tears upon persecuted genius, upon talents ne-glected, and upon virtue in distress. From thence it is, that we pour forth impre-cations on those who deceive mankind, and those who oppress them and devote them to ignominy. From thence it is that we see the proud head of the tyrant hum-bled and covered with dust, while the modest front [i.e., brow] of the just man reaches to the vault of the skies. From thence it is, that I have been enabled to cry out, I am free, and feel myself upon a level with the subject I treat.[2]

Having shaken off worldly interests, Raynal's philosophe assumes two relations to the globe: that of an all-seeing eye that dispassionately seeks out universal truth and that of the engaged, enlightened man of feeling, bent on justice and the vindication of the rights of those wronged by history.

Yet a bird's-eye perspective on the globe is by no means exhaustive. From such heights, one glimpses the results of progress without the origins, the effects of historical change without their apparent cause. Even spread before Raynal's eagle eye, the world poses as many questions as it answers:

> It is from thence, in a word, that, viewing [*voyant à mes pieds*] those beautiful regions, in which the arts and sciences flourish, and which have been for so long a time obscured by ignorance and barbarism, I have said to myself: Who is it that hath digged these canals? Who is it that hath dried up these plains? Who is it that hath founded these cities? Who is it that hath collected, clothed, and civilized these people? Then have I heard the voice of all the enlightened men among them, who have answered: This is the effect of commerce [*c'est le commerce, c'est le commerce*].
> (1.intro.4; 1.4)

The force that has dissipated barbarism, founded cities, and united peoples proves to be, not a person, but a system that embraces everything in its activity. Superseding the agency of any one individual or any one set of people, commerce is proclaimed by enlightened voices to be the cause and engine of global change across history.

But only the progressive, transformative powers of commerce are visible from above. The bird's-eye perspective obscures the devastation wrought by the pursuit of wealth in the colonies—the effects of the very commerce Raynal would celebrate. The singular, universal perspective of Raynal's omnivoyant, errant narrator dissolves before a cacophony of voices, as the authoritative chorus of enlightened men ("c'est le commerce, c'est le commerce") is supplanted by the apostrophized and ventriloquized victims of European colonization. Throughout the *Histoire*, the reader is invited to relinquish the comprehensive gaze of the philosophe for the partial, sentimental vision of the man of feeling. It is not the objective stance of Raynal's omnivoyant philosophe but rather the fractured outpourings of the sentimental subject that furnish the social glue that holds the globe together.

This chapter asks how Raynal uses the sentimental to imagine the global, as well as what the global was imagined to be. The first part of my argument explores Raynal's depiction of commerce as an agent of global unification. As a system, Raynal's global economy is more than the sum of its parts; it cannot be fully understood through analogies with individual behavior. Raynal thus personifies abstractions like commerce and collective entities like nations in order to elaborate a concept of commercial causality and individual accountability able to act over great distances. Such personifications create the means of imagining agency in a world system in which effective reach outstrips imaginative grasp. The second part of the argument turns to the way Raynal's apostrophes to the victims and perpetrators of colonization draw home the effects of commerce to metropolitan readers. The text alternately addresses and lends a voice to (among others) the infanticidal women of the Orinoco, rapacious Spaniards and brutalized Native Americans, the ancestors of the Dutch colonists in the Cape and future generations called upon to judge the deeds of the present time. Addressed both to colonized and colonizer, written from the point of view of both victim and executioner, Raynal's text creates a shared tabula on which figures divided by space and time can communicate, as the ostensibly spontaneous torrents of sentimental emotion attest to the existence of a common humanity. It is the sentimental tropes that personalize history—personify it—and make possible a properly philosophical response.

The philosophe pours his heart out into a variety of speaking vessels, punctuating his text with speeches by Native Americans, Africans, Batavians (i.e., Indonesians), and slaves, who both articulate the claims of colonial populations to political and literary representation and invite metropolitan readers to recognize their own oppression in the guise of another.[3] Yet the ventriloquism of these speaking others—the sentimental animation of the oppressed—does not necessarily confer historical agency. To have a voice in the *Histoire* is not necessarily to have a history. Among the questions we should ask of the *Histoire*, J. G. A. Pocock notes, "is what capacity its authors display for depicting the others in all these encounters as having histories of their own and acting in them. Are they unintelligible to the philosophe; are they merely those Others about whom we now write so much?"[4] By reinforcing a historiographical divide between the agents of historical narrative and its passive victims, the rhetorical and affective constitution of sentimental subjects in the *Histoire* helps consolidate the image of indigenous populations as "people without history." Although the text's assorted victims are embroiled in sentimental exchanges with the feeling narrator, they are barred from equal partnership in commerce, progress, and history. What Johannes Fabian famously calls the "denial of coevalness" relegates whole groups to an anterior phase in a progressive history that takes European commercial society as its endpoint.[5] Inasmuch as the timelessness of the *Histoire*'s sentimental figures feeds into the teleological model of history that authorizes nineteenth-century imperial ventures, these figures help justify the very empire they ostensibly resist.

Commerce as the Motor of the World

At more than 4,800 octavo pages in its third edition of 1780, the *Histoire* constitutes one of the great Enlightenment attempts to represent global commerce in a systematic fashion. Raynal methodically catalogues the marketable commodities of each territory; expatiates on the uses, abuses, and deficiencies of a wide array of indigenous products, and suggests ways to run factories and plantations more efficiently—which implicitly involves more effective exploitation of available resources (natural and human). At the same time, the text speaks out against the results of this commerce: the exploitation and annihilation of native populations, the toppling of indigenous governments, the heedless and insatiable pursuit of profit, the disregard for Enlightenment principles of equality, freedom, and property.[6] Raynal's indictment of the horrors of slavery in the French Antilles thus nestles against proposals for the amelioration of slavery as the best means to forestall revolution.

The text's focus on the mobility of persons, goods, and ideas across geopolitical frontiers exposes its antecedents in commerce manuals like Jacques Savary's *Le parfait négociant, ou, Instruction générale pour ce qui regarde le commerce* (1675); philosophical histories like Voltaire's *Le Siècle de Louis le Grand* (1751) and Montesquieu's *De l'esprit des lois* (1748); and collections of voyages like the abbé Prévost's *Histoire générale des voyages* (1746–89). Indeed, the transnational content of the *Histoire* is echoed in the history of its reception: the book itself travels around the globe as commodity, as *porte-parole* of revolutionary principles, as manual of colonial conquest, and as protest against its consequences. The text became one of the international best sellers of the eighteenth century, with over seventy French editions (legitimate and pirated), and translations into English, Spanish, Italian, Dutch, German, Russian, Hungarian, and Polish.[7] Napoleon notoriously carried it with him on his Egyptian campaign in 1798.

A brief résumé of the text's history is perhaps merited. The seven-volume first edition appeared anonymously in 1772 with a Dutch imprint dated 1770; it was followed by a second edition in 1774 and a substantially revised third edition in 1780. All three versions were the labor of multiple hands. Raynal had an enormous network of informants and correspondents from Russia to North America from whom he obtained archival records, statistics, journal articles, and accounts of voyages. He pillaged (with and without permission) from Buffon, Cornelius de Pauw, Tom Paine, Jean-Baptiste Labat, Pierre-François-Xavier de Charlevoix, and Jean-Baptiste du Tertre, among others, while orchestrating the participation of numerous unacknowledged contributors, including Diderot, Antoine-Laurent de Jussieu, Alexandre Deleyre, Jean de Pechméja, Jean-François de Saint-Lambert, and Jacques-André Naigeon. Such ghostwriters were and are called *nègres* in French.[8] Notwithstanding its collaborative origins, this *is* indisputably a book with an author: it was Raynal's body that stood as the pledge of his accountability for the text following its condemnation by the Paris parlement in 1781. The book was burned by the executioner and orders were issued for Raynal's arrest, sending the author into exile and the book to the top of the charts.

Not unlike the myriad personifications discussed in this chapter, Raynal as author gives voice to a spirit that ostensibly supersedes the mere individual, condensing the myriad hands behind the text into one. As Diderot put it in his *Lettre apologétique de l'abbé Raynal à M. Grimm,* "it is not a subject, it is a deputy of the nation who speaks. It is the organ of virtue, of reason, of equity, of humanity, of justice, of clemency, of the law."[9] Although many of the examples in this chapter are drawn from the some 700 pages Diderot contributed to the 1780 edition, I allude to the text as Raynal's throughout the chapter.[10] Simply to call the text Diderot's, as some critics have, is to occlude the complex history outlined above, while parsing the contributions imposes an artificial coherence upon the different strands of argument by attributing, for example, the radical bits to Diderot and the conciliatory passages to Raynal. Nevertheless, Diderot's participation is by no means immaterial to the argument of this chapter. The *Histoire* employs many of the rhetorical strategies used in Diderot's *Supplément au voyage de Bougainville* (written ca. 1772); its use of tableaux, its mediated invitations to identify with isolated suffering figures, and its deliberate incitement of feeling as a call to collective action draw on both Diderot's theoretical considerations of the sentimental and his experiments with the mode in, for example, *Le fils naturel* (1757) and *La religieuse* (1760). As noted in the discussion of the elegy to Eliza Draper in Chapter 2, the collective authorship of the *Histoire* poses questions both about the authenticity of the sentimental effusions and about the identity or consistency of the *moi* who surfaces intermittently throughout the text, "usually," Pocock dryly notes, "in floods of tears."[11]

The *Histoire*'s sudden shifts from how-to tips for colonial administrators to thundering indictments of colonial policies to sentimental set pieces make it difficult to assign a consistent position to the narrator, although the division of the text according to spheres of European domination and conquest—and the subdivision of these sections by European power—structures the work around a resolutely Western center. As the full title of the book suggests, Europe—"that part of the globe which has most influence over the rest [*qui agit le plus sur toutes les autres*]" (6.1.198; 6.239)—is depicted as the agent and prime mover behind all commercial activity. The text's geographical divisions between Europe and the two Indies also reify an emerging distinction between the timeless world of anthropology and the (progressive) diachrony of history described by Michèle Duchet in *Anthropologie et histoire au siècle des lumières*, in which, as Srinivas Aravamudan puts it, "the non-European parts of the world that enter history do so as objects acted upon by European imperial agents."[12] The four corners of the world are collapsed into the "two Indies," with the European nations serving as rapacious *entremetteurs* between them. If this is a globe, it is one already spatially organized according to commercial precepts, fragmented into a hierarchy of parts.

These parts are unified through the extraordinary mobility of Raynal's philosophe narrator (as we saw above) and by the all-powerful force of commerce: "By pervading the earth, by crossing the seas, by raising the obstacles which opposed themselves to the intercourse of nations, by extending the sphere of wants, and the thirst of enjoyments, it [commerce] multiplies labour, it encourages industry; and becomes, in some measure, the moving principle of the world [*le moteur du monde*]." The engine and fairy godmother of history, commerce relentlessly breaks down borders, drawing persons into reciprocal exchanges that forge connections by satisfying mutual needs. "Commerce," Raynal tells us, "produces nothing of itself; for it is not of a plastic nature [*il n'est pas créateur*]." It is an agent that moves the unequally distributed goods of nature among nations, producing plenitude where there was lack. It giveth and it taketh away from individuals in a zero-sum game of reciprocity: through commerce, "a town, a province, a nation, a part of the globe are disencumbered of what is useless to them; and receive what they are in want of. It is perpetually engaged in supplying the respective wants of men" (19.6.140–41; 19.179). Seen from this point of view, commerce fosters sociability by obliging men to exchange; even where it contains the nefarious ingredients of avarice and self-interest, it silently reconciles parties to each other.[13]

Serenely confident of the powers of free trade, Raynal regards it as the harbinger of world peace. "Commerce is established without difficulty among men who have reciprocal wants," he announces, "and they soon accustom themselves to consider, as friends and as brethren, those whom interest or other motives have brought into their country" (9.1.3; 9.360). No coercive structure, no inequity, mars Raynal's happy vision of collective reciprocity. The needs and desires of the whole are consonant with those of the parts. "Universal society exists as well for the common interest of the whole, as by the mutual interest [*l'intérêt réciproque*] of all the individuals that compose it. An increase of felicity must, therefore, result from a general intercourse" (5.33.154–55; 5.189). Raynal does not acknowledge the existence of surplus value or the possibility that exchanges result in disequilibrium. Indeed, where inequity exists, it stems from restrictions on trade that hamper the workings of the system as a whole. Thus Raynal advocates the removal of all protective trade barriers: "Would you wish to put an end to the calamities which ill-contrived plans [*des systêmes mal combinés*] have brought upon the whole earth, you must pull down the fatal walls with which they [nations] have encompassed themselves" (19.6.167; 19.213).

Commerce, for Raynal, "supposes an inclination and a liberty between all nations to make every exchange that can contribute to their mutual satisfaction. The inclination and the liberty of procuring enjoyments [*Désir de jouir, liberté de jouir*] are the only two springs of industry, and the only two principles of social intercourse among men" (5.33.156; 5.191). Commerce thus depends upon and promotes universal and benevolent sentiments through complementary relations of supply and demand, although foreshadowed in Raynal's exuberant "désir de jouir, liberté de jouir" are intimations of a freedom unchecked by acknowledgment of other's rights. Raynal's initial jubilance at the potential benefits to all nations of a "general intercourse [*échange mutuel*] of opinions, laws and customs, diseases and remedies, virtues and vices" (1.intro.2; 1.2) opens up onto a darker prospect. Commerce may unite the globe, but it also drives peoples apart; it is, for Raynal, simultaneously the herald of civilization and the purveyor of European diseases, weapons, and vices.

At the same time as the movement of goods creates and expresses connections among discrete peoples, the desire to possess singles out the individual as self-interested, sundering him from all others. "[I]f the spirit of commerce unites nations," as Montesquieu had observed earlier in the century, "it does not in the same manner unite individuals. We see, that in countries where the people move only by the spirit of commerce, they make a traffick of all the humane, all the moral virtues; the most trifling things, those which humanity would demand, are there done, or there given, only for money."[14] Raynal likewise acknowledges that commerce produces two diametrically opposed relations between persons: it both invites interchange, the commingling of desire necessary for giving and getting, *and* carves out an inscribed sphere from which the covetous consumer clutches his goods to himself while glaring at others' possessions in baleful avidity. The dazzling array of products that colonial expansion thrusts onto European markets transforms both the individual desiring subject and what might be called national spirit. If, as Raynal contends, "the discovery of a new species of sensations excited a desire of preserving them, and a propensity to find out others [*la cu-riosité d'en imaginer d'une autre espèce*]" (5.33.156; 5.190), the influx of goods and pleasures changes the way the consumer desires and acquires in ways that menace Raynal's depiction of commerce as a series of ostensibly sociable exchanges. Commerce placates existing desires in a global symbiosis but invents novel appetites, easily whetted and never cloyed, that prove to be insatiable in their quest for new objects. On the one hand, exchange is said to foster mutuality, parity, equity; on the other, the engine that drives trade is the accumulation of surplus wrung from another's loss.

Once one moves beyond reasoned need, the equilibrium that renders exchanges fair tips over into a quest for *more* at all costs. Europeans have forgotten that "nature hath set certain bounds to the felicity of every considerable portion of the human species, beyond which we have nearly as much to lose as to gain" (6.23.320; 6.395). Untempered by reason, the drive to acquire will produce the same scenes of devastation in every nation touched by the Europeans: "they will be uninterruptedly repeat[ed] in those immense regions which remain for us to go over. The sword will never be blunted; we shall not see it stop 'till it meets with no more victims to strike" (7.1.2; 7.2–3). The thirst for gold feeds a lust for blood. Reduced to the blades they wield, Europeans destroy everything in their path until there is nothing left to devour.

Sociable exchange crumbles before the mimetic nature of desire; the neat proposition that "you want what I don't want" and vice versa falters before a structure in which my desire is incited and stoked by your desire. The idealized dyad of reciprocal and zero-sum exchange in which both parties get and give what they want mutates into a triangle of competitive avarice. Scarcity creates competition for the same objects. Social bonds strain and crack before these burgeoning appetites: "In vain have society, morality, and politics, been improved amongst us: those distant countries have only been witnesses of our rapaciousness, our restlessness, our tyranny" (5.16.77–78; 5.97). Commercial reciprocity falters before competitive desire for the same thing.[15] "Envy," as Johnson's Imlac succinctly words it, "is commonly reciprocal."[16]

Raynal grapples with this tension at the heart of commerce by oscillating between an attempt to depict commerce as a global system and its local and particular effects. Yet how is one to conjoin the limited and partial vision offered by discrete acts of exchange to a notion of a unified globe? Mere compilation or accumulation does not produce a sense of the global. The pages consecrated to the uses and abuses of rubber or the possible utility of the breadfruit do not offer a view of the interconnectedness of the world. The sheer profusion of detail defeats a unified perspective; the catalogues of heterogeneous goods at times prod the reader into a paratactic model of reading in which one cannot see the forest for the trees. How can one move from the sequential nature of the encyclopedic catalog—even one with pretensions to a Bouvard and Pécuchet–like exhaustiveness—to something approaching a global or synthetic perspective?

Raynal's analysis uses the reasoned causality of commerce to fetch objects home to the imagination, enabling individuals to perceive connections between themselves and people far away, between actions in one place and consequences elsewhere. In much the same way, Adam Smith invites us in *The Theory of Moral Sentiments* to contemplate the possibility that "the great empire of China, with all its myriads of inhabitants, was suddenly swallowed up by an earthquake."[17] A man of humanity in Europe would, Smith argues, express every necessary and correct sentiment upon hearing the news: "he would make many melancholy reflections upon the precariousness of human life, and the vanity of all the labours of man. . . . He would too, perhaps, if he was a man of speculation, enter into many reasonings concerning the effects which this disaster might produce upon the commerce of Europe, and the trade and business of the world in general." Yet the ability to make these connections is a necessary but insufficient condition for humane feelings. As Smith points out, the smallest injury to the self supersedes the catastrophes of others. "If he was to lose his little finger to-morrow, he would not sleep to-night; but, provided he never saw them, he will snore with the most profound security over the ruin of a hundred millions of his brethren" (136). Space and time annihilate the commonality of feeling that excites compassion, because "the sentiment of humanity" is dissipated when given too broad a field. The intensity of feeling exists in direct proportion to the proximity of its object. Smith's little finger dwarfs the death of millions.

Smith's man of "speculation" is significantly not a philosopher but a merchant, and it is commerce, for Raynal as for Smith, that allows the individual to associate local deeds with remote consequences. As Thomas Haskell has controversially argued of the swelling of abolitionist sentiment at the close of the eighteenth century, commerce helps inculcate a new humanitarian sensibility. By obliging merchants to keep promises and to trust others to do the same, extensive trade networks enlarge the perceived extent of an individual's causal power in both self-interested and in altruistic ways: "what links the capitalist market to a new [humanitarian] sensibility," Haskell argues, "is not class interest so much as the power of market discipline to inculcate altered perceptions of causation in human affairs."[18] Once the abstract connections made by the market liberate causality from the restraints of contiguity, things and people need no longer be near to be dear. Commerce forces people to think beyond their parochial bounds; it enables them to envision agency over intervals of time and space. Random acts of kindness do not perform themselves; the individual must not only feel connected to the suffering other but also be able to recognize his or her relation to a collective body able to act over great distances. To "pay it forward," one must have an entity able to disburse the payment. Commerce provides the tools to envision this entity.

The ideal aims and ends of commerce do not, however, necessarily reflect the real practices of trade and of empire: dispatches between metropolitan clerks and colonial factors betray suspicion, skepticism, and paranoia, the fear of insufficient control rather than serene faith in the causal links between colony and metropole. The correspondence and records of the East India Company, for example, are riddled with reprimands for shoddy bookkeeping and questions about fishy transactions and fudged accounts.[19] Nor is the consciousness fostered by the causal reasoning of commerce distinguished by much feeling or sensitivity. Smith's "man of humanity," for example, doesn't feel at all: he falls back on a set of moral *sententiae* (the precariousness of human life, the vanity of the labors of man), but never becomes absorbed in the plight of others. The market may expand the imagined sphere of individual power, but it does not necessarily create right-thinking men and women. The pseudonymous Africanus furnishes an instructive counterexample to Smith in his *Remarks on the Slave Trade:*

> As the death of thousands in battle is often read of almost without concern, so the cruelties of the Slave Trade from Africa to the West-Indies has been talked of (though we hope it will be so no longer) with an indifference, common to other commercial considerations. A cargo of slaves, like a cargo of lumber, may have foundered at sea without exciting a sigh, if it were but insured; or if it arrived at its destined port, the condemnation of thousands of Human Beings, to the rank and labour of brutes, without any prospect of release, may have been considered as a consequence of state policy, and justified by the plea of commercial necessity.[20]

Haskell's commercial imagination here seizes upon persons and things as goods; it reinforces rather than undermines inhumane practices. The "cargo of slaves" is interchangeable with the "cargo of lumber," a matter of pecuniary rather than personal interest. Complicity with broader structures of exploitation is underwritten by the poverty of the imagination; to be felt, loss must be made personal. Without the imaginative labor that stirs the mind to right action by compelling it to trace the origins, nature or fate of an object, readers can easily forget that the commodities in the slave trade are human. A kind of emotional entropy dilutes sympathy over distance, while disbelief in what is not witnessed furnishes an alibi of ignorance.

The intense feelings inspired by sentimental reading are made possible by the *impression* of proximity. Only by particularizing objects and drawing them close to home can the individual come to feel with the kind of intensity that moves to right action. Raynal offers the reader the tools to think about the remote consequences of local deeds by concretizing the effects of the market as particular persons and specific scenes. Thus in his discussion of slavery, Raynal appeals to his interlocutor as a witness. "Behold," he commands,

> Behold that proprietor of a vessel, who leaning upon his desk, and with the pen in his hand, regulates the number of enormities he may cause to be committed on the Coasts of Guinea; who considers at leisure, what number of firelocks he shall want to obtain one Negro, what fetters will be necessary to keep him chained on board his ship, what whips will be required to make him work; who calculates with coolness, every drop of blood which the slave must necessarily expend in labour for him, and how much it will produce; who considers whether a Negro woman will be of more advantage to him by her feeble labours, or by going through the dangers of child-birth. You shudder! (11.24.123; 11.294–95)

The leisurely musing of the shipowner on the distant violent acts of which he is the origin and agent makes the sanctuary of his study in Europe into a stark contrast with the objects of his reflections: whips, guns, chains, blood. This passage combines abstract calculation and concrete detail to produce a powerful rhetorical effect on its interpellated reader, the "you" who is called upon to "behold" and "shudder." The passage describes a series of equivalencies: between drops of blood and the price paid for the slave, between the manual and reproductive labor of a slave woman, between the anodyne pen strokes that record the shipowner's orders and their horrific execution abroad. The passage meticulously traces the trajectory of *making* the slave: the material objects embroiled in the exchange, the chains required to subjugate the African, the weapons needed to enforce the master's dominance and to coerce the slave's labor. In a perverse sense, Raynal defetishizes the slave by recreating the material process of his or her production. The synecdoches of the gun, the whip, the chain, and the drop of blood represent in small the violence of a series of transactions. It is by fragmenting the big picture—the totality of the Atlantic trade—into concrete details and material objects that its enormity—its cost in human terms—is made legible.[21]

For Raynal, commerce not only creates a global system; it also furnishes the imaginative tools that enable readers to conceive of that system. Not unlike Raynal's omnivoyant philosophe, the merchant possesses the extraordinary capacity to consider the world as a whole: in tracing the progress of commercial peoples across the planet, he shows "the same understanding that Newton had to calculate the motion of the stars." The merchant "takes in both worlds at one view, and directs his operations upon an infinite variety of relative considerations, which it is seldom given to the statesman, or even to the philosopher, to comprehend and estimate. Nothing must escape him." He extrapolates from historical precedent—knowledge of a predictable chain of cause and effect—to recognize secondary and tertiary consequences across time and space. His calculations project beyond the immediate and the contiguous to account for "the effect that the fall of any European power in India, may have over Africa and America; the stagnation that may be produced in certain countries, by the blocking up of some channels of industry" (19.6.149–50; 19.190–92).

Yet even the merchant's ability to cast beyond the local does not itself constitute a global perspective. Although merchants, like kings and their counselors, command a view above the fray, their perspective is tainted by interest: "The politician is guided only by his views; the merchant by his interest. There is none but the philosopher who knows when to doubt; who is silent, when his knowledge fails him; and who tells the truth, when once he resolves to speak" (5.32.153; 5.187). The philosophe alone is impartial enough and feeling enough to paint a true picture of the world. Only he can put the raw material gleaned from voyagers and merchants into global perspective, and only once that work is done does its world historical significance become apparent.[22]

Raynal figures commerce both as a body and as the ligature that binds that body together. It creates and constitutes a system in which the parts cannot be dissevered from the whole. "Commerce," Raynal tells us, "connects people and fortunes together, and establishes the intercourse of exchanges. It is one entire whole, the several parts of which, attract, support, and balance each other. It resembles the human body, all the parts of which are affected, when one of them doth not fulfil the functions that were destined to it" (19.6.167; 19.212–13). Raynal's homeostatic commercial body is a far cry from the body politic of early political theory with its monarchical head and subordinated parts. The system here ("un tout dont les diverses parties s'attirent") has taken on a life of its own. It is like a body, yet it is more than a body. The parts are indissolubly connected, yet it is difficult to identify which part governs. There is something afoot in Raynal that cannot be described in terms of individual acts or sequential causal chains, but the vocabulary of systemic causality is not yet fully in place (which is part of what distinguishes Raynal's sense of the global from modern conceptualizations thereof.)[23]

Although the abstract connections made by the market allow one to conceive of noncontiguous causality, they do not necessarily enable individuals to imagine the remote consequences of their deeds. In an era in which global capacities surpass the intellectual and imaginative tools available to understand them, what is to make abstract and immaterial forces like commerce intelligible? Let us return to the tropes of personification and prosopopoeia discussed in Chapter 3. These figures, we saw, give shape to the invisible, abstract forces (of the economy, of religion, of a global market) that govern everyday life. They confer agency, form, and intention on things that lack readily comprehensible or tangible form. "Prosopopoeia," the *Encyclopédie* tells us, "represents things that are not; it opens tombs, summons spirits, resuscitates the dead, makes speak gods, the sky, the earth, peoples, cities, in a word, all real, abstract, imaginary beings."[24]

Systems like commerce need to be personified in order to be intelligible. "People know what they do," Foucault once remarked; "they frequently know why they do what they do; but what they don't know is what what they do does."[25] Walter Benn Michaels's gloss on this is useful for my purposes: personification, he notes, mediates between the fact that the economy is man-made, but that it is not a person (and is not even composed of people; it's a system, objective, autonomous). "[T]he desire to personify the economy," Michaels writes, "is the desire to bridge the gap between our actions and the consequences of our actions by imagining a person who does not do what we do but who does do what what we do does."[26] The need to explain how and why things happen fosters personifications. In the *Histoire,* personified abstractions—history, commerce, and ventriloquized voices that vehiculate collective intent—fetch and carry goods, ideas, and bodies from the far reaches of the globe. By imaginative proxy, they carry out the deeds performed by the ineffable forces of a systemic economy; they describe masses of people as if they were possessed of shared purposes. In the guise of such personifications, we witness not only the return of Cartesianism but also the limits of our capacity to envision global forces without the specter of some kind of agent.

Although "commerce" in Raynal's text is not a full-fledged personification like Milton's Sin, it functions as an agent of historical revolution. So, too, "nations" become personified collectives, with the capacity to intend, to choose, to

desire, to reflect. Greed stalks after commerce, dismantling the progress it brings:
"it seems as if from one region to another prosperity had been pursued by an evil
genius which speaks our several languages, and which diffuses the same calamities in all parts" (4.33.340; 4.431). Elsewhere Raynal condenses the emotions and
intentions that fuel self-interested trade into a "spirit of monopoly" that "in the
paroxysm of its phrensy," pronounces "at all times, and among all nations, the
following decree":

> Let my country perish, let the region I command perish likewise; perish the citi-
> zen and the foreigner; perish my associate, provided I can but enrich myself with
> his spoils. All parts of the universe are alike to me. When I have laid waste, ex-
> hausted, and impoverished one country, I shall always find another, to which I may
> carry my gold, and enjoy it in peace. (3.41.164; 3.207–8)

Impartial in its gluttony as it shifts from one set of victims to another, the "spirit
of monopoly" insatiably moves from one land to another, leaving devastation in
its wake. Likewise, the philosophe gives the power of speech to "private interest," taxing the British, those "privileged robbers," with the specter of revenge
(3.41.162–63; 3.205). By lending a voice to the underlying motives and nefarious
intentions of collective entities or abstractions, Raynal renders the broader economic system thinkable.

The sprawling nature of global commerce supersedes the agency of singular
individuals; many people may be implicated in the execution of the simplest
deed. If agency extends beyond the boundaries of the self, how is one to appraise
accountability on a grand scale? "The tyrant," Raynal reminds us, "can do nothing of himself; he is only the *primum mobile* of those efforts which all his subjects exert to their own mutual oppression. . . . [L]ike the blood which flows in
his veins, all crimes originate from his heart, and return thither as to their primary source" (11.24.128; 11.301). The figure of the tyrant simultaneously disguises the multitude of hands necessary to execute barbaric deeds and offers a
neat explanation for the impetus that propels masses of people into joint action.
We crystallize agency in singular figures to tender a sacrificial scapegoat to ap-
pease the consciences of all: "Caligula used to say, that if the whole human race
had but one head, he should have taken pleasure in cutting it off. Socrates would
have said, that if all crimes were heaped upon one head, that should be the one
which ought to be stricken off" (11.24.128–29; 11.301). The fancy that evil can be
localized (or demonized) in a particular vessel creates accountability for historical events, but it is not possible to identify the head from which all crimes spring,
any more than it is possible to isolate one aspect of the commercial system from

another. The messy workings of the world may not always be condensed into a solitary figure.

From a moral or ethical standpoint, Raynal argues, the deeds performed by nations should be appraised as if they were the acts of individuals. "The individual who should think of acting the same part in the midst of his country, which they [the great powers] do among other nations, would be looked upon as the most execrable of malefactors" (5.4.21; 5.26). Such analogies strip away the alibi of collective action. War crimes perpetrated by the many, Raynal argues, should be judged as if they were the acts of particular private people: "Any number of men, however considerable, coming into a foreign and unknow'n country, are to be considered only as one single man. Strength increases with numbers, but the right is still the same. If one or two hundred men can say, *this country belongs to us;* one man may say the same" (8.1.151–52; 8.192). Conquest is composed of numerous individual acts of murder; it amounts to collective theft. Justice should not be scaled to size; might does not make right. By condensing the acts of the many into a single figure representative of the multitude, Raynal makes the agency behind or within the system visible, creating the possibility of resistance and revolt. It is when individuals cannot see that systems are composed of and by individuals that they bow down before the yoke as if it were inevitable. "Multitudes of the human race," the *Histoire* tells us, "really believe themselves to be the property of a small number of men who oppress them" (1.8.77; 1.98). Whereas sentimental writers concentrate upon a single figure to magnify the reader's sense of his or her suffering, Raynal encapsulates the swarming activity of multitudes into a single figure in order to create both an accountable agent and, as we shall see below, a visible victim.

Although personifications turn abstractions into graspable entities, these personified abstractions may sprout legs and outrun us. "[T]he projection of historical agency onto formal abstractions that are anthropomorphized and given a life of their own," as Anne McClintock argues of terms like *discourse* and *ambivalence,* enables "social relations between humans [to] appear to metamorphize into structural relations between forms—through a formalist fetishism that effectively elides the messier questions of historical change and social activism."[27] Raynal tries to prevent relations between abstractions from supplanting relations between humans by inviting the victims of commerce and history to address kings and commoners, rapacious merchants and compassionate consumers, fanatical ecclesiasts and tolerant readers. He uses the trope of apostrophe in order to call into being colonial subjects able to display their wounds and to reclaim their rights. By moving the right-feeling reader to sympathetic tears,

Raynal seeks to produce a model of universal humanity that endures despite the failures of commercial reciprocity. The world that cannot be united by commerce can be drawn together in sentimental feeling.

Lachrymose Intolerance

Raynal's *oeil vivant* sheds tears. Copiously. "My view is to write history," he informs us, "and I almost always write it with my eyes bathed in tears" (7.1.1; 7.1). The fact that "the traces of our pen have been constantly marked with blood" means that "our heart hath . . . constantly been oppressed, agonized, and tor'n" (6.23.323; 6.398). Indeed, the atrocities committed by Europeans are so horrific that he is obliged to lay down his pen: "Let me be allowed to pause here for a moment. My eyes overflow with tears, and I can no longer discern what I am writing" (6.7.223; 6.270). The act of writing fuses with the process of historical representation, as the task of documenting the external world is superseded by the transcription of interior feeling. The narrator's description of his own affect is meant to be a lesson to the reader, instructing him or her in the proper or improper responses to the scenes described. Only interest, Raynal insists, can denature the feeling heart: "I have already said too much for the honest and feeling man. I shall never be able to say enough for the inhuman trader" (11.24.131; 11.304). The citizen of the world must also be a man of feeling.

In its solicitation of the reader's sensibilities, Raynal's mode of history writing is a far cry from Émile Benveniste's description of the modern *récit historique:* "The historian will never say *je* or *tu* or *maintenant*, because he will never make use of the formal apparatus of discourse, which resides primarily in the relationship of the persons: je: tu. . . . The events are set forth chronologically, as they occurred. [*Les événements sont posés comme ils se sont produits à mesure qu'ils apparaissent à l'horizon de l'histoire.*] No one speaks here; the events seem to narrate themselves."[28] The removal of personal address from history allows for events to appear to be the result of impersonal forces, documented by a dispassionate authority, removed from the here and now. The response solicited by the descriptions of events is not explicitly articulated within Benveniste's historical text. By contrast, the "I" of the *Histoire* who addresses "you" both stages his own response and invites the reader to join in.

The sentimental ploys Raynal devises allow his reader to reel the world home, dissolving the distance between colonial devastation and the scene of metropolitan reading. Split between a hypothetical colonial addressee and a metropolitan interlocutor, the text alternately calls for reform and revolt, for empathy and in-

surrection. Raynal's reader, a kind of affective yo-yo, is alternately invited to sympathize with the oppressed and to repudiate the role of the oppressor; to join an
audience of weeping witnesses and to engage in disinterested philosophical appraisal; to confer rights on others and to seize them for himself. The fiction of
sentimental solidarity would seem to negate Raynal's analysis of specific colonial
situations, as all victims of colonial oppression—the Hottentots, the Indians, the
Africans—assume a kind of formal equivalence in the text. Sentimentality tan-
talizingly holds out the promise of equity through feeling, as communal emotion
absorbs people into the global world without admitting them to the rights of autonomous subjects. (I return below to the way the text invites the oppressed to
rise up and seize political as well as affective privileges.)

The frontispiece to book 15 of the *Histoire* (fig. 5.1), which shows a group of
unarmed French sailors supplicating a benevolent Amerindian, stages one such
scene of intercultural sympathy for the consumption of a metropolitan audience.
The open-handed gestures of the Native American, who is surrounded by his
family rather than depicted as the isolated noble savage, neatly convert into a gift
of the continent to the encroaching French, while his welcoming pose and the
clutching hands of the child temper the potential threat implied by his superior
height and commanding position. By imagining these encounters as relations of
giving and receiving, supplicating and bestowing, such images disguise the violence of colonial contact by depicting it as an exchange between mutually benevolent peoples. Depicted in sentimental postures of helplessness, the sailors beg
rather than take, are passive victims rather than marauding conquerors. The
overt theatricality of the image reminds us that sentimental gestures are displayed signs of an internal disposition, contrived to prove that an "innate spirit
of benevolence" characterizes savages as well as civilized men (15.4.21; 15.446).
In such tableaux, as Jay Caplan has argued, "social relations are momentarily
both repaired and arrested; that is, they are *fixed.*"[29]

The scene is both captured as a tableau in the frontispiece and narrated in the
text; we are offered the freeze-frame of its entirety in the engraving and then
read the account of the event in sequential time. The lines Raynal places in the
mouth of his Amerindian *père de famille* might have issued from the lips of any
eighteenth-century sentimental hero: "*brethren,* said the chief of this lonely
family, addressing himself affectionately to them, *the wretched are entitled to our
pity and our assistance. We are men, and the misfortunes incident to any of the human race affect us in the same manner as if they were our own*" (15.4.21; 15.446).
To be human is to feel for others. Raynal's Amerindian elaborates a sentimental
ethic based on the golden rule: one not only does unto others, one also feels for

Figure 5.1. "Bienveillance d'une famille sauvage du Canada envers des François." Frontispiece by J. M. Moreau le jeune to vol. 8, bk. 15 of the abbé Raynal's *Histoire philosophique et politique des établissements et du commerce des Européens dans les deux Indes,* 3rd ed. (Geneva: Jean-Léonard Pellet, 1781).

others, as one would feel for oneself. The universality of humanity, recognized through feeling, creates instant rights to succor.

Yet the Amerindian *père de famille* does not have a monopoly on human emotion for long. Raynal invites the reader to "preserve the sensations which my narrative hath raised in you" (15.4.22; 15.446). Savages, it would seem, are ideally suited to inspire undiluted, spontaneous feeling. The most exquisite air-brushed portrait of the accomplishments and arts of civilized life, drawn by the greatest genius of Europe, might elicit admiration, Raynal notes, "but do you imagine that it will leave in your minds that delicious emotion which you experience at present? Will the writer inspire you with those sentiments of esteem, love, and veneration, which you have just granted the savages?" (15.4.22; 15.447). The New World offers not only new opportunities for wealth, but also a wealth of opportunities to feel what Diderot elsewhere calls the delicious "pleasure of being touched [*s'attendrir*] and shedding tears."[30] The uncorrupted man of nature affords a superior strain of sentiment to the jaded palate of the metropolitan reader. The superior pleasures afforded by Raynal's portrait of the savage enable the reader to acknowledge what is lost to civilized refinement and to find himself elevated and restored by sentiment to a happier state. The humanity of the savage redounds back onto the humanity of the European, who siphons off the delicious surplus of sentiment. Such moments carve out a space of abstract humanity, to be occupied by any and all who feel.

Although sympathy allows metropolitan readers to recognize the common humanity of colonial populations, other kinds of social and cultural differences cut individuals off from the happy family of humankind. "Are we not all brethren, all children of one common father," Raynal asks, "and are we not all called to fulfill the same destiny? Is it necessary that I should thwart the prosperity of my fellow creature, because nature hath placed a river or a mountain between him and me? Doth this barrier authorise me to hate and to persecute him?" (6.18.291; 6.356–57). Arbitrary boundaries sunder the human race; geographic contingency divides a world that would otherwise be one. National chauvinism and mercantilist competition benefit no one and damage all. Superficial differences of custom or appearance legitimate treating others as less than human. It is the failure of the Spaniards to recognize "the image of an organisation similar to their own (a similarity which is the foundation of all moral duties)," for example, that enables them to treat "their new-discovered brethren as they did the wild beasts of the other hemisphere, and to do it with as little remorse" (8.32.244; 8.310).

Humanity, it seems, does not travel well. Although Raynal often depicts commerce as a redemptive or progressive activity, the motives that lure sailors, soldiers, explorers, and traders from their native land are rarely of unmingled nobility. While the merchant who remains tethered to his home is capable of conducting virtuous commerce, colonialism produces curiously deracinated human beings, transformed by travels, sundered from their origins. Those who quit their country are by definition bad members of any club, while those who do not return to the *patrie* become outcasts, "amphibious creatures, who live upon the surface of the waters; who come on shore only for a moment; to whom every habitable latitude is equal; who have, in reality, neither fathers, mothers, children, brothers, relations, friends, nor fellow-citizens" (19.15.289; 19.370). Such passages indicate, as Anthony Pagden contends, that the "target of the *Histoire*'s most eloquent criticism is . . . not so much the colonial process itself—although Raynal had much to say about that—as the individual whom that process had created."[31]

As the European moves away from the mother country, he reverts to a Hobbesian state of nature. For Raynal, stripping off the encrustations of civilization does not return humanity to the state of the noble savage; instead, the mask of civility dissolves, leaving the European free to pursue unbridled conquest unchecked:

> In proportion as the distance from the capital increases, this mask detaches itself; it falls off on the frontiers; and, between one hemisphere and another, is totally lost. When a man hath crossed the line, he is neither an Englishman, a Dutchman, a Frenchman, a Spaniard, or a Portugueze. He preserves nothing of his country, except the principles and prejudices which give a sanction to his conduct, or furnish him with an excuse for it. Servile when he is weak, and oppressive when he is strong; eager to acquire wealth, and to enjoy it; and capable of all the enormities which can contribute most speedily to the completion of his designs; he is a domestic tiger [*tigre domestique*] again let loose in the woods, and who is again seized with the thirst of blood. Such have all the Europeans, indiscriminately, shew'n themselves in the regions of the New World, where they have been actuated with one common rage, the passion for gold [*la soif de l'or*]. (9.1.2; 9.359)

As he recedes from the geographical heart of civilization, crosses the line between hemispheres, man regresses from his civil state and sheds his national identity. Subject to unchecked impulses and desires, man turns indiscriminately savage: the "domestic tiger" preys on all alike. The avaricious and rapacious individual is not driven by natural or animal instincts, however, but by the economic imperatives of conquest. National character may anchor the European in a moral structure, but once carried beyond the sight of his fellow countryman, nothing

restrains him. The fact that civility of character is described as a theatrical ac-
coutrement, a mask, suggests the fragility of the outer carapace of civilization.
The human *de base* in Raynal's early modern voyage into the heart of darkness
is not a beneficent soul.

The model of human identity proffered in the *Histoire* is shaped by the
specific nature of eighteenth-century colonial endeavors. Whereas the expanding city-states of the classical empires of Rome and Athens preserved cultural
homogeneity by absorbing contiguous populations through voluntary or coerced
assimilation or by exterminating them, eighteenth-century empires consisted of
scattered discrete colonial possessions, separated from the metropole by great ex-
panses of sea and land. The heterogeneous cultures embraced by these modern
empires undermine the commonality of heritage and interest that creates social
unity, making it difficult to find a vocabulary of commonality anywhere other
than in the abstract promise of a universal human nature. As the gyre of empire
widens, moreover, the center ceases to hold; the pull of the colony as a separate
gravitational force becomes a factor to grapple with. Distended beyond its just
limits, the original community loses its proper shape and identity. "By what firm
tie shall we secure a possession, from which we are separated by an immense in-
terval?" Raynal demands. "Can colonies interest themselves to a certain degree
in the misfortunes or prosperity of the mother-country? and can the mother-
country be very sincerely rejoiced or afflicted at the fate of the colonies?" (13.1.2–
3; 13.3).

It is in order to reinvigorate interest attenuated by distance that Raynal
lingers over scenes of exploitation and suffering. Thus he calls upon the reader
as witness, as judge, as defendant and as chief mourner in his description of the
horrific Bengal famine of 1770, in which an estimated ten million died (roughly
one-third of the population). The protracted drought and the failure of successive harvests were compounded by the refusal of the East India Company to open
its granaries to the starving populace or to suspend the collection of its tithes.[32]
Raynal paints a "tableau" designed to "make humanity tremble" and then invites the reader to embroider upon the details of the scene in his or her imagination in order to draw home its full magnitude:

> They were to be seen in their villages, along the public ways, in the midst of our
> European colonies, pale, meagre, fainting, emaciated, consumed by famine; some
> stretched on the ground in expectation of dying, others scarce able to drag them-
> selves on to seek for any food, and throwing themselves at the feet of the Euro-
> peans, intreating them to take them in as their slaves. To this description, which

makes humanity shudder, let us add other objects equally shocking; let imagination enlarge upon them, if possible; let us represent to ourselves infants deserted,
some expiring on the breasts of their mothers; every where the dying and the dead
mingled together; on all sides the groans of sorrow, and the tears of despair; and
we shall then have some faint idea of the horrible spectacle Bengal presented for
the space of six weeks. (3.38.148–49; 3.187–88)

Raynal does not locate the witnessing gaze. He simply tells us that such things
"were to be seen." Nor does he position the "pale, meager, fainting, emaciated"
bodies against a local context or scenic backdrop. We are given a catalog of victims in an array of postures of supplication and abjection. No active verbs animate these figures; even the "groans of sorrow" and "tears of despair" seem to
issue from the air. Raynal invites the reader to compound the interest of the scene
with the addition of "equally shocking" objects that create a visual and aural theater of cruelty. In replicating such scenes in his or her imagination, the reader
participates in a mass reenactment of the scenes ("let us add," "let us represent").
She or he becomes both the engineer and the witness of these horrors, implicitly
precipitated into the position of the British agents in India who saw and refused
to act.

The frame set around the Indians' suffering implicitly strips them of their
agency; the scenes that have the greatest affective impact are typically those that
are the most disempowering for the victims. Like the other eighteenth-century
European representations of the Bengal famine studied by David Arnold, Raynal's rendition excludes the long months of active struggle and ingenious con-
trivances that preceded these last desperate moments. Thus the spectacular tableaux of dead and dying bodies offered by Raynal confirm emerging European
stereotypes about Indian passivity. Indeed, Raynal reinforces this image by attributing the fact that the Indians did not revolt against the British to an orien-
tal submissiveness, speculating that the same circumstances would cause mass in-
surrection in Europe. The sequence meant to inspire action on the part of the
European reader does so at the expense of the Indian: the less agency the Indians possess, the greater the scope of the interlocutor's intervention. If we cannot,
as J. G. A. Pocock has argued, "read Raynal and Diderot in search of a historiography which permits those who are not Europeans—whether Asian, African or
American, savages, settlers or slaves—to exist in a history of their own making"
(44), it is at least in part because the sentimental figures who stand for indigenous peoples have a restricted range of motion and a limited repertoire of gestures and speeches at their command.

Even where Raynal confers a voice upon the Indians, inviting them to address the inhumane British, he reinforces images of their essential inertia:

> Might not the poor wretches, expiring before the eyes of the Europeans, with rea-
> son have cried out, ". . . what have you done for our preservation? What steps have
> you taken to remove from us the scourge that threatened us? Deprived of all au-
> thority, stripped of our property, weighed down by the terrible hand of power, we
> can only lift our hands to you to implore your assistance. Ye have heard our groans;
> ye have seen famine making very quick advances upon us; and then ye attended to
> your own preservation." (3.38.150−51; 3.189−90)

Raynal's Indians do not offer a comprehensive description of the material causes of their suffering; they speak to describe their own helplessness at the hands of the British rather than to proffer their own history. A speaking part in the *Histoire* does not come with approval over the script. Indeed, the portraits are adorned with barely enough decorative cultural detail—the equivalent of Barthes's Roman forelock—to locate them in time and space, an absence of particulariz-ing detail that reinforces the impression that these figures are timeless and in-terchangeable. The poor will always be with us (or, Raynal sometimes suggests, against us). The Indians' second-person address (to the British, to the reader) col-lapses the distance between witnessing and complicity, precipitating the reader into the empowered position of the one being supplicated. The fact that the speech condemns Europeans only partly disguises its essential solipsism. As Pocock points out, "what we call Eurocentricity can be the product of European self-hatred as well as of European self-flattery."[33]

Yet Raynal ultimately has little faith in the self-reforming powers of senti-mental feeling. All too often, sympathy produces pleasurable but fruitless emo-tion rather than political action.

> Those great catastrophes which subvert the globe, and the description of which, is
> pleasing to all readers, from the violence of the shocks they receive from them, and
> from the tears, partly delicious, and partly bitter, which they draw from their eyes,
> will soon sully the remainder of these deplorable annals. Readers, are ye wicked,
> or are ye good? If ye were good, ye would not, it should seem, listen to the recital
> of these calamities; if ye were wicked, ye would hear them without shedding a tear.
> Yet, I perceive your eyes are overflowing. Ye pant after happiness, and yet misfor-
> tune alone can awaken your attention. The reason of it is plain. The afflictions of
> others, afford you comfort in your own, and your self-estimation is increased, by
> the compassion you bestow upon them. (6.23.323; 6.398−99)

Unmoved by such scenes, the stoic reader is clearly wicked, while his or her tender-hearted counterpart, like Rousseau's novel-reading girl, is guilty for seeking out such scenes in the first place. Accused of historical rubbernecking, Raynal's reader must justify his or her appetite for scenes of suffering. While the weeping reader possesses a feeling heart, she or he also delights in these half-bitter, half-delicious, tears. As an ethical litmus test, tears fail.

The barbarous conduct of Europeans in the Indies allows the affective tourist to rack up sentimental mileage in record time, although the consolatory pleasures of frequent crying create their own reward. "All Europe hath for this century past," Raynal tells us, "been filled with the most sublime, and the soundest sentiments of morality. Writings, which will be immortal, have established in the most affecting manner, that all men are brethren" (11.22.102; 11.267–68). Yet such universally acknowledged truths prove to be flimsy. There is no shortage of tears on the domestic front, but real scenes of suffering leave readers sublimely unmoved: "Even imaginary distresses draw tears from our eyes, both in the silent retirement of the closet, and especially at the theatre. It is only the fatal destiny of the Negroes which doth not concern us. They are tyrannized, mutilated, burnt, and put to death, and yet we listen to these accounts coolly and without emotion" (11.22.102; 11.268). Readers weep before fictions but are impervious to accounts of colonial depredations. Economic interest, Raynal tells us, denatures men's hearts and leads to the misapplication of otherwise good maxims. The very fact that one profits from another's suffering annihilates pity. "The torments of a people, to whom we owe our luxuries," he concludes, "can never reach our hearts" (11.22.103; 11.268). The flood of goods from the colonies drowns out sympathy for the oppressed.

Sentiment alone is inadequate to initiate change. Thus, although the rulers of the globe "cannot but have been sensibly affected" by the portraits of the oppressed the narrator has sketched, it is necessary to provide additional incentive to nudge them into action: "I have warned them, that if they turned their eyes away, those true but dreadful pictures would be engraven on the marble of their tombs, and accuse their ashes" (19.14.291; 19.373). Pleas for change must be backed by force or sustained by self-interest. The Indians' pathetic address to the East India Company must be supplemented by a warning to the British from the philosophical narrator:

> You are precipitating yourselves into ruin. Your tyranny is hastening to its end. . . . The earth now covers the carcases [*sic*] of three millions of men, who have perished through your fault or neglect; but they will be taken up again out of the

ground; they will cry out to Heaven, and to the earth for vengeance, and will ob-
tain it. Time and circumstances will only suspend your punishment. I see the period approaching when you will be recalled, and your souls impressed with terror.
(3.41.163; 3.206)

Inhumanity is a poor long-term investment strategy; the resuscitation of the
dead promises an apocalypse in which the British will reap what they have sown.
Yet even here the Indians are curiously passive: revenge is exacted by the corpses
of Indians who rise up out of the ground, rather than by their living compatri-
ots. It is not, moreover, the Indian but the dispassionate philosophical observer
who anticipates—and seeks to provoke—the revolt of the oppressed.

The apostrophe is meant to incite action by calling into being the figures it
addresses. It is, Jonathan Culler tells us, "a device which the poetic voice uses to
establish with an object a relationship which helps to constitute him. The object
is treated as a subject, an *I* which implies a certain type of *you* in its turn. One
who successfully invokes nature is one to whom nature might, in its turn,
speak."[34] By addressing an object, the speaker wills it to function as a subject, enjoins it to respond. Thus the narrator's initial address to the Indians—"Unfortunate Indians! endeavour to reconcile yourselves to your chains" (3.41.162;
3.205)—is superseded by an invitation to the populace to rise up against their
tyrants: "People, whose clamours have so often caused your masters to tremble,
what are you now waiting for? For what occasion do you reserve your torches, and
the stones that pave your streets? Tear them up" (3.41.164; 3.207). Such exhorta-
tory passages seem to allude immediately to the downtrodden European reader
as well as the Indian—a possibility reinforced by the fact that the passage employs the same rhetoric as contemporary French attacks on the royal monopoly
on grain.[35]

Apostrophe is closely related to the trope of prosopopoeia, what Paul de Man
defines as "the fiction of an apostrophe to an absent, deceased, or voiceless entity,
which posits the possibility of the latter's reply and confers upon it the power of
speech."[36] De Man warns against the chiasmic or reversible structure of apostrophe: to speak to the dead or inanimate (apostrophe) and to make them speak
back (prosopopoeia) creates a potentially terrible symmetry. "By making the
death [*sic*] speak," de Man writes, "the symmetrical structure of the trope implies, by the same token, that the living are struck dumb" (78). It is all very well
to address another in order to invite that party to answer back, but such conjured
revenants are not invariably friendly ghosts. De Man's fear is that they *will* respond, that the trope will turn and produce its own revolution. (Prosopopoeia, as

Decan says in his 1779 *Essai sur la littérature*, creates "a new order of things; it makes the absent speak; it even resuscitates the dead.")[37]

The *Histoire* flirts with and even aspires to this revolutionary possibility. The apostrophes in Raynal's text turn into harangues as the silent interlocutors stir to life and begin to speak or indeed act. Although his discussion of slavery in book 11 begins with a plea for reciprocal recognition ("Men! you are all brethren. How long will you defer to acknowlege [*sic*] each other?" [11.9.37; 11.186]), Raynal's address to the slave turns to the revolutionary reversal of positions, as the slave hijacks the narrative and declares his right to revolt against tyranny. "If thou dost think thyself authorised to oppress me, because thou are stronger or more dextrous than I am, complain not if my vigorous arm shall rip up thy bosom in search of thy heart" (11.24.124; 11.295). The European's unjust arrogation of right based on might justifies the slave's retribution, as the slave slits open the master's body in a literal and figurative quest for his feeling heart. Raynal's text thus acknowledges the possibility of the violent reversal of its tropes: the reclaiming by the oppressed of his or her rights to liberty, autonomy, and self-propriety, the supplanting, as Raynal powerfully puts it, of the French *code noir* with the *code blanc* of the slave's vengeance. Like Raynal's famous invocation of the New Spartacus, the slave who will rise and lead the others in rebellion, such passages turn the reciprocity of exchange into the violent symmetry of an eye for an eye.

Human Interest

The possibility that the oppressed may reply to Raynal's apostrophes and rise up to claim their rightful place depends upon a scene of reading that Raynal's text attempts to foreclose. His harangue to the "Hottentots" of the Cape—which invites them to massacre the falsely benevolent Dutch—concludes with an address to the metropolitan reader: "And you, barbarous Europeans, be not incensed at this harangue. It will neither be hear'd by the Hottentot, nor by the inhabitant of those regions which still remain for you to lay waste. If you should be offended at my words, it is because you are not more humane than your predecessors; it is because you perceive in the hatred I have vowed against them, that which I entertain against you" (2.18.249; 2.312). Past, present, and future victims are only the *imagined* interlocutors of Raynal's call to arms; the European alone, Raynal claims, hears his message. It is certainly true that portions of the eighteenth-century European public read *through* the ostensible colonial representation to a radical anti-clerical and anti-monarchical referent, interpreting Raynal's revolutionary discourse as a plea for Europeans to liberate themselves.

The colonial glass darkly reflects metropolitan not colonial oppression, antici-
pating French rather than African or Indian revolt.[38] The fact that metropolitan
readers of the *Histoire* discover the possibility of resistance by identifying with
"the grievances, disenfranchisement, and indeed the slavery of tropicopolitan
subjects," Srinivas Aravamudan has suggested, offers a "heterodox account of the
rise of the Jacobin democratic subject," one that challenges the historical prece-
dence of European "center" over colonial periphery.[39]

The text's reception history reveals that the message did reach at least some
colonial recipients. The *Histoire* was not only read by anti-slavery factions like
the Amis des noirs under the Revolution but also by plantation owners in the
slave colonies of Bourbon and the Île de France. Latin American Creole revolu-
tionaries, including Simon Bolívar, owned the text, but so too did estate managers
and colonial administrators in the Spanish and Portuguese empires.[40] C. L. R.
James postulates that Toussaint L'Ouverture read the *Histoire*, while Srinivas Aravamudan offers a speculative history of Toussaint's hypothetical female counterpart as a possible revolutionary reader.[41] The diversity of the text's audience
hints at the volatility and plurality of sentimental and political identifications
made possible by the *Histoire* and suggests that its revolutionary significance
stems not only from *who* read it but also from *how* it was read. It is as much the
structure or phenomenology of reading enabled by the text as its radical content
that fosters historical change.

The revolutionary effect of the *Histoire* stems in part from the way the text's
apostrophes cast readers in unexpected parts, inciting acts of sympathetic identification that enable them to shake off the myopia of their own worldview. The
fact that the oppressed who speak out in Raynal's text are more virtual than
real—the "Hottentots" had ceased to exist as discrete populations at the time of
the text's composition, and his new Spartacus had not yet come into being—potentially makes it easier to identify with them, in much the same way that fiction, as Catherine Gallagher has argued, "by representing feelings that belong to
no other body," offers "the illusion of immediately appropriable sentiments, free
sentiments belonging to nobody and therefore identifiable with ourselves."[42]
Such sentimental interchangeability might in turn be extended to suggest, for
example, that anyone can assume the role of a subject endowed with rights, as
the fictional "nobody" becomes the political "anybody" of revolutionary ideals.
The affective extension of humanity to hitherto disenfranchised subjects may
come to imply the inclusiveness of a claim to political and legal rights. Substitution paves the way for the kind of appeal to universality upon which a document
like the Declaration of the Rights of Man and of the Citizen is based, although it

is perhaps worth recalling in this context that the philosophes, like the senti-mentalists, were interested less in equality per se than in a just order.[43] If the sentimental reversal of self and other has a leveling effect, it is because tropes at times outstrip the aims and intentions of their authors. The radical work per-formed by the form of a text may supersede the revolutionary promises of its content.

Yet the fact that tears often surface at moments of identification with suffer-ing others may also forestall such truly revolutionary effects. The sentimental irrupts into Raynal's text at the moments of greatest commercial and political inequality: when other forms of exchange fail, the reader's tears serve as provi-sional compensation for the violent extraction of material surplus elsewhere. As Michelle Burnham has argued, the "tears which are so often a sign of senti-mental identification—of the successful establishment of this relation of ap-parent equivalence—result . . . not from the seamless substitution of self for other but from the necessary margin of inequivalence produced by such an exchange."[44] Raynal's apostrophes show that commerce fails to knit the globe together: happy visions of commercial reciprocity falter before scenes of unchecked rapacity and violent appropriation. The tribute of tears, the gratuity of sentimental affect, al-low vicarious suffering to be redressed through the easy consolatory pleasures of right feeling. The tear-filled eyes of Raynal's omnivoyant philosophe behold a globe united, not by commerce, but by the chimerical promise of a sentimental union intended to palliate the very inequities commerce sustains.

The Peripheral Vision
of the Enlightenment

We won't know. We'll all be dead.

—*George W. Bush's response to Bob Woodward's question about how history will judge the American war in Iraq*

In the *Histoire des deux Indes,* Raynal mocks the efforts of kings and generals to control the verdict of history. Monarchs who raise monuments to commemorate their deeds for future generations cannot even dictate the opinions of their contemporaries. Indeed, memorials often testify to the failings of those they are meant to honor. The gilt statue throws into relief the rags of the indigent prone at its feet; the figure of a tyrant reminds the people of his crimes. "If you wish to immortalize your name," Raynal tells the monarch, "consider, that monuments of bronze are more or less rapidly destroyed by time. Intrust the care of your reputation to beings who will perpetuate it by regeneration. The statue is silent, but mankind will speak. Let them, therefore, speak of you with praise."[1] Human feeling creates a more lasting legacy than stone or bronze; through it, the goodness of the righteous transcends the ravages of time. Sentiment alone is the true vehicle of history.

The ultimate tribunal of colonial deeds Raynal elevates for the monarch is not history but its victims. Spaniards who have a ticklish conscience about the slaughter and enslavement of Native Americans cannot absolve themselves, Raynal contends. Indeed, given the current state of the Americas, there can be no present expiation:

Posterity will not forgive you, 'till harvests shall arise in those fields which you have manured with so much innocent blood; and 'till those immense spaces which you have laid waste shall be covered with happy and free inhabitants. If ye would know the period in which you may perhaps be absolved of all your crimes, it will be when you shall revive, in idea, some one of the antient monarchs of Mexico and Peru, and placing him in the midst of his possessions, shall be able to say to him, BEHOLD THE PRESENT STATE OF YOUR COUNTRY, AND OF YOUR SUB-JECTS; INTERROGATE THEM, AND FORM YOUR JUDGMENT OF US. (8.35.280; 8.357)

Raynal does not offer the plenitude of a "native" perspective (whatever that might be) on the conquest. Instead, he invites the Spanish to judge their deeds from the hypothetical perspective of their victims' shades. He creates a structure of reading that makes the Spaniards of the present time accountable to their past victims for the future of the nation they have destroyed. Raynal, that is, resuscitates the long-dead monarchs of Mexico and Peru to pass judgment, not on crimes already committed, but on the postcolonial world Raynal insists the Spaniards must make. Fruitless and self-indulgent hand-wringing over past and present injustice must be superseded by concrete amends. Accountability resides in the future consequences. Nor can the devastation wrought by conquest be repaired by decolonization or unilateral withdrawal from a country one has invaded; the harm must be remedied by sustained political commitment to rebuilding the prosperity of a just postcolonial world. The refusal to anticipate the judgment of the world to come—"We won't know; we'll all be dead"—constitutes a refusal to admit that we are answerable to questions posed by people we may not even be able to imagine.

Yet Raynal's condemnation of imperial depredations may perversely pave the way for a kinder, gentler version of colonialism; demands for postconquest reconstruction, then as now, all too often entail a society rebuilt in the image of those who destroyed it. Harbored in Raynal's dreams of expiation and reconciliation is a teleological model of improvement that plants non-Western societies on a progressive continuum leading to European Enlightenment. "The century," as Michèle Duchet puts it, "that shed tears so willingly over the fate of savage peoples and waxed indignant over the barbarism of the civilized only really knew one antidote: the civilization of the savages, the only moral basis for a humanism of conquest."[2] The sentimental depiction of non-European subjects as passive victims in need of moral, economic, and cultural salvation helps fuel the later imperial discourses of improvement and civilization—a sentimental genealogy that may help explain the fact that some of the most enthusiastic proponents of empire in nineteenth-century Britain and France were liberal thinkers like Alexis de Tocqueville and John Stuart Mill.[3] The sentimental figures of empire discussed in this book are stamped upon the moral banner of universal human progress under which the French *mission civilisatrice* advances across the globe; the passive victims in need of benevolent aid are the poster children of the humanitarianism, which, as Andrew Porter notes, had become a "vital component of Britain's national or Imperial identity" by the 1840s.[4] As Anthony Pagden has argued, "the languages in which the nineteenth-century empires sought to frame themselves were the transfigured products . . . not of the [early modern] languages of empire but instead of the critique which the enemies of imperialism had levelled against them in the closing years of the eighteenth century."[5] The discourses of trusteeship and paternalist protection, of evangelicalism and enlightenment, of progress and the white man's burden, are the ideological offspring of the sentimental figures described above.

The transformation of sentimental rhetoric from critique to justification in the early years of the nineteenth century is in part the by-product of the changing nature of empire. It is perhaps for this reason that the mixed languages of sentimental denunciation and imperial redemption surface so powerfully in Edmund Burke's condemnation of British conduct in the country that would become the mainstay of Britain's second empire, India. Implicit in Burke's 1783 "Speech on Fox's India Bill"—a bill designed to render the East India Company accountable to the British government—are the principles that would later become central to nineteenth-century justifications of empire. Rewriting the causal logic subtending imperial commerce into a humanitarian impetus—"if we are the very cause of the evil, we are in a special manner engaged to the redress"— Burke advocates an "administration in England at once protecting and stable."[6] The tearful acknowledgment of the injury inflicted upon other nations cannot be fully disentangled from the recognition that what Burke characterizes as criminal acts are necessary for imperial success: "it is our protection," he notes, "that destroys India. . . . [I]t is our friendship" (402).

No noblesse oblige, Burke notes, has hitherto characterized British activities in India; the Company has pillaged without making any material or symbolic return, degrading Britons even below "their ferocious, bloody, and wasteful" predecessors, the "Arabs, Tartars, and Persians" (401). Not yet refashioned into the bold young adventurers central to the ideology of the Raj, the rapacious "young men (boys almost)" of the East India Company have pillaged India and made no return:

Every rupee of profit made by an Englishman is lost for ever to India. With us are no retributory superstitions, by which a foundation of charity compensates,

through ages, to the poor, for the rapine and injustice of a day. With us no pride
erects stately monuments which repair the mischiefs which pride had produced,
and which adorn a country, out of its own spoils. England has erected no churches,
no hospitals, no palaces, no schools; England has built no bridges, made no high
roads, cut no navigations, dug out no reservoirs. Every other conqueror of every
other description has left some monument, either of state or beneficence, behind
him. Were we to be driven out of India this day, nothing would remain, to tell that
it had been possessed, during the inglorious period of our dominion, by any thing
better than the ouran-outang or the tiger. (402)

Consolidated into a single personified entity, Burke's "England" is capable of acting over great distances. But it is not Britain's deeds that Burke condemns, but its
failure to act; not the presence of Britons in India, but the fact that they have
made an insufficient mark. Burke represents houses, schools, churches—the ideological state apparatus—and bridges, roads, canals—the commercial infrastructure—as compensatory return for conquest, without acknowledging that
such "improvements" are necessary components for the effective exploitation of
labor and resources that consolidate rather than mitigate English dominion. His
condemnation of the failure to bestow the fruits of European superiority upon
the Indians implies that Company dominion would be acceptable had they done
so. We have here the scaffolding of what would become the liberal platform for
empire over the next century: although Burke rails against the usurpation and
abuses of power and political authority by the Company, he simultaneously
sketches out an ideal of benevolent stewardship. "[A]ll political power which is
set over men, and . . . all privilege claimed or exercised in exclusion of them," he
proclaims, "ought to be some way or other exercised ultimately for their benefit. . . . [S]uch rights, or privileges, or whatever you choose to call them, are all in
the strictest sense a *trust*" (385).

By the 1790s, the terms of Burke's critique are already being refashioned into
the language of imperial protection in characterizations of Lord Cornwallis, who
succeeded Warren Hastings, first governor-general of India, upon his impeachment before Parliament (1787–95). The astonishing popularity of depictions of
Cornwallis's paternal care for the sons of Tipu Sultan, delivered to the British as
hostages following Tipu's defeat, suggests the pleasure Britons took in this be-
nign and benevolent image of empire.[7] Cornwallis is extolled for his "mildness
and beneficence" in ushering in a new era of protective improvement: "Thy kind
controul, thy parentlike command, / Thy mild protection of an injur'd land, /
Shall form the epoch whence whole realms shall date, / With hearts exultant,

their amended fate."[8] An orator at the East India Company's General Court lauds the Permanent Act of Settlement passed in 1793 by Cornwallis as "the greatest Revolution that had ever taken place for the happiness of mankind," praising those "two stupendous schemes of philanthropy, the Reformation of Criminal Jurisprudence, and the utter abolition of Feudal Tyranny. The first gave to the natives security, the latter liberty."[9] Yet the violent idealism of these colonial Samaritans requires a touch of sentimental refashioning for its goodness to be made visible. While Henry Dundas, president of the ministerial Board of Control for India, praises "the wise and benevolent system established by the marquis Cornwallis" for effecting "the growing happiness and increasing prosperity of that country,"[10] others rather cynically note that "the resources of our Asiatic possessions will more and more unfold themselves from the enlightened measures of Lord Cornwallis's government."[11] A moral empire is also a more profitable one.

Towards the end of the century, sentimental denunciations of slavery likewise produce a fresh mandate for imperial activity. Thus although abolitionist poetry like Hannah More's "Slavery" unmasks the mystification that recasts plunder in epic terms—whether under the guise of "Hero or robber," More insists, "Conquest is pillage with a nobler name"—visions of imperial carnage give way to a kinder, gentler version of empire, modeled after the "mild and liberal plan" of a Cook or a William Penn.[12] Benevolence and mutual reciprocity, More contends, will preside over a world in which the "social hands" of "blessed philanthropy" link "dissevered worlds in brothers' bands" (ll. 239–40). The celebrated liberty of Britons distinguishes their empire both from the rapacity of other nations and from the failed models of the Spanish and the Romans. "Oh let the nations know," More rhapsodizes, "The liberty she [Britain] loves she will bestow; / Not to herself the glorious gift confined, / She spreads the blessing wide as hu[m]ankind" (ll. 253–56). A sentimentally reformed empire becomes the vanguard of moral and intellectual enlightenment, as God, with the British riding shotgun, "bursts their [Africans'] two-fold bands," so that "Faith and Freedom spring from Mercy's hands" (ll. 293–94). The beneficiaries of empire, it turns out, are not the conquerors but the conquered.

Whereas for More commerce and Christianity trump conquest, French writers stress the ways enlightenment redeems empire. Notwithstanding the "no conquests" formula incorporated into the French Revolutionary Constitution of 1791—"the French nation renounces the undertaking of any war with a view toward conquests, and will never use its forces against the liberty of any people"[13]—the abstract universals of the Declaration of the Rights of Man and of

the Citizen "gave birth to the idea that France was the 'universal' nation, the nation that represented the future of civilization and was charged with rescuing
other peoples from tyranny and ignorance."[14] Condorcet's *Outlines of an Historical View of the Progress of the Human Spirit*, composed while he was impris-
oned under the Terror and published following his death in 1794, condemns the
devastation inflicted by "our monopolies, our treachery, our sanguinary contempt for men of a different complexion or a different creed, and the proselyt-
ing [*sic*] fury or the intrigues of our priests."[15] Yet such depredations find a
panacea in the redemptive power of European civilization. The advent of Europeans in new territories becomes the opportunity for lesser peoples to wrest
themselves from what Dipesh Chakrabarty has called the "imaginary waiting
room of history," launching the inexorable march of progress towards political
and social modernity under the guise of a beneficent union of all humankind.[16]
Indeed, Condorcet claims that colonial incursions occur because there's no more
good to be done at home:

> [T]he love of truth is also a passion; and when it shall have at home no gross prej-
> udices to combat, no degrading errors to dissipate, it will naturally extend its re-
> gards, and convey its efforts to remote and foreign climes. These immense coun-
> tries will afford ample scope for the gratification of this passion. In one place will
> be found a numerous people, who, to arrive at civilization [*pour se civiliser*], appear
> only to wait till we shall furnish them with the means; and who, treated as broth-
> ers by Europeans, would instantly become their friends and disciples. In another
> will be seen nations crouching under the yoke of sacred despots or stupid con-
> querors, and who, for so many ages, have looked for some friendly hand to deliver
> them.[17]

By depicting the world as a site awaiting the bright beams of cultural and economic Enlightenment, Condorcet unites all peoples in a progressive history. The
language of common humanity provides the shared raw material that allows
different peoples to be located on the same continuum: similar enough to become
(eventually) like, but still not quite there. Plowshares not swords are the protagonists in Condorcet's happy vision: it is "the love of truth" rather than the love
of power or profit that propels Europeans "to remote and foreign climes." Condorcet's natives passively await the arrival of history in the form of the Europeans; in this historical game of hide-and-seek, the players are rapturous to "be
found." Once Westerners have recognized the humanity of other people and tendered a "friendly hand to deliver them," these populations will scatter roses before their liberators. The familiar sentimental fiction that the natives have only

to be "treated as brothers by Europeans . . . [to] instantly become their friends and disciples" transforms the affective bonds of proffered kinship into a voluntary moral and cultural apprenticeship. What is lauded as recognition of the humanity and dignity of other people masks the desire for other people to recognize and refashion themselves in a Western image.

Notwithstanding its ostensible function—to facilitate comprehension and thence sympathy—the instantly recognizable nature of the sentimental figure only rarely blossoms into a scene of mutual legibility or reciprocal reading. More often, sentimental figures—the dying Indian, the generous savage, the grateful Negro—serve up entire populations in specially marked packages, making self-contained vessels of diversity available for ease of consumption or comparison. At best, sentimental figures are invited to make themselves at home in the pigeonhole to which they have been assigned. Summoned into being at the will and convenience of the reader, sentimental figures reconstitute humanity—just add tears and stir—as attributed content, rather than recognizing it as a form of *being* already claimed by the people in question. Literary history runs the risk of repeating this error by assuming that the attribution of increasingly nuanced affect gradually shifts the status of the native from caricature to character in a kind of stadial theory of novelistic progress in which successive iterations of marginal figures ultimately result in acknowledgment of the lesser figure's full humanity.

Nor is the dream of human plenitude the exclusive province of the sentimental text. The desire to find and restore the traces of the human subject is discernible even in the most knowing histories of Enlightenment, in the canniest, most tortuously self-reflective theories, and, of course, in literary histories like this one. This desire presents in many guises: in the desire to make the subaltern speak or to identify places where she or he can speak or has spoken, in the retroactive discovery or attribution of resistance (subversion, doubleness, mimicry); in the quest for the historical roots of future deeds, the sowing of agency that it may be subsequently reaped. Certainly, the trajectory—from the voiceless to the speaking, from dehumanized exploited thing to articulate autonomous human— seems inherently desirable and intuitively progressive, but we must be aware that there may be something dangerously sentimental about such projects.

Postcolonial theory has drawn attention to the hazards of making subjects, exposing the sentimental fetishism of the "rediscovered" voice, the scholarly trophy life. The act of fleshing out such figures, endowing them with the shape and habits of the human, may become a scholarly repetition of what Gayatri Spivak has famously called the "terrorism of the categorical imperative," the attempt to "*make* the heathen into a human so that he can be treated as an end in himself."[18] In yearning to restore it is possible to seize on an image of the subject that blocks out the recognition that all subjects, as sufferer beings (or as the agents of suffering), also exist as objects of leaden force. We must be aware, Rey Chow warns, that the desire to wrest colonial peoples away from their "status as symptom or object" may also be a desire to glean "the surplus value of the oppressed, a surplus value that results from *exchanging* the defiled image for something more noble."[19] Seen from this angle, the writing of restorative histories bears an uncanny and discomfiting resemblance to the practices of sentimental fiction. What eighteenth-century philosophers describe as a human "propension to spread a resemblance of ourselves over all other things"[20] forms not only gods but other men and women. In composing accounts of eighteenth-century colonialism that seek to avoid making objects of others, it is perhaps important to be cautious about making the semblance of subjects as well.

Yet the fact that eighteenth-century writers were alive to the faults and limits of sentimental form—to the very problems Spivak and Chow describe—ought to forestall too ready an assumption of superiority. Indeed, the "romance of the voice"—the recapturing of the lost figure—and the vehement repudiation of that project might have more in common than is apparent at first glance. "I thought I loved the man," Sterne remarks, "but I fear I mistook the object—'twas my own way of thinking."[21] Sentimentality is not entirely ignorant of its own ignorance, and the fact that it contains its own internal critique makes it difficult to issue an unequivocal indictment of its practices. Neither can one easily dismiss the charges of narcissism, solipsism, myopia, and self-indulgence so frequently leveled against it. Inasmuch as sentimental figures never become discrete cultural entities—subjects or agents with their own histories—they remain the playthings of a self-seeking and self-serving imagination, at best only pressing the reader up against the limits of an identity gleaned from a parasitical identification with or appropriation of another person's history, feelings, and experience. "[W]hatever the advisability of attempting to 'identify' (with) the other as subject in order to know her," as Spivak puts it, "knowledge is made possible and is sustained by irreducible difference, not identity. What is known is always in excess of knowledge. Knowledge is never adequate to its object."[22] The fact that eighteenth-century writers are as interested in the failure of sympathy as they are in its ostensible successes suggests that they recognize the existence of these irreducible differences, the inadequacy of sentimental knowledge to its object.

The possibility that a sentimental model of recognition—on which humanitarian sensibility is in some sense based—might be incorporated into a form of subject making that does not just involve puppetry or wish fulfillment depends upon modes of reading—habits of sympathy—that enable readers to think about (and maybe even think beyond) the parochialism of their own identities and coveted identifications. Even if the content of the sentimental text is all too often reductive, its formal apparatus may also make possible a way of imagining other people that is grounded, not in the instant legibility of a preconstructed identity or the identification of some lowest common denominator of humanity, but rather in the acknowledgement of what Frantz Fanon calls the "zone of occult instability where . . . people dwell," and what Uday Singh Mehta terms the "unfamiliar."[23] On these terms, the sentimental recognition of another's humanity would not entail the wanton projection of self onto other or the vacuous celebration of an impossible mutual transparency, but might instead produce an awareness of what is *not* to be assimilated in a master template of the human: the intransigent singularities that elude or defy sentimental representation.

Introduction • *The Great World Without*

1. Sterne, *Life and Opinions of Tristram Shandy*, ed. New and New (Florida edition), 1.7.10.

2. Sterne, *Vie et les opinions de Tristram Shandy*, trans. Frénais, 1.22, qtd. in Texte, *Jean-Jacques Rousseau et les origines du cosmopolitisme littéraire*, 344.

3. P. J. Marshall, "Introduction," *Oxford History of the British Empire*, 2.2.

4. Parker, *Military Revolution*, 5; Colley, *Britons*, 323.

5. Henry, *Historical Account of All the Voyages*, 1.v–vi, vii.

6. Barbara Johnson, "Anthropomorphism in Lyric and Law," 550.

7. Burke, "Speech on Fox's India Bill," in *Writings and Speeches*, ed. Marshall, 5.403–4.

8. Hawkesworth, *Account of the Voyages*, 1.iv, vii.

9. See, e.g., Barker-Benfield, *Culture of Sensibility*; Denby, *Sentimental Narrative and the Social Order in France*; Mullan, *Sentiment and Sociability*.

10. Pinch, *Strange Fits of Passion*, 7.

11. See, e.g., Ellison, *Cato's Tears*; Claudia Johnson, *Equivocal Beings*.

12. See, e.g., Laura Brown, *Ends of Empire*; Douthwaite, *Exotic Women*; Nussbaum, *Limits of the Human* and *Torrid Zones*; Wheeler, *Complexion of Race*; and Kathleen Wilson, *Island Race*.

13. Wahrman, *Making of the Modern Self*, xiii.

14. See esp. Ellis, *Politics of Sensibility*.

15. Pratt, *Imperial Eyes*.

16. Aravamudan, *Tropicopolitans*, 4.

17. Ferguson, *Essay on the History of Civil Society*, ed. Oz-Salzberger, 145.

18. *Lettres de Mentor à un jeune seigneur*, trans. Prévost (London: Paul Vailland, 1754), v–vi, qtd. in McMurran, "Translation and the Novel," 12.

19. Colley, "Britishness and Otherness," 321.

20. See Mornet, "Enseignements des bibliothèques privées"; Grieder, *Anglomania* and *Translations*.

21. Joseph-Pierre Frénais, qtd. in Brissenden, *Virtue in Distress*, 20.

22. John Wesley, qtd. in Erämetsä, "Study," 22.

23. On the relation of sensibility to radicalism in the 1790s, see Todd, *Sensibility*, 130; Butler, *Jane Austen and the War of Ideas*, 7–28; and Chris Jones, *Radical Sensibility*.

24. Chow, *Writing Diaspora*, 37.

One • *The Distinction of Sentimental Feeling*

1. E.g., Frye, "Towards Defining an Age of Sensibility"; Crane, "Suggestions Toward a Genealogy"; Greene, "Latitudinarianism and Sensibility."

2. *Monthly Review*, August 1799, 467, qtd. in Tompkins, *Popular Novel in England*, 93n.

3. "Character of Modern Poetry," *Scots Magazine* 34 (November 1772): 619.

4. Ellis, *Politics of Sensibility*, 7.

5. Kames, *Essays on the Principles of Morality and Natural Religion*, 17.

6. Coleridge, "On the Slave Trade," in *Collected Works*, 2.139.

7. "Question: Ought Sensibility to Be Cherished, or Repressed?" *Monthly Magazine* 2 (October 1796): 706.

8. Markley, "Sentimentality as Performance"; Langford, *Polite and Commercial People*, esp. 461–518.

9. Hulme, *Colonial Encounters*, 229.

10. See Maza, *Myth of the French Bourgeoisie*.

11. On the dialectical relation between aristocratic and bourgeois claims over the novel, see McKeon, *Origins of the English Novel*, and DiPiero, *Dangerous Truths and Criminal Passions* (for France).

12. Stuart Hall, "Blue Election, Election Blues," *Marxism Today* (July 1987): 33, qtd. in Bhabha, "Commitment to Theory," 28.

13. Bhabha, "Commitment to Theory," 29.

14. See Ellis, *Politics of Sensibility*; Andrew, *Philanthropy and Police*; Donzelot, *Policing of Families*.

15. On the physiological basis of sensibility in France, see Vila, *Enlightenment and Pathology*; for England, see Van Sant, *Eighteenth-Century Sensibility and the Novel*, and G. S. Rousseau, "Nerves, Spirits, and Fibres."

16. *Dictionnaire de l'Académie française* (1694), ARTFL database, s.v. *sentiment*.

17. Raymond Williams, *Keywords*, rev. ed., 280–83; Erämetsä, "Study"; and Brissenden, *Virtue in Distress*.

18. Berthelin, *Abrégé du… Dictionnaire de Trévoux*, s.v. *sentiment*. See also Trusler, *Difference Between Words*, 1.128–29.

19. Trusler, *Difference Between Words*, 1.129.

20. Long, *Sentimental Exhibition*, iii–iv.

21. Johnson, *Dictionary of the English Language on CD-ROM*, ed. McDermott.

22. Rorty, "From Passions to Emotions and Sentiments," 159.

23. Richelet, *Dictionnaire de la langue françoise*, s.v. *émotion*.

24. Chambers, *Cyclopaedia* (1783), 4.379.

25. Jaucourt, *Encyclopédie*, s.v. *sensibilité*.

26. Campbell, *Philosophy of Rhetoric*, ed. Bitzer, 80.

27. See Mornet, "Introduction," in Rousseau, *Nouvelle Héloïse*, 1.255; Price, *Anthology*

and the Rise of the Novel, 48. On the French collections, see Chisick, *Limits of Reform,* 225–38.

28. Knox, *Winter Evenings,* 2.264.

29. See Arthur Wilson, "Sensibility in France," 45.

30. Hester Thrale Piozzi, entry of Oct. 1, 1791, in *Thraliana,* ed. Balderston, 2.823; Lady Louisa Stuart, letter to Sir Walter Scott, Sept. 4, 1826, in *Private Letter-Book of Sir Walter Scott,* ed. Partington, 273.

31. Coleridge, "Lecture on the Slave Trade," in *Collected Works,* 1.249.

32. Rousseau, *Lettre à d'Alembert,* 134, trans. in id., *Letter... to M. d'Alembert,* 25.

33. *Sensibilité*—alternately the "disposition des sens à recevoir les impressions des objets" or the "qualité de celui ou celle qui est sensible"—is not ascribed to objects: one does not talk, except metaphorically, about the sensibility of a rock. Berthelin, *Abrégé du... Dictionnaire de Trévoux,* s.v. *sensibilité.* For Johnson, *sensibility* is quickness of both sensation and perception (1755); later editions add "delicacy" of sense.

34. Hume, *Treatise of Human Nature,* ed. Selby-Bigge, 2nd ed. rev. Nidditch, 319.

35. Pinch, *Strange Fits of Passion,* 34.

36. Mullan, *Sentiment and Sociability,* 25–26.

37. Pinch, *Strange Fits of Passion,* 1.

38. Lamb, *Preserving the Self in the South Seas, 1680–1840,* 9. On self-preservation, see esp. 17–48; 250–80.

39. Smith, *Theory of Moral Sentiments,* ed. Raphael and Macfie, 9.

40. David Marshall, *Figure of Theater,* 175, 176.

41. David Marshall, "Adam Smith and the Theatricality of Moral Sentiments," 599.

42. On the self-disciplinary aspects of this gaze, see Bender, *Imagining the Penitentiary,* 218–28.

43. *Correspondence of Adam Smith,* ed. Mossner and Ross, 43, 51.

44. Lynch, *Economy of Character,* 95.

45. See Gallagher, *Nobody's Story,* 168–72.

46. Saint-Amand, *Laws of Hostility,* 5.

47. Árdal, *Passion and Value in Hume's Treatise,* 46.

48. Sterne, *Sentimental Journey,* ed. Stout, 202.

49. De Man, "Rhetoric of Temporality," in id., *Blindness and Insight,* 214. For an alternate reading of the relation between sentimentality and irony, see Cohen, "Sentimental Communities," in *Literary Channel,* ed. Cohen and Dever, 115.

50. De Riccoboni to Garrick, 1769, qtd. Brissenden, *Virtue in Distress,* 83.

51. Campbell, *Romantic Ethic.*

52. Rousseau, *Lettre à d'Alembert,* 172; id., *Letter to M. d'Alembert,* 63.

53. Rousseau, *Lettre à d'Alembert,* 164; id., *Letter to M. d'Alembert,* 55–56.

54. Newton, *Authentic Narrative,* 90.

55. Féraud, *Dictionnaire critique,* s.v. *identifier.*

56. Fuss, *Identification Papers,* 10.

57. Taussig, *Mimesis and Alterity,* 150–51.

58. Fisher, *Hard Facts,* 4.

59. Although my focus in this book is on the human, animals of course also possess sensi-

bility and inspire pity in humans confronted with their suffering. Some of the most interesting debates during the period revolve around the human/animal divide, but they fall beyond the purview of this book.

60. Rousseau, *Discours sur l'origine et les fondements de l'inégalité*, ed. Starobinski, in *Oeuvres complètes*, 3.126; id., *Discourse on the Origins of Inequality*, in *Collected Writings*, 3.15.

61. Lamb, *Preserving the Self*, 257.

62. Rousseau, *Essai sur l'origine des langues*, ed. Starobinski, in *Oeuvres complètes*, 5.396; id., *Essay on the Origin of Languages*, 7.306.

63. De Man, "Metaphor (*Second Discourse*)," in id., *Allegories of Reading*, 151.

64. David Marshall, *Surprising Effects of Sympathy*, 150. On Rousseau's efforts to regulate sensibility's effects on moral behavior, see Vila, *Enlightenment and Pathology*, 182–224.

65. Rousseau, *Dialogues, ou Rousseau juge de Jean-Jacques*, ed. Osmont, in *Oeuvres complètes*, 1.805; id., *Rousseau, Judge of Jean-Jacques: Dialogues*, in *Collected Writings*, 1.112.

66. Rousseau, *Émile, ou de l'éducation*, ed. Wirz, in *Oeuvres complètes*, 4.505; id., *Emilius and Sophia*, 2.164–65. An identical passage is in the *Essay on the Origin of Languages*, 7.306

67. Rousseau, *Émile*, 4.505–6; *Emilius and Sophia*, 2.165.

68. Derrida, *Of Grammatology*, 190.

69. Arnaud, *Épreuves du sentiment*, 1.v.

70. Ibid., 1.vn.

71. Rousseau, preface, *Julie*, ed. Gagnebin and Raymond, in *Oeuvres complètes*, 2.12; id., *Julie*, in *Collected Writings*, 6.7.

72. Locke, *Essay Concerning Human Understanding*, ed. Nidditch, 3.6.37; p. 462.

73. De Man, "Epistemology of Metaphor," 19.

74. Beattie, *Elements of Moral Science*, 1.180.

75. Wollstonecraft, *Works*, 7.50.

76. See Steintrager, *Cruel Delight*, esp. 3–17.

77. *Man: A Paper for Ennobling the Species* 43 (Oct. 22, 1755): 4.

78. "On Benevolence," *London Magazine* 49 (January 1780): 31.

79. Laporte and Chaudon, *Nouvelle bibliothèque*, 4.103.

80. Brooke, *History of Emily Montague*, 303.

81. Arnaud qtd. in May, *Dilemme du roman*, 150.

82. Diderot, "Éloge de Richardson," in *Oeuvres esthétiques*, ed. Vernière, 39–40.

83. See Alliston, "Transnational Sympathies, Imaginary Communities," in *Literary Channel*, ed. Cohen and Dever, 133–48.

84. Smith, *Theory of Moral Sentiments*, ed. Raphael and Macfie, 229.

85. Anderson, *Imagined Communities*, 7.

86. Renan, "What Is a Nation?" in *Nation and Narration*, ed. Bhabha, 18.

87. Kathleen Wilson, *Island Race*, 4.

88. Sahlins, "Natural Frontiers Revisited," 1451.

89. Trumpener, *Bardic Nationalism.*

90. Colley, *Britons*, 6. See also Kathleen Wilson, *Sense of the People*, and Armitage, *Ideological Origins of the British Empire*.

91. Bell, *Cult of the Nation*, 104.

92. Le Blanc, *Letters on the English and French Nations*, 1.27.

93. *Observateur françois*, qtd. in Grieder, *Anglomania in France*, 17.

94. Bowen, *Elites, Enterprise, and the Making of the British Overseas Empire*. For a comparison of the French and English economies in the eighteenth century, see Crouzet, *Britain Ascendant*.

95. See Maza, "Luxury, Morality, and Social Change," 213.

96. See Pluchon, *Histoire de la colonisation française*, 1.1020, 1021, 1018.

97. P. J. Marshall, *Making and Unmaking of Empires*, 183.

98. Ferguson, *Essay on the History of Civil Society*, ed. Oz-Salzberger, 257.

99. Kathleen Wilson, "Citizenship, Empire, and Modernity," 86.

100. Although its racial terminology—*noir* for *esclave*—suggests a French consolidation of racial categories, it also stemmed from the "Paris Parlement's refusal to register legislation containing the word *esclave*" (Peabody, *"There are no slaves in France,"* 7–8). On Mansfield, see Shyllon, *Black Slaves in Britain*.

101. For overtly racist language in the wake of the Mansfield decision and fears of miscegenation, see Estwick, *Considerations*, 94–95; Long, *Candid Reflections*, 48–49.

102. Burnham, "Between England and America," in *Cultural Institutions of the Novel*, ed. Lynch and Warner, 53.

103. Diderot, "Éloge de Richardson," 30–31. First published in the January 1762 *Journal étranger*, the "Éloge" appeared as a pamphlet shortly afterwards and was subsequently reprinted with later editions of Richardson translations.

104. Diderot, "Éloge de Richardson," 44. For an alternate reading of this passage, see Cohen, "Sentimental Communities," in *Literary Channel*, ed. Cohen and Dever, 122.

105. See Caplan, *Framed Narratives*.

106. Burnham, "Between England and America," in *Cultural Institutions of the Novel*, ed. Lynch and Warner, 53.

107. Prévost, *Cleveland, ou le philosophe anglais*, in *Oeuvres*, ed. Sgard, 2.17.

108. Burke, *Philosophical Enquiry*, ed. Womersley, 84–85.

109. Jameson, *Political Unconscious*, 118.

110. Quint, *Epic and Empire*, 23.

111. Bakhtin, "Novel and Epic," in id., *Dialogic Imagination*, 17.

112. Charpentier, *Relation*, 11.

113. Pagden, *Lords of All the World*, 10; see also 66–73. Miller, *Defining the Common Good*.

114. Henry, *Historical Account of All the Voyages*, 1.iv.

115. Ferguson, *Essay*, 191.

116. Blondel, *Des hommes tels qu'ils sont et doivent être*, 30.

117. See, e.g., Kaiser, "Louis le Bien-Aimé," in *From Royal to Republican Body*, ed. Melzer and Norberg, 131–61.

118. Montesquieu, *De l'esprit des lois*, ed. Goldschmidt, bk. 20, chap. 1; 2.9; id., *Spirit of the Laws*, 2.1.

119. Merish, *Sentimental Materialism*, 31.

120. See Cohen, "Sentimental Communities," in *Literary Channel*, 110, and Van Kley, ed., *French Idea of Freedom*.

121. Roach, "Body of Law," in *From the Royal to Republican Body*, ed. Melzer and Norberg, 113–30.

122. Aubert, "Blood of France," 452; Axtell, *Invasion Within.*

123. Belmessous, "Assimilation and Racialism," para. 6.

124. Mirabeau, *Ami des hommes,* 347.

125. Pagden, *Lords of All the World,* 74.

126. Ibid., 35; Porter, *Religion Versus Empire?* 40.

127. Cheek, *Sexual Antipodes,* 10. On eighteenth century discussions of race, see Hudson, "From 'Nation' to 'Race'"; Boulle, "In Defense of Slavery," in *History from Below,* ed. Krantz.

128. Raynal, *Histoire philosophique et politique des… deux Indes,* 3rd ed., 9.2; id., *Philosophical and Political History of… the East and West Indies,* trans. Justamond, 9.359–60.

129. Wheeler, *Complexion of Race,* 138–75.

130. Diderot, letter to Falconet, July 1767, qtd. in Brissenden, *Virtue in Distress,* 279.

131. Cheek, *Sexual Antipodes,* 8.

132. Prévost, *Histoire générale des voyages,* 13.iii.

133. Mackenzie, *Man of Feeling,* ed. Vickers, 93.

134. Ellison, *Cato's Tears,* 15.

135. Lavallée, *Nègre,* 1.xiii.

136. Gordon, *Citizens Without Sovereignty.*

137. Hume, *Treatise,* 482.

Two • Sterne's Snuffbox

1. Colley, *Britons,* 103.

2. Koehn, *Power of Commerce,* 50–51.

3. Brewer, *Sinews of Power,* 114; Anderson, *Crucible of War,* 561.

4. Colley, *Britons,* 103.

5. Sterne, *Sentimental Journey,* ed. Stout, 99. Subsequent citations are given parenthetically in text (SJ).

6. Derrida, *Given Time,* 14.

7. See Mullan, *Sentiment and Sociability;* Ellis, *Politics of Sensibility,* esp. 129–59.

8. Lamb, "Language and Hartleian Associationism," 297.

9. Appadurai, "Introduction," in *Social Lives of Things,* ed. id., 11–12.

10. Frow, "Gift and Commodity," in id., *Time and Commodity Culture,* 131. See also Gregory, *Gifts and Commodities.*

11. Pietz, "Bosman's Guinea," 3. Pietz's argument does not accommodate commodities that *acquire* their exchange value from their cultural particularity.

12. Henry Mackenzie, "Attachment to Inanimate Objects," *The Mirror* 61 (December 1780), in id. et al., *Mirror,* 6th ed., 2.12.

13. Beattie, *Elements of Moral Science,* 1.171–72.

14. Blair, *Lectures on Rhetoric and Belles Lettres,* 1.384–85.

15. For useful accounts of commerce in Sterne, see Lamb, "Language and Hartleian Associationism," 295–99; Seidel, "Narrative Crossings"; Markley, "Sentimentality as Performance," in *New Eighteenth Century,* ed. Nussbaum and Brown, 210–30.

16. Weiner, *Inalienable Possessions,* 5, 43.

17. Derrida, *Given Time*, 14.

18. Walter's money in *Tristram Shandy* comes in part from the Turkey trade and a £1,000 legacy from Walter's sister. See Visser, "*Tristram Shandy* and the Straight Line of History."

19. In Dorothy Kilner's 1781 *Adventures of a Hackney Coach*, thieves cynically speculate on whether the falsified sentimental provenance of a snuffbox will allow it to fetch "as great a price as the Monk's horn-box—if Yorick's heirs would dispose of it." Kilner, *Adventures of a Hackney Coach*, 3rd ed., 73.

20. Jacobi in Howes, ed., *Sterne: The Critical Heritage*, 429–30. See also subsequent citations given parenthetically in the text (Howes).

21. Thayer, "Laurence Sterne in Germany," 87–88. See also Longo, *Laurence Sterne und Johann Georg Jacobi*, 39–44.

22. Lynch, *Economy of Character*, 19.

23. Sterne to Dr. John Eustace, Feb. 9, 1768, in *Letters of Laurence Sterne*, ed. Curtis, 411.

24. On the relation between the laugh track and the Greek chorus, see Žižek, *Sublime Object of Ideology*, 35

25. "Pharisee and Publican in the Temple," in Sterne, *Sermons*, ed. New (Florida edition), 6.63 [1.6]. References are to the sermon number and page number in the Florida edition followed by the volume and sermon number from the original edition in brackets.

26. *Sermons*, 19.184 [3.4]. The same sentiments are echoed in sermon 37.351 [6.10].

27. Sterne, *Tristram Shandy*, ed. New and New, 2.17.159. Citations are to book, chapter, and page numbers in this edition.

28. Sterne, *Sermons*, 14.137 [2.14].

29. Ibid.

30. Extract from Jean Baptiste Suard's notice of volumes 7 and 8 of *Tristram Shandy*, in the *Gazette littéraire de l'Europe*, translated and printed in the *London Chronicle* 17, no. 1299 (Apr. 10–18, 1765): 373, qtd. in Howes, ed., *Sterne: The Critical Heritage*, 169.

31. Extract from an unsigned review of volumes 7 and 8 of *Tristram Shandy* in the *Critical Review* 19 (January 1765): 65–66; qtd. in Howes, ed., *Sterne: The Critical Heritage*, 160.

32. *Letters of Oscar Wilde*, ed. Hart-Davis, 501; quoted in Tanner, "Sentimentality," 127.

33. Sterne to Kitty Fourmantel, April 1760, in *Letters of Laurence Sterne*, ed. Curtis, 105.

34. Sterne to John Hall-Stevenson, June 1761, in *Letters of Laurence Sterne*, ed. Curtis, 140.

35. Donoghue, *Fame Machine*, 56–85.

36. Sterne to David Garrick, Mar. 16, 1765, in *Letters of Laurence Sterne*, ed. Curtis, 235.

37. See Ellis, *Politics of Sensibility*, 71–79; Lamb, *Preserving the Self*, 264–67; Frank, "A Man who laughs is never dangerous," 109–11.

38. Kant, *Critique of Judgment*, trans. Bernard, 145. See also Lichtenstein, *Eloquence of Color*, 169–74.

39. Ellis, *Politics of Sensibility*, 75.

40. Born in 1729 in a slave ship and brought to England at the age of two, Sancho attracted the interest of the 2nd duke of Montagu, and eventually entered the Montagu household, where he rose to the rank of butler. Upon his retirement from service, Sancho and his West Indian wife ran a shop in Westminster, where he corresponded with Sterne, Johnson, Garrick, and George Cumberland.

41. Trimmer, *Family Magazine,* 3.206.

42. Review, "Considerations of the Abolition of Slavery and the Slave Trade," *Critical Review: or, the Annals of Literature* 67 (1789): 454.

43. Sterne, "Job's Account of the Shortness . . . of Life," in *Sermons* 10.99 [2.10]; also SJ, 199–200.

44. *Letters of Ignatius Sancho,* ed. Edwards and Rewt, 86.

45. Aravamudan, *Tropicopolitans,* 44.

46. See Sterne, *Sentimental Journey,* ed. Stout, 205–6n.

47. *Beauties of Sterne,* viii.

48. On Sterne's reception, see Howes, *Yorick and the Critics;* Oates, *Shandyism and Sentiment;* Bandry, "Imitations of *Tristram Shandy,*" in *Critical Essays on Laurence Sterne,* ed. New, 39–52.

49. See Lamb, "Sterne's System of Imitation," in *Critical Essays on Laurence Sterne,* ed. New, 19–38; and Fanning, "Things Themselves," 29–45.

50. Ferriar, *Illustrations of Sterne,* 6–7. "[I]n the ludicrous," Ferriar admits, "he is generally a copyist" (7).

51. Extracts from "Critical Comments on Sterne, Smollett, and Fielding," *The Port Folio,* 3rd ser., 6 (November 1811), qtd. in Howes, ed., *Sterne: The Critical Heritage,* 340.

52. Sterne to Dr. John Eustace, Feb. 9, 1768, in *Letters of Laurence Sterne,* ed. Curtis, 411. See also *Tristram Shandy:* "a man should ever bring one half of the entertainment along with him" (8.19.682).

53. See *Letters of Laurence Sterne,* ed. Curtis, 362n; see also 12n–15n.

54. Lanham, *Tristram Shandy,* 56.

55. Lamb, *Sterne's Fiction and the Double Principle,* 8.

56. Bakhtin, "Discourse in the Novel," in id., *Dialogic Imagination,* 293–94.

57. Bakhtin, *Dialogic Imagination,* 294.

58. Ibid., 352.

59. The curses came to Sterne secondhand; see *Tristram Shandy,* ed. New and New (Florida edition), 2.952–57 (app. 8).

60. New et al., *Tristram Shandy,* vol. 3: *The Notes* (Florida edition), 219.

61. Barbara Johnson, "Using People," in *Turn to Ethics,* ed. Garber et al., 52. "Winnicott," Johnson argues, "is capable of *using* language in just the way he speaks of *using* objects—using language to play fort-da with, and letting language play him" (61).

62. H. F. Jones, *Samuel Butler,* 1.136–37, qtd. in Howes, *Yorick and the Critics,* 166.

63. Lamb, *Sterne's Fiction and the Double Principle,* 4.

64. For the details of her life, see Wright and Sclater, *Sterne's Eliza;* Guest, "Sterne, Elizabeth Draper, and Drapery," 9–33; Strugnell, "À la recherche d'Eliza Draper," in *Abbé Raynal,* ed. Bancarel and Goggi, 173–86.

65. Cash, *Laurence Sterne: The Later Years,* 275, 275n54, 365.

66. Lamb, "Sterne's System of Imitation," 36.

67. J. H. Miller, "Narrative Middles," 375.

68. Guest, "Sterne, Eliza Draper, and Drapery," 28.

69. Lamb, "Sterne's System of Imitation," 36.

70. Sterne, letter of May 25, 1767, in *Letters of Laurence Sterne,* ed. Curtis, 346.

71. Simmel, *Philosophy of Money*, 67.

72. Sterne, "On the Duty of Setting Bounds to our Desires," in *Sermons* 13.127–28. [2.13]

73. Nunokawa, *Afterlife of Property*, 7.

74. Sterne to Eliza Draper, March 1767, in *Letters of Laurence Sterne*, ed. Curtis, 313.

75. Raynal 3.15.71; 3.90. The citations in this chapter refer respectively to Raynal's *Histoire philosophique et politique des... deux Indes*, 3rd ed., and to the English translation by J. O. Justamond, *Philosophical and Political History of... the East and West Indies*, 3d ed. On the inkstand, see Strugnell, "À la recherche d'Eliza Draper," 179.

76. On Eliza's importance to the frontispiece, see Ette, "Mise en scène de la table de travail," in *Icons*, ed. Wagner, 185–88. The passage first appeared in the third edition of 1780. Raynal probably met Eliza during her sojourn in Paris upon returning home from India, a friendship that was renewed in 1778 during a visit to London upon his election to the Royal Society. See Strugnell, "À la recherche d'Eliza Draper," 173–86. The elegy was published in four of the five French editions of *Yorick's Letters to Eliza* and was translated into English in the *European Magazine* 5 (1784), 171–73.

77. Grimm, *Correspondance littéraire*, 12.520–21.

78. Lydia Sterne to Mrs. Montagu, April 5, 1768, in *Letters of Laurence Sterne*, ed. Curtis, 434.

Three • Tales Told by Things

1. Hutton, *Ladies' Diary*, 27.

2. Smollett, *History and Adventures of an Atom*, ed. Day.

3. Kilner, *Adventures of a Hackney Coach*, 3rd ed., 5; Scott, *Adventures of a Rupee*, vii.

4. Bridges, *Adventures of a Bank-note*, 1.111–13; *Flagel, or A Ramble of Fancy*, 21–24; *Adventures of a Watch*, 203–4.

5. *Adventures of a Black Coat*, vi.

6. *Adventures of a Cork-screw*, xiii–xiv.

7. *Birmingham Counterfeit*, 1.40.

8. Douglas, "Britannia's Rule," 71.

9. Marx, *Capital*, 1.42–43; *History of a Pin*, 22.

10. Marx, *Capital*, 1.44. On the "chiasmus between people and things," see also Pietz, "Fetishism and Materialism," in *Fetishism*, ed. Apter and Pietz, 148.

11. Marx, *Capital*, 1.55. Subsequent citations given parenthetically in the text.

12. De Grazia et al., eds., "Introduction," in *Subject and Object*, 4.

13. On tropes in *Capital*, see Keenan, "Point," in *Fetishism*, ed. Apter and Pietz.

14. Stallybrass, "Marx's Coat," in *Border Fetishisms*, ed. Spyer, 184.

15. Marx also acknowledges that the commodity cannot do without its owner. "It is plain that commodities cannot go to market and make exchanges of their own account. We must, therefore, have recourse to their guardians, who are also their owners. Commodities are things, and therefore without power of resistance against man. If they are wanting in docility he can use force; in other words, he can take possession of them" (*Capital*, 1.56).

16. Kopytoff, "Cultural Biography of Things," in *Social Life of Things*, ed. Appadurai, 64–91.

17. Addison, *The Tatler*, no. 249, reprinted in *Commerce of Everyday Life*, ed. Mackie, 183–87.

18. Scott, *Adventures of a Rupee*, 137–38.

19. Ibid., 138.

20. See de Grazia, "Ideology of Superfluous Things," in *Subject and Object*, ed. id. et al, 17–42.

21. *Adventures of a Watch*, 205.

22. Ibid., 205–6.

23. *Adventures of a Black Coat*, 13.

24. *Adventures of an Ostrich Feather of Quality*, 70–71; *Adventures of a Watch*, 209–10.

25. *History of a Pin*, 107.

26. Scott, *Adventures of a Rupee*, 59.

27. Ibid., 13, 27, 43.

28. Ibid., 197.

29. Theophilus Johnson, *Phantoms*, 1.4, 1.10.

30. *Argentum*, 3.

31. "Adventures of a Mirror," *Lady's Magazine* 22 (January 1791): 16; (May 1791): 263.

32. Johnstone, *Chrysal*, 1.6.

33. *Aureus*, 9.

34. See *Adventures of a Rupee*, 214. Also Douglas, "Britannia's Rule," 74.

35. *Memoirs and Interesting Adventures of an Embroidered Waistcoat, Part II*, 8.

36. Other instances of French object narratives include *Le canapé couleur de feu* (The Flame-Colored Couch [1741]; attributed to Jean-Louis Fougeret de Montbron), in which the spirit of a man is infused into a sofa, and the abbé de Voisenon's *Le sultan Misapouf et la princesse Grisemine* (1746), in which the hero becomes a bathtub. On the Orientalist strain running through these books, see Dobie, *Foreign Bodies*, 83–120.

37. Jerrold, *Story of a Feather*, 86.

38. *Memoirs of the Shakespear's Head*, 1.7.

39. Caracioli, *Chiron*, 2.163.

40. Lynch, *Economy of Character*, 94–102.

41. Burn, *Second Address*, 8; "Anthropos," *Rights of Man*, 40–41.

42. Fox, *Address to the People of Great Britain*, 11th ed., 3.

43. Sussman, "Women and the Politics of Sugar, 1792," 51–58; Coleman, "Conspicuous Consumption," esp. 344–49.

44. Scarry, *Body in Pain*, 256.

45. Bill Brown, "How to Do Things with Things," 953.

46. *Genuine and Most Surprising Adventures of a Very Unfortunate Goose-Quill*, 25.

47. See Flint, "Speaking Objects."

48. *History of a Bible*, 3–4.

49. "Adventures of a Quire of Paper," *London Magazine* 48 (October 1779): 451.

50. Carroll, *Alice's Adventures*, 92.

51. De Man, "Autobiography as De-Facement," in id., *Rhetoric of Romanticism*, 75–76. Johnson's *Dictionary* defines *personification* as a "prosopopoeia; the change of things or per-

sons: as '*Confusion* heard his voice'"; *prosopopoeia*, with neat reciprocity, is defined as "personification; figure by which things are made persons."

52. De Man, "Autobiography as De-Facement," 76.

53. Addison, *Tatler*, 184.

54. *Story of a Needle*, 10–11; *History of a Pin*, 4.

55. On catachresis, see Barbara Johnson, "A Hound, A Bay Horse, and a Turtle Dove," in id., *World of Difference*, 53; and Kaplan, *French Lessons*, 149–50.

56. De Man, "Epistemology of Metaphor," 21.

57. Barbara Johnson, "Deconstruction, Feminism, and Pedagogy," in id., *World of Difference*, 45.

58. Chambers, "Preface," in *Cyclopaedia* (1728), 1.xii.

59. Lamb, "Modern Metamorphoses and Disgraceful Tales," 158.

60. As Werner Sollors notes, "with the exception of the *Narrative* itself, a single letter from 1789, and one use of the signature 'Aethiopianus,' Equiano appears to have signed publications, letters, and legal documents with the name Gustavus Vassa." Sollors, "Introduction," in *Interesting Narrative of Olaudah Equiano*, x.

61. See Carretta, "Olaudah Equiano or Gustavus Vassa?"; Acholonu, "Home of Olaudah Equiano."

62. Knapp, *Personification and the Sublime*, 2. The object narratives are not personifications in the sense Knapp discusses. Knapp is interested in allegorical personifications, wherein the fictional agent is saturated "by the thematic idea it represents" (3).

63. Bhabha, "Of Mimicry and Man," in id., *Location of Culture*, 87. At the time, *person* was a differential term. "The objects of dominion or property are *things*, as contradistinguished from *persons*," Blackstone writes (*Commentaries*, 2.16).

64. Hinds, "Spirit of Trade," 635.

65. See the debate between Adam Potkay, Srinivas Aravamudan, and Roxann Wheeler in "Forum: Teaching Equiano's *Interesting Narrative*."

66. Fichtelberg, "Word Between Worlds," esp. 463–69; Potkay, "Olaudah Equiano and the Art of Spiritual Autobiography," 680.

67. Equiano, *Interesting Narrative*, ed. Sollors, 44. Subsequent citations given parenthetically in the text.

68. Gates, *Signifying Monkey*, 156.

69. De Grazia et al., "Introduction," in *Subject and Object*, 3.

70. On Equiano's use of eighteenth-century theories of human difference, see Wheeler, *Complexion of Race*, esp. 260–87.

71. Pels, "Spirit of Matter," in *Border Fetishisms*, ed. Spyer, 100.

72. The taciturn Bible in the slave narratives has a speaking counterpart in the 1812 *History of a Bible*. Taken to the West Indies by its owner, the Bible is handed on to a "poor native, who," it tells us, "desired me to speak to his companions. A few were greatly affected with what I said. They often called upon me" (21–22).

73. Gronniosaw, "Narrative of the Most Remarkable Particulars," in *Pioneers of the Black Atlantic*, ed. Gates and Andrews, 40–41.

74. Gates, *Signifying Monkey*, 137.

75. Ferguson, *Pornography*, 12.

76. Gates, *Signifying Monkey*, 157.

77. Ibid., 156.

78. Ibid., 130.

79. Aravamudan, *Tropicopolitans*, 270.

80. Thomas, *Man and the Natural World*, 25n.

81. Owned by people who could not read, the Bible was (not unlike the African fetish) called into service for the swearing of oaths, curing diseases, bibliomancy, or even the divination of thieves; see Cressy, "Books as Totems." On the projection of book fetishism *onto* native populations as a sign of the European fetishism of literacy, see Wogan, "Perceptions of European Literacy," and Warkentin, "In Search of 'The Word of the Other.'"

82. Stedman, *Stedman's Surinam*, 263.

83. See also Bhabha, "Signs Taken for Wonders," in id., *Location of Culture*, 102–22.

84. Aravamudan, *Tropicopolitans*, 271.

85. Baker, *Blues, Ideology and Afro-American Literature*, 35.

86. Ibid., 36.

87. Alleine, *Solemn Warnings of the Dead*, 13.

88. Potkay, "Olaudah Equiano and the Art of Spiritual Autobiography," 687.

89. De Man, "Anthropomorphism and Trope in the Lyric," in id., *Rhetoric of Romanticism*, 241.

90. Alleine, *Solemn Warnings of the Dead*, 50, 7–8.

91. Chambers, *Cyclopaedia* (1728), 1.107, s.v. *anthropology*.

92. Hume, "Natural History of Religion," in id., *Essays and Treatises*, 4.266.

93. Ibid., 258.

94. Ibid., 283. Gronniosaw refuses the plurality of African Gods: "Then says I, who made the First Man? and who made the first cow, and the first lion, and where does the fly come from, as no one can make him?" (36–37).

95. Hume, "Natural History of Religion," in id., *Essays and Treatises*, 4.266–68. See also Brosses, *Du Culte des dieux fétiches*, 215–16.

96. Hume, *Treatise of Human Nature*, ed. Selby-Bigge, 2nd ed., rev. Nidditch, 224–25.

97. See Barbara Johnson, "Anthropomorphism in Lyric and Law."

98. Foucault, *Herculine Barbin*, xiii.

Four • *Making Humans Human*

1. Newton, *Journal of a Slave Trader*, ed. Martin and Spurrell, 45.

2. "Extract from the *Judith's* ledger, 1728, Account of Rice and Slaves Purchesed and Whatt Goods Paid," in *Documents Illustrative... of the Slave Trade*, ed. Donnan, 2.372.

3. On the trade ounce, see Polanyi, "Sortings and 'Ounce Trade'"; Marion Johnson, "Ounce in Eighteenth-Century West African Trade"; and Metcalf, "Gold, Assortments and the Trade Ounce."

4. Quoted in Anstey, *Atlantic Slave Trade and British Abolition*, 10.

5. Phillips, "Journal of a Voyage ... in the Years 1693, and 1694," in *Collection of Voyages and Travels*, ed. Churchill and Churchill, 6.227.

6. Francis Moore, *Travels in Africa*, qtd. in *Documents Illustrative ... of the Slave Trade*, ed. Donnan, 2.396–97.

7. De Man, "Epistemology of Metaphor," 21.

8. *Documents Illustrative ... of the Slave Trade*, ed. Donnan, 2.17n.

9. Matthews, *Voyage to the River Sierra-Leone*, 175.

10. Pietz, "Bosman's Guinea," 3. See also id., "Problem of the Fetish."

11. Cobbett, *Parliamentary History of England*, 29.1233. Hereafter cited parenthetically by volume and page number.

12. Sharp, *Appendix*, 9, 10.

13. Blackstone, *Commentaries*, 1.412.

14. Samuel Sewell, *The Selling of Joseph* (1700), 162, qtd. in Davis, *Problem of Slavery in Western Culture*, 345.

15. Day, *Dying Negro*, 1st ed. (1773), 5. Page numbers cited parenthetically in the text are from this edition.

16. Berlant, "Female Complaint," 243.

17. Day, *Dying Negro*, 2nd ed., viii. The second edition includes a dedication to Rousseau.

18. On the choice of "Hosier's Ghost," see Kaul, *Poems of Nation*, 247. On Cowper's popularity, see Wood, *Slavery, Empathy, and Pornography*, 82.

19. Lady Hesketh, letter to Cowper, Mar. 21, 1788, in Cowper, *Letters and Prose Writings*, ed. King and Ryskamp, 3.130; id., "The Negro's Complaint," in *Poems*, ed. Baird and Ryskamp, 3.13–14 (citations are given in text by line number).

20. Kaul, *Poems of Nation*, 246.

21. Cheng, *Melancholy of Race*, 7.

22. Ibid., 6.

23. Cowper, *Letters and Prose Writings*, 3.127n; Clarkson, *History*, 2.153.

24. The medallion was the product of important technological advances. Wedgwood had developed a clay that could be colored effectively; "the ground was a most delicate white, but the Negro, who was seen imploring compassion in the middle of it, was in his own native colour" (Clarkson, *History*, 2.153).

25. Ibid., 2.154.

26. For the myriad forms in which the medallion circulated, see Oldfield, *Popular Politics*, 155–67.

27. Cowper, letter to Lady Hesketh, June 23, 1788, in *Letters and Prose Writings*, 3.185.

28. Cooper, *Letters on the Slave Trade*, 5.

29. Knapp, *Personification and the Sublime*, 3.

30. Kames, *Elements of Criticism*, 3.70.

31. Deirdre Coleman has argued that the question must remain unanswered because the collapse of the metaphor of fraternity introduces the literal possibility of "a nightmare confusion of the races through interracial sex." See Coleman, "Conspicuous Consumption," 342.

32. Wexler, "Tender Violence," in *Culture of Sentiment*, ed. Samuels, 17.

33. *Capital*, 1.21n.

34. See Yellin, *Women and Sisters*, 10.

35. Marx, *Capital*, 1.26n. Things are complicated by the fact that the template is mutable: "A, for instance, cannot be 'your majesty' to B, unless at the same time majesty in B's eyes as-

sumes the bodily form of A, and, what is more, with every new father of the people, changes its features, hair, and many other things besides" (20).

36. What Marx calls a fetishistic inversion occurs because commodity A relates to commodity B as if A would not be a "reflexive determination" of B. See Marx, *Capital*, 1.21. Commodities "forget" that their value is relative: thus commodity A acts as if B would "*already in itself*" be the equivalent of A" (Žižek, *Sublime Object of Ideology*, 24). The fact that B expresses the value of A is seen as a property of B, belonging to it even when it is not placed in relation to A.

37. Hume, *Treatise of Human Nature*, ed. Selby-Bigge, 2nd ed. rev, Nidditch, 340. Subsequent citation given parenthetically in the text.

38. Parsons, "Arts of Abolition," in *Interpreting Colonialism*, ed. Wells and Stewart, 345–68.

39. See Blackburn, *Overthrow of Colonial Slavery*.

40. Whitbread qtd. in Walvin, "Public Campaign in England," in *Abolition of the Atlantic Slave Trade*, ed. Eltis and Walvin, 68.

41. Kowaleski-Wallace, *Consuming Subjects*, 38.

42. See Bohls, *Women Travel Writers*, 46–65; Sandiford, *Cultural Politics of Sugar*, 88–117; and Coleman, "Janet Schaw and the Complexions of Empire."

43. Schaw, *Journal of a Lady of Quality*, 28.

44. Fisher, *Hard Facts*, 100.

45. Žižek, *Sublime Object*, 106. See Burnham, "Between England and America," in *Cultural Institutions of the Novel*, ed. Lynch and Warner, 47–72.

46. Barbauld, "Inquiry," in id., *Works*, 2.222.

47. Smith, *Theory of Moral Sentiments*, ed. Raphael and Macfie, 36.

48. Montag, "Universalization of Whiteness," in *Whiteness*, ed. Hill, 284.

49. Bellamy, *Benevolent Planters*, in *Slavery, Abolition and Emancipation, vol. 5: Drama*, ed. Cox, 5.127.

50. Chatterton, ed., *Memorials, Personal and Historical of Admiral Lord Gambier*, 1.170. On More's involvement with the abolition movement, see Stott, *Hannah More*, 86–95.

51. Wood, *Blind Memory*, 17. For a history of the image from its origins to the present, see ibid., 17–36, and Oldfield, *Popular Politics*, 165–66.

52. More to her sister, April 1789, in Roberts, *Memoirs of the Life and Correspondence of Mrs. Hannah More*, 1.310.

53. Clarkson, *History*, 2.91–92.

54. Wood, *Blind Memory*, 19; Spillers, "Mama's Baby, Papa's Maybe," 72.

55. Wood, *Blind Memory*, 29; Fox, *Speeches*, 372.

56. Clarkson, letter to Honoré Gabriel Riquetti, comte de Mirabeau, Nov. 13, 1789, Huntington Library MS CN 35, p. 4.

57. Great Britain, Parliament, House of Commons, *Abridgment of the Minutes*, no. 3 (n.p., 1790), 37. Countertestimony to Dr. Trotter's account was offered by Clement Nobele, ship's master on the *Brookes* (ibid., 51).

58. Cobbett, *Parliamentary History of England*, 27.586. For another instance of the air-pump analogy, see Cobbett, 27.643.

59. Stanfield, *Observations on a Guinea Voyage*, 30.

60. Newton, *Thoughts upon the African Slave Trade*, 33–34. For another comparison of books and slaves, see Cobbett, *Parliamentary History of England*, 27.642.

61. Mitchell, "Soul that dreams," para. 11.

62. All quotations are cited by line number from Cowper, "Sweet Meat has Sour Sauce," in *Poems*, ed. Baird and Ryskamp, 3.15–16, ll. 9–11.

63. Wood, *Slavery, Empathy and Pornography*, 84.

64. Keith, "Formal Challenges of Antislavery Poetry," 110.

65. Kaul, *Poems of Nation*, 248.

66. Žižek, *Sublime Object*, 106.

67. Mitchell, "Soul that dreams," para. 11.

68. Burke, *Philosophical Enquiry*, ed. Womersley, 91.

69. A full survey of the literature is not possible here. For discussions of the parliamentary debates, see Anstey, *Atlantic Slave Trade*, esp. 239–320. On the economic underpinnings, see Williams, *Capitalism and Slavery*; Drescher, *Econocide*; Ragatz, *Fall of the Planter Class*. On the intellectual, philosophical and social aspects, see Davis, *Problem of Slavery in Western Culture* and *Problem of Slavery in the Age of Revolution*.

70. On the petition campaigns, see Oldfield, *Popular Politics;* on women's role in the campaigns, see Sussman, *Consuming Anxieties;* Midgley, *Women Against Slavery;* Ferguson, *Subject to Others*.

71. Ellison, *Cato's Tears*, 20.

72. Claudia Johnson, *Equivocal Beings*, 14.

73. Cobbett, *Parliamentary History*, 28.42. All subsequent references are given parenthetically in text.

74. Fox, *Speeches*, 60.

75. Horkheimer and Adorno, *Dialectic of Enlightenment*, 3.

76. *Debate on a Motion for the Abolition . . . 1791*, 114.

77. Great Britain, Parliament, House of Commons, *Abridgement of the Minutes*, no. 4 (1791), 141. In the *Debate on a Motion for the Abolition . . . 1791*, the woman is "tied up to a beam by her wrists, entirely naked" (114).

78. *Debate on a Motion for the Abolition . . . 1791*, 114.

79. Ibid. Crafton, *Short Sketch of the Evidence*, 19–20, also cites this passage.

80. Smith, *Theory of Moral Sentiments*, ed. Raphael and Macfie, 190.

81. See Halttunen, "Humanitarianism and the Pornography of Pain," 329. See also Wood, *Slavery, Empathy and Pornography*.

82. Stanfield, *Observations on a Guinea Voyage*, 33.

83. *Debates in the British House of Commons . . . on . . . the Abolition of the Slave Trade*, 5.

84. Wexler, "Tender Violence," 15.

85. *Selected Writings of Benjamin Rush*, ed. Runes, 15.

86. Stanfield, *Observations on a Guinea Voyage*, 33.

87. Sade, *Philosophie dans le boudoir,* in *Oeuvres*, ed. Delon, 3.89.

88. Newton, *Thoughts upon the African Slave Trade*, 17–18. See also Cobbett, *Parliamentary History of England*, 29.1068.

89. Krafft-Ebbing, *Psychopathia Sexualis*, case # 57, p. 96; Freud, "Child," in *Standard Edition*, 17.180.

90. Favret, "Flogging," in *Romanticism and Gender*, ed. Janowitz, 29.

91. Great Britain, Parliament, House of Commons, *Sessional Papers of the Eighteenth Century*, ed. Lambert, 82.54.

92. Ibid., 152, 154.

93. Ibid., 199.

94. Ibid., *Sessional Papers*, 199.

95. The flogging of women gained even greater prominence in abolitionist polemics of the 1820s and 1830s. See Paton, "Decency, Dependence and the Lash."

96. Alexander, *History of Women*, 1.291.

97. Great Britain, Parliament, House of Commons, *Abridgement of the Minutes*, no, 4 (1791), 30. Additional anecdotes on pp. 68; 72–73; 81; 83.

98. "Character of the English Ladies, from Dr. Wendeborn's View of England," *Lady's Magazine* 22 (February 1791), 72.

99. Wollstonecraft, *Vindication of the Rights of Men*, in *Works*, ed. Butler and Todd, 5.45.

100. Ibid.

101. Wollstonecraft, *Vindication of the Rights of Woman*, in *Works*, ed. Butler and Todd, 5.215.

102. Review of "A Poem on the Bill lately passed for regulating the Slave Trade," by Helen Maria Williams, *Monthly Review* 80 (1789): 237–38, also qtd. in Davies, "Moral Purchase," in *Women, Writing and the Public Sphere*, ed. Eger et al., 136; and in Ferguson, *Subject to Others*, 163 (but incorrectly attributed to the *Critical Review*).

103. On women's abolitionist poetry and the bid for cultural authority, see also Mellor, "Am I not a Woman . . . ?" in *Romanticism, Race and Imperial Culture*, ed. Richardson and Hofkosh; Davies, "Moral Purchase," in *Women, Writing and the Public Sphere*, ed. Eger et al.

104. Johnson, *Equivocal Beings*, 12.

105. Wollstonecraft, *Wrongs of Woman*, in *Works*, ed. Todd and Butler, 1.83.

106. Wollstonecraft attacked Barbauld for resigning the public domain of reason to men and excoriated Barbauld's comparison of woman to a delicate flower in "To Mrs. P," prompting Barbauld to retaliate with her poem, "The Rights of Woman." See Wollstonecraft, *Vindication of the Rights of Woman*, in *Works*, ed. Butler and Todd, 5.122–23n, and Barbauld, "The Rights of Woman," in *Poems*, ed. McCarthy and Kraft, 121–22 (ll. 29–32).

107. Barbauld, "Epistle to William Wilberforce," in *Poems*, ed. McCarthy and Kraft, 114–18 (ll. 3–10). Subsequent line numbers are given parenthetically in the text.

108. Žižek, *Sublime Object*, 29.

109. Ellison, *Cato's Tears*, 110.

110. See Ross, *Contours of Masculine Desire*, 222–23; Coleman, "Conspicuous Consumption," 353–54.

111. *Debate on a Motion for the Abolition . . . 1792*, 47.

112. Ibid., 100–101.

113. *Very New Pamphlet Indeed*, 1.

114. *Debate on a Motion for the Abolition . . . 1791*, 37.

115. Ibid. See also Fox, *Speeches*, 375.

Five • Global Commerce in Raynal's Histoire des deux Indes

1. Raynal, *Histoire philosophique et politique des... deux Indes*, 3rd ed., 1.introduction.3; trans. Justamond as *Philosophical and Political History of... the East and West Indies*, 3rd ed., 1.4. Because of deviations in the pagination of the French third edition, each citation gives the book, chapter, and page number of the octavo French edition, followed by the book and page number of the English one.

2. Raynal, 1.intro.3–4; 1.4. See Delon, "Appel au lecteur," in *Lectures de Raynal*, ed. Lüsebrink and Tietz, esp. 53–55.

3. On the status of the harangue as a mode of historical writing, see Pujol, "Formes de l'éloquence," in *"L'Histoire des deux Indes": Réécriture et polygraphie*, ed. Lüsebrink and Strugnell, esp. 358–62; on the relation of reader and narrator in the *Histoire*, see Penke, "Figures du narrateur et du destinataire," in ibid., 69–78, and Ette, "Tour de l'univers," in *Abbé Raynal*, ed. Bancarel and Goggi, 255–72. On sentimentality in the writing of history in eighteenth-century Britain, see Phillips, "Relocating Inwardness."

4. Pocock, "Commerce, Settlement, and History," in *Articulating America*, ed. Starr, 16.

5. Fabian, *Time and the Other*, 31.

6. Raynal acknowledges the possibility of a "bad reader" who will perversely skip the revolutionary moral parts to get to the "good bits" that will allow him to exploit the colonies with greater efficacy. An "avaricious mortal, and destitute of taste" may read the revolutionary treatise as a mercantile dictionary: "thou hast entered upon the reading of my work, with the same spirit as the ferocious Europeans entered upon these rich and unhappy countries; I see that thou wert worthy to accompany them, because thy propensities are the same as theirs [*tu avois la meme âme qu'eux*]" (7.29.117; 7.150). Franz Christian Lorenz Karsten's epitome of the *Histoire des deux Indes* published in 1780 under the title *Europens Handel mit beyden Indien* did precisely this, it would seem. See Lüsebrink, "*L'Histoire des deux Indes* et ses 'extraits'," 37.

7. See Feugère, *Précurseur de la Révolution*. On the pan-European and pan-American reception of Raynal, see the essays in Lüsebrink and Tietz, eds., *Lectures de Raynal*. Celebrated as one of the "fathers of the French Revolution," Raynal was inducted into the Panthéon, but his 1791 condemnation of the excesses of the Revolution in his Address to the Assemblée nationale led to his repudiation by Robespierre and the Left. See Hans-Jürgen Lüsebrink, "La Réception de l'*Adresse à l'Assemblée nationale*," in *De la polémique à l'histoire*, ed. Bancarel and Goggi, 333–44.

8. On plagiarism and the *Histoire*, see Brot, "Réécritures des lumières," esp. 627–32; on the term *nègre*, see Brot, 628.

9. Diderot, *Oeuvres philosophiques*, ed. Vernière, 641.

10. Muthu, *Enlightenment Against Empire*, 73. On Diderot's contributions, see Duchet, *Diderot et "L'histoire des deux Indes"*; Dieckmann, *Inventaire du fonds Vandeul, et inédits de Diderot*; Bénot, *Diderot*.

11. Pocock, "Commerce, Settlement, and History," 17.

12. Aravamudan, "Progress Through Violence or Progress from Violence?" in *Progrès et violence*, ed. Cossy and Dawson, 263.

13. See Skrzypek, "Le commerce instrument de la paix mondiale," in *De la polémique à l'histoire,* ed. Bancarel and Goggi, 243–54.

14. Montesquieu, *De l'esprit des lois,* ed. Goldschmidt, bk. 20, chap. 2; 2.10; id., *Spirit of the Laws,* 2.2.

15. See Saint-Amand, *Laws of Hostility.*

16. Samuel Johnson, *History of Rasselas,* ed. Enright, 77.

17. Smith, *Theory of Moral Sentiments,* ed. Raphael and Macfie, 136. See also Hancock, *Citizens of the World.*

18. Haskell, "Capitalism and the Rise of Humanitarian Sensibility, Part I," in *Antislavery Debate,* ed. Bender, 111. Haskell's argument has been subjected to significant critique among historians. See the other essays in the Bender volume.

19. Joseph, "Bookkeeping and the Informatics of Empire" (paper presented at the Modern Language Association, Washington, D.C., December 2004).

20. Africanus [pseud.], *Remarks on the Slave Trade,* 2.

21. Africanus paraphrases this passage. See ibid., 42.

22. Raynal is very specific about who can tell us the meaning of the discovery of the New World: "Barbarous soldiers and rapacious merchants were not proper persons to give us just and clear notions of this hemisphere. It was the province of philosophy alone," Raynal announces, "to avail itself of the informations scattered in the accounts of voyages and missionaries, in order to see America such as nature hath made it, and to find out it's [*sic*] analogy to [*ses rapports avec*] the rest of the world" (17.3.201–2; 17.142–43).

23. The modern global economy is more than the sum of its parts. Thus it is not enough, as Žižek notes, to point out that there are real people and real things behind the abstraction of a capitalist economy, or to say that the abstraction is a misperception of social reality; one must recognize that these abstract forms are "'real' in the precise sense of determining the very structure of material social processes" (Žižek, *Fragile Absolute,* 15).

24. Jaucourt, *Encyclopédie,* s.v. *prosopopée.*

25. Foucault qtd. in Michaels, *Gold Standard,* 179.

26. Michaels, *Gold Standard,* 179.

27. McClintock, *Imperial Leather,* 63–64.

28. Benveniste, *Problèmes de linguistique générale,* 1.239, 241; *Problems in General Linguistics,* 206–7, 208.

29. Caplan, *Framed Narratives,* 24–25.

30. Diderot, "De la poésie dramatique," in *Oeuvres esthétiques,* ed. Vernière, 189.

31. Pagden, *Lords of All the World,* 165.

32. See Arnold, "Hunger in the Garden of Plenty," in *Dreadful Visitations,* ed. Johns, 81–111.

33. Pocock, "Commerce, Settlement, and History," 20.

34. Culler, *Pursuit of Signs,* 142.

35. Aravamudan, "Progress Through Violence or Progress from Violence?" 270–71n.

36. De Man, "Autobiography as De-Facement," in id., *Rhetoric of Romanticism,* 75–76.

37. Decan, *Essai sur la littérature,* 161.

38. Books of extracts like the 1774 supplement, the *Tableau de l'Europe,* use the *Histoire*

to present a portrait of Europe without reference to the colonies. See Lüsebrink, "*Histoire des deux Indes* et ses 'extraits,'" 28–41.

39. Aravamudan, "Progress Through Violence or Progress from Violence?" 269.

40. See Bénot, "Traces de l'*Histoire des deux Indes*," in *Lectures de Raynal*, ed. Lüsebrink and Tietz, 141–54; Venturo, "Lectures de Raynal en Amérique latine," in ibid., 341–59; and Racault, "Effet exotique," in *"Histoire des deux indes": Réécriture et polygraphie*, ed. Lüsebrink and Strugnell, 119.

41. See James, *Black Jacobins*, 24–25; Aravamudan, *Tropicopolitans*, 289–325.

42. Gallagher, *Nobody's Story*, 171.

43. See Gordon, *Citizens Without Sovereignty*.

44. See Burnham, "Between England and America," in *Cultural Institutions*, ed. Lynch and Warner, 53.

Coda • The Peripheral Vision of the Enlightenment

Epigraph: Paul Slansky, "The Twelfth Hundred Days: The Quiz," *New Yorker*, May 24, 2004, "Shouts & Murmurs," 98. www.newyorker.com/shouts/content/articles/040524.sh_shouts (accessed January 10, 2006).

1. Raynal, *Histoire philosophique et politique... des deux Indes*, 3rd ed., 4.5.188; trans. Justamond as *Philosophical and Political History of... the East and West Indies*, 3rd ed., 4.239.

2. Duchet, *Anthropologie et histoire au siècle des Lumières*, 18.

3. See Pitts, *Turn to Empire*.

4. Porter, "Trusteeship, Anti-Slavery, and Humanitarianism," in *Oxford History*, vol. 3: *Nineteenth Century*, ed. id., 198. Since, Porter contends, "Empire provided the sphere within which benevolent government action was most readily conceivable, ... humanitarians rarely questioned the continued existence of territorial Empire" (204).

5. Pagden, *Lords of All the World*, 10.

6. Burke, "Speech on Fox's India Bill," in id., *Writings and Speeches*, vol. 5: *India*, ed. Marshall, 385, 427. On Burke and India, see Suleri, *Rhetoric of English India*, esp. 24–68.

7. P. G. Marshall, "Free though conquering People," in id., *"Free though conquering People,"* 18–19.

8. "The Hero: A Poetic Epistle respectfully Addressed to Marquis Cornwallis" (Cambridge: n.p., 1794), 15; qtd. in P. J. Marshall, "Moral Swing to the East," in id., *"Free though conquering People,"* 72.

9. East India House, *Continuation of the... Debates... at the India-House*, 8–9, 8.

10. Cobbett, *Parliamentary History*, 32.1400, Dec. 20, 1796, also qtd. in P. J. Marshall, "Moral Swing to the East," in id., *"Free though conquering People,"* 72.

11. Law, *Sketch of Some Late Arrangements*, i.

12. More, "Slavery," cited by line number from *Romantic Women Poets*, ed. Wu, pp. 43–50, ll. 213, 226, 237.

13. Godechot, *Grande nation*, 66.

14. Pitts, *Turn to Empire*, 166.

15. Condorcet, *Esquisse*, 268; id., *Outlines*, 321.

16. Chakrabarty, *Provincializing Europe*, 8.

17. Condorcet, *Esquisse*, 269; id., *Outlines*, 324.

18. Spivak, "Three Women's Texts," 248.

19. Chow, *Writing Diaspora*, 31, 30.

20. Blair, *Lectures*, 1.384.

21. Sterne, *Sentimental Journey*, ed. Stout, 181.

22. Spivak, *In Other Worlds*, 254.

23. Fanon, *Wretched of the Earth*, 227; Mehta, *Liberalism and Empire*, 20.

Primary Sources

Addison, Joseph, and Richard Steele. *The Commerce of Everyday Life: Selections from "The Tatler" and "The Spectator."* Edited by Erin Mackie. Boston: Bedford/St. Martins's, 1998.

Adventures of a Black Coat. London: J. Williams & J. Burd, 1760.

The Adventures of a Cork-screw. London: T. Bell, 1775.

"Adventures of a Mirror." *Lady's Magazine, or Entertaining Companion for the Fair Sex* 22, January 1791, 14–18; February 1791, 89–93; May 1791, 261–64.

The Adventures of an Ostrich Feather of Quality. London: Sherwood, Neely & Jones, 1812.

"Adventures of a Quire of Paper." *London Magazine, or Gentleman's Monthly Intelligencer* 48, August 1779, 355–58; September 1779, 395–98; October 1779, 448–52.

The Adventures of a Watch. London: G. Kearsley, 1788.

Africanus [pseud.]. *Remarks on the Slave Trade, and the Slavery of the Negroes.* London: J. Phillips, 1788.

Alexander, William. *The History of Women from the Earliest Antiquity, to the Present Time.* 2 vols. London: W. Strahan & T. Cadell, 1779.

Alleine, Joseph. *The Solemn Warnings of the Dead, or, An Admonition to Unconverted Sinners.* 1672. New York: John C. Totten, 1804.

Alletz, Pons Augustin. *Tableau de l'humanité et de la bienfaisance.* Paris: Chez Musier fils, 1769.

"Anthropos." *The Rights of Man (Not Paine's,) but the Rights of Man, in the West Indies.* London: Knight & Lacey, 1824.

Argentum: or, Adventures of a Shilling. London: J. Nichols, 1794.

Arnaud, François-Thomas-Marie de Baculard d'. *Les épreuves du sentiment.* 1772–73. Vols. 1–3 in *Oeuvres de d'Arnaud.* 12 vols. 1803. Geneva: Slatkine, 1972.

Barbauld, Anna Laetitia. "An Inquiry into Those Kinds of Distress Which Excite Agreeable Sensations." In *The Works of Anna Laetitia Barbauld, with a Memoir, by Lucy Aikin.* 2 vols. London: Longman, Hurst, Rees, Orme, Brown, & Green, 1825.

———. *Poems of Anna Letitia Barbauld.* Edited by William McCarthy and Elizabeth Kraft. Athens: University of Georgia Press, 1994.

Baxter, Richard. *A Call to the Unconverted to Turn and Live.* London: Nevil Simmons, 1658.

Beattie, James. *Elements of Moral Science.* 2 vols. Edinburgh: T. Cadell, 1790–93.

The Beauties of Sterne, including all his pathetic tales, and most distinguished observations on life, selected for the heart of sensibility. London: T. Davies, 1782.

Behn, Aphra. *Oroonoko or, The Royal Slave.* Edited by Lore Metzger. New York: Norton, 1973.

Bellamy, Thomas. *The Benevolent Planters.* In *Slavery, Abolition and Emancipation: Writings in the British Romantic Period.* Vol. 5: *Drama.* Edited by Jeffrey N. Cox. London: Pickering & Chatto, 1999.

Bellegarde, Jean Baptiste Morvan, abbé. *The Modes, or, a Conversation upon the Fashions of all Nations.* Trans. anon. London, 1735.

Bernardin de Saint-Pierre, Henri. *Paul et Virginie.* 1787. Edited by Robert Mauzi. Paris: Garnier-Flammarion, 1966.

Berthelin, Pierre-Charles. *Abrégé du dictionnaire universel, françois et latin, vulgairement appellé Dictionnaire de Trévoux.* 3 vols. Paris: Libraires associés, 1762.

The Birmingham Counterfeit, or, Invisible Spectator: A Sentimental Romance. 2 vols. London: S. Bladon, 1772.

Blackstone, William. *Commentaries on the Laws of England: A Facsimile of the First Edition of 1765–1769.* 4 vols. Chicago: University of Chicago Press, 1979.

Blair, Hugh. *Lectures on Rhetoric and Belles Lettres.* 3 vols. Dublin: Whitestone, Colles, Burnet, Moncrieffe, Gilbert, 1783.

Blondel, Jean. *Des hommes tels qu'ils sont et doivent être: Ouvrage de sentiment.* 1758. Hamburg: Chrétien Hérold, 1760.

Borges, Jorge Luis. "On Exactitude in Science." In *Collected Fictions,* trans. Andrew Hurley, 325. New York: Viking, 1998.

Bridges, Thomas. *The Adventures of a Bank-note.* 4 vols. London: T. Davies, 1770–71.

Brooke, Frances Moore. *The History of Emily Montague.* 1769. Toronto: McClelland & Stewart, 1995.

Brosses, Charles de. *Du culte des dieux fétiches.* Paris: n.p., 1760.

———. *Histoire des navigations aux terres australes.* Paris: Durand, 1756.

Burke, Edmund. *A Philosophical Enquiry into the Origin of Our Ideas of the Sublime and the Beautiful.* 1757. Edited by David Womersley. New York: Penguin Books, 1998.

———. "Speech on Fox's India Bill." In *Writings and Speeches of Edmund Burke.* Vol. 5: *India, Madras and Bengal, 1774–1785,* ed. P. J. Marshall, 378–451. Oxford: Clarendon Press, 1981.

Burn, Andrew. *A Second Address to the People of Great Britain: Containing a New, and Most Powerful Argument to Abstain from the Use of West India Sugar.* 2nd ed. London: M. Gurney, 1792.

Burney, Frances. *Cecilia; or, Memoirs of an Heiress.* 1782. Edited by Peter Sabor and Margaret Anne Doody. Oxford: Oxford University Press, 1988.

———. *Evelina; or, The History of a Young Lady's Entrance into the World.* 1778. Edited by Kristina Straub. Boston: Bedford Books, 1997.

Campbell, George. *The Philosophy of Rhetoric.* 1776. Edited by Lloyd Bitzer. Carbondale: Southern Illinois University Press, 1963.

Caracioli, Charles. *Chiron: or, The Mental Optician.* 2 vols. in one. London: J. Robinson, 1758.

Caraccioli, Louis-Antoine. *Paris, le modèle des nations étrangères; ou, l'Europe française.* Paris: Duchesne, 1777.

Carroll, Lewis. *Alice's Adventures in Wonderland.* 1865. New York: Magnum Books, 1968.

Chambers, Ephraim. *Cyclopaedia; or, An Universal Dictionary of Arts and Sciences.* 2 vols. London: James & John Knapton, 1728.

———. *Cyclopaedia; or, An Universal Dictionary of Arts and Sciences.* 5 vols. London: W. Strahan, J. F. & C. Rivington, 1778–88.

"Character of Modern Poetry with a Specimen." *Scots Magazine* 34 (November 1772): 619.

"Character of the English Ladies, from Dr. Wendeborn's View of England." *Lady's Magazine* 22 (February 1791): 72.

Charpentier, François. *Relation de l'établissement de la compagnie françoise pour le commerce des Indes orientales.* 1666. Rpt. Saint-Clothilde, Réunion: CRI, 1986.

Chatterton, Georgiana, Lady, ed. *Memorials personal and historical of Admiral Lord Gambier, G.C.B. With original letters from William Pitt first lord Chatham, Lord Nelson, Lord Castlereagh, Lord Mulgrave, Henry Fox first lord Holland, the Right Hon. George Canning, etc.* 2nd ed. London: Hurst & Blackett, 1861.

Clarkson, Thomas. *History of the Rise, Progress, and Accomplishment of the Abolition of the African Slave Trade by the British Parliament.* 2 vols. Philadelphia: James P. Parke, 1808.

———. Letter to Honoré Gabriel Riquetti, comte de Mirabeau. Nov. 13, 1789. Huntington Library MS CN 35.

Cobbett, William. *The Parliamentary History of England from the Earliest Period to the Year 1803.* 36 vols. London: T. C. Hansard, 1806–20.

Le code noir, ou, Recueil des reglements. Rpt. Basse-Terre: Société d'histoire de la Guadeloupe, 1980.

Coleridge, S. T. "Lecture on the Slave Trade." In *Lectures 1795: On Politics and Religion.* Edited by L. Patton and P. Mann. Vol. 1 in *The Collected Works of Samuel Taylor Coleridge.* 16 vols. Princeton: Princeton University Press, 1969.

———. "On the Slave Trade." *The Watchman.* Edited by L. Patton. Vol. 2 of *The Collected Works of Samuel Taylor Coleridge.* 16 vols. Princeton: Princeton University Press, 1969.

Condorcet, Jean-Antoine-Nicolas de Caritat, marquis de. *Esquisse d'un tableau historique des progrès de l'esprit humain.* 1795. Paris: Garnier-Flammarion, 1988. Translated by anon. as *Outlines of an Historical View of the Progress of the Human Mind* (London: J. Johnson, 1795.)

Cook, James [attrib.]. *Journal of a Voyage Round the World in His Majesty's Ship Endeavour, in the Years 1768, 1769, 1770 and 1771.* London: T. Becket & P. A. de Hondt, 1771.

Cooper, Thomas. *Letters on the Slave Trade.* Manchester: C. Wheeler, 1787.

Cowper, William. *The Letters and Prose Writings of William Cowper.* Edited by James King and Charles Ryskamp. 5 vols. Oxford: Clarendon Press, 1979–86.

———. *The Poems of William Cowper.* Edited by John D. Baird and Charles Ryskamp. 3 vols. Oxford: Clarendon Press, 1980–95.

Crafton, William Bell. *A Short Sketch of the Evidence Delivered before a Committee of the House of Commons for the Abolition of the Slave Trade.* 3rd ed. London: M. Gurney, 1792.

Day, Thomas. *The Dying Negro, A Poetical Epistle, supposed to be written by a Black, (who lately shot himself on board a vessel in the river Thames;) to his intended Wife.* London: W. Flexney, 1773.

———. *The Dying Negro, a Poetic Epistle.* 2nd ed., with additions. London: W. Flexney, 1774.

Debate on a Motion for the Abolition of the Slave-Trade in the House of Commons on Monday and Tuesday, April 18 and 19, 1791. London: W. Woodfall, 1791.

Debate on a Motion for the Abolition of the Slave-Trade in the House of Commons on Monday the second of April, 1792. London: W. Woodfall, 1792.

Debates in the British House of Commons, Wednesday May 13th, 1789, on the Petitions for the Abolition of the Slave Trade. Philadelphia: Joseph Crukshank, 1789.

Decan, F. *Essai sur la littérature.* London: G. Bigg, 1779.

Démeunier, Jean-Nicolas. *L'esprit des usages et des coutumes des différens peuples.* 3 vols. Londres: Pissot, 1776.

Dictionnaire de l'Académie française. ARTFL database, University of Chicago.

Diderot, Denis. "De la poésie dramatique." 1758. In *Oeuvres esthétiques,* ed. Paul Vernière, 179–287. Paris: Garnier, 1994.

———. "Éloge de Richardson." 1762. In *Oeuvres esthétiques,* ed. Paul Vernière, 29–48. Paris: Garnier, 1994.

———. "Lettre apologétique de l'abbé Raynal à Monsieur Grimm." 1781. In *Oeuvres philosophiques,* ed. Paul Vernière, 627–44. Paris: Garnier, 1964.

———. *La religieuse.* Written 1760. Paris: Garnier-Flammarion, 1968.

———. *Supplément au voyage de Bougainville.* Written 1772. Edited by Herbert Dieckmann. Geneva: Droz, 1955.

East India House. *A Continuation of the Series of the Several Debates that have taken place at the India-House on... the general principles of the Company's new Charter.* London: William Woodfall, 1793.

L'Encyclopédie, ou Dictionnaire raisonné des sciences, des arts et des métiers. ARTFL Encyclopédie Project, University of Chicago, 1996.

Equiano, Olaudah. *The Interesting Narrative of the Life of Olaudah Equiano, or Gustavus Vassa, the African, Written by Himself.* 1789. Edited by Werner Sollors. New York: Norton, 2001.

Estwick, Samuel. *Considerations on the Negroe Cause, commonly so called addressed to the Right Honourable Lord Mansfield, Lord Chief Justice of the Court of the King's Bench.* 2nd ed. London: J. Dodsley, 1773.

Étrennes de la vertu. Paris: n.p., 1783 [?].

Falconbridge, Alexander. *An Account of the Slave Trade on the Coast of Africa.* 1788. New York: AMS Reprints, 1973.

Féraud, Jean-François. *Dictionnaire critique de la langue française.* 3 vols. Marseille: Mossy, 1787–88.

Ferguson, Adam. *An Essay on the History of Civil Society.* 1767. Edited by Fania Oz-Salzberger. Cambridge: Cambridge University Press, 1995.

Ferriar, John. *Illustrations of Sterne.* London: Cadell & Davies, 1798.

Fielding, Sarah. *The Adventures of David Simple and Volume the Last.* 1744. Edited by Peter Sabor. Lexington: University Press of Kentucky, 1998.

Flagel, or A Ramble of Fancy through the Land of Electioneering in the Manner of the Devil Upon Two Sticks. London: G. Kearsly, 1768.

Formey, Jean-Henri-Samuel. *L'Esprit de Julie, ou Extrait de La nouvelle Héloïse, ouvrage utile à la société et particulierement à la jeunesse.* Berlin: J. Jasperd, 1763.

Fougeret de Montbron, Louis Charles. *Préservatif contre l'anglomanie.* Minorca: n.p., 1757.

Fox, Charles James. *The Speeches of the Right Honourable Charles James Fox.* 3rd ed. London: Aylott, 1853.

Fox, William. *An Address to the People of Great Britain, on the Utility of Refraining from the Use of West India Sugar and Rum.* 11th ed. London: M. Gurney, 1791.

Freud, Sigmund. "A Child Is Being Beaten." In vol. 17 of *The Standard Edition of the Complete Psychological Works of Sigmund Freud,* ed. and trans. James Strachey et al., 175–204. 24 vols. London: Hogarth Press and the Institute of Psycho-Analysis, 1955.

Fromageot, abbé. *Anecdotes de la bienfaisance.* Paris: Chez Nyon l'aîné, 1777.

Furetière, Antoine. *Dictionnaire universel.* 3 vols. La Haye: Arnout & Renier Leers, 1690.

A General and Descriptive History of the Ancient and Present State of the Town of Liverpool. Liverpool: R. Phillips, 1795.

The Genuine Memoirs and Most Surprising Adventures of a Very Unfortunate Goose-Quill with an Introductory Letter to Mrs. Midnight's Tye-Wig. London: M. Cooper & G. Woodfall, 1751.

Great Britain. Parliament. House of Commons. *Abridgment of the Minutes of the Evidence taken before a Committee of the Whole House, to whom it was referred to consider of the slave-trade,* nos. 1–4. London, 1789–91.

———. *House of Commons Sessional Papers of the Eighteenth Century,* edited by Sheila Lambert, vol. 82: *George III: Slave Trade 1791 and 1792.* Wilmington, Del.: Scholarly Resources, 1975.

Grimm, Friedrich Melchior, Freiherr von, et al. *Correspondance littéraire, philosophique et critique par Grimm, Diderot, Raynal, Meister, etc.* 16 vols. Paris: Garnier, 1877–82.

Gronniosaw, James Albert Ukawsaw. "A Narrative of the Most Remarkable Particulars in the Life of James Albert Ukawsaw Gronniosaw, an African Prince, as Related by Himself." In *Pioneers of the Black Atlantic: Five Slave Narratives from the Enlightenment, 1772–1815.* Edited by Henry Louis Gates Jr. and William L. Andrews. Washington, D.C.: Civitas, 1998.

Harlow, Lawrence. *The Conversion of an Indian, in a Letter to a Friend.* London: n.p., 1774.

Hawkesworth, John. *An Account of the Voyages undertaken . . . by Commodore Byron, Captain Carteret, Captain Wallis, and Captain Cook.* 3 vols. London: W. Strahan & T. Cadell, 1773.

Henry, David. *An Historical Account of All the Voyages Round the World, Performed by English Navigators.* 4 vols. London: F. Newbery, 1773–74.

The History of a Bible. Utica, N.Y.: Ira Merrell, 1812.

The History of a Pin, as Related by Itself. Dublin: T. Jackson, 1799.

Horace. *The Works of Horace in English Verse. By Several Hands. Collected and published by Mr. Duncombe.* London: R. & J. Dodsley, 1757–59.

Hume, David. *Essays: Moral, Political, and Literary.* Edited by Eugene F. Miller. Indianapolis: Liberty Fund, 1987.

———. "Natural History of Religion." 1757. In id., *Essays and Treatises on Several Subjects.* 4 vols. London: A. Millar, 1760.

———. *A Treatise of Human Nature.* 1739–40. Edited by L. A. Selby-Bigge. 2nd ed. rev. P. H. Nidditch. Oxford: Clarendon Press, 1980.

Hutton, Charles. *Ladies' Diary; or Woman's Almanack, for the year of our lord 1786 . . . no. 83.* London: Robert Horsfield, 1786.

James, Henry. *Roderick Hudson.* Boston: Houghton Mifflin, 1917.

Jerrold, Douglas. *The Story of a Feather.* London: Bradbury, Evans, 1867.

Johnson, Samuel. *A Dictionary of the English Language on CD-ROM.* Edited by Anne Mc-Dermott. Cambridge: Cambridge University Press, 1996.

———. *The History of Rasselas, Prince of Abissinia.* 1759. Edited by D. J. Enright. New York: Penguin Books, 1980.

Johnson, Theophilus. *Phantoms: or, The Adventures of a Gold-Headed Cane.* 2 vols. London: William Lane, 1783.

Johnstone, Charles. *Chrysal; or The Adventures of a Guinea.* 1760–65. 4 vols. New York: Garland, 1979.

Kames, Henry Home, Lord. *Elements of Criticism.* 3 vols. Edinburgh: A. Millar and A. Kinkaid & J. Bell, 1762.

———. *Essays on the Principles of Morality and Natural Religion.* Edinburgh: R. Fleming, 1751.

Kant, Immanuel. *Critique of Judgment.* 1790. Translated by J. H. Bernard. New York: Hafner, 1951.

Kilner, Dorothy. *Adventures of a Hackney Coach.* 3rd ed. London: G. Kearsly, 1781.

Knox, Vicesimus. *Winter Evenings: or, Lucubrations on Life and Letters.* 3 vols. London: Charles Dilly, 1788.

Krafft-Ebbing, Richard von. *Psychopathia Sexualis.* 1902. Translated by Franklin Klaf. New York: Arcade Publishing, 1998.

Lacombe de Prézel, Honoré. *Les Annales de la Bienfaisance, ou Les hommes rappellés à la bienfaisance, par les exemples des peoples anciens et moderns.* 3 vols. Lausanne: Lacombe, 1772.

Laporte, Joseph de, and Louis-Mayeul Chaudon. *Nouvelle bibliothèque d'un homme de gout.* 4 vols. Paris: Grand Corneille, 1777.

Lavallée, Joseph. *Le Nègre comme il y a peu de blancs.* 3 vols. in 2. Paris: Buisson, 1789. Translated by Phyllis Wheatley as *The Negro equalled by few Europeans* (Philadelphia: William W. Woodward, 1801).

Law, Thomas, of Washington. *A Sketch of Some Late Arrangements, and a View of the Rising Resources, in Bengal.* London: John Stockdale, 1792.

Le Blanc, Jean-Bernard, abbé. *Letters on the English and French Nations.* Trans. anon. 2 vols. London: J. Brindley, 1747.

Locke, John. *An Essay Concerning Human Understanding.* 1689. Edited by Peter Nidditch. Oxford: Clarendon Press, 1979.

———. *Two Treatises of Government.* 1690. Edited by Peter Laslett. New York: Mentor, 1965.

Long, Edward. *Candid Reflections upon the Judgment Lately awarded by the Court of King's Bench in Westminster-Hall, on what is commonly called the Negroe-Cause.* London: T. Lowndes, 1772.

———. *The Sentimental Exhibition; or, Portraits and Sketches of the Times.* London: T. Lowndes, 1774.

Mackenzie, Henry. *The Man of Feeling.* 1771. Edited by Brian Vickers. New York: Oxford University Press, 1967.

Mackenzie, Henry, et al. *The Mirror: A Periodical Paper published at Edinburgh in the years 1779 and 1780.* 6th ed. 2 vols. Dublin: R. Marchbank, 1790.

Man: A Paper for Ennobling the Species. London: J. Haberkorn, 1755.

Marx, Karl. *Capital: A Critical Analysis of Capitalist Production. Vol. 1.* 1867. Translated by Samuel Moore and Edward Aveling. 3 vols. London: George Allen & Unwin, 1971.

Matthews, John. *A Voyage to the River Sierra-Leone.* 1788. London: B. White & Son, 1791.

Maupertuis, Pierre-Louis Moreau de. *Lettre sur le progrès des sciences.* N.p.: 1752.

———. *Vénus physique: contenant deux dissertations, l'une, sur l'origine des hommes et des animaux, et l'autre, sur l'origine des noirs.* The Hague: Jean Martin Husson, 1746.

The Memoirs and Interesting Adventures of an Embroidered Waistcoat. Part II, in which is introduced the episode of a petticoat. London: J. Brooke, 1751.

Memoirs of the Shakespear's Head in Covent Garden, by the Ghost of Shakespear. 2 vols. London: Noble & Noble, 1755.

Mercier, Louis-Sébastien. *L'an deux-mille quatre cent quarante.* Londres: n.p., 1775.

Mirabeau, Victor de Riquetti, marquis de. *L'ami des hommes, ou Traité de la population.* Avignon: n.p., 1756.

Mistelet. *De la sensibilité par rapport aux drames, aux romans, et à l'éducation.* Amsterdam: Mérigot jeune, 1777.

Montesquieu, Charles de Secondat, baron de. *De l'esprit des lois.* 1748. Edited by Victor Goldschmidt. 2 vols. Paris: Garnier-Flammarion, 1979. Translated by Thomas Nugent as *The Spirit of the Laws* (2 vols.; London: J. Nourse & P. Vaillant, 1750).

More, Hannah. "Slavery" and "Sensibility." In *Romantic Women Poets: An Anthology,* ed. Duncan Wu, 43–50. Oxford: Blackwell, 1997.

Newton, John. *An Authentic Narrative of Some Remarkable and Interesting Particulars in the Life of ******.* London: R. Hett, 1764.

———. *Journal of a Slave Trader (John Newton), 1750–1754.* Edited by Bernard Martin and Mark Spurrell. London: Epworth Press, 1962.

———. *Thoughts upon the African Slave Trade.* London: J. Buckland & J. Johnson, 1788.

Oakley, Peregrine. *Aureus; or, The Life and Opinions of a Sovereign, written by himself.* London: George Wightman, 1824.

"On Benevolence." *London Magazine, or Gentleman's Monthly Intelligencer* 49 (January 1780): 30–33.

Owen, Nicholas. *Journal of A Slave-Dealer: A View of Some Remarkable Axcedents [sic] in the Life of Nics. Owen on the Coast of Africa and America from the Year 1746 to the Year 1757.* Edited by Eveline Martin. London: G. Routledge, 1930.

Peckard, Peter. *Am I not a Man? and a Brother? With all humility addressed to the British Legislature.* Cambridge: J. Archdeacon, 1788.

Phillips, T. "A Journal of a Voyage from England to Africa, and so forward to Barbadoes, in the Years 1693, and 1694." In *A Collection of Voyages and Travels,* ed. Awnsham Churchill and John Churchill, 6.173–239. 6 vols. London: Churchill, 1732.

Picquenard, J.-B. *Adonis, ou le Bon nègre, anecdote coloniale.* Paris: Didot jeune, an VI (1798).

———. *Zoflora, ou la Bonne négresse.* 2 vols. Paris: Didot jeune, an VIII (1799–1800). Translated as *Zoflora, or, The generous negro girl: a colonial story* (2 vols.; London: Lackington, Allen, 1804).

Prévost d'Exiles, Antoine-François (abbé Prévost). *Cleveland, ou le philosophe anglais.* Vol. 2 in *Oeuvres de Prévost.* Edited by Jean Sgard. 8 vols. Grenoble: Presses universitaires de Grenoble, 1978.

———. *Histoire générale des voyages.* 19 vols. Paris: Didot, 1746–70.

———. *Journal étranger: Ouvrage périodique.* Paris: Bureau du Journal étranger, Feb. 1755.

"Question: Ought Sensibility to Be Cherished, or Repressed?" *Monthly Magazine* 2 (October 1796): 706–9.

Ramsay, James. *An Essay on the Treatment and Conversion of African Slaves in the British Sugar Colonies.* London: James Phillips, 1784.

Raynal, Guillaume-Thomas-François, abbé. *Histoire philosophique et politique des établissements et du commerce des Européens dans les deux Indes.* 1770. 3rd ed. 10 vols. Geneva: Jean-Léonard Pellet, 1781. Translated by J. O. Justamond as *Philosophical and Political History of the Settlements and Trade of the Europeans in the East and West Indies* (3rd ed., 8 vols., London: W. Strahan & T. Cadell, 1783). Epitomized under the title *Europens Handel mit beyden Indien: Ein Auszug aus Raynals Geschichte* by Franz Christian Lorenz Karsten (Rostock: Verlegts Johann Christian Koppe, 1780).

Review of "A Poem on the Bill lately passed for regulating the Slave Trade," by Helen Maria Williams. *Monthly Review* 80 (1789): 237–38.

Review of "Considerations on the Abolition of Slavery and the Slave Trade, upon Grounds of Natural, Religious, and Political Duty." *Critical Review: or, the Annals of Literature* 67 (1789): 452–54.

Riccoboni, Marie-Jeanne. *Lettres de Milady Juliette Catesby à Milady Henriette Campley, son amie.* 1759. Paris: Desjonqueres, 1983.

Richardson, Samuel. *Clarissa or, The History of a Young Lady.* 1747–48. 3rd ed. 1751. Edited by Florian Stuber. New York: AMS Press, 1990.

———. *The Correspondence of Samuel Richardson.* Edited by Anna Laetitia Barbauld. 6 vols. London: R. Phillips, 1804.

———. *Pamela, or, Virtue Rewarded.* 1740–42. Edited by T. C. Duncan Eaves and Ben Kimpel. Boston: Houghton Mifflin, 1971.

Richelet, Pierre. *Dictionnaire de la langue françoise, ancienne et moderne.* 2 vols. Amsterdam: au dépens de la compagnie, 1732.

Roberts, William. *Memoirs of the Life and Correspondence of Mrs. Hannah More.* 2 vols. New York: Harper & Bros, 1836.

Romance de Mesmon, Germain-Hyacinthe, marquis de. *De la lecture des romans: Fragment d'un manuscrit sur la sensibilité.* Paris: P.-D. Pierres, 1776.

Rousseau, Jean-Jacques. *The Collected Writings of Rousseau.* 10 vols. Edited by Roger D. Masters and Christopher Kelly. Hanover, N.H.: University Press of New England, 1990–2004.

———. *Dialogues, ou Rousseau juge de Jean-Jacques.* Composed 1772–76; published 1780. Edited by Robert Osmont. In *Oeuvres complètes,* vol. 1. Translated by Judith R. Bush, Christopher Kelly, and Roger D. Masters as *Rousseau, Judge of Jean-Jacques: Dialogues* in *Collected Writings,* vol. 1.

———. *Discours sur l'origine et les fondements de l'inégalité.* 1755. Edited by Jean Starobinski. In *Oeuvres complètes,* vol. 3. Translated by Judith R. Bush, Roger D. Masters, Christopher Kelly, and Terence Marshall as *Discourse on the Origins of Inequality (Second Discourse)* in *Collected Writings,* vol. 3.

———. *Émile, ou De l'éducation.* 1762. Edited by Charles Wirz. In *Oeuvres complètes,* vol. 4.

Translated by William Kenrick as *Emilius and Sophia: or, a New System of Education* (2 vols., London: R. Griffiths, 1762).

———. *Esprit, maximes, et principes de M. Jean-Jacques Rousseau.* Neuchatel: Chez les Libraires associés, 1764.

———. *Essai sur l'origine des langues.* Posthumously published 1781. Edited by Jean Starobinski. In *Oeuvres complètes,* vol. 5. Translated by John T. Scott as *Essay on the Origin of Languages* in *Collected Writings,* vol. 7.

———. *Julie, ou la Nouvelle Héloïse.* 1761. Edited by Bernard Gagnebin and Marcel Raymond. In *Oeuvres complètes,* vol. 2. Translated by Philip Stewart and Jean Vaché as *Julie, or the New Heloise* in *Collected Writings,* vol. 6.

———. *Lettre à d'Alembert sur les spectacles.* 1758. Edited by Léon Fontaine. Paris: Garnier, 1889. Translated by anon. as *Letter from M. Rousseau, of Geneva, to M. d'Alembert, concerning the effects of theatrical entertainments on the manners of mankind* (London: J. Nourse, 1759).

———. *Oeuvres complètes.* Edited by Bernard Gagnebin, Marcel Raymond, et al. 5 vols. Bibliothèque de la Pléiade. Paris: Garnier, 1959–95.

———. *Pensées de J. J. Rousseau, citoyen de Geneve.* Amsterdam: n.p., 1763.

Rush, Benjamin. *The Selected Writings of Benjamin Rush.* Edited by Dagobert D. Runes. New York: Philosophical Library, 1947.

Sade, Donatien-Alphonse-François, marquis de. *La philosophie dans le boudoir.* 1795. Vol. 3 in *Oeuvres.* Edited by Michel Delon. 3 vols. Paris: Gallimard, 1998.

Sancho, Ignatius. *The Letters of Ignatius Sancho.* 1782. Edited by Paul Edwards and Polly Rewt. Edinburgh: Edinburgh University Press, 1994.

Schaw, Janet. *Journal of a Lady of Quality; being the Narrative of a Journey from Scotland to the West Indies, North Carolina, and Portugal in the Years 1774 to 1776.* Edited by E. W. Andrews and C. M. Andrews. New Haven: Yale University Press, 1921.

Scott, Helenus. *The Adventures of a Rupee, wherein are interspersed various anecdotes, Asiatic and European.* London: J. Murray, 1782.

Scott, Sarah. *The History of Sir George Ellison.* 1766. Edited by Betty Rizzo. Lexington: University Press of Kentucky, 1996.

Scott, Sir Walter. *The Private Letter-Book of Sir Walter Scott.* Edited by Wilfred Partington. New York: Frederick Stokes, 1930.

"Sensibility: An Irregular Ode." *Scots Magazine* 45 (December 1783): 660.

Shaftesbury, Anthony Ashley Cooper, earl of. *Characteristics of Men, Manners, Opinions, Times.* 1711. Edited by Lawrence Klein. Cambridge: Cambridge University Press, 1999.

Sharp, Granville. *An Appendix to the Representation . . . of the Injustice and Dangerous Tendency of Tolerating Slavery.* London: Benjamin White & Robert Horsefield, 1772.

———. *Extract from a Representation of the Injustice and Dangerous Tendency of Tolerating Slavery.* Philadelphia: Joseph Crukshank, 1771.

Smith, Adam. *The Correspondence of Adam Smith.* Edited by Ernest Campbell Mossner and Ian Simpson Ross. Indianapolis: Liberty Classics, 1987.

———. *The Theory of Moral Sentiments.* 1759. Edited by D. D. Raphael and A. L. Macfie. Indianapolis: Liberty Classics, 1982.

Smollett, Tobias. *The Expedition of Humphry Clinker.* 1771. Edited by Lewis M. Knapp. London: Oxford University Press, 1966.

———. *The History and Adventures of an Atom.* 1769. Edited by O. M. Brack Jr. Introduction and notes by Robert Adams Day. Athens: University of Georgia Press, 1989.

Stanfield, James Field. *Observations on a Guinea Voyage.* London: James Phillips, 1788.

Stedman, John Gabriel. *Stedman's Surinam: Life in Eighteenth-Century Slave Society.* Edited by Richard Price and Sally Price. Baltimore: Johns Hopkins University Press, 1992.

Sterne, Laurence. *Letters of Laurence Sterne.* Edited by Lewis Perry Curtis. Oxford: Clarendon Press, 1935.

———. *The Life and Opinions of Tristram Shandy, Gentleman.* 1759–67. Edited by Melvyn New and Joan New. Vols. 1–2 in the Florida Edition of the Works of Laurence Sterne. Gainesville: University Press of Florida, 1978.

———. *A Sentimental Journey Through France and Italy by Mr. Yorick.* 1768. Edited by Gardner D. Stout Jr. Berkeley: University of California Press, 1967.

———. *"A Sentimental Journey Through France and Italy" with "The Journal to Eliza."* Edited by Ian Jack. Oxford: Oxford University Press, 1984.

———. *The Sermons of Laurence Sterne.* Edited by Melvyn New. Vols. 4–5 in the Florida Edition of the Works of Laurence Sterne. Gainesville: University Press of Florida, 1996.

———. *The Sermons of Mr. Yorick: vols. 1 & 2.* London: R. & J. Dodsley, 1760.

———. *The Sermons of Mr. Yorick: vols. 3 & 4.* London: T. Becket & P. A. de Hondt, 1766.

———. *The Sermons of Mr. Yorick: vols. 5, 6 & 7.* London: W. Strahan, T. Cadell, & T. Becket, 1769.

———. *La vie et les opinions de Tristram Shandy.* Translated by Joseph-Pierre Frénais. 2 vols. Paris: n.p., 1776.

Stewart, John. *An Account of Jamaica.* London: Longman, Hurst, Rees, & Orme, 1808.

The Story of a Needle. New York: Robert Carter, 1862.

Thrale Piozzi, Hester. *Thraliana: The Diary of Mrs. Hester Lynch Thrale.* Edited by Katharine C. Balderston. 2 vols. Oxford: Clarendon Press, 1942.

Trimmer, Sarah. *The Family Magazine: or, A Repository of Religious Instruction and Rational Amusement.* 18 vols. London: John Marshall, 1788–89.

Trusler, John. *The Difference Between Words, esteemed Synonymous, in the English Language.* 2 vols. London: J. Dodsley, 1766.

Vandermonde, Charles-Augustin. *Essai sur la manière de perfectionner l'espèce humaine.* Paris: Vincent, 1756.

A Very New Pamphlet Indeed, Being the Truth Addressed to the People at Large. London: n.p., 1792.

Wilde, Oscar. *The Letters of Oscar Wilde.* Edited by Rupert Hart-Davis. London: Rupert Hart-Davis, 1962.

Wilson, Thomas. *The Knowledge and Practice of Christianity Made Easy for the Meanest Capacities, or, An Essay towards an Instruction for the Indians.* London: J. Osborn & W. Thorn, 1740.

Wollstonecraft, Mary. *The Works of Mary Wollstonecraft.* Edited by Marilyn Butler and Janet Todd. 7 vols. New York: New York University Press, 1989.

Secondary Sources

Abraham, Nicholas, and Maria Torok. "Mourning *or* Melancholia: Introjection *Versus* Incorporation." In *The Shell and the Kernel: Renewals of Psychoanalysis.* Ed. and trans. Nicholas T. Rand, 125–38. Chicago: University of Chicago Press, 1994.

Acholonu, Catherine Obianju. "The Home of Olaudah Equiano: A Linguistic and Anthropological Search." *Journal of Commonwealth Literature* 22.1 (1987): 5–16.

Acomb, Frances. *Anglophobia in France (1763–1789): An Essay in the History of Constitutionalism and Nationalism.* Durham, N.C.: Duke University Press, 1950.

Alliston, April. "Transnational Sympathies, Imaginary Communities." In *The Literary Channel: The Inter-National Invention of the Novel,* ed. Margaret Cohen and Carolyn Dever, 133–48. Princeton: Princeton University Press, 2002.

———. *Virtue's Faults: Correspondences in Eighteenth-Century British and French Women's Fiction.* Stanford: Stanford University Press, 1996.

Anderson, Benedict. *Imagined Communities: Reflections on the Origin and Spread of Nationalism.* London: Verso, 1991.

Anderson, Fred. *The Crucible of War: The Seven Years' War and the Fate of Empire in British North America, 1754–1766.* New York: Knopf, 2000.

Andrew, Donna. *Philanthropy and Police: London Charity in the Eighteenth Century.* Princeton: Princeton University Press, 1989.

Anstey, Roger. *The Atlantic Slave Trade and British Abolition, 1760–1810.* Atlantic Highlands, N.J.: Humanities Press, 1975.

Appadurai, Arjun. "Introduction: Commodities and the Politics of Value." In *The Social Lives of Things: Commodities in Cultural Perspective,* ed. Arjun Appadurai, 3–63. Cambridge: Cambridge University Press, 1986.

Aravamudan, Srinivas. "Progress Through Violence or Progress from Violence? Interpreting the Ambivalences of the *Histoire des deux Indes.*" In *Progrès et violence au XVIIIe siècle,* ed. Valérie Cossy and Deidre Dawson, 259–80. Paris: Champion, 2001.

———. "Trop(icaliz)ing the Enlightenment." *Diacritics* 23.3 (1993): 48–68.

———. *Tropicopolitans: Colonialism and Agency, 1688–1804.* Durham, N.C.: Duke University Press, 1999.

Árdal, Páll S. *Passion and Value in Hume's Treatise.* Edinburgh: Edinburgh University Press, 1966.

Armitage, David. *The Ideological Origins of the British Empire.* Cambridge: Cambridge University Press, 2000.

———, ed. *Theories of Empire, 1450–1800.* Brookfield, Vt.: Ashgate, 1998.

Arnold, David. "Hunger in the Garden of Plenty: The Bengal Famine of 1770." In *Dreadful Visitations: Confronting Natural Catastrophe in the Age of Enlightenment,* ed. Alessa Johns, 81–111. New York: Routledge, 1999.

Aubert, Guillaume. "'The Blood of France': Race and Purity of Blood in the French Atlantic World." *William and Mary Quarterly* 61.3 (2004): 439–78.

Axtell, James. *The Invasion Within: The Contest of Cultures in Colonial North America.* New York: Oxford University Press, 1985.

Baker, Houston A. *Blues, Ideology and Afro-American Literature: A Vernacular Theory.* Chicago: University of Chicago Press, 1984.

Bakhtin, Mikhail. *The Dialogic Imagination: Four Essays.* Translated by Caryl Emerson and Michael Holquist. Austin: University of Texas Press, 1981.

Bandry, Anne. "Imitations of *Tristram Shandy.*" In *Critical Essays on Laurence Sterne,* ed. Melvyn New, 39–52. New York: G. K. Hall, 1998.

Barker-Benfield, G. J. *The Culture of Sensibility: Sex and Society in Eighteenth-Century Britain.* Chicago: University of Chicago Press, 1992.

Barthes, Roland. "The Romans in Films." In *Mythologies.* Translated by Annette Lavers, 26–28. New York: Hill & Wang, 2000.

Bataille, Georges. *The Accursed Share: An Essay on General Economy.* Translated by Robert Hurley. 3 vols. New York: Zone Books, 1988–91.

Bayly, C. A. *Imperial Meridian: The British Empire and the World, 1780–1830.* London: Longman, 1989.

Bell, David A. *The Cult of the Nation in France: Inventing Nationalism, 1680–1800.* Cambridge, Mass.: Harvard University Press, 2001.

Bellamy, Liz. *Commerce, Morality and the Eighteenth-Century Novel.* Cambridge: Cambridge University Press, 1998.

Belmessous, Saliha. "Assimilation and Racialism in Seventeenth and Eighteenth-Century French Colonial Policy." *American Historical Review* 110.2 (2005): 56 paras. www .historycooperative.org/journals/ahr/110.2/belmessous.html (accessed Jan. 9, 2006).

Bender, John. *Imagining the Penitentiary: Fiction and the Architecture of Mind in Eighteenth-Century England.* Chicago: University of Chicago Press, 1987.

Bender, Thomas, ed. *The Antislavery Debate: Capitalism and Abolitionism as a Problem in Historical Interpretation.* Berkeley: University of California Press, 1992.

Benedict, Barbara. *Framing Feeling: Sentiment and Style in English Prose Fiction, 1745–1800.* New York: AMS Press, 1994.

Bénot, Yves. *Diderot: De l'athéisme à l'anticolonialisme.* Paris: Maspero, 1981.

———. "Traces de l'*Histoire des deux Indes* chez les anti-esclavagistes sous la Révolution." In *Lectures de Raynal: "L'Histoire des deux Indes" en Europe et en Amérique au XVIIIe siècle,* ed. Hans-Jürgen Lüsebrink and Manfred Tietz, 141–54. Studies on Voltaire and the Eighteenth Century 286. Oxford: Voltaire Foundation, 1991.

Benveniste, Émile. *Problèmes de linguistique générale.* 2 vols. Paris: Gallimard, 1966–74. Translated by Mary Elizabeth Meek as *Problems in General Linguistics* (Coral Gables, Fla.: University of Miami Press, 1971).

Berlant, Lauren. "The Female Complaint." *Social Text* 19–20 (Fall 1988): 237–59.

Bhabha, Homi K. "The Commitment to Theory." In id., *The Location of Culture,* 19–39. London: Routledge, 1994.

———. "Of Mimicry and Man." In id., *The Location of Culture,* 85–92. London: Routledge, 1994.

———. "Signs Taken for Wonders: Questions of Ambivalence and Authority Under a Tree Outside Delhi, May 1817." In id., *The Location of Culture,* 102–22. London: Routledge, 1994.

Blackburn, Robin. *The Overthrow of Colonial Slavery, 1776–1848.* London: Verso, 1988.

Bohls, Elizabeth. *Women Travel Writers and the Language of Aesthetics, 1716–1818.* Cambridge: Cambridge University Press, 1995.

Boulle, Pierre. "In Defense of Slavery: Eighteenth-Century Opposition to Abolition and the Origins of a Racist Ideology in France." *History from Below: Studies in Popular Protest and Popular Ideology in Honour of George Rudé*, ed. Frederick Krantz, 221–41. Montreal: Concordia University, 1985.

Bowen, H. V. *Elites, Enterprise, and the Making of the British Overseas Empire, 1688–1775.* New York: St. Martin's Press, 1996.

Brewer, John. *The Sinews of Power: War, Money, and the English State, 1688–1783.* Cambridge, Mass.: Harvard University Press, 1988.

Brissenden, R. F. *Virtue in Distress: Studies in the Novel of Sentiment From Richardson to Sade.* London: Macmillian, 1974.

Brot, Muriel. "Réécritures des Lumières." *Critique* 58 (2002): 627–37.

Brown, Bill. "How to Do Things with Things (A Toy Story)." *Critical Inquiry* 24 (Summer 1998): 935–64.

Brown, Laura. *Ends of Empire: Women and Ideology in Early Eighteenth-Century English Literature.* Ithaca, N.Y.: Cornell University Press, 1993.

Burnham, Michelle. "Between England and America: Captivity, Sympathy, and the Sentimental Novel." In *Cultural Institutions of the Novel*, ed. Deidre Lynch and William Warner, 47–72. Durham, N.C.: Duke University Press, 1996.

Butler, Marilyn. *Jane Austen and the War of Ideas.* Oxford: Clarendon Press, 1987.

Campbell, Colin. *The Romantic Ethic and the Spirit of Modern Consumerism.* Oxford: Basil Blackwell, 1987.

Caplan, Jay. *Framed Narratives: Diderot's Genealogy of the Beholder.* Minneapolis: University of Minnesota Press, 1985.

Carretta, Vincent. "Olaudah Equiano or Gustavus Vassa? New Light on an Eighteenth-Century Question of Identity." *Slavery and Abolition* 20.3 (1999): 96–105.

Cash, Arthur. *Laurence Sterne: The Early and Middle Years.* London: Methuen, 1975.

———. *Laurence Sterne: The Later Years.* London: Methuen, 1986.

Chakrabarty, Dipesh. *Provincializing Europe: Postcolonial Thought and Historical Difference.* Princeton: Princeton University Press, 2000.

Cheek, Pamela. *Sexual Antipodes: Enlightenment Globalization and the Placing of Sex.* Stanford: Stanford University Press, 2003.

Cheng, Anne Anlin. *The Melancholy of Race: Psychoanalysis, Assimilation, and Hidden Grief.* Oxford: Oxford University Press, 2001.

Chisick, Harvey. *The Limits of Reform in the Enlightenment: Attitudes Towards the Education of the Lower Classes in Eighteenth-Century France.* Princeton: Princeton University Press, 1981.

Chow, Rey. *Writing Diaspora: Tactics of Intervention in Contemporary Cultural Studies.* Bloomington: Indiana University Press, 1993.

Cohen, Margaret, and Carolyn Dever. "Introduction." In *The Literary Channel: The Inter-National Invention of the Novel*, ed. Margaret Cohen and Carolyn Dever, 1–34. Princeton: Princeton University Press, 2002.

———. "Sentimental Communities." In *The Literary Channel: The Inter-National Invention of the Novel,* ed. Margaret Cohen and Carolyn Dever, 106–32. Princeton: Princeton University Press, 2002.

———. *The Sentimental Education of the Novel.* Princeton: Princeton University Press, 1999.

Cohen, William B. *The French Encounter with Africans: White Response to Blacks, 1530–1880.* Bloomington: Indiana University Press, 1980.

Coleman, Deirdre. "Conspicuous Consumption: White Abolitionism and English Women's Protest Writing in the 1790s." *ELH* 61.2 (1994): 341–62.

———. "Janet Schaw and the Complexions of Empire." *Eighteenth-Century Studies* 36 (2003): 169–93.

Colley, Linda. "Britishness and Otherness: An Argument." *Journal of British Studies* 31 (October 1992): 309–29.

———. *Britons: Forging the Nation, 1707–1837.* New Haven: Yale University Press, 1992.

Colwill, Elizabeth. "Sex, Savagery, and Slavery in the Shaping of the French Body Politic." In *From the Royal to the Republican Body: Incorporating the Political in Seventeenth- and Eighteenth-Century France,* ed. Sara Melzer and Kathryn Norberg, 198–223. Berkeley: University of California Press, 1998.

Crane, R. S. "Suggestions Toward a Genealogy of the 'Man of Feeling.'" *ELH* 1.3 (1934): 205–30.

Craton, Michael. *Testing the Chains: Resistance to Slavery in the British West Indies.* Ithaca, N.Y.: Cornell University Press, 1982.

Cressy, David. "Books as Totems in Seventeenth-Century England and New England." *Journal of Library History* 21.1 (1986): 92–106.

Crouzet, François. *Britain Ascendant: Comparative Studies in Franco-British Economic History.* Translated by Martin Thom. Cambridge: Cambridge University Press, 1990.

Culler, Jonathan. *The Pursuit of Signs: Semiotics, Literature, Deconstruction.* Ithaca, N.Y.: Cornell University Press, 1981.

Curtin, Philip D. *The Atlantic Slave Trade: A Census.* Madison: University of Wisconsin Press, 1969.

———. *The Image of Africa: British Ideas and Action, 1780–1850.* Madison: University of Wisconsin Press, 1964.

Damrosch, Leo. *Fictions of Reality in the Age of Hume and Johnson.* Madison: University of Wisconsin Press, 1989.

Davies, Kate. "A Moral Purchase: Femininity, Commerce and Abolition, 1788–1792." In *Women, Writing and the Public Sphere, 1700–1830,* ed. Elizabeth Eger, Charlotte Grant, Cliona O'Gallchoir, and Penny Warburton, 133–59. Cambridge: Cambridge University Press, 2001.

Davis, David Brion. *The Problem of Slavery in the Age of Revolution, 1770–1823.* New York: Oxford University Press, 1998.

———. *The Problem of Slavery in Western Culture.* New York: Oxford University Press, 1988.

De Grazia, Margreta. "The Ideology of Superfluous Things: *King Lear* as Period Piece." In *Subject and Object in Renaissance Culture,* ed. Margreta de Grazia, Maureen Quilligan, and Peter Stallybrass, 17–42. Cambridge: Cambridge University Press, 1996.

De Grazia, Margreta, Maureen Quilligan, and Peter Stallybrass, eds. "Introduction." In *Sub-*

ject and Object in Renaissance Culture, ed. Margreta de Grazia, Maureen Quilligan, and Peter Stallybrass, 1–13. Cambridge: Cambridge University Press, 1996.

Delon, Michel. "L'appel au lecteur dans *l'Histoire des deux Indes.*" In *Lectures de Raynal: "L'Histoire des deux Indes" en Europe et en Amérique au XVIIIe siècle,* ed. Hans-Jürgen Lüsebrink and Manfred Tietz, 53–66. Studies on Voltaire and the Eighteenth Century 286. Oxford: Voltaire Foundation, 1991.

De Man, Paul. "Anthropomorphism and Trope in the Lyric." In id., *The Rhetoric of Romanticism,* 239–62. New York: Columbia University Press, 1984.

———. "Autobiography as De-Facement." In id., *The Rhetoric of Romanticism,* 67–81. New York: Columbia University Press, 1984.

———. "The Epistemology of Metaphor." *Critical Inquiry* 5 (Autumn 1978): 13–30.

———. Metaphor (*Second Discourse*)." In id., *Allegories of Reading: Figural Language in Rousseau, Nietzsche, Rilke and Proust,* 135–59. New Haven: Yale University Press, 1979.

———. "The Rhetoric of Temporality." In id., *Blindness and Insight: Essays in the Rhetoric of Contemporary Criticism,* 187–228. Minneapolis: University of Minnesota Press, 1983.

Denby, David. *Sentimental Narrative and the Social Order in France, 1760–1820.* Cambridge: Cambridge University Press, 1994.

Derrida, Jacques. *Given Time: 1. Counterfeit Money.* Translated by Peggy Kamuf. Chicago: University of Chicago Press, 1992.

———. *Of Grammatology.* Translated by Gayatri Spivak. Baltimore: Johns Hopkins University Press, 1976.

Dieckmann, Herbert. *Inventaire du fonds Vandeul, et inédits de Diderot.* Geneva: Droz, 1951.

DiPiero, Thomas. *Dangerous Truths and Criminal Passions: The Evolution of the French Novel, 1569–1791.* Stanford: Stanford University Press, 1992.

Dobie, Madeleine. *Foreign Bodies: Gender, Language, and Culture in French Orientalism.* Stanford: Stanford University Press, 2001.

Donnan, Elizabeth, ed. *Documents Illustrative of the History of the Slave Trade to America.* 4 vols. Washington, D.C.: Carnegie Institution of Washington, 1930–35.

Donoghue, Frank. *The Fame Machine: Book Reviewing and Eighteenth-Century Literary Careers.* Stanford: Stanford University Press, 1996.

Donzelot, Jacques. *The Policing of Families.* Translated by Robert Hurley. New York: Pantheon Books, 1979.

Douglas, Aileen. "Britannia's Rule and the It-Narrator." *Eighteenth-Century Fiction* 6.1 (1993): 65–82.

Douthwaite, Julia. *Exotic Women: Literary Heroines and Cultural Strategies in Ancien Régime France.* Philadelphia: University of Pennsylvania Press, 1992.

Drescher, Seymour. *Econocide: British Slavery in the Era of Abolition.* Pittsburgh: University of Pittsburgh Press, 1977.

Duchet, Michèle. *Anthropologie et histoire au siècle des Lumières.* 1971. Paris: Albin Michel, 1995.

———. *Diderot et "L'Histoire des deux Indes," ou l'écriture fragmentaire.* Paris: A. G. Nizet, 1978.

Dziembowski, Edmond. *Un nouveau patriotisme français, 1750–1770: La France face à la puissance anglaise a l'époque de la guerre de Sept Ans.* Studies on Voltaire and the Eighteenth Century 365. Oxford: Voltaire Foundation, 1998.

Ellis, Markman. *The Politics of Sensibility: Race, Gender and Commerce in the Sentimental Novel.* Cambridge: Cambridge University Press, 1996.

Ellison, Julie. *Cato's Tears and the Making of Anglo-American Emotion.* Chicago: University of Chicago Press, 1999.

Eltis, David. "Europeans and the Rise and Fall of African Slavery in the Americas: An Interpretation." *American Historical Review* 98.5 (1993): 1399–1423.

Erämetsä, Erik. "A Study of the Word 'Sentimental' and of Other Linguistic Characteristics of Eighteenth-Century Sentimentalism in England." *Annales Academiae Scientiarum Fennicae* (Helsinki), ser. B, 74.1 (1951).

Ette, Ottmar. "La mise en scène de la table de travail: poétologie et épistémologie immanentes chez Guillaume-Thomas Raynal et Alexander von Humboldt." In *Icons—Texts—Iconotexts: Essays on Ekphrasis and Intermediality,* ed. Peter Wagner, 175–209. Berlin: Walter de Gruyter, 1996.

———. "'Le tour de l'univers sur notre parquet': Lecteurs et lectures dans l'*Histoire des deux Indes.*" In *L'Abbé Raynal: De la polémique à l'histoire,* ed. Gilles Bancarel and Gianluigi Goggi, 255–72. Studies on Voltaire and the Eighteenth Century 2000:12. Oxford: Voltaire Foundation, 2000.

Fabian, Johannes. *Time and the Other: How Anthropology Makes its Object.* New York: Columbia University Press, 1983.

Fanning, Christopher. "'The Things Themselves': Origins and Originality in Sterne's Sermons." *The Eighteenth Century: Theory and Interpretation* 40.1 (1999): 29–45.

Fanon, Frantz. *The Wretched of the Earth.* Translated by Constance Farrington. New York: Grove Press, 1981.

Favret, Mary A. "Flogging: The Anti-Slavery Movement Writes Pornography." In *Romanticism and Gender,* ed. Anne Janowitz, 19–43. *Essays and Studies* 51. Cambridge: D. S. Brewer, 1998.

Ferguson, Frances. *Pornography: The Theory.* Chicago: University of Chicago Press, 2004.

Ferguson, Moira. *Subject to Others: British Women Writers and Colonial Slavery, 1670–1834.* New York: Routledge, 1992.

Feugère, Anatole. *Un précurseur de la Révolution: l'abbé Raynal (1713–1796).* Geneva: Slatkine, 1970.

Fichtelberg, Joseph. "Word Between Worlds: The Economy of Equiano's *Narrative.*" *American Literary History* 5 (1993): 459–80.

Fisher, Philip. *Hard Facts: Setting and Form in the American Novel.* New York: Oxford University Press, 1987.

Flint, Christopher. "Speaking Objects: The Circulation of Stories in Eighteenth-Century Prose Fiction." *PMLA* 113.2 (1998): 212–26.

Foucault, Michel. *Herculine Barbin, being the Recently Discovered Memoirs of a Nineteenth-Century French Hermaphrodite.* Translated by Richard McDougall. New York: Pantheon Books, 1980.

Frank, Judith. "'A Man who laughs is never dangerous': Character and Class in Sterne's *A Sentimental Journey*." *ELH* 56.1 (1989): 97–124.

Fried, Michael. *Absorption and Theatricality: Painting and Beholder in the Age of Diderot.* Chicago: University of Chicago Press, 1980.

Frow, John. *Time and Commodity Culture: Essays in Cultural Theory and Postmodernity.* Oxford: Clarendon Press, 1997.

Frye, Northrop. "Towards Defining an Age of Sensibility." *ELH* 23.2 (1956): 144–52.

Fryer, Peter. *Staying Power: The History of Black People in Britain.* London: Pluto Press, 1984.

Fuss, Diana. *Identification Papers.* New York: Routledge, 1995.

Gallagher, Catherine. *Nobody's Story: The Vanishing Acts of Women Writers in the Marketplace, 1670–1820.* Berkeley: University of California Press, 1994.

Gates, Henry Louis, Jr. *The Signifying Monkey: A Theory of Afro-American Literary Criticism.* New York: Oxford University Press, 1988.

Gilroy, Paul. *The Black Atlantic: Modernity and Double Consciousness.* Cambridge, Mass.: Harvard University Press, 1993.

Godechot, Jacques. *La grande nation: L'expansion révolutionnaire de la France dans le monde de 1789 à 1799.* 1956. Paris: Aubier Montaigne, 1983.

Gordon, Daniel. *Citizens Without Sovereignty: Equality and Sociability in French Thought, 1670–1789.* Princeton: Princeton University Press, 1994.

Greene, Donald. "Latitudinarianism and Sensibility: The Genealogy of the 'Man of Feeling' Reconsidered." *Modern Philology* 75 (1977): 159–83.

Gregory, Chris R. *Gifts and Commodities.* London: Academic Press, 1982.

Grieder, Josephine. *Anglomania in France, 1740–1789: Fact, Fiction, and Political Discourse.* Geneva: Droz, 1985.

——— . *Translations of French Sentimental Prose Fiction in Late Eighteenth-Century England.* Durham, N.C.: Duke University Press, 1975.

Guest, Harriet. "Sterne, Elizabeth Draper, and Drapery." *The Shandean* 9 (November 1997): 9–33.

Halttunen, Karen. "Humanitarianism and the Pornography of Pain in Anglo-American Culture." *American Historical Review* 100.2 (1995): 303–34.

Hancock, David. *Citizens of the World: London Merchants and the Integration of the British Atlantic Community, 1735–1785.* Cambridge: Cambridge University Press, 1997.

Harlow, Vincent T. *The Founding of the Second British Empire, 1763–1793.* 2 vols. London: Longmans, Green, 1952–64.

Haskell, Thomas. "Capitalism and the Rise of Humanitarian Sensibility, Parts 1 and 2." In *The Antislavery Debate: Capitalism and Abolitionism as a Problem in Historical Interpretation*, ed. Thomas Bender, 107–60. Berkeley: University of California Press, 1992.

Hinds, Elizabeth Jane Wall. "The Spirit of Trade: Olaudah Equiano's Conversion, Legalism, and the Merchant's *Life*." *African American Review* 32.4 (1998): 635–47.

Hirschman, Albert. *The Passions and the Interests: Political Arguments for Capitalism Before its Triumph.* Princeton: Princeton University Press, 1977.

Horkheimer, Max, and Theodor W. Adorno. *Dialectic of Enlightenment.* Translated by John Cumming. New York: Continuum, 1972.

Howes, Alan B., ed. *Sterne: The Critical Heritage*. London: Routledge & Kegan Paul, 1974.

———. *Yorick and the Critics: Sterne's Reputation in England, 1760–1868*. New Haven: Yale University Press, 1958.

Hudson, Nicholas. "From 'Nation' to 'Race': The Origin of Racial Classification in Eighteenth-Century Thought." *Eighteenth-Century Studies* 29 (1996): 247–64.

Hulme, Peter. *Colonial Encounters: Europe and the Native Caribbean, 1492–1797*. London: Methuen, 1986.

James, C. L. R. *The Black Jacobins: Toussaint L'Ouverture and the San Domingo Revolution*. New York: Vintage Books, 1963.

Jameson, Fredric. *The Political Unconscious: Narrative as a Socially Symbolic Act*. Ithaca, N.Y.: Cornell University Press, 1981.

Johnson, Barbara. "Anthropomorphism in Lyric and Law." *Yale Journal of Law and the Humanities* 10.2 (1998): 549–74.

———. "Deconstruction, Feminism, and Pedagogy." In id., *A World of Difference*, 42–46. Baltimore: Johns Hopkins University Press, 1989.

———. "A Hound, A Bay Horse, and a Turtle Dove: Obscurity in *Walden*." In id., *A World of Difference*, 49–56. Baltimore: Johns Hopkins University Press, 1989.

———. "Using People: Kant with Winnicott." In *The Turn to Ethics*, ed. Marjorie Garber, Beatrice Hanssen, and Rebecca Walkowitz, 47–63. New York: Routledge, 2000.

Johnson, Claudia. *Equivocal Beings: Politics, Gender, and Sentimentality in the 1790s: Wollstonecraft, Radcliffe, Burney, Austen*. Chicago: University of Chicago Press, 1995.

Johnson, Marion. "The Ounce in Eighteenth-Century West African Trade." *Journal of African History* 7 (1966): 197–214.

Jones, Chris. *Radical Sensibility: Literature and Ideas in the 1790s*. London: Routledge, 1993.

Jones, Henry Festing. *Samuel Butler*. 2 vols. London: Macmillan, 1919.

Joseph, Betty. "Bookkeeping and the Informatics of Empire." Paper Presented at the Modern Language Association, Washington, D.C., December 2004.

Kaiser, Thomas. "Louis le Bien-Aimé and the Rhetoric of the Royal Body." In *From Royal to Republican Body: Incorporating the Political in Seventeenth-and Eighteenth-Century France*, ed. Sara Melzer and Kathryn Norberg, 131–61. Berkeley: University of California Press, 1998.

Kaplan, Alice. *French Lessons: A Memoir*. Chicago: University of Chicago Press, 1993.

Kaul, Suvir. *Poems of Nation, Anthems of Empire: English Verse in the Long Eighteenth Century*. Charlottesville: University Press of Virginia, 2000.

Kay, Carol. *Political Constructions: Defoe, Richardson, and Sterne, in Relation to Hobbes, Hume, and Burke*. Ithaca, N.Y.: Cornell University Press, 1988.

Keenan, Thomas. "The Point Is to (Ex)Change It: Reading *Capital*, Rhetorically." In *Fetishism as Cultural Discourse*, ed. Emily Apter and William Pietz, 152–85. Ithaca, N.Y.: Cornell University Press, 1993.

Keith, Jennifer. "The Formal Challenges of Antislavery Poetry." *Studies in Eighteenth-Century Culture* 34 (2005): 97–124.

Kelly, Gary. *Women, Writing, and Revolution, 1790–1827*. Oxford: Clarendon Press, 1993.

Knapp, Steven. *Personification and the Sublime: Milton to Coleridge*. Cambridge, Mass.: Harvard University Press, 1985.

Koehn, Nancy. *The Power of Commerce: Economy and Governance in the First British Empire.* Ithaca, N.Y.: Cornell University Press, 1994.

Kopytoff, Igor. "The Cultural Biography of Things: Commoditization as Process." In *The Social Lives of Things: Commodities in Cultural Perspective,* ed. Arjun Appadurai, 64–91. Cambridge: Cambridge University Press, 1986.

Kowaleski-Wallace, Elizabeth. *Consuming Subjects: Women, Shopping, and Business in the Eighteenth Century.* New York: Columbia University Press, 1997.

Lamb, Jonathan. "Language and Hartleian Associationism in *A Sentimental Journey.*" *Eighteenth-Century Studies* 13 (1980): 285–312.

———. "Modern Metamorphoses and Disgraceful Tales." *Critical Inquiry* 28 (Autumn 2001): 133–66.

———. *Preserving the Self in the South Seas, 1680–1840.* Chicago: University of Chicago Press, 2001.

———. *Sterne's Fiction and the Double Principle.* Cambridge: Cambridge University Press, 1989.

———. "Sterne's System of Imitation." In *Critical Essays on Laurence Sterne,* ed. Melvyn New, 19–38. New York: G. K. Hall, 1998.

Langford, Paul. *A Polite and Commercial People: England, 1727–1783.* Oxford: Clarendon, 1989.

Lanham, Richard. *"Tristram Shandy": The Games of Pleasure.* Berkeley: University of California Press, 1973.

Lichtenstein, Jacqueline. *The Eloquence of Color: Rhetoric and Painting in the French Classical Age.* Translated by Emily McVarish. Berkeley: University of California Press, 1993.

Longo, Joseph. *Laurence Sterne und Johann Georg Jacobi.* Vienna: J. Eisenstein, 1898.

Lowe, Lisa. *Critical Terrains: French and British Orientalisms.* Ithaca, N.Y.: Cornell University Press, 1991.

Lüsebrink, Hans-Jürgen. "*L'Histoire des deux Indes* et ses 'extraits': Une mode de dispersion textuelle au XVIIIe siècle." *Littérature* 69 (1988): 28–41.

———. "La réception de l'*Adresse à l'Assemblée nationale.*" In *L'Abbé Raynal: De la polémique à l'histoire,* ed. Gilles Bancarel and Gianluigi Goggi, 333–44. Studies on Voltaire and the Eighteenth Century 2000:12. Oxford: Voltaire Foundation, 2000.

Lüsebrink, Hans-Jürgen, and Anthony Strugnell, eds. *"L'Histoire des deux indes": Réécriture et polygraphie.* Studies on Voltaire and the Eighteenth Century 333. Oxford: Voltaire Foundation, 1995.

Lüsebrink, Hans-Jürgen, and Manfred Tietz, eds. *Lectures de Raynal: "L'Histoire des deux Indes" en Europe et en Amérique au XVIIIe siècle.* Studies on Voltaire and the Eighteenth Century 286. Oxford: Voltaire Foundation, 1991.

Lynch, Deidre Shauna. *The Economy of Character: Novels, Market Culture, and the Business of Inner Meaning.* Chicago: University of Chicago Press, 1998.

Macpherson, C. B. *The Political Theory of Possessive Individualism: Hobbes to Locke.* Oxford: Clarendon Press, 1962.

Markley, Robert. "Sentimentality as Performance: Shaftesbury, Sterne, and the Theatrics of Virtue." In *The New Eighteenth Century: Theory, Politics, English Literature,* ed. Felicity Nussbaum and Laura Brown, 210–30. New York: Methuen, 1987.

Marshall, David. "Adam Smith and the Theatricality of Moral Sentiments" *Critical Inquiry* 10 (June 1984): 592–613.

———. *The Figure of Theater: Shaftesbury, Defoe, Adam Smith, and George Eliot.* New York: Columbia University Press, 1986.

———. *The Surprising Effects of Sympathy: Marivaux, Diderot, Rousseau, and Mary Shelley.* Chicago: University of Chicago Press, 1988.

Marshall, P. J. "'A free though conquering people': Britain and Asia in the Eighteenth Century." In id., *"A free though conquering People": Eighteenth-Century Britain and Its Empire.* Burlington, Vt.: Ashgate, 2003.

———. "Introduction." In *The Oxford History of the British Empire*, vol. 2: *The Eighteenth Century*, ed. P. J. Marshall, 1–27. Oxford: Oxford University Press, 1998.

———. *The Making and Unmaking of Empires: Britain, India, and America c. 1750–1783.* Oxford: Oxford University Press, 2005.

———. "The Moral Swing to the East: British Humanitarianism, India and the West Indies." In id., *"A free though conquering people": Eighteenth-Century Britain and Its Empire.* Burlington, Vt.: Ashgate, 2003.

Marshall, P. J., and Glydwr Williams. *The Great Map of Mankind: Perceptions of New Worlds in the Age of Enlightenment.* Cambridge, Mass.: Harvard University Press, 1982.

Mauss, Marcel. *The Gift: Forms and Functions of Exchange in Archaic Societies.* Translated by Ian Cunnison. New York: Norton, 1967.

May, Georges. *Le dilemme du roman au XVIIIe siècle: Étude sur les rapports du roman et de la critique, 1715–1761.* New Haven: Yale University Press, 1963.

Maza, Sarah. "Luxury, Morality, and Social Change: Why There was No Middle-Class Consciousness in Prerevolutionary France." *Journal of Modern History* 69.2 (1997): 199–229.

———. *The Myth of the French Bourgeoisie: An Essay on the Social Imaginary, 1750–1850.* Cambridge, Mass.: Harvard University Press, 2003.

McClintock, Anne. *Imperial Leather: Race, Gender, and Sexuality in the Colonial Conquest.* New York: Routledge, 1995.

McGann, Jerome. *The Poetics of Sensibility: A Revolution in Literary Style.* Oxford: Clarendon Press, 1996.

McKeon, Michael. *The Origins of the English Novel, 1600–1740.* Baltimore: Johns Hopkins University Press, 1987.

McMurran, Mary Helen. "Translation and the Novel, 1660–1800." Ph.D. diss., New York University, 1999.

Meeker, Richard K. "Bank Note, Corkscrew, Flea and Sedan: A Checklist of Eighteenth-Century Fiction." *Library Chronicle* 35 (1969): 52–57.

Mehta, Uday Singh. *Liberalism and Empire: A Study in Nineteenth-Century British Liberal Thought.* Chicago: University of Chicago Press, 1999.

Mellor, Anne. "'Am I not a Woman, and a Sister?': Slavery, Romanticism, and Gender." In *Romanticism, Race and Imperial Culture, 1780–1834*, ed. Alan Richardson and Sonia Hofkosh, 311–29. Bloomington: Indiana University Press, 1996.

Merish, Lori. *Sentimental Materialism: Gender, Commodity Culture, and Nineteenth-Century American Literature.* Durham, N.C.: Duke University Press, 2000.

Metcalf, George. "Gold, Assortments and the Trade Ounce: Fante Merchants and the Problem of Supply and Demand in the 1770s." *Journal of African History* 28 (1987): 27–41.

Michaels, Walter Benn. *The Gold Standard and the Logic of Naturalism.* Berkeley: University of California Press, 1987.

Midgley, Clare. *Women Against Slavery: The British Campaigns, 1780–1870.* London: Routledge, 1992.

Miller, J. Hillis. "Narrative Middles: A Preliminary Outline." *Genre* 11 (Fall 1978): 375–87.

Miller, Peter N. *Defining the Common Good: Empire, Religion, and Philosophy in Eighteenth-Century Britain.* Cambridge: Cambridge University Press, 1994.

Mitchell, Robert E. " 'The Soul that dreams it shares the power it feels so well': The Politics of Sympathy in the Abolitionist Verse of Williams and Yearsley." *Romanticism on the Net* 29–30 (February–May 2003): 35 paras. www.erudit.org/revue/ron/2003/v/n29/007719ar.html (accessed Jan. 9, 2006).

Montag, Warren. "The Universalization of Whiteness: Racism and Enlightenment." In *Whiteness: A Critical Reader,* ed. Mike Hill, 281–93. New York: New York University Press, 1997.

Mornet, Daniel. "Les enseignements des bibliothèques privées (1750–1780)." *Revue d'histoire littéraire de la France* 17 (1910): 449–96.

———. "Introduction." In *La Nouvelle Héloïse,* by Jean-Jacques Rousseau, vol. 1. 4 vols. Paris: Hachette, 1925.

Mullan, John. *Sentiment and Sociability: The Language of Feeling in the Eighteenth Century.* Oxford: Clarendon Press, 1988.

Muthu, Sankar. *Enlightenment Against Empire.* Princeton: Princeton University Press, 2003.

New, Melvyn, Richard Davies, and W. G. Day. *The Life and Opinions of Tristram Shandy: The Notes.* Vol. 3 of *The Florida Edition of the Works of Laurence Sterne.* Gainesville: University Press of Florida, 1984.

Newman, Gerald. *The Rise of English Nationalism: A Cultural History, 1740–1830.* New York: St. Martin's Press, 1987.

Nunokawa, Jeff. *The Afterlife of Property: Domestic Security and the Victorian Novel.* Princeton: Princeton University Press, 1994.

Nussbaum, Felicity. *The Limits of the Human: Fictions of Anomaly, Race, and Gender in the Long Eighteenth Century.* Cambridge: Cambridge University Press, 2003.

———. *Torrid Zones: Maternity, Sexuality, and Empire in Eighteenth-Century English Narratives.* Baltimore: Johns Hopkins University Press, 1995.

Oates, J. C. T. *Shandyism and Sentiment, 1760–1800.* Cambridge: Cambridge Bibliographical Society, 1968.

Oldfield, J. R. *Popular Politics and British Anti-Slavery: The Mobilisation of Public Opinion Against the Slave Trade, 1787–1807.* London: Frank Cass, 1998

Olshin, Toby. "Form and Theme in Novels About Non-Human Characters." *Genre* 2 (1969): 43–56.

Oxenhandler, Neal. "The Changing Concept of Literary Emotion: A Selective History." *New Literary History* 20.1 (1988): 105–21.

Pagden, Anthony. *Lords of All the World: Ideologies of Empire in Spain, Britain and France, 1500–1800.* New Haven: Yale University Press, 1995.

Parker, Geoffrey. *The Military Revolution: Military Innovation and the Rise of the West, 1500–1800.* Cambridge: Cambridge University Press, 1988.

Parsons, Sarah Watson. "The Arts of Abolition: Race, Representation and British Colonialism, 1768–1807." In *Interpreting Colonialism,* ed. Byron Wells and Philip Stewart, 345–68. Studies on Voltaire and the Eighteenth Century 2004:09. Oxford: Voltaire Foundation, 2004.

Paton, Diana. "Decency, Dependence and the Lash: Gender and the British Debate over Slave Emancipation, 1830–1834." *Slavery and Abolition* 17.3 (1996): 163–84.

Peabody, Sue. *"There are no slaves in France": The Political Culture of Race and Slavery in the Ancien Régime.* New York: Oxford University Press, 1996.

Pels, Peter. "The Spirit of Matter: On Fetish, Rarity, Fact, and Fancy." In *Border Fetishisms: Material Objects in Unstable Spaces,* ed. Patricia Spyer, 91–121. New York: Routledge, 1998.

Penke, Olga. "Les figures du narrateur et du destinataire dans l'*Histoire des deux Indes*." In *"L'Histoire des deux indes": Réécriture et polygraphie,* ed. Hans-Jürgen Lüsebrink and Anthony Strugnell, 69–78. Studies on Voltaire and the Eighteenth Century 333. Oxford: Voltaire Foundation, 1995.

Perry, Ruth. "Mary Astell and the Feminist Critique of Possessive Individualism." *Eighteenth-Century Studies* 23 (1990): 444–57.

Phillips, Mark Salber. "Relocating Inwardness: Historical Distance and the Transition from Enlightenment to Romantic Historiography." *PMLA* 118.3 (2003): 436–49.

Pietz, William. "Bosman's Guinea: The Intercultural Roots of an Enlightenment Discourse." *Comparative Civilizations Review* 11 (Fall 1982): 1–22.

———. "Fetishism and Materialism: The Limits of Theory in Marx." In *Fetishism as Cultural Discourse,* ed. Emily Apter and William Pietz, 119–51. Ithaca, N.Y.: Cornell University Press, 1993.

———. "The Problem of the Fetish." Parts 1, 2, and 3. *Res* 9 (Spring 1985): 5–17; *Res* 13 (Spring 1987): 23–45; *Res* 16 (Autumn 1988): 105–23.

Pinch, Adela. *Strange Fits of Passion: Epistemologies of Emotion, Hume to Austen.* Stanford: Stanford University Press, 1996.

Pitts, Jennifer. *A Turn to Empire: The Rise of Imperial Liberalism in Britain and France.* Princeton: Princeton University Press, 2005.

Pluchon, Pierre. *Histoire de la colonisation française.* 2 vols. Paris: Fayard, 1991.

Pocock, J. G. A. "Commerce, Settlement, and History: A Reading of the *Histoire des deux Indes*." In *Articulating America: Fashioning a National Political Culture in Early America, Essays in Honor of J. R. Pole,* ed. Rebecca Starr, 15–44. Lanham, Md.: Rowman & Littlefield, 2000.

———. *Virtue, Commerce, and History: Essays on Political Thought, Chiefly in the 18th Century.* Cambridge: Cambridge University Press, 1985.

Polanyi, Karl. "Sortings and 'Ounce Trade' in the West African Slave Trade." *Journal of African History* 5 (1964): 381–93.

Popkin, Richard. "The Philosophical Basis of Eighteenth-Century Racism." In *Racism in the Eighteenth Century,* vol. 3 of *Studies in Eighteenth-Century Culture,* ed. Harold Pagliaro, 245–62. Cleveland: Press of Case Western Reserve, 1973.

Porter, Andrew. *Religion Versus Empire? British Protestant Missionaries and Overseas Expansion, 1700–1914.* Manchester: Manchester University Press, 2004.

———. "Trusteeship, Anti-Slavery, and Humanitarianism." In *The Oxford History of the British Empire*, vol. 3: *The Nineteenth Century,* ed. Andrew Porter, 198–221. Oxford: Oxford University Press, 1999.

Potkay, Adam, Srinivas Aravamudan, and Roxann Wheeler. "Forum: Teaching Equiano's *Interesting Narrative.*" *Eighteenth-Century Studies* 34 (2001): 601–24.

———. "Olaudah Equiano and the Art of Spiritual Autobiography." *Eighteenth-Century Studies* 27 (1994): 677–92.

Pratt, Mary Louise. *Imperial Eyes: Travel Writing and Transculturation.* London: Routledge, 1992.

Price, Leah. *The Anthology and the Rise of the Novel: From Richardson to George Eliot.* Cambridge: Cambridge University Press, 2000.

Prickett, Stephen. *Words and "The Word": Language, Poetics and Biblical Interpretation.* Cambridge: Cambridge University Press, 1986.

Pujol, Stéphane. "Les formes de l'éloquence dans l'*Histoire des deux Indes.*" In *"L'Histoire des deux indes": Réécriture et polygraphie,* ed. Hans-Jürgen Lüsebrink and Anthony Strugnell, 357–69. Studies on Voltaire and the Eighteenth Century 333. Oxford: Voltaire Foundation, 1995.

Quint, David. *Epic and Empire: Politics and Generic Form from Virgil to Milton.* Princeton: Princeton University Press, 1993.

Racault, Jean-Michel. "L'effet exotique dans *L'Histoire des deux Indes* et la mise en scène du monde colonial de l'océan indien." In *"L'Histoire des deux indes": Réécriture et polygraphie,* ed. Hans-Jürgen Lüsebrink and Anthony Strugnell, 119–32. Studies on Voltaire and the Eighteenth Century 333. Oxford: Voltaire Foundation, 1995.

Ragatz, Lowell J. *The Fall of the Planter Class in the British Caribbean, 1763–1833.* New York: Octagon, 1963.

Renan, Ernest. "What Is a Nation?" 1882. In *Nation and Narration,* ed. Homi K. Bhabha, 8–22. London: Routledge, 1990.

Richetti, John. *Philosophical Writing: Locke, Berkeley and Hume.* Cambridge, Mass.: Harvard University Press, 1983.

Roach, Joseph. "Body of Law: The Sun King and the Code Noir." *From the Royal to the Republican Body: Incorporating the Political in Seventeenth- and Eighteenth-Century France,* ed. Sara Melzer and Kathryn Norberg, 113–30. Berkeley: University of California Press, 1998.

Rorty, Amélie Oksenberg. "From Passions to Emotions and Sentiments." *Philosophy* 57 (1982): 159–72.

Ross, Marlon. *The Contours of Masculine Desire: Romanticism and the Rise of Women's Poetry.* New York: Oxford University Press, 1989.

Rousseau, G. S. "Nerves, Spirits, and Fibres: Towards Defining the Origins of Sensibility." In *Studies in the Eighteenth Century: Papers Presented at the Third David Nichol Smith Memorial Seminar, Canberra, 1973,* ed. R. F. Brissenden and J. C. Eade, 137–57. Toronto: Toronto University Press, 1976.

Sahlins, Peter. "Natural Frontiers Revisited: France's Boundaries Since the Seventeenth Century." *American Historical Review* 95.5 (1990): 1423–51.

Said, Edward. *Culture and Imperialism*. New York: Knopf, 1994.

———. *Orientalism*. New York: Pantheon Books, 1978.

Saint-Amand, Pierre. *The Laws of Hostility: Politics, Violence, and the Enlightenment*. Translated by Jennifer Curtiss Gage. Minneapolis: University of Minnesota Press, 1996.

Sandiford, Keith. *The Cultural Politics of Sugar: Caribbean Slavery and Narratives of Colonialism*. Cambridge: Cambridge University Press, 2000.

Scarry, Elaine. *The Body in Pain: The Making and Unmaking of the World*. New York: Oxford University Press, 1985.

Schiebinger, Londa. "The Anatomy of Difference: Race and Sex in Eighteenth-Century Science." *Eighteenth-Century Studies* 23 (1990): 387–405.

Seidel, Michael. "Narrative Crossings: Sterne's *A Sentimental Journey*." *Genre* 18 (Spring 1985): 1–22.

Shyllon, F. O. *Black Slaves in Britain*. London: Oxford University Press, 1974.

Skrzypek, Marian. "Le commerce instrument de la paix mondiale." In *L'Abbé Raynal: De la polémique à l'histoire*, ed. Gilles Bancarel and Gianluigi Goggi, 243–54. Studies on Voltaire and the Eighteenth Century 2000:12. Oxford: Voltaire Foundation, 2000.

Simmel, Georg. *The Philosophy of Money*. Translated by Tom Bottomore and David Frisby. London: Routledge & Kegan Paul, 1978.

Solkin, David. *Painting for Money: The Visual Arts and the Public Sphere in Eighteenth-Century England*. New Haven: Yale University Press, 1993.

Sollors, Werner. "Introduction." *The Interesting Narrative of Olaudah Equiano or Gustavus Vassa, the African*. New York: Norton, 2001.

———. *Neither Black nor White yet Both: Thematic Explorations of Interracial Literature*. New York: Oxford University Press, 1997.

Spillers, Hortense J. "Mama's Baby, Papa's Maybe: An American Grammar Book." *Diacritics* 17.2 (Summer 1987): 65–81.

Spivak, Gayatri Chakravorty. *In Other Worlds: Essays in Cultural Politics*. New York: Methuen, 1987.

———. *Outside in the Teaching Machine*. New York: Routledge, 1993.

———. "Three Women's Texts and a Critique of Imperialism." *Critical Inquiry* 12 (Autumn 1985): 243–61.

Stallybrass, Peter. "Marx's Coat." In *Border Fetishisms: Material Objects in Unstable Spaces*, ed. Patricia Spyer, 183–207. New York: Routledge, 1998.

Steintrager, James. *Cruel Delight: Enlightenment Culture and the Inhuman*. Bloomington: Indiana University Press, 2004.

Stott, Anne. *Hannah More: The First Victorian*. Oxford: Oxford University Press, 2003.

Streeter, Harold Wade. *The Eighteenth-Century English Novel in French Translation: A Bibliographical Study*. 1936. Rpt. New York: Benjamin Blom, 1970.

Strugnell, Anthony. "À la recherche d'Eliza Draper." In *L'Abbé Raynal: De la polémique à l'histoire*, ed. Gilles Bancarel and Gianluigi Goggi, 173–86. Studies on Voltaire and the Eighteenth Century 2000:12. Oxford: Voltaire Foundation, 2000.

Suleri, Sara. *The Rhetoric of English India*. Chicago: University of Chicago Press, 1992.

Sussman, Charlotte. *Consuming Anxieties: Consumer Protest, Gender, and British Slavery, 1713–1833*. Stanford: Stanford University Press, 2000.

———. "Women and the Politics of Sugar, 1792." *Representations* 48 (Fall 1994): 48–69.

Sypher, Wylie. *Guinea's Captive Kings: British Anti-Slavery Literature of the Eighteenth Century*. Chapel Hill: University of North Carolina Press, 1942.

Tanner, Michael. "Sentimentality." *Proceedings of the Aristotelian Society*, n.s., 77 (1976–77): 127–47.

Taussig, Michael. *Mimesis and Alterity: A Particular History of the Senses*. New York: Routledge, 1993.

Texte, Joseph. *Jean-Jacques Rousseau et les origines du cosmopolitisme littéraire: Étude sur les relations de la France et de l'Angleterre au XVIIIe siècle*. Paris: Hachette, 1909.

Thayer, Harvey Waterman. "Laurence Sterne in Germany: A Contribution to the Study of Literary Relations of England and Germany in the Eighteenth Century." *Columbia University Germanic Studies* 2.1. New York: Columbia University Press, 1905.

Thomas, Helen. *Romanticism and Slave Narratives: Transatlantic Testimonies*. Cambridge: Cambridge University Press, 2000.

Thomas, Keith. *Man and the Natural World: A History of the Modern Sensibility*. New York: Pantheon Books, 1983.

Todd, Janet. *Sensibility: An Introduction*. London: Methuen, 1986.

Tompkins, J. M. S. *The Popular Novel in England, 1770–1800*. Lincoln: University of Nebraska Press, 1961.

Trumpener, Katie. *Bardic Nationalism: The Romantic Novel and the British Empire*. Princeton: Princeton University Press, 1997.

Van Kley, Dale, ed. *The French Idea of Freedom: The Old Regime and the Declaration of Rights of 1789*. Stanford: Stanford University Press, 1994.

Van Sant, Ann Jessie. *Eighteenth-Century Sensibility and the Novel: The Senses in Social Context*. Cambridge: Cambridge University Press, 1993.

Ventura, Roberto. "Lectures de Raynal en Amérique latine aux XVIIIe et XIXe siècles." In *Lectures de Raynal: "L'Histoire des deux Indes" en Europe et en Amérique au XVIIIe siècle*, ed. Hans-Jürgen Lüsebrink and Manfred Tietz, 341–59. Studies on Voltaire and the Eighteenth Century 286. Oxford: Voltaire Foundation, 1991.

Vila, Anne. *Enlightenment and Pathology: Sensibility in the Literature and Medicine of Eighteenth-Century France*. Baltimore: Johns Hopkins University Press, 1998.

Visser, Nicholas. "*Tristram Shandy* and the Straight Line of History." *Textual Practice* 12.3 (1998): 489–502.

Wahrman, Dror. *The Making of the Modern Self: Identity and Culture in Eighteenth-Century England*. New Haven: Yale University Press, 2004.

Walvin, James. "The Public Campaign in England Against Slavery, 1787–1834." In *The Abolition of the Atlantic Slave Trade: Origin and Effects in Europe, Africa and the Americas*, ed. David Eltis and James Walvin, 63–79. Madison: University of Wisconsin Press, 1981.

Warkentin, Germaine. "In Search of 'The Word of the Other': Aboriginal Sign Systems and the History of the Book in Canada." *Book History* 2.1 (1999): 1–27.

Wasserman, Earl. "The Inherent Values of Eighteenth-Century Personification." *PMLA* 65.4 (1950): 435–63.

Watt, Ian. *The Rise of the Novel: Studies in Defoe, Richardson and Fielding.* Berkeley: University of California Press, 1965.

Weiner, Annette. *Inalienable Possessions: The Paradox of Keeping-While-Giving.* Berkeley: University of California Press, 1992.

Wexler, Laura. "Tender Violence: Literary Eavesdropping, Domestic Fiction, and Educational Reform." In *The Culture of Sentiment: Race, Gender, and Sentimentality in Nineteenth-Century America*, ed. Shirley Samuels, 9–38. New York: Oxford University Press, 1992.

Wheeler, Roxann. *The Complexion of Race: Categories of Difference in Eighteenth-Century British Culture.* Philadelphia: University of Pennsylvania Press, 2000.

Williams, Eric. *Capitalism and Slavery.* Chapel Hill: University of North Carolina Press, 1944.

Williams, Raymond. *Keywords: A Vocabulary of Culture and Society.* Rev. ed. New York: Oxford University Press, 1983.

Wilson, Arthur. "Sensibility in France in the Eighteenth Century: A Study in Word History." *French Quarterly* 13.1–2 (1931): 35–46.

Wilson, Kathleen. "Citizenship, Empire, and Modernity in the English Provinces, c. 1720–1790." *Eighteenth-Century Studies* 29 (1995): 69–96.

———. *The Island Race: Englishness, Empire, and Gender in the Eighteenth Century.* London: Routledge, 2002.

———. *The Sense of the People: Politics, Culture and Imperialism in England, 1715–1785.* Cambridge: Cambridge University Press, 1995.

Wogan, Peter. "Perceptions of European Literacy in Early Contact Situations." *Ethnohistory* 41 (1994): 407–29.

Wood, Marcus. *Blind Memory: Visual Representations of Slavery in England and America, 1780–1865.* New York: Routledge, 2000.

———. *Slavery, Empathy and Pornography.* Oxford: Oxford University Press, 2002.

Wright, Arnold, and William Lutley Sclater. *Sterne's Eliza: Some Account of her Life in India with her Letters Written Between 1757 and 1774.* New York: Knopf, 1923.

Yellin, Jean Fagan. *Women and Sisters: The Antislavery Feminists in American Culture.* New Haven: Yale University Press, 1989.

Žižek, Slavoj. *The Fragile Absolute: or, Why Is the Christian Legacy Worth Fighting For?* London: Verso, 2000.

———. *The Sublime Object of Ideology.* London: Verso, 1989.

Page numbers followed by *f* refer to illustrations.